Endorsements for *Dissolving into Being*

"This is an exquisitely beautiful and sharply insightful contemporary engagement with Ibn 'Arabi's ideas. With charm and remarkable lucidity, W. Rory Dickson makes complex metaphysical concepts, theological debates and perennial philosophy both accessible and compelling to the reader. This is indeed delightfully 'fresh food' for the spiritual seeker and the intellectual. Truly one of the most valuable, discerning and useful contemporary contributions to the study of Ibn 'Arabi's ideas."
Sa'diyya Shaikh, Department for the Study of Religions, University of Cape Town, South Africa

"William Rory Dickson brings Ibn 'Arabi's Gemstones of Wisdom *into conversation with modern spirituality.* Dissolving into Being *dives deep into a rich variety of themes in Islamic mysticism and comparative religion, and provides an engaging and accessible modern commentary that is a pleasure to read.*"
Aydogan Kars, School of Philosophical, Historical, and International Studies, Monash University, Australia

"Of interest to both the academic and the general reader, William Rory Dickson offers profound insights into the work of the great Sufi Master, Ibn 'Arabi. Of particular relevance to our present fractured time, he explores how everything in our world is a manifestation of a singular Essence or One Being, and how this singular Ultimate Reality can also be found in Buddhist teachings, among others. Ibn 'Arabi's understanding of the unity of life and the reality of love speak directly to the mind and the heart. Dissolving into Being *is a valuable addition to contemporary Sufi studies.*"
Llewellyn Vaughan-Lee, author of *Sufism, the Transformation of the Heart*

"Dissolving into Being *is a must-read for anyone seeking a clear and lively exposition of Sufi metaphysics.*"
Mohammed Rustom, Carleton University, Canada, author of *Inrushes of the Heart: The Sufi Philosophy of 'Ayn al-Quḍāt*

Dissolving into Being

The Wisdom of Sufi Philosophy

WILLIAM RORY DICKSON

Published by Anqa Publishing
PO Box 1178
Oxford OX2 8YS, UK
www.anqa.co.uk

© William Rory Dickson 2024

William Rory Dickson has asserted his moral right under the Copyright, Designs and Patents Act, 1988, to be identified as the author of this work.

All rights reserved. No part of this publication may be reproduced, stored in a retrieval system, or transmitted, in any form or by any means, without the prior permission in writing of the publisher.

A CIP catalogue record for this book is available from the British Library

ISBN: 978-1-905937-77-6 (Hardback)
ISBN: 978-1-905937-78-3 (Paperback)
ISBN: 978-1-905937-79-0 (eBook)

Cover and interior design: meadencreative.com
Cover image: "Breath of the Compassionate", Lateefa Spiker
Calligraphy: Abdul Kayyum Silawat

Contents

Preface	1
Acknowledgments	9
Introduction	13
1 What Does it Mean to be Human? Adam's Secret and the Wisdom of Divinity	57
2 The Abrahamic Paradigm: the Wisdom of Love and the Mystery of Destiny	93
3 What Does it Mean to Have a Heart? Shu'ayb and the Heart's Wisdom	123
4 Jonah and The Wisdom of Breath: Compassion, Remembrance and Life after Death	161
5 What do you Really Know? The Transcendent Wisdom of Elijah–Enoch	193
6 Things are Even Stranger Than You Think: Moses and the Wisdom of Sublimity	231
7 Between Divinity and Humanity: Jesus and the Wisdom of Prophecy	265
8 Muhammad and the Wisdom of Singularity: Marrying Sense and Spirit	295
Index	345

Preface

by Meena Sharify-Funk

*All that is left
to us by tradition
is mere words.*

*It is up to us
to find out what they mean.*[1]

According to traditional Sufi wisdom, our knowledge of reality will always be incomplete if it arises primarily from linear, rational thinking and from received conceptual frameworks. To truly know something, Sufis have taught, one must acquire a 'taste' (*dhawq*) of it through direct, unmediated experience – through bridging the gap between subject and object and experiencing an underlying unity of knower and known. The title of this book, *Dissolving into Being: The Wisdom of Sufi Philosophy*, evokes this Sufi epistemological position, which stipulates that deep and authentic knowledge of reality comes from merging with the real and not simply through thinking about it.

In his efforts to communicate this Sufi wisdom, and to convey its relevance to contemporary cultural and intellectual contexts, William Rory Dickson has centered his narrative on core writings and teachings of a singular Sufi Muslim philosopher, Ibn 'Arabi (d. 1240). There is a reason for this. Ibn 'Arabi was both a great synthesizer and (to use a word that evokes our present-day internet multiverse) a larger-than-life influencer. Born in 12th-century Andalusia, at a major point of intersection among medieval Islamic, Christian and Jewish cultures, Ibn 'Arabi traveled extensively throughout North Africa

---

[1] Ibn 'Arabi, as quoted in Stephen Hirtenstein, 'Muhyiddin Ibn 'Arabi: The Treasure of Compassion,' *Beshara Magazine*, Issue 12 (Autumn 1990). https://ibnarabisociety.org/the-treasure-of-compassion-stephen-hirtenstein/ (accessed January 27, 2024).

and the Middle East, from southern Spain to the Fertile Crescent, the Arabian Peninsula and Anatolia, eventually settling in Damascus. At each waystation of his journey he engaged new communities of learning, courted patrons, and shared his unique articulation of Sufi philosophy, building a network of appreciative students and readers that would eventually extend from the eastern Atlantic to the Pacific Rim, from Central Asia to the Sahel in Africa. No Sufi thinker was more influential, or had a greater impact on the development of mystical philosophy in Islamic contexts, as it would subsequently be expressed and appreciated among poets, teachers of the way, and even official representatives of the Ottoman Empire. Subsequent generations of writers in the Sufi philosophical tradition made frequent use of honorific terms when referring to Ibn 'Arabi, the most pervasive of which was *al-Shaykh al-Akbar*, the Greatest Teacher.

Despite Ibn 'Arabi's many centuries as a key intellectual and spiritual influence throughout the Islamic world, today his legacy is less well tended. His works and contributions are not well known in the West, and have become controversial or obscure in lands that once received his teachings enthusiastically. There are many reasons for this. As many scholars have observed, Ibn 'Arabi's writings are deep, complex and multilayered, and frequently refer to experiences and insights that, on their surface, sound paradoxical and challenging. To address these challenges, Dickson has sought to articulate Ibn 'Arabi's significance as simply, elegantly and accessibly as possible, by selecting some central themes and ideas that convey to the contemporary reader a taste of the underlying, unifying vision. In the process of decoding Ibn 'Arabi's teachings and relating them to 21st-century vernacular culture, Dickson offers commentary on core ideas of Sufis philosophy, frequently described as the mystical wisdom of the Islamic tradition. He presents this wisdom ecumenically and with an attunement to universal aspects of human experience and the spiritual quest, whatever its time or setting.

Throughout his text, Dickson seeks to demonstrate that key insights of Sufi philosophy, and of Ibn 'Arabi as its representative, are more accessible and resonant than is generally recognized. Even if Ibn

'Arabi's prose and verse may not soon propel him to iconic pop culture status akin to that of Rumi or St. Francis, there should be no barriers to understanding his message. As Dickson's culturally and philosophically eclectic narrative suggests, Ibn 'Arabi should be appreciated as an important figure in global intellectual history, whose manner of conveying the heart of Sufi philosophy can be gainfully contemplated by diverse present-day readers, wherever they may stand in relation to Islam and Sufism. In addition to providing intrinsically rewarding material for deep reflection on issues of human identity and purpose, Dickson's appreciative introduction to Ibn 'Arabi and Sufi philosophy can also be helpful to readers in other, more ordinary ways, as a basis for correcting misperceptions and rebalancing worldviews.

Recognizing that a thinker and mystic such as Ibn 'Arabi was historically *central* to the Islamic and Sufi intellectual experiences requires a direct confrontation with stereotypes, and indeed with subtle as well as gross forms of Islamophobia. Sadly, it remains commonplace for many Western readers to presume that there is little in the Islamic tradition that holds broader ecumenical, spiritual or world-historical significance. Historians, of course, have explored the profound interconnections of Abrahamic religions and indeed of Europe with southwest Asian and North African experiences, and have recognized Muslim contributions to intellectual history such as transmitting Aristotelian philosophy from Mediterranean antiquity to the European Renaissance. Popular misperceptions of Islam, however, remain stubbornly persistent. Among these misperceptions is the notion that Islamic culture can be reduced to arbitrary and restrictive rules colored by male privilege, conservatism and scriptural literalism, and therefore offers little that might be experienced as intellectually stimulating or resonant with contemporary concerns. From this standpoint, Sufi philosophy appears anomalous, as an intellectual form that is neither representative of Islam nor especially useful in a modern technological civilization. In the absence of a suitable introduction such as Dickson's, it may also seem abstruse, cryptic and 'hard to crack' – perhaps a nut that is not worth opening.

Muslim preconceptions and self-understandings, however, have also contributed to the problem. Although the Islamic intellectual heritage was richly engaged with the deepest of existential issues, modern Muslim thought has been more intensely preoccupied with problems wrought by the colonial experience – problems of identity and politics, and of asserting a manageable sense of 'authenticity' against intrusive outside forces. As understandable as this may be, strong preoccupation with identity revival and the politics of culture has contributed to a pattern of forgetfulness within intellectual circles – and indeed to a narrowing or pruning of the Islamic intellectual tradition, often in a mode influenced by Ibn 'Arabi's detractor, Ibn Taymiyya (d. 1328). Although a new trend seeks to resuscitate elements of Sufi philosophy, such as the synthesis of orthodoxy and mysticism produced by Abu Hamid al-Ghazali (d. 1111), Ibn 'Arabi's vast corpus and its phenomenal impact on spiritual curricula are too frequently neglected. Whether focused on pathways to a Muslim postmodernity or on ways of making the fundamentals of Islam portable and defensible in modern contexts, contemporary Muslim intellectuals have often preoccupied themselves with problems of collective recovery or revival that differ from the more existential and spiritual priorities of Sufi philosophy and its contemplative traditions.

Dickson's narrative offers a corrective to both of these ways of overlooking Ibn 'Arabi and Sufi philosophy – not through polemic, but rather through demonstration. Dickson excavates nuggets of profound wisdom from the complex layers of Ibn 'Arabi's thought, spotlighting ideas and questions that go to the core of spirituality and religion whatever one's context. He does this by asking some crucial questions:

- Why does religion still matter? Why do humans need prophets and saints?

- Of what use is the symbolic, cosmological language of Ibn 'Arabi and others with whom he was in conversation? How might this language still speak to us today, in an age of ultra-high-tech innovation ecosystems, artificial intelligence, secular thought and individualism?

- What does it mean to be a 'complete', universal or fully developed human being?
- What is the value and purpose of human life, as a process of being and becoming? How can the legacies of thinkers such as Ibn 'Arabi assist us in reaching for our deeper potential?

In offering an introduction to Ibn 'Arabi and Sufi philosophy, Dickson distils important ideas for the lay, non-specialist reader. At the same time, he interprets the heart of Ibn 'Arabi's tradition in ways that can also be rewarding to the specialist, through creative connections and insightful presentation. Throughout his narrative, he also offers careful citations for those seeking a deeper dive into source material.

Thanks to the work of dedicated scholars such as William C. Chittick, English-language academic investigations of Ibn 'Arabi's extensive writings are no longer difficult for the Western reader to locate. Though tremendously valuable for grasping nuances and contexts of important textual passages, these works are sometimes daunting to more casual readers, because the discourse is embedded in broader and often quite technical conversations among scholars, and can require a prohibitive investment of time and intellectual energy for readers who are seeking first and foremost to gain a feel for the underlying ideas and vision.

Dissolving into Being is richly informed by this literature, as well as by the primary source material. However, Dickson's aim in this book is to explore Sufi philosophy in a manner that is reminiscent of more oral philosophical traditions, in which deep ideas are considered in a conversational style and in a spirit of dialogue. Ibn 'Arabi's mode of philosophy, Dickson suggests, is not just for academic and traditional Islamic intellectual contexts, and can enrich a wide range of contemporary discussions. Although well documented and infused with scholarship, his book aims to serve as an accessible resource, relevant not just to the classroom or study but also to the subway, coffee bar, or bedside table. Furthermore, the key ideas are presented not just for comprehension of their original terms of expression, but also for their perennial relevance to the human condition.

Even as the book's narrative unfolds in a conversational, engaging, and accessible manner, Dickson draws actively on key themes expressed in one of Ibn 'Arabi's more influential works, the *Fusus al-hikam*, or 'The Gemstones of Wisdom' – a book that is for many the quintessential summary of Ibn 'Arabi's cosmological and philosophical as well as metaphysical thought. The format of the *Fusus*, which was composed late in Ibn 'Arabi's life, is structured as a commentary on the essential wisdom of the various prophets of the Abrahamic and Islamic traditions. For Ibn 'Arabi, each prophet manifested and expressed enduring teachings about being, reality, and human purpose. In engaging this material as well as North American and cosmopolitan cultural contexts, Dickson shows an eye for significant details from the text that communicate perennial teachings of Sufi spirituality, from the privilege and peril of being human to the perennial cosmic dance, in relationship and (paradoxically) in union with the Divine.

Many readers are sure to enjoy this presentation of spiritual ideas, conveyed in a manner that emphasizes connections – of past and present, of East and West, of diverse religions and philosophies, and of the traditional and contemporary. Dickson harmonizes insights from many quarters and communities, as if speaking to a diverse audience of travellers gathering to engage him at a postmodern caravanserai. In the process he shows how Ibn 'Arabi's Sufi philosophy can contribute vibrantly to contemporary ecumenical and philosophical engagement.

Part of the freshness of Dickson's narrative owes to the manner in which he openly acknowledges aspects of Ibn 'Arabi's thought that can be experienced as 'edgy' or unsettling, whatever the context in which they are received. Traditional thinkers, to be sure, found ways to work with challenging and seemingly unorthodox ideas and metaphors, and with Ibn 'Arabi's insistence on wrestling with intellectual paradoxes while progressing towards transrational forms of perception and awareness. While recognizing the value of contributions made by Ibn 'Arabi's many generations of interpreters, Dickson invites readers to consider how it is precisely the possibility of reading Ibn 'Arabi in more than one way (for example, as thoroughly orthodox *or* surprisingly unorthodox) that enables his thinking to remain alive and speak to multiple audiences.

Even while probing complex themes with subtle understanding and serious purpose, Dickson also writes with a light touch. In so doing, he demonstrates that philosophy need not be a dour exercise, and is well served by humorous allegorical stories, poetic metaphors, and provocative paradoxes as well as by tight, sequential connections. Through his own style of expression and choice of references, Dickson also subverts the idea that philosophy must somehow be insulated from popular culture, as a sort of 'high culture' practice that is, at best, indifferent to 'low culture'. He demonstrates that 'doing philosophy' is compatible with cultural literacy, through using current linguistic expressions and cultural references. Dickson's accessible, non-technical introduction to Sufi philosophy welcomes a broad and diverse readership that finds significance in the mundane as well as the sacred, and which sees the potential for connections between Western and Eastern forms of thought.

From Dickson's standpoint, Sufi philosophy is relevant to everyday life no matter what one's setting or culture. Sufi philosophy is a way of seeing and interacting with the worlds within and around us, and provides means of exploring all aspects of human experience. In insisting that self and other – and indeed, other dualities such as subject and object, seeker and sought, worshipper and worshipped, lover and beloved – are in communion and union with each other, Sufi philosophy proposes that the very ground of being from which all beings spring is ever present. Moreover, the heart has ways of knowing that can be harnessed by a nimble mind that recognizes the integral role of love in religion and spirituality.

Such ideas arguably deserve to occupy a greater amount of real estate in contemporary philosophical deliberations, especially considering the extent to which present-day discussions of epistemology underscore alienation of self and other, and arise from profound doubts about the human capacity to transcend tragically self-serving, destructive, and exploitative entanglements of nations, cultures, religions, genders and racial groups. While there are lessons to glean from present-day discussions of how knowledge is both informed and circumscribed by identity and positionality – lessons that can inspire more inclusive and indeed liberating forms of dialogue – thinkers arguably sell their readers short when they insist on boundary-reinforcing limits to identity and knowledge rather than on encounters with others and with truths that expand and transform identity. It is this latter possibility that is at the heart of Ibn 'Arabi's philosophy, according to which transformation of identity and of knowledge is the means to ever-greater realization, and in which the profundity and expansiveness of truth can never be exhausted by a singular vantagepoint or positionality. 'Beware,' Ibn 'Arabi teaches, 'of being bound up by a particular religion and rejecting all others as unbelief! If you do that you will fail to obtain a great benefit. Nay, you will fail to obtain the true knowledge of the reality.'[2] Does not a contemporary reading of this admonition challenge us to actively transcend our own boundaries, through respectful and appreciative encounters with the seeming 'other'?

Ibn 'Arabi's philosophy invites us not just to know ourselves in the deepest possible way, but also to empathize with one another across all divisions. There is potential here to draw from his teachings a healing epistemology that points beyond alterity and alienation, and towards transformation – towards an embrace of everyday 'unity in diversity' and not just retreat. As a decidedly non-monastic contemplative tradition, Sufi philosophy has long offered its teachings as integral forms of everyday spirituality – as ways of being and engaging with truth in backstreet alleys as well as in daily work and in congregations. Such a spirit is creatively evoked by Dickson's prose, which transcends the sacred/mundane dichotomy and transposes philosophy into communication and rapport that extends well beyond a classroom, infusing the routines, experiences, and encounters with deeper meaning. 'Dissolving into being' does not mean ceasing to be or to do, but rather discovering the wellspring of unity between self and other, traditional and modern, Easts and Wests.

---

2   Ibn 'Arabi, *Fusus al-hikam*, as quoted in Toshihiko Izutsu, *Sufism and Taoism: A Comparative Study of Key Philosophical Concepts* (Berkeley, 1983), 254.

Acknowledgments

'Boon' is, perhaps, a strange word. At least it sounds strange to my ears. But its meaning is a beautiful one. Coming from the old Norse *bón*, a boon is a gratuitous favor, an overflowing gift, a lottery win, a rare prize. It is simply given, apparently with little concern for the merit of the receiver. I have received two great boons in my life. The first is to be born to my parents Bev and Kevin Dickson. Merry, prairie hearts, meticulously fair and equitable, they make whatever they come across better with work and care and appreciation. Their genuineness and humor, generosity and creativity, fostered the best possible environment within which to emerge into this world and later to grow and thrive. Their companionship continues to offer the choicest food for the soul. To gratefully acknowledge my parents is to also gratefully acknowledge my grandparents: on my mother's side, Arline and Michael Lozensky, and on my father's side, Bill and Janice Dickson. Their many virtues continue to benefit those of us who are fortunate enough to come from them.

The second great boon I received is to have Meena Sharify-Funk kindly accept me as a PhD student at Wilfrid Laurier University, and later co-author, mentee and honorary member of her beautiful family. Alongside a socially engaged academic training, she and her husband Nathan Funk received from their doctoral supervisor, Professor Abdul Aziz Said, a very old, very organic path of wisdom, and I am an equally unworthy and fortunate beneficiary of this stream of enlightenment, as ancient as the Tigris and Euphrates. We can call it Sufism, and the word is certainly a good one, and yet realities transcend names and meanings go beyond forms. I bow in gratitude for their sharing and for Meena's generous guidance, invaluable inspiration and sublime *sohbet* over the years. Simply put, this book would not remotely exist without her (though its limitations are very much my own). I am honored to count their son Mikael as a nephew and friend, and I am quite sure that I can neither imagine the horizons he will encounter nor the contributions to our world he will make.

The seeds for this book were planted over many conversations about *The Gemstones of Wisdom* with Ben Baader, Bilquis and Shahid Khan, Najam and Sumera Sahar, and Patricia Robertson, in our humble Sufi Book Club in Winnipeg, and I greatly appreciate the sapiential sustenance they've offered over the years (alongside some truly epic meals). In addition, Ben, Bilquis, Shahid, Najam, Sumera and Patricia read and discussed drafts of this work's chapters, and their many insights and fulsome feedback have improved it considerably. Ben's suggestions for the chapter on Jesus were particularly helpful.

I must thank my brilliant brother, Rhett Dickson, whose intellectual curiosity raised a question that, at least in good measure, inspired this book. His inquiry about what books I might recommend on Sufi philosophy made clear to me the absence of available literature that conveys the tradition's profound depth and insight, without requiring a background in Islamic studies. I couldn't have written the result of my brother's inquiry without the companionship of Rachel Brown (sister of the soul), Andre Furlong (co-flaneur in terrestrial wanderings and existential musings) and Naniece Ibrahim (or Shams, the generous sun), each of whom provide grounding and inspiration in equal measure. Special thanks to Naniece (and to Olivia Psooy and Hend Amin) for helping me complete my *wajib* and find Dhu'l-Nun in the City of the Dead in Cairo in 2022. I also want to give shout outs to Joel Fink, Zach Frieg, Zabeen Khamisa, Peter McCullough, Kent Olsen, Evdoxia Sotiriadou and Shobhana Xavier, for not only their valuable friendship but for their helpful feedback on early drafts of this work. I would be remiss if I didn't acknowledge here my oldest friends, Brad Benner and Ryan McLeod, who I hope will read this book and see that all of that 'free' time they roasted me about having has amounted to something!

I especially appreciate Mohammed Rustom's kind and encouraging feedback on a later draft of this work, and Aydogan Kars's invitation to speak about this project as part of the *Hidden Treasures: Ibn 'Arabi*

Seminar series at Monash University in 2021. This work has been greatly improved by Stephen Hirtenstein's paramount expertise and generous, thorough comments, especially regarding the technicalities of translation. I must also thank Elizabeth Alexandrin for kindly sharing resources in Arabic and English on Ibn 'Arabi's works. I remain grateful to Llewellyn Vaughan-Lee for his prompt and rich responses to my inquiries about contemporary Sufism over the years, and for sharing his time and presence in 2014. Thank you to Abdul Kayyum Silawat for his amazing calligraphy work in this book. And thank you to Lateefa Spiker for the beautiful cover image, entitled "Breath of the Compassionate."

This book was made possible by the University of Winnipeg and United Church of Canada's Research Chair in Contemporary Theology, which I held from 2021 to 2024. This freed me up from teaching enough that I could devote the time to this work that it deserves, and I hope it proves worthy of their kind support. As I was baptized in the United Church as an infant, it felt like connecting the proverbial circle to draw upon the United Church's support to produce a book that reflects my Christian roots, Islamic-Sufi branches and wide-ranging religious and philosophical interests.

In what follows, I begin this book with *Bismillah al-Nafi'* - an Arabic phrase that can be translated as, 'In the Name of God, the Benefactor' – with *al-Nafi'* meaning something like 'the One who gives benefit, profit, favor and good'. Meena shared with me that Professor Asad Ali would always begin his public lectures at the University of Damascus with this blessing. In my case, it is a prayer that what is beneficial in this work find its way to the reader, and what, inevitably, is the dross of my own misunderstandings remain hidden. May we, like the honey bee, always draw the nectar of enlivening essence and leave behind what holds us back from seeing Reality (*al-Haqq*) as it is.

بسم الله النافع

Introduction

Discovering Sufism

Although I have pleasant memories of the rural Canadian church I attended as a child,[3] with its upbeat, liberal theology and plethora of post-sermon snacks, by adolescence I was a precocious atheist, convinced that religions were long-outdated mythologies. They appeared to have a sum total of zero data to support their claims about unseen beings. I even tried to dissuade a friend of mine from getting confirmed in their church. It seemed to me they would be joining a fairy-tale club that had somehow managed to gain widespread social traction over the centuries, despite lacking any evidence to support its outlandish propositions.

My perspective changed quite unexpectedly in my first year of university, when I had several surprising experiences that we might call 'spiritual'. Although these experiences were likely of the garden-variety sort, they would have a profound impact on my life. I was dumbfounded to discover that claims about the nature of existence I had thought of as silly at best, turned out to be verifiably *real*. I had inadvertently stumbled upon the evidence I was so sure did not exist. I remember thinking that, left to my own devices and never having had those experiences, even if I lived for a thousand years, I would never have suspected how much was going on beyond surface appearances. I felt as though I had found a priceless treasure, an ocean of being lying just beneath life's surface, a luminosity and overwhelming positivity beyond birth and death.

---

[3] My mother, Bev Dickson, regularly took my brother and me to the Balzac United Church, located just outside of Calgary, Alberta. When we attended in the late 1980s and early 1990s, this irenic little church community was led by the indefatigably positive Reverend Gordon Saville (d.2018), whose overall message seemed to be embodied in a short phrase he repeated often in his sermons (usually to conclude them): 'Thanks be to God.'

Now that this depth-dimension of reality had, even in a small way, opened up to me, I naturally became intrigued by what others far more experienced had said about it: the teachings of humanity's prophets and sages suddenly became a lot more interesting. Religion no longer appeared to be a strange mythology from another, more ignorant, time. On the heels of my cursory encounter with some of what it spoke of, religion now glowed with the promise of insight into the deep structure of our existence and tried and true methods to sustainably connect with it.

The summer after my first year of undergrad, between shifts in an oilfield warehouse in Northern Alberta, I haunted local book stores and libraries reading everything about religion that I could get my hands on. One of the first I came across was Huston Smith's (d.2016) *The World's Religions,* a classic introduction that brimmed with Smith's own enthusiasm for the subject.[4] As I voraciously read and re-read each chapter sitting in my car on lunch breaks, I fell in love with every religion I came across.[5] I was enchanted by Buddhism, with its highly developed philosophy of mind and intractable practicality in dealing with human suffering. I was struck by the explanatory power of Hindu cosmology and impressed with the subtle depth of Daoist teachings. Although the Bible had previously held little appeal for me, I was now moved by the concision and profundity of the words of Jesus.

Alongside my steady diet of reading, I was seeking a way of life to connect me with reality's deeper dimensions. I began attending meditation sessions with a Tibetan Buddhist teacher in Calgary,[6]

---

4   Huston Smith's *The World's Religions* (New York, 2009) was initially published in 1958 as *The Religions of Man*. I was actually fortunate enough to meet Huston Smith the day after his 90th birthday at his retirement home in Berkeley, California, through the kind arrangement of M. Darrol Bryant, a professor of mine at the University of Waterloo, and long-time friend and colleague of Huston's. We had a lovely dinner together and I was impressed that Professor Smith still had book projects on the go. As his hearing was not strong, however, he misheard my name when I introduced myself and thought I had said I was 'Dorky Dickson'. I didn't have the heart (or verve) to correct him, so he innocently referred to me as Dorky during our time together.

5   For what remains one of the best genealogical critiques of the 'world religions' model, see Tomoko Masuzawa's *The Invention of World Religions* (Chicago, 2005).

6   I was fortunate to attend meditation (*shiné*) lessons with Jetsun Rigdzin Khandro, appointed by Karma Thinley Rinpoche to lead the Marpa Gompa Meditation Society (see https://www.marpagompa.org).

and considered running off to a monastery in Nepal to pursue enlightenment full-time. I also felt the need to make my way in the world and figure out career and relationships. Having made some Muslim friends, I started exploring Islam. As I struggled to integrate my draw toward the newly discovered transcendent with the earthly demands of establishing a viable adult life, the Islamic tradition grew in appeal for me, offering a grounding balance, organically weaving spirituality into the everyday. I soon joined a local mosque, grew my beard and tried to maintain the basics of Islamic practice.[7] Ultimately, however, I found myself unsatisfied with what American sociologist Robert Wuthnow calls a 'spirituality of dwelling', where religion is rooted in communal conformity and doctrinal certainty.[8] This 'local mosque Islam' had a lot of virtues, but did not offer what I was ultimately looking for: the visceral, experiential connection with God/Ultimate Reality. I still wanted to find a spiritual path that could offer real transformation and sustained access to deeper dimensions of consciousness, one that could grapple with existential questioning and experimentation.

The few books on Sufism I came across during my initial foray into literary spiritual seeking tended to be introductory in nature, delving little into its deeper philosophy. Whereas the boom in Buddhist publishing since the 1990s means that you can find an abundance of texts on Buddhist philosophy in most major North American

---

7   My first Muslim friends in the Calgary area were not born into particularly religious families, but had themselves become religious in early to mid-adulthood, through encounters with the Tablighi Jama'at. Although originating in India in the 1920s, by the 1990s the Jama'at had emerged as a massive global missionary movement, seeking not so much to convert non-Muslims, but rather to revive the practice of Islam among those already Muslim. For about a year or so after my conversion I joined my friends for several Tablighi outings in Alberta, usually spending a weekend in a mosque in another city, where we would attend talks by Tablighi members, and in some cases find Muslim households in the phonebook and knock on their doors in an attempt to get the men to join us at the mosque. I can only imagine the surprise of the Pakistani university students we tracked down in Edmonton, for example, when I showed up at their door (probably in a thawb or shalwar kameez) inviting them to a talk at the mosque. I later wrote about the group in Waterloo, Ontario. See William Rory Dickson, 'The *Tablighi Jama'at* in Southwestern Ontario: Making Muslim Identities and Networks in Canadian Urban Spaces', *Contemporary Islam*, 3 (2009), 99–112.

8   Robert Wuthnow, *After Heaven: Spirituality in America since the 1950s* (Berkeley, CA, 1998), pp. 3–4.

bookstores,⁹ it remains a rarity to come across Sufi equivalents. It was only years later, in graduate school, that I really began to encounter Sufism, both as a philosophy and practice. I planned to write my PhD dissertation on Sufism's pre-eminent philosopher, Muhyi al-Din Ibn 'Arabi (d.1240), but eventually pivoted to focus on Sufism in North America, engaging in several road trips throughout Canada and the United States to meet with and interview Sufi teachers, and explore how they were adapting Sufi practice in the West. During this time, I found that Sufi practices resonated with me in ways that others had not – there seemed to be a naturalness and 'fit' to the Sufi approach to spiritual development. Since then, and with the kind mentorship of my PhD supervisor, Professor Meena Sharify-Funk, I have pursued not only the academic study of Sufism but also its practice, and yet remain what Sufis have long described as a sort of 'wannabe', a *mutasawwif*: one who tries to be a Sufi but doesn't really get that far down the road.¹⁰

The Book's Purpose

In retrospect, the fact that I encountered Sufism in an academic setting is not all that surprising. Many scholars of Sufism have a personal connection to the spiritual path, and books about Sufism – especially those that deal with its deeper philosophical dimensions – rarely circulate outside of academic circles. Perhaps one reason for the limited availability of these texts is simply that, for many in the broader culture, Islam is not what comes to mind when we think of things like mystical spirituality or philosophy.¹¹ Too many only know an Islam distorted

---

9   It is not uncommon to find texts readily available on some of the more sophisticated and subtle systems of Buddhist philosophy, such as Madhyamaka, Yogacara or Dzogchen.

10 Early Sufis like 'Ali al-Hujwiri (d.1077) and 'Umar al-Suhrawardi (d.1234) defined the *mutasawwif* as the Sufi aspirant or seeker, unlike the Sufi proper, one who has been purified and accomplished their spiritual aspirations, at least to a significant degree.

11 Simply browsing the religion and spirituality shelves of major North American bookstores usually demonstrates just how much more there is available on the contemplative philosophies of Buddhism or Hinduism than can be found on analogous Islamic traditions. Translations or renderings of Rumi's poetry have been quite popular, but they are something of an exception in terms of the broader Sufi tradition and popular reading in the contemporary West.

by the spiritually bankrupt extremist groups that flail about the post-colonial landscape, themselves largely disconnected from the tradition they claim to represent (except of course for its surface symbols and accoutrement). In recent decades these numerically negligible groups, so often born of invasion, occupation and instability, have been platformed by various media for their sensational, violent actions. Those unfamiliar with Islam may come to perceive these groups as somehow representative of global Islamic culture, a diverse, spiritually rich and deeply humanistic matrix that stands in stark contrast to extremists who suffer from a uniformity of moral failing and spiritual shallowness.

Although a great deal more amenable than extremists, popular Muslim preachers frequently present Islam as a set of rules and rituals that function like a prepackaged program for paradise, or a blueprint for building a utopian society. Islam's deeper currents of spiritual wisdom seem to be largely ignored, not only by misinformed outsiders but even by influential insiders. In either case, Islamic spirituality/mysticism ends up being thought of as a misnomer or dismissed as something marginal when, in fact, what today we call Sufism (*tasawwuf* in Arabic) was at the heart of Islamic thought, practice and culture for most of its history, long understood by Muslims not as a separate 'ism' somehow grafted onto Islam, but rather as Islam's own deepest teachings. If we conceive of Islam as a walled garden, the outer walls of Islamic law and theology (shari'a) enclose the garden of Sufi philosophy and spirituality within. Its flowers of wisdom blossomed abundantly in every Muslim culture, and yet today we catch so little of their fragrance, or see so little of their color.

Besides aiding in the larger task of sharing some of the depth dimension of the Islamic tradition in a time of shallow stereotypes, this book is intended to offer practical insights for contemporary seekers, of whatever background: it is both an introduction to the deeper cuts of the Islamic 'mixtape' and something of a philosophically grounded self-help guide (at least implicitly). It addresses universal human questions about the nature of our world, about the reality of love and the meaning of destiny, about peace and conflict, religious diversity, the possibility of enlightenment, and the implacably mysterious nature of life. Sufism offers unique insights on these subjects for people navigating particularly perplexing times. Although there are already several phenomenal books exploring Sufi philosophy, especially in terms of Ibn 'Arabi's thought,[12] these tend to be more exclusively academic in nature and hence remain somewhat difficult to get into for those without a background in Islamic intellectual traditions.[13]

What follows then is a bit like a guided tour of a particularly verdant Sufi garden, an attempt to make its colors and fragrances available to those who are unsure how to navigate its myriad pathways, or even how to open the gate. The metaphorical garden I'm referring to is the *Fusus al-hikam* or, in English, *The Gemstones of Wisdom*. It is a short, mysterious work that has had an enormous impact over the centuries. Its author, Ibn 'Arabi, has long been revered the greatest master of the Sufi way and 'probably the most influential thinker of the second half of Islamic history'.[14] In his hundreds of written works, Ibn 'Arabi draws upon the semantic depths of the Qur'an and the spiritual template offered by the Prophet Muhammad to develop a staggering philosophical vision that facilitates harmonization at all levels of human experience, emphasizing our world's inevitable diversity while ever pointing to its deep unity. Although his view is rooted in the very heart of Islam, it aligns remarkably well with other spiritual philosophies, an alignment that I will gesture toward throughout this book.

---

12 I'm thinking here of the many excellent academic books and articles on Ibn 'Arabi's thought by scholars such as Mukhtar H. Ali, William C. Chittick, Michel Chodkiewicz, Gerald T. Elmore, Stephen Hirtenstein, Toshihiko Izutsu, Fitzroy Morrisey, Sachiko Murata, Mohammed Rustom, Sa'diyya Shaikh and Cyrus Ali Zargar, among others, whose works I will be drawing upon extensively throughout this book.

13 My brother, Rhett Dickson, is a software engineer and musician with broad reading interests. As I alluded to in the Acknowledgments, some years ago he was delving into material on philosophy and meditation and asked what books I might recommend to him on Sufi philosophy. I realized that most of the books I could think of would certainly be comprehensible, but not necessarily all that accessible or interesting for the non-expert. Hence this book is an attempt to bridge this gap between a) purely academic translations of Ibn 'Arabi's works and philosophical explanations of them, and b) a more accessible, general introduction to the Sufi philosophical tradition.

14 William C. Chittick, *Imaginal Worlds: Ibn al-'Arabi and the Problem of Religious Diversity* (Albany, NY, 1994), p.1.

The Gemstones of Wisdom is a concentrated synthesis of Ibn 'Arabi's entire body of writing, and was soon recognized as his *pièce de résistance*. Its main themes include the unity of the cosmos, the centrality of love, the diversity of religions and the vast potential of the human being. Its dissemination in Sufi circles helped foster a vibrant Islamic humanism that permeated Muslim cultures globally. Generations of the best minds wrote philosophical commentaries on the text. Their commentaries formed the foundation of Sufi philosophy, which then circulated among poets, artisans and educators, shaping Islamic cultures in lasting and profound ways.[15]

Its traces remain in every corner of Islamic civilization. Echoes of *Gemstones* can be found in the architectural design of the Taj Mahal.[16] It had pride of place in the advanced curricula in the Ottoman Empire's network of Islamic universities.[17] We find themes of Ibn 'Arabi's masterwork in the poetry and folk music of countries as varied as Bosnia and Morocco, Indonesia and Pakistan.[18] It is no exaggeration

---

15 I use the term 'Sufi philosophy' here to refer to what scholars tend to call 'philosophical Sufism.' Mukhtar H. Ali helpfully defines philosophical Sufism as the convergence of philosophy and Sufism in the school of Ibn 'Arabi. See his *Philosophical Sufism: An Introduction to the School of Ibn al-'Arabi* (New York, 2022). Mohammed Rustom observes that Ibn 'Arabi's Sufi school did not 'invent an entirely new philosophical vocabulary' but drew upon well-established terminology and conceptual frameworks in Islamic philosophy. Mohammed Rustom, 'Philosophical Sufism', in *The Routledge Companion to Islamic Philosophy*, ed. Richard C. Taylor and Luis Xavier Lopez-Farjeat (New York, 2016), p.400.

16 As Stephen Hirtenstein pointed out to me, Ibn 'Arabi's encyclopedic *al-Futuhat al-Makkiyya* is most likely the source of the possible connection between his work and the design of the Taj Mahal. See W. E. Begley's 'The Myth of the Taj Mahal and a New Theory of its Symbolic Meaning', *The Art Bulletin*, 61 (1979), 7–37.

17 Even the Ayatollah Khomeini (d.1989), in his 1989 letter to Mikhail Gorbachev (d. 2022), suggested that a study of the works of Ibn 'Arabi could help Russians build a more inclusive and holistic future after the Soviet Union's fall. For more on Khomeini's relationship with Ibn 'Arabi's works, see Alexander Knysh, '*Irfan* Revisited: Khomeini and the Legacy of Islamic Mystical Philosophy', *The Middle East Journal*, 46 (1992), 631–53.

18 Despite its popularity, Ibn 'Arabi's masterwork is also one of Islam's most controversial books: less esoterically – inclined theologians have attacked it for centuries as a text so radical that it falls into the most obvious and blatant sort of heresy. Beginning with Taqi al-Din Ahmad Ibn Taymiyya (d.1328), the foremost medieval opponent of Ibn 'Arabi's 'philosophical Sufism', a segment of Sunni's clerical class (the 'ulama') would condemn Ibn 'Arabi's works as ones that totally stray outside of borders of orthodoxy, or at least their own conception of it. In the centuries immediately following Ibn Taymiyya, Osman Yahia notes 34 books and 138 *fatawa* (religious rulings) opposed to Ibn 'Arabi and his teachings. Michel Chodkiewicz, *Seal of the Saints: Prophethood and Sainthood in the Doctrine of Ibn 'Arabi*, translated by Liadain Sherrard (Cambridge, UK, 1993), pp.19–20.

to suggest that much of the classical Islamic tradition bears its imprint.

In his preface to *The Gemstones of Wisdom*, Ibn 'Arabi describes the origin of the text in a sublime encounter with the spiritual form of the Prophet Muhammad, in Damascus in the year 1229 (or 627 in the Islamic Hijri calendar).[19] He says that the Holy Prophet handed the *Gemstones* to him and asked that he share it with people so that they may benefit from it. He then carefully transcribed the visionary text into written form, without any alteration or addition of his own.[20] As a result, Ibn 'Arabi says that the book is not drawn from his own wisdom, but is simply a faithful transmission of what the Prophet gave him in the ancient city.[21]

As the Qur'an suggests that Muhammad is a *mercy to the cosmos* (Q 21:107) it follows that the *Gemstones*, coming from Muhammad's hand and spiritual level, is itself intended as a mercy, bringing benefit to those in need, regardless of background, shedding light in otherwise persistent corners of darkness. This book is an attempt to consider some of the many lights this revelatory text offers us today and to make its rainbow-like spectrum of insight as accessible as possible to those

---

19 It seems Damascus has a special place in the history of spiritual experience, whether we think of the Apostle Paul encountering the spiritual form of Jesus Christ on a road to Damascus in the 1st century, or Ibn 'Arabi encountering the spiritual form of the Prophet Muhammad there in the 13th. Perhaps it has something to do with the city's ancient and storied past, as one of the world's oldest continuously inhabited cities. With its manifold layers of civilization – Nabatean, Roman, Arabic – the echoes of millions of lives across the spectrum of human history reverberate among its ancient streets, impregnating the city with presence, and, perhaps, thinning the border between this world and the invisible one.

20 His son-in-law and foremost disciple, Sadr al-Din al-Qunawi (d.1274), in his famous commentary on the Fusus, described it as the summation and quintessence of his work, emerging from Muhammad's spiritual level, which he describes as 'the Fountainhead of Essence (*mashrab al-dhat*), and the Unitary All-Comprehensiveness (*al-jam' al-ahadi*)'. Al-Qunawi suggests that the *Fusus* 'contains the epitome of spiritual perception (*dhawq*) of our Prophet – God's blessing be upon him – concerning the knowledge of God', and that the book functions as something like a key unlocking spiritual knowledge: 'It leads everyone of spiritual insight to the peak of their spiritual perceptions, the objects of their intentions and aspirations.' William C. Chittick, 'The Chapter Headings of the *Fusus*', *Journal of the Muhyiddin Ibn 'Arabi Society*, 2 (1984), 42–3.

21 Ibn 'Arabi describes this as a revelation (using an Arabic term for revelation found in the Qur'an), but clearly distinguishes himself from a prophet, affirming instead that he is merely an heir to prophetic wisdom. Whereas prophets receive their wisdom directly from God, saints receive it via the mediation of a prophetic presence. We will dive deeper into the relationship between prophets and saints in the sixth chapter on Moses. Binyamin Abrahamov, *Ibn al-'Arabi's Fusus al-hikam: An Annotated Translation of 'The Bezels of Wisdom'* (New York, 2015), p.57.

who may benefit from it. In the process of doing so, the book further sheds light on some of the deeper dimensions of the broader Islamic-Sufi tradition. Before exploring the *Gemstones* and Sufi philosophy in the chapters that follow, I will first briefly discuss a) what Sufism is, before considering b) the author of the *Gemstones*, Ibn 'Arabi, and then finally c) the book itself.

What is Sufism?

Sufism is a term that we use to capture a wide range of human activity, from meditation and virtue cultivation to popular fraternities, festivals and art, all of which flourished in Muslim societies.[22] More simply, we can think of Sufism as Islam's spiritual path. During the faith's early centuries Sufi masters worked with the teachings of the Qur'an and the Prophet Muhammad's example to develop systems of spiritual practice and personal development that facilitate the fulfillment of human potential. They sought to purify the heart so that the human being can directly encounter the transcendent majesty of Divine presence and channel the healing beauty of Divine love into the world.

In one sense, then, Sufism is simply the inward (or esoteric) aspect of Islam and Sufis have generally understood their path to be the inner dimension of the Prophet Muhammad's Way, or, in Arabic, his *Sunnah*. On the other hand, Sufis tell us that the soul's quest to discover its own nature is as old as humanity and that Sufism as we know it is just the latest expression of this ancient journey. Sufis believe that not only Muhammad but all of the great prophets before him like Moses and Jesus taught accessible forms of law and morality for society as a

---

22 For example, each year there is a massive birthday celebration held in Tanta, Egypt, for Ahmad al-Badawi (d.1276), a legendary Sufi saint buried there. Thousands from the Middle East and Africa congregate for procession, chanting, lights and charity, in honor of al-Badawi. For more on this, see Catherine Mayeur-Jaouen, *The Mulid of Sayyid al-Badawi of Tanta: Egypt's Legendary Sufi Festival*, translated by Colin Clement (Cairo, 2019). Such saintly birthday celebrations can be found throughout Muslim countries. Sufism is also associated with ancient traditions of virtue and chivalry, and Sufis developed religious orders and craft guilds to help Muslims embody these virtues. In terms of the arts, Sufis have inspired ecstatic music like *qawwali* in South Asia, made popular in the twentieth century through the remarkable voices of Nusrat Fateh Ali Khan (d.1997), the Sabri Brothers and Abida Parveen.

whole, and more hidden, inward paths of spiritual discovery, reserved for those with the requisite need and receptivity. Later Sufis would speak of the 'Sufism' of the Christians and the Jews, believing that each religion had its own unique inner path, though all sharing the same goal of human transformation. In its deepest essence then, Sufism is the spiritual heart of every religion and yet not limited to any one of them. Turkish Sufi master Sheikh Muzaffer Ozak al-Jerrahi (d.1985) expressed this metaphorically as follows: 'A river passes through many countries and each claims it for its own. But there is only one river.'[23]

Sufism is a path of knowledge, knowledge of the *transformational* rather than *informational* sort. When pursued whole-heartedly, this transformative knowledge leads to human completion, or the maturation of human potential, whereby the individual becomes a vessel of the most sublime qualities in the universe. The fully flowered human being that results from this transformative path radiates a creative, compassionate, life-giving energy field, one that inspires myriad cultural forms wherever they go. Where we find Sufis, we soon find exquisite art and music, profound philosophy, and innovative forms of social organization springing up around them. Sufis are associated with Islam's celebrated *madhhab-i 'ishq* or 'way of love'. They wrote untold volumes of love poetry, drawing upon the suffering and sorrow, the ecstasy and elation of romantic love, as a metaphor for the soul's longing for its primordial home. Sufis are also philosophers who have produced complex commentaries on the hidden meanings of the Qur'an, and metaphysical systems mapping the various modalities of existence. Sufis established global spiritual fraternities – the great Sufi orders of the medieval period – which, during the political fragmentation following the devastation wrought by the Mongol invasions, offered Muslims social security, community, culture and, most importantly, access to Islam's deeper spiritual reality.

Tracing back its origins, *Sufi* was a term first used in Islam's early

---

23 Muzaffer Ozak, *Love is the Wine: Talks of a Sufi Master in America*, edited and compiled by Ragip (Robert) Frager (Prescott, AZ, 2009), p.1.

centuries[24] to describe individuals who took the Qur'an's message particularly close to heart, those whom *neither trade nor commerce distract from the remembrance of God* (Q 24:37).[25] Like the Bible, the Qur'an repeatedly warns us of the fleeting nature of the world's pleasures and the precarity of our lives in it. As everything is passing, it is only with what is ultimately Real that we find stable, lasting value. Alongside calling us to orient ourselves toward the ground of our reality (*al-Haqq* or the Real), the Qur'an warns that the implications of our deeds reverberate far beyond this life. It affirms the preciousness of the human soul, and the success that accrues to those who care for and purify it, alongside the inevitable suffering experienced by those who abuse and corrupt it (Q 91:7–10).

The Qur'an calls upon us to avoid obsessing over the 'shiny objects' found on life's surface, which can offer neither sustainable peace nor satisfaction. Instead, its verses, in various ways, suggest we gravitate toward life's center, within our own heart, where we find not only our deepest connections with others, but also with our very Origin. It is only here in the depths of our own being that what is most real can be known and lasting joy can be found.[26] To access the deeper dimensions of the self, however, we need to break our addiction to these 'shiny objects' – the distracting draws and desires of our world – the metaphorical 'wines' we get drunk on. To accomplish this, we don't need to somehow force ourselves to abandon these wines, but can instead find something much better to drink, after which the appeal of lesser varieties will naturally dissolve. Jalal al-Din Rumi (d.1273), for

---

24 Christopher Melchert notes that the historical emergence of the term 'Sufi' has not been 'convincingly mapped in detail', though it can be traced to an Iraqi 'mystical trend' of the ninth century, with various eighth-century ascetics pointed to as their predecessors. The first person recorded to have been called a Sufi is Abu Hashim (d.767), associated with the pious wearing of wool (suf in Arabic). Christopher Melchert, 'Origins and Early Sufism', in *The Cambridge Companion to Sufism*, ed. Lloyd Ridgeon (New York, 2014), pp.3, 13.

25 As we will see in the fourth chapter on Jonah, the Qur'an declares, above all else commanded, that *dhikr Allah* or the *remembrance of God* is the greatest (Q 29:45), and Sufis are those who build their lives around this practice, integrating an awareness of God with every moment and facet of life.

26 Sara Sviri, a scholar of Sufism, defines the spiritual path as 'a quest for a center from which everything emerges and to which everything returns'. Sara Sviri, *The Taste of Hidden Things: Images on the Sufi Path* (Inverness, CA, 1997), p.1.

example (probably the most famous of Sufi poets) admonishes us to not get drunk on any old wine, spending our lives on mediocre swill, but rather, like a connoisseur, to find the best vintage in the universe:

> *There are thousands of wines*
> *that can take over our minds.*
>
> *Don't think all ecstasies*
> *are the same!*
>
> *Jesus was lost in his love for God.*
> *His donkey was drunk with barley.*[27]

From Islam's inception we find reports of individuals who focused on purifying their souls through intensive worship, drawing their attention away from outward ambitions and worries, toward the inward reality of the heart, and its mysterious essence, a love beyond time and space. In other words, we find those who sought the purest wine in the cosmos, forgoing the everyday sorts in the hopes of tasting God's own vintage, a 'dark wine so potent that, drinking it, we leave the two worlds'.[28] Once they tasted this wine of divine love, they weren't all that concerned with trying other, lesser varieties.

Various accounts suggest that a life of spiritual purification and inwardness is precisely how the Prophet Muhammad and his closest companions lived: owning very little, fasting frequently, spending significant amounts of time in prayer and meditation. 'Sufi' seems to be the name given to Muslims who attempted to maintain the levels of spiritual awareness, devotion and ethical scrupulousness found among the first generations of Muslims, known as the *salaf*. In this sense

---

27 Jalal al-Din Rumi, *The Essential Rumi*, translated by Coleman Barks and John Moyne (New York, 1997), p.6. Barks admittedly takes creative license with an English translation of the original Persian works of Rumi, though in the case of the verses quoted above, they remain quite close to the original. These particular verses are from Rumi's *Masnavi* IV.2687–91. For the original Persian, and a more literal translation, see www.masnavi.net (accessed January 25, 2023).

28 God's 'wine' is a metaphor for spiritual experience. Sufis have described proximity to God's presence as a rich, dark drink that intoxicates such that 'the two worlds' seem to fade into insignificance. The 'two worlds' Rumi refers to here are likely either a) the world of our current life (*dunya*) and the world of the afterlife (*akhira*), or b) the worlds of the seen and unseen, the material and spiritual. *Masnavi* IV.2683.

Sufism is simply the process of taking Islamic teachings to heart, of following the way of the Prophet and his followers, and yet in another sense Sufism is very much a continuation of what was being done for centuries by Christian sages – monks and nuns who withdrew from the many distractions of the world to devote themselves to a life of prayer and spiritual purification. Known as the Desert Mothers and Fathers, these ascetic contemplatives flourished in the deserts and wild places of the Middle East in the centuries before Muhammad's birth. They were spiritual power stations that would charge medieval Christianity with vitality, as their intensive religiosity crystalized in the form of monasteries, some of the most famous in the region including St. Pachomius in Egypt, Mar Saba in Palestine and St. Simeon in Syria.

Considering the centrality of monasteries to Christian life in the Middle East, it is not all that surprising that Sufi doctrines and practices overlapped significantly with Christian monasticism. Even the word *Sufi* itself may have some connection with the wearing of wool (in Arabic *suf*), a coarse fabric that signified abandonment of worldly comfort among Christian ascetics. Medieval Sufi literature abounds with admiration for the spiritual discipline and devotion of Christian holy women and men.[29] More broadly, we can observe that Islam and Christianity were basically 'pickled' in the same ancient spiritual culture of the Near East, with its Mesopotamian, Egyptian, Greek and Persian streams of wisdom – streams that we will explore further as this book unfolds.

One of the ways that Sufism *differed* from medieval Christian spirituality is that it was premised on taking the religious life of the monk or nun outside of the cloister walls or desert cave – integrating spiritual practice with the hustle of worldly challenges.[30] The Prophet Muhammad is celebrated by Muslims as an archetype and model of human completion, fully integrating spirituality with all aspects of life in the world. He worked as a shepherd and trader, functioned as a community leader, was married and had children. Islam's institution

---

29 Alexander Knysh, *Sufism: A New History of Islamic Mysticism* (Princeton, NJ, 2017), p.20.
30 The Prophet Muhammad is reported to have said, 'There is no monasticism (*rahbaniyya*) in Islam.' Quoted in Knysh, *Sufism*, p.16.

of ritual prayers marking the cycle of the sun throughout the day (dawn, noon, mid-afternoon, sunset, night), and fasting from dawn to sunset during the month of Ramadan, are both ways of integrating the constant prayer and frequent fasting of a monastic with everyday life. Islamic sacred law (shari'a) facilitates a way of being that enables the mammalian needs of human beings (food, shelter and family) to be equitably met, while ensuring that the drives and desires for such things do not derail the pursuit of spiritual enlightenment. Muslims understand the Prophetic paradigm as a model that calibrates human life such that its outward aspects and inward possibilities are harmonized as best as possible, with neither totally subsuming the other. In these respects, Islam more closely resembles Judaism, which similarly joins an awareness of the transcendent with family and community life, all regulated by sacred law.

The Prophet Muhammad was incredibly active in his work to establish the Muslim community in early seventh-century Arabia, an environment largely hostile to the new religion. He engaged in everything from resolving disputes between neighbors and spouses, leading armies, securing tribal alliances and establishing a more compassionate economy. And yet this social activism was the expression of an inner life of intense prayer, visionary experience and a perpetual awareness of the unity underlying our world's apparent multiplicity. If we envision our lives as a metaphorical mountain, the Prophet was busy with all of the 'hustle and bustle' taking place at the mountain's base while his heart remained 'alone with the Alone'[31] atop the mountain's silent peak.[32]

The spiritual energy field that developed around the Prophet – an energy of blessing, healing and peace, known as *baraka* – infused the lives of those closest to him, allowing the mountain peak's pristine air to circulate among the base. His family and friends were transformed

---

31 I should give a nod here to Henry Corbin's *Alone with the Alone: Creative Imagination in the Sufism of Ibn 'Arabi* (Princeton, NJ, 1969).

32 'Ali ibn Abi Tabib characterized those who are close to God as follows: 'With their bodies they keep company with the world, while their spirits are tied to the transcendent realm.' Quoted in the famous record of 'Ali's discourses, the *Nahj al-Balagha*. Reza Shah-Kazemi, *Justice and Remembrance: Introducing the Spirituality of Imam 'Ali* (London, 2006).

by their intimate companionship with him, as well as by their recitation of the revelation he was given, the Qur'an. They inherited from Muhammad not only this profound spiritual energy, but also the Qur'an's deep meanings and inner wisdom (*hikma*), teachings not always shared with the larger community. This *baraka* and *hikma* transformed the Prophet's loved ones and they themselves became conduits of it.

Both Sunni and Shi'i Muslims believe that Muhammad's Way, in all of its dimensions, was fully transmitted to his son-in-law, cousin and close companion, 'Ali ibn Abi Talib (d.661). Besides his role as the fourth successor to the Prophet and leader of the Muslim community (*khalifa*), 'Ali is celebrated in Muslim tradition as a paragon of nobility, chivalry, integrity and wisdom. He was an archetypal warrior-sage, as famous for his peerless valour and consummate skill on the battlefield (symbolized by his two-pronged sword, *Zulfiqar*), as he was for his philosophical and spiritual insight, his profound aphorisms and learning. The Prophet is reported to have said, 'I am the city of knowledge and 'Ali is its gate.'[33] Most Sufi orders trace their spiritual lineage back to the Prophet Muhammad through 'Ali. This means that Sufi and Shi'i Muslims share veneration of 'Ali as one of the community's most important guides, and the esoteric wisdom of

---

33   This hadith is recorded in both Shi'i and Sunni sources (see, for example, Hakim al-Nishapuri's *Mustadrak* 3.127).

both systems of Islamic spirituality go through him.³⁴ 'Ali was further associated with a group of particularly devout Muslims who embraced a life of poverty, essentially living on the stoop of Muhammad's Mosque in Medina in constant prayer and meditation, an area known as the *suffa*. They became known then as the 'people of the *suffa*' and their term may be another source for the name 'Sufi'.³⁵

The students of 'Ali and others among Muhammad's closest companions, including Abu Bakr (d.634),³⁶ continued to transmit the Prophet's deepest teachings and living spiritual energy to those with the necessary aptitude and receptivity. Those who received these teachings were themselves transformed, with their hearts opened to inner wisdom, spiritual realities and even a direct experience of God. Within a few generations study circles formed around those who had received this deeper Prophetic transmission, in the urban centers of the expanding Arab-Muslim empire. These proto-Sufis eventually

---

34 However, Shi'i Muslims also believe that Muhammad's spiritual and political authority is inherited *exclusively* through the line of descent beginning with 'Ali and the Prophet's daughter Fatima (d.c.632), through their children Hasan (d.670) and Husayn (d.680). Collectively they are the 'People of the House' or *ahl al-bayt* – the people of the Prophet's own household. Beginning with 'Ali, and continuing through Hasan and Husayn, leaders among the *ahl al-bayt* are known as Imams, and are thought to have inherited some of the Prophet's light, wisdom and guidance, much along the lines of the various familial lineages of prophecy described in the Qur'an, such as Abraham and his sons Isaac and Ishmael. This inherited holiness enabled the Imams to lead the Muslim community and guide them in their understanding of the faith. Although Sunnis acknowledged the paramount spiritual importance of the *ahl al-bayt*, and a great many Sufi orders trace their lineage through the first Imams, this prophetic inheritance was believed to be more widely available, and hence any particularly devout and spiritually purified Muslim may have access to this, even if not related to the Prophet through a direct line of descent. One particularly important figure for both Sunni and Shi'i Muslims is Ja'far al-Sadiq (d.765), who lived before the Sunni–Shi'a divide crystalized. Besides being credited with founding his own school of law, some of the earliest mystical commentary on the Qur'an is traced to him, and many Sufis see Ja'far as a key link in their connection back to the Prophet. For more on al-Sadiq's mystical teachings, see *Spiritual Gems: The Mystical Qur'an Commentary, Ascribed to Ja'far al-Sadiq*, translated by Farhana Mayer (Louisville, 2011).

35 See Martin Lings's chapter on 'The People of the Bench', in his *Muhammad: His Life Based on the Earliest Sources* (Rochester, VT), pp.172-4.

36 Other companions of Muhammad's are thought to have been taught some of the Prophet's deeper teachings and inner wisdom, such as Abu Dharr al-Ghifari (d.652) and Salman al-Farsi (d.657).

attracted public attention, in places like Iraq and Persia.[37] Not all of this attention was friendly, as some Muslim theologians feared that early Sufis were straying from orthodoxy in their claims of first-hand knowledge of God, and in their descriptions of divine encounter using the language of love and desire.

If you prefer your religion sober and static, sensible and scholarly, you may understandably get a bit perturbed when someone shows up claiming to have had a direct encounter with God that totally transcends rational categories and causes their hearts to overflow with love beyond their wildest imaginings. Some Sufis even expressed divine love in terms of passionate desire (*'ishq*), which scandalized those theologians more prone to see God as a great King to be obeyed from afar, rather than an intimate Companion of the heart. Although the Qur'an does indeed point to God's transcendence totally beyond likeness to any created thing, it further affirms His profound closeness to us, stating that God is nearer to us than our own jugular vein (Q 50:16).[38] Against accusations of heresy, early Sufis affirmed that their path was nothing but the deepest heart of Qur'anic teachings, and that the best Muslims were those who not only knew the texts and traditions of Islam, but actualized their meaning within their own bodies, minds and souls.[39]

Perhaps the most celebrated of early Sufis is Rabi'a al-'Adawiyya (d.801), of Basra, Iraq. She was as relentless in her call for sincerity

---

37 These 'proto-Sufis' were known by various terms, including renunciant (*zahid*), impoverished one (*faqir*), worshipper (*'abid*) or righteous one (*salih*). For more on the early development of Sufism, see Arthur F. Buehler, *Recognizing Sufism: Contemplation in the Islamic Tradition* (London, 2016).

38 Paradoxically, Iranian philosopher Jawadi Amuli observes that God's 'invisibility is due to the intensity of His manifestation, and His remoteness is because of His extreme proximity'. As quoted by Ali, *Philosophical Sufism*, p.41.

39 Gerhard Bowering points out that early Sufis produced essentially three genres of text: 1) the Sufi treatise, which defined central Sufi ideas and spiritual terminology, perhaps best represented by Abu Talib al-Makki's (d.996) *Qut al-Qulub*; 2) the Sufi hagiography, which contained stories of Sufi saints, their lives, teachings and miracles, best represented by Abu 'Abd al-Rahman al-Sulami's (d.1021) *Tabaqat al-Sufiyya* and finally 3) the Sufi manual, which was in a sense a synthesis of the first two genres, including both doctrine and stories, as well as practices, representing a maturation of the *'ilm al-tasawwuf* or 'Sufi Science', with this genre best represented by 'Abd al-Karim al-Qushayri's (d.1072) *Risala*. Gerhard Bowering, *The Mystical Vision of Existence in Classical Islam: The Qur'anic Hermeneutics of Sahl al-Tustari* (d. 283/896) (New York, 1980), pp.19–20.

and love as she was in her critique of shallow, performative religion.⁴⁰ She is reported to have said, 'Oh Lord, if I worship you out of fear of hell, burn me in hell. If I worship you in the hope of paradise, forbid it for me. And if I worship you for your own sake, do not deprive me of your eternal beauty.'⁴¹ Rabiʿa is further depicted as frequently 'one-upping' her male Sufi interlocutors. In one narrative she is said to have heard the famed ascetic Salih al-Murri (d.793) preaching that 'if you constantly knock, one day the door will be opened for you'. She called out in reply: 'The door is always open, but who wishes to enter?'⁴² For Muslims, Rabiʿa remains an archetype of unflinching love of God, spiritual mastery, wisdom and critique of official versions of religion that failed to embody these deeper values. Rabiʿa's approach would become central to later Sufi developments.

Sufism and 'Establishment' Islam

By the medieval period, in most Muslim contexts, Sufism went totally mainstream, forming a series of popular religious orders that would become the standard-bearers of Islamic devotion from Morocco to Malaysia.⁴³ Sufis gained public admiration as spiritual exemplars, endorsements from establishment jurists and theologians (and in many cases were themselves these jurist-theologians – collectively known as the 'ulama'), and received the patronage of sultans. From market stalls to palace halls, Sufis were celebrated by Muslims as the most profound representatives of Islamic teachings. The lineage of masters at the

---

40 Although much of what we know of her is filtered through later, often legendary accounts, she remains 'an important part of Islamic cultural memory', and is celebrated for her peerless piety. See Rkia Elaroui Cornell, *Rabiʿa: From Narrative to Myth* (London, 2019).

41 As quoted in Michael Sells, *Early Islamic Mysticism: Sufi, Qurʾan, Miraj, Poetic and Theological Writings* (New York, 1996), p.169.

42 I've slightly paraphrased the description of this story by Rkia Elaroui Cornell, *Rabiʿa from Narrative to Myth: The Many Faces of Islam's Most Famous Woman Saint, Rabiʿa al-ʿAdawiyya* (London, 2019), p.72.

43 Michel Chodkiewicz notes that Ibn ʿArabi's era was a pivotal one in this respect. Within decades of his death the Mongols destroyed the ʿAbbasid Caliphate in Baghdad (1258), inaugurating a political shift in Muslim societies with wide-ranging implications. 'It was no accident that this was also the period of transition in Sufi doctrine from implicit to explicit, and the start, sociologically speaking, of its transition from informality to formality, fluidity to organization.' *Seal of the Saints*, p.10.

heart of a Sufi order offered regular Muslims a chance to connect with individuals that perpetuated the spiritual blessing and wisdom of the Prophet Muhammad.

As the various disciplines of Islamic learning crystalized into schools of thought, the foremost Sunni theologians, following Abu Hamid al-Ghazali, categorized these disciplines as the inward (esoteric) and the outward (exoteric) aspects of Islam. For al-Ghazali Sufism was simply Islam's inner science parallel to its outward sciences like jurisprudence and scriptural commentary.[44] Interestingly, he observed that the jurists often dealt with the mundane matters of worldly life, things like business contracts, marriage and divorce, criminal acts, and building regulations, and may have had little understanding of spirituality and ultimate reality. He called those Sufis who specialize in spiritual matters the *'ulama al-akhira* or the scholars of the afterlife, the scientists of the unseen.[45] Although we cannot credit al-Ghazali solely with the almost universal acceptance of Sufism as one of the integral disciplines of the Islamic tradition, 'soon after Ghazali, in fact, the majority of Sunni scholars would become affiliated with a Sufi path'.[46]

The most common form of conceptualizing Sufism at this time was based upon a popular hadith, in which the Angel Gabriel appears before the Prophet Muhammad in the form of a man. Gabriel asks Muhammad to tell him about *Islam*, *Iman* (faith) and *Ihsan* (the perfection of faith or spiritual excellence). The answers given by the Prophet came to define the three 'layers' of the Islamic tradition for Muslims.

> The Prophet said, 'Islam is to testify there is no God but God and Muhammad is the Messenger of God, to establish prayer, to give charity, to fast the month of Ramadan, and to perform pilgrimage

---

[44] Al-Ghazali also characterizes Sufism as the 'science of unveiling' (*'ilm al-mukashafa*). His most detailed discussion classifying the various sciences (*'ulum*) of Islam is found in the first book (*Kitab al-'Ilm*) of his *Ihya 'Ulum al-Din*. For a helpful breakdown of his schema, see Alexander Trieger, 'Al-Ghazali's Classifications of the Sciences and Descriptions of the Highest Theoretical Science', *Dîvân: Disiplinler Arası Çalışmalar Dergisi*, 16:30 (2011), 1–32.

[45] Khaled Abou El Fadl, 'What Type of Law is Islamic Law', in *Routledge Handbook of Islamic Law*, edited by Khaled Abou El Fadl, Ahmad Atif Ahmad and Said Fares Hassan (New York, 2019), p.27.

[46] Samer Dajani, *Sufis and Shari'a: The Forgotten School of Mercy* (Edinburgh, 2023), p.2.

to Mecca if a way is possible.' The man said, 'You have spoken truthfully.' ... He said, 'Tell me about Iman.' The Prophet said, 'Iman is to believe in God, His angels, his Books, His Messengers, the Last Day, and to believe in destiny, its good and its evil.' The man said, 'You have spoken truthfully. Tell me about Ihsan.' The Prophet said, 'Ihsan is to worship God as if you see Him, and if you do not see Him, to know that He surely sees you.'[47]

Islam is essentially *what Muslims are to do* (the Five Pillars, consisting of the testimony, daily prayer, annual charity, fasting and pilgrimage), whereas Iman represents *what Muslims are to believe*, particularly the six core beliefs: God, His prophets, scriptures, angels, the afterlife and destiny. Ihsan is the topmost layer representing *how Muslims are to be*, what states of being and awareness should be cultivated, foremost being awareness of God's presence. We may also think of this as the body, mind and soul of the Islamic tradition. By al-Ghazali's time the accepted schools of law (*fiqh*) were thought to define Islam, the schools of theology (*kalam*) clarified the content of Iman, while the Sufi orders represented the path of Ihsan.[48]

Valued as masters of both Islam's deeper philosophy and spirituality, as well as its outward rituals and ethical norms, Sufis were given prestigious positions of religious authority by the various dynasties ruling Muslims in the medieval period. Despite the fact that many Sufis functioned within the bureaucracy of 'establishment' Islam, Sufis were frequently critical of ruling elites and the dangers that the halls of power posed to a genuine spiritual life. There were also Sufis on the margins of respectable Muslim society, living what we might now see as a sort of 'punk rock' approach to spirituality. These rebel Sufis, often called dervishes, purposefully transgressed social norms, drew

---

[47] This hadith is found in the two most revered Sunni hadith collections, *Sahih-al-Bukhari* and *Sahih Muslim*.

[48] In fact, it was widely agreed upon among Muslim authorities that one cannot be a complete Muslim *without* Sufism, for the inner aspects of Muhammad's path (things like purity of intention, awareness of God, compassion) were more important than their outward practices and rules: one's performance of Islamic ritual and obedience to Islamic law were only truly valid if there was a corresponding inward intention and sincerity, a moral development and an opening of the heart.

attention to the hypocrisy of establishment forms of religion and called to the divine within. If they wore hats at all they wore them crookedly, and in some cases these Sufis were pierced, dreadlocked, drug-taking wanderers.

Sufism from the Inside Out

If we take a step out of the perspective of history and attempt to discuss Sufism from the inside – as a spiritual path – things get a bit trickier. Sufis tell us that their way is best found, not in words, but in silence. So, we begin by acknowledging that anything you read about Sufism, including this book, is not going to *remotely* suffice in conveying what it really is. Hazrat Inayat Khan (d.1927) was a classically trained Indian musician and Sufi master. He was also the first Sufi teacher in the West. He put it this way: 'Sufism avoids words, words from which differences and distinctions arise. Words can never express the truth fully.'[49] The speaker of words so often means something different by them than what the listener hears, and hence endless misunderstanding can ensue.[50] This is particularly so when it comes to words about the more subtle dimensions of existence.

In *Gemstones,* in the chapter on Ezra, Ibn 'Arabi writes that 'hearing about something falls far short of perceiving it through direct tasting'.[51] The deeper you go within, the less you are able to say anything about what you find. The spiritual journey goes increasingly beyond words and its exquisitely subtle waystations – entire worlds of meaning – must be 'tasted' for oneself. As such, Sufism is better thought of as a science of experience rather than a collection of concepts or arrangement of words. Sufi practices are meant to allow the practitioner to directly verify the vast spectrum of reality for themselves. In Arabic this verification is called *dhawq* (taste), *kashf*

---

49 Hazrat Inayat Khan, *Mastery through Accomplishment* (New Lebanon, NY, 2011).

50 In chapter 54 of his *Futuhat,* Ibn 'Arabi discusses *ishara,* or allusions. In particular, he relates that many Sufis have *purposefully* spoken in allusive ways, in part to protect themselves from the machinations of religious clerics.

51 Muhyi al-Din Ibn 'Arabi, *Fusus al-hikam,* edited by Mahmud Erol Kilic and Abdurrahim Alkis (Istanbul, 2016), p.122.

(unveiling), *tahqiq* (realization), *mushahada* (direct witnessing) or *ma'rifa* (experiential knowledge).

Why this Sufi emphasis on direct experience? Well, as an analogy, you can imagine trying to explain what an orange tastes like to someone who has never tried a citrus fruit. You could use words like 'sweet' or 'acidic' but no collection of words, however well-woven together, however expressive, will come anywhere close to conveying the utterly unique, unmistakable taste of an orange. At the end of the day, such knowledge is only available through experience, as the experience of tasting is inestimably richer than any set of words can possibly convey. Rumi expresses this pointedly, in describing spiritual realization:

> Oneness is on the other side of descriptions and states. Nothing but duality enters speech's playing-field. So, either live in this duality, like the double-seeing man, or sew up your mouth and be happily silent![52]

In particular, according to Sufis, sewing up one's mouth and entering into silence attunes one to the remarkable depth of the living moment. When we rest in silence, we find ourselves immersed in the mysterious presence of our own being. Tuning into this presence quiets the mind, clears the heart center and allows the energy of life to flow freely. Ironically, although our own presence is what we *are*, we tend to be strangers to it, with our attention focused outward. Ibn 'Arabi invites us to reverse this outward flow of attention: 'So let us turn our contemplation to our [own human] Essence, which is the way of our liberation!'[53]

If we consistently follow Ibn 'Arabi's invitation, we may eventually discover that our own essence has no end, and realize that we are the limitless being of the universe, temporarily condensed into a human

---

52 Jalal al-Din Rumi, *Masnavi* VI.2034–5. As quoted in William C. Chittick, *The Sufi Path of Love: The Spiritual Teachings of Rumi* (Albany, NY, 1983), p.275.

53 I've slightly altered Gerald T. Elmore's translation of Ibn 'Arabi's quote here from his *'Anqa' Mughrib*, in *Islamic Sainthood in the Fullness of Time: Ibn al-'Arabi's Book of the Fabulous Gryphon* (Boston, 1999), p.11.

body and personality.⁵⁴ The 20th-century Sri Lankan Sufi master Bawa Muhaiyaddeen (d.1986) defined Sufism very much along these lines, stating simply, 'Sufism is the vast open space of the heart.'⁵⁵ Similarly, Professor Abdul Aziz Said (d.2021),⁵⁶ who was the doctoral supervisor of my doctoral supervisor (Professor Sharify-Funk), and a close student of Ibn 'Arabi, defined spirituality as 'attaining the widest possible context'.⁵⁷

As we open to the wide context of existence and dissolve into the boundless presence of the moment, we discover its inherent peace. We find that, as Professor Sharify-Funk shared with me, 'contentment is our essential being'. We see that existence is inherently good, that we can trust the entire process of life and death. And the more we rest in the natural state, the more the conflicted elements of the self spontaneously harmonize. This inner harmony emanates outward as balance and awareness, and a profound love expressed in compassion for others. Sufism then is found in the silent vastness of our own presence, a heart attuned to natural goodness and love, and an empty, open mind. This is what is known in Islam as the *fitra*, the original human state that

---

54 The Prophet Muhammad is reported to have said that 'one who knows their self knows their Lord', or in Arabic, *man 'arafa nafsuhu faqad 'arafa rabbuhu*. Ibn 'Arabi notes that this saying (hadith) remains unconfirmed in terms of its chain of narration, but is confirmed through spiritual experience. For more see Dom Sylvester Houedard, 'Notes on the More than Human Saying: "Unless you know yourself you cannot know God"', *Newsletter of the Muhyiddin Ibn 'Arabi Society*, Summer 1990, http://www.ibnarabisociety.org/articles/notesonsaying.html (accessed April 26, 2020).

55 As related to me by Bawa's student, Michael Green, in an interview conducted on June 26, 2010, in Coatesville, Pennsylvania.

56 Hailing from Mesopotamia, or the *balad bayn al-nahrayn* (Land Between the Two Rivers) in Syria, Professor Abdul Aziz Said (d.2021) was the founding director of the International Peace and Conflict program at the American University in Washington, D.C. Having suffered from war as a child, Professor Said sought to foster a more cooperative model of international relations, informed by spiritual values like justice and reconciliation. He was affectionately called AU's 'Living Legend of Peace'. Alongside training scholars and public servants, he was also a behind-the-scenes diplomat and Sufi teacher, connecting seekers, teachers and friends from various Sufi orders and backgrounds. For an overview of Abdul Aziz Said's life and work, see Nathan C. Funk and Meena Sharify-Funk's edited volume, *Abdul Aziz Said: A Pioneer in Peace, Intercultural Dialogue, and Cooperative Global Politics* (Berlin, 2022). Also see Nathan C. Funk and Abdul Aziz Said, *Peacemaking in the Middle East* (Boulder, CO, 2008), and Abdul Aziz Said and Meena Sharify-Funk (editors), *Cultural Diversity and Islam* (Lanham, MD, 2003).

57 As quoted by Kabir Helminski, 'Requiem for Abdul Aziz Said 1931–2021', *Threshold Society Newsletter*. https://sufism.org/?na=archive&email_id=6 (accessed September 1, 2023).

the prophets and guides are here to help us return to. It is in this state that the human being is both at peace within themselves and of use to others, positioned to respond to life's challenges with wisdom and grace, and to plant seeds of love and creativity wherever they go.

Recovering this natural human existence is what the inner aspect of every prophetic teaching is for. Prophets like Moses, Jesus and Muhammad not only brought scripture, law and moral teachings for the community at large – they also brought a living spirituality that animated these outward elements of revelation, a stream of *baraka* that transformed generations of followers thereafter. To ears inclined toward a skepticism of religious claims, this may sound like flowery nonsense. And yet Sufis have always suggested that the claims made by humanity's prophets and guides are not simply a series of emotionally pleasant thoughts, or a set of interesting notions that can be related to only through belief or rejection, but rather that spiritual truth can be directly and unmistakably confirmed for oneself, in a way that gives certainty deeper than any other sort of knowledge, as this knowledge is a result of *being* what one knows, rather than merely hearing or observing it.[58]

As a vehicle of *baraka*, the mysterious energy of blessing traced back to God through the Prophet Muhammad, and *hikma*, his esoteric knowledge and wisdom, Sufism is the spiritual heart of Islam, and the vast majority of Sufis were and are devout Muslims. And yet the essence of Sufism is the realization of truth, which is, as the Sufis say, beyond all time, form, name and place: the meaning of truth always transcends the forms of its expression. As Muzaffer Ozak put it, the river is not owned by any of the lands it runs through. This formless, universal essence enabled Sufism to take on many shapes and forms

---

58 Indeed, René Descartes (d.1650) famously applied a rigorous skepticism to our various forms of knowledge and found that he could legitimately question the validity of any sense perception or thought, but could not question that there was *someone* perceiving and thinking. He found, I think accurately, that we can question all forms of knowledge but in doing so must admit that there is in fact *something or someone* that questions – this *being* is the only thing we can have truly certain knowledge of. He articulates this in various works of his, including his *Discourse on the Method of Rightly Conducting One's Reason* (1637) and in his *Meditations on First Philosophy* (1641).

historically. In places like India for example, Sufis opened the doors of their path to Hindus, and in places like Syria and Egypt, to Christians and Jews, seeing one's religion of birth as secondary to the path of one's heart.[59]

In my research on contemporary Sufi movements and meetings with Sufi teachers, I have encountered *baraka* and *hikma* among Sufis who are practicing Muslims and among Sufis who do not identify as Muslim at all. Although some may suspect that this wide spectrum of approaches is a distinctly modern development, in fact, over the centuries Sufi masters designed systems of spiritual transformation that are premised upon outward Islamic practice and systems that, though rooted in the essence and meaning of Islam, are more formless in nature.[60] A close study of Sufism across the variety of cultures it has infused suggests that Sufi masters prepared a variety of spiritual dishes for those with different tastes and dietary needs and hence we find a diverse feast of Sufi systems. Some will find one system to be more palatable than another, and yet, at least for me, that is not sufficient grounds to dismiss their respective nutritional value.[61]

---

59 For a discussion of some of this history of the transmission of Sufism to Hindus, see William Rory Dickson, 'The Golden Sufi Center: A Non-Islamic Branch of the Naqshbandiyya-Mujaddidiyya', in *Varieties of American Sufism: Islam, Sufi Orders, and Authority in a Time of Transition*, ed. Marcia Hermansen and Elliott Bazzano (Albany, NY, 2020), pp. 27–54.

60 Historical forms of Sufism with notably less focus on adherence to Islamic law and practice include some branches of the Qalandariyya (about whom more will be said in Chapter Seven), the Bektashiyya, some expressions of the Malamatiyya (whom we will discuss in Chapter Eight) and later, some forms of Chishti and Naqshbandi Sufism. Generally speaking, what I've found in my own research is that being a 'card-carrying' Muslim does not appear to be the most important thing in terms of being a Sufi. That is, if by 'Muslim' we mean an identity, a formal adherence, a set of creeds, practices and historical laws. If, however, we look at the universal way that the Qur'an uses the word *muslim*, as a general term for those who have submitted to God, for those who live in harmony with Reality, then the two words Muslim and Sufi seem much more intimately related. It is also why Muzaffer Ozak could joke that sometimes Muslims are the most difficult folk to make *muslim*: a religious identity can actually get in the way of a truly religious life, as Ozak alluded to. That being said, some forms of Sufism are unequivocally premised on a committed Islamic practice.

61 This is, of course, not to suggest that there are no fake Sufis. The problem of spiritual charlatanry is universal, and Sufis have, from very early on, developed things like lineage, in part to try to weed out the fakes, though people are well advised to be wary of spiritual charlatans in any form, and lineage is not always a guarantee. Genuine lineage can further be, at times, difficult to conclusively establish.

Sufism and Sainthood

Historically, Sufi masters were known as God's 'friends', His allies here on Earth.[62] Each of God's friends is tasked with the incredible responsibility of carrying out God's will in the inner and outer planes of existence, of transmitting wisdom, blessing and love-energy to the world and its inhabitants. Scholar of Sufism Michel Chodkiewicz (d.2020) says, 'Sufism and sainthood are inseparable. In the absence of saints there is no Sufism.'[63] These saintly friends of God have been around since humanity's origin and are found in every culture. Sometimes hidden and sometimes visible, they ally themselves with Life and hence Life allies itself with them. They dedicate themselves to sharing the love and wisdom of which they are vessels, bringing peace to those around them, opening the 'doors of perception' for those seeking knowledge, and leading to spontaneous healing and transformation of those in need of it.[64]

The transmission of living love-energy and wisdom requires that God's friends carefully protect what they have received and ensure that it can be accessed, digested and integrated by those they are living with, whether they be urban cosmopolitans, nomadic pastoralists, warriors or artists. This inevitably requires some level of adaptation. Thus Sufism, at least in appearance, changes quite a bit in different times and places.[65] This may lead some to conclude that two presentations of Sufism are two totally different phenomena, when they are better thought of as the same water flowing through different channels.

---

62 In Arabic the terms are *wali* (singular) and *awliya'* (plural), with the phenomenon of friendship with God known as *walaya* – a concept that we will discuss at length in Chapter Six. See, for example, Qur'an 10:62-4. Derivates from the root *waw-lam-ya* occur 227 times in the Qur'an. See Chodkiewicz, *Seal of the Saints*, p.23, and Mukhtar H. Ali (translator and commentator), *The Horizons of Being: The Metaphysics of Ibn al-'Arabi in the Muqaddimat al-Qaysari* (Leiden, 2020), p.13.

63 Chodkiewicz, *Seal of the Saints*, p.13.

64 This is also why a guide is so important on the spiritual path – as Rumi put it, without the guidance of one who has traversed the terrain, a two-day journey can take two hundred years. A saint *radically* speeds up one's healing, insight and transformation.

65 Sufi orders further developed different methodologies that transmit spiritual energy in quite different ways, utilizing different energy centers within the human body and engaging with contrasting techniques, whether we think of music, meditation, breathwork, fasting or spiritual retreat.

Simply put, different people have different needs, and one form of Sufism may be appropriate for some and totally inappropriate for others, based upon their cultural and psychological proclivities, styles of embodiment or the nature of the times within which they live. Sufi masters thus adapted Sufism in myriad ways over the centuries to suit the needs of their followers. As a result, discerning the authenticity of a particular Sufi tradition is something that I believe might be more subtle than many who casually dismiss Sufi expressions they find objectionable may realize. We are well advised to seek the reality behind appearances rather than stop at appearances as such, as reality can (and often does) show up to the party in a strange outfit.[66]

This mysterious phenomenon of God's friends – these enlightened souls enlivening and adapting religious teachings to ensure that their wisdom is not obscured, that blessing energy can flow as needed – is central not just to Islam but really to every genuine tradition of spiritual development. Without these friends of God to draw out religion's essential point and transmit its enlivening spiritual energy, religion becomes like a body without a soul. You get something along the lines of 'zombie religion': zombie Islam or zombie Christianity, for example. Religion becomes the 'walking dead', having all of faith's outward appearances (clothing, ritual, rules, buildings, authorities, claims to scriptural adherence, etc.) but with none of the soul. And just like zombies do in horror movies, zombie religions also eat brains, robbing people of their intellect and intuition, cornering them in an

---

66   On a practical note, for those interested in pursuing a Sufi path or really any spiritual process, I think the best approach is to thoroughly educate yourself on the nature of the path you are interested in (in other words, do your homework). Then, have the humility to be open to guidance but the gumption to trust one's own 'nose' in sniffing out what is a good fit for oneself. Ideally, one can follow one's nose long enough to find a teacher that one resonates reasonably well with – spiritually, philosophically and ethically – and, if one is finding genuine spiritual fruit, to stick with that path. If a teacher is not available, one can of course proceed as best as possible on one's own or with friends. If you find a path that's working, it may be natural to think of it as uniquely efficacious and to, correspondingly, question the efficacy of other paths. However, I think we do well to adopt a basic spiritual humility, one that acknowledges that there may be paths that seem strange to us, and yet lead to water for another. This approach prevents casting aspersions on people and groups that may be walking to the same place via a different road, even if it seems like it is going in an odd direction. Perhaps humanity is like that old couple having a never-ending argument about the best route to take home ...

attack of soulless, oppressive dogma bereft of spiritual life.

This is why we see so much abuse in the name of religion over the centuries and so many moribund forms of extremism, dogmatism, corruption and persecution by people acting in religion's name. We can all think of examples of people and groups who *look* incredibly religious and *claim* to be following scripture better than anyone else, but then live staggeringly awful and cruel lives. As a historical phenomenon, religion, like any social movement or organization, is only as good as the people who constitute it, and hence the importance of God's friends: purified souls who can ensure that religion remains an open channel of wisdom and compassion, enlightenment and ease, rather than decaying into a brain-eating zombie apocalypse.[67]

To avoid this problematic zombie religion, lineages of Sufi masters were tasked with training their disciples in the way of sincerity, self-reflection, humility, tolerance and concealing the failings of others. An early Islamic spiritual movement known as the *Malamatiyya* (the 'people of blame'), for example, purposefully avoided any sort of public display of piety. They remained as ordinary as possible, to blend in with average folk, but also, in some cases, behaved in ways that brought judgment and blame from others, all to avoid developing an

---

67 In Islamic history, the dangers of zombie religion were noted very early on, with the phenomenon of the Khawarij: the first extremist splinter-group in Islam. Within decades of the Prophet Muhammad's death, the Khawarij emerged as a small, break-away group of Muslims who separated themselves from the broader community and waged a violent insurgency against fellow Muslims for their failure to live up to the Khawarij's uncompromising, simplistic notion of religious purity. The Prophet Muhammad is reported to have predicted the rise of the Khawarij, describing them as people whose prayer and piety seem perfect, whose Qur'an recitation is better than yours, and yet he said that the Qur'an 'does not go past their throats', meaning that theirs is a performative, shallow piety. Despite the perfection of their ritual and recitation, the meaning of the Qur'an does not even remotely penetrate their hearts. Interestingly, Jesus is reported in the Gospels to similarly condemn this sort of performative zombie religion, noting the false piety of those clerics with carefully programmed religiosity, that masks the malice within their own hearts. Jesus describes them as cleaning the outside of their cup and dish, while the inside is filled with filth and greed, or as sparkling white tombstones that conceal the bones and decay within (Matthew 23:25–7). For more on the Khawarij and their relationship to contemporary extremist movements, see Muhammad al-Yaqoubi, *Refuting ISIS: A Rebuttal of Its Religious and Ideological Foundations* (Herndon, VA, 2015).

egotistical religiosity that feeds off approval and veneration.[68] Sufism is a path to becoming nobody,[69] an absence through which love, the essence of life, can flow unencumbered, and hence it is an enemy of egotism, self-righteousness or any sense of superiority and specialness.

Sufism and the Qur'an

Despite Sufism's rich diversity, its many expressions can be traced back, in some form or another, to the Qur'an. Although the sacred text does not always strike readers – especially in English translation – as particularly mystical, much like the Bible, the closer one looks, the more its spiritual depths unfold.[70] Ibn 'Arabi, for example, shares that all of his many works are drawn from the treasury of the Qur'an, and describes it as an ocean or sea:

> Immerse yourself in the sea of the Qur'an, if your breath is strong enough. And, if not, then be content to study the commentaries on its outward meaning; in such a case do not immerse yourself, for you would drown. The sea of the Qur'an is deep, and if he who plunges into it does not keep close to the shore, he never returns. The prophets and those who preserve their legacy undertake the pursuit of remote places out of compassion for the universe. Those who are gone (*al-waqifun*), however, who reached their destination but remained there and never returned again, are of no use to anyone and no one is of any use to them: they aspired to reach the middle of the sea – no, the middle of the sea aspired to reach them – and

---

68 For more on the Malamatiyya, see Yannis Toussulis, *Sufism and the Way of Blame: Hidden Sources of a Sacred Psychology* (Wheaton, IL, 2010). We will also discuss this phenomenon in more detail in the book's final chapter on the Prophet Muhammad.

69 This 'nobody' is someone who lives without constant self-reference, or in Sufi terminology, one who is living a state of fana' – the self's annihilation in the Real.

70 Ja'far al-Sadiq was one of the first to map out the Qur'an's layered depths, suggesting that each verse has an 'expression, for the common people; allusion, for the [spiritually] privileged or elite; touches of grace (*lata'if*), for the saints; and finally the "realities," for the prophets'. *Mystical Dimensions of Islam* (Chapel Hill, 1975), p.41.

they are immersed forever and will never come back out of the sea.[71]

According to Ibn ʿArabi, the Qur'an's depths are such that one can get lost in them and never found again. Although communicating such fathomless depths is not always easy, I believe that Asad Ali can help point us in the right direction. Ali is a visionary Sufi master, poet and professor of Arabic language and literature in Damascus, Syria – whom Professor Sharify-Funk had the good fortune to study with. He has even been described as a modern-day Ibn ʿArabi. Much of his poetry is an extended commentary on each chapter of the Qur'an. In a talk he gave on a February evening in Damascus in 2005, recorded in *Civilization of Paradise: Revelation Poems* (2014), Professor Ali discusses a short poem of his and explains its various levels of connection to the Qur'an. He considers the following verses of *Surah al-Waqiʿah* (Q 56:75–80):

> *I vow by the places of the stars. And it is indeed a great vow if you only knew! It is truly a noble recital in a book that is hidden like a pearl that cannot be touched except by those who are purified, a bestowal from the Lord of the Worlds.*

Ali begins by asking, 'what is the relationship between the places of the stars and the Noble Quran? What's the story here, what's going on, eh? ... The Earth is but a head of a pin compared to the places of the stars, so what is the relationship between the structure of the universe and God telling us that only the pure can touch the Qur'an? ... We have the stars in the heaven and verses in the Quran, what is the connection?'[72]

He continues to explain, 'With each new discovery in space we find that our previous knowledge of the universe is as small as an olive pit! And the expanses of the stars are ever-expanding, so the more we explore, the more wonders we see. This is why the Qur'an tells us, *And*

---

71   Ibn ʿArabi, Fut.I.76. Quotation and translation by Navid Kermani in *God is Beautiful: The Aesthetic Experience of the Quran*, translated by Tony Crawford (Cambridge, UK, 2014), p.316. As Stephen Hirtenstein pointed out, the more literal translation of *al-waqifun* is 'those who have stopped'.

72   Asad Ali, *Civilizations of Paradise: Revelation Poems*, translated by Kabir and Camille Helminski, with Mahmoud Mostafa and Ibrahim Shihabi (Louisville, KY, 2014), pp.56–7.

truly it is indeed a great vow if only you knew!'[73] Just as the places of the stars are hidden from us in their vastness, so the Qur'an is *hidden like a pearl,* meaning that, 'no matter how much you fathom of it, it is still unknown'.[74] Despite their hiddenness, Ali suggests that we can *scientifically* study both the stars and the Qur'an. However, the science of the Qur'an is closely tied to the nature of the scientist: here the knowing subject determines what can be known. The Qur'an asserts that only the pure can touch it, only those pure in heart can actually touch the meanings of the 'hidden book' (*maknun*) as it describes itself. Ali suggests that *maknun* means that the Qur'an 'holds universes within it', that its words contain 'veiled universes' within themselves, much in the way that a person's name (a word, simply a set of letters) represents the unfathomable richness of a unique human being, the person who is 'the pearl that is hidden inside the letters'.[75]

So, the science of the Qur'an (and really any genuine scripture) is something closely tied to the nature of our own self – our soul's condition determines how much of scripture we can 'touch', or understand – how many of its hidden universes will unveil themselves before us. He concludes his discussion of these verses as follows:

> So here is the connection between the places of the stars and the Noble Qur'an that is in a state of constant generous giving, with the condition that one approaches it in accordance, in resonance with the hidden book. This discourse is impossible for anyone to grasp unless they are in a state of complete and total purity in body, thoughts, emotions, and intentions.[76]

Along these lines, Rumi describes scripture as a 'shy bride' that refuses to remove her veil, even as we tug at it, until we first serve her from afar, after which she removes it for us freely.[77] He explains

---

73 Ibid., p.57.
74 Ibid., p.58.
75 Ibid., pp.58–9.
76 Ibid., p.59.
77 For more on Rumi's interpretation of the Qur'an, see Amer Latif, *Qur'anic Narrative and Sufi Hermeneutics: Rumi's Interpretation of Pharaoh's Character* (PhD Thesis, Stony Brook University, 2009). Latif translates Rumi's comparison of the Qur'an to a shy bride (from Rumi's *Fihi ma fihi*) on page 18.

that 'everyone sees the unseen in proportion to the clarity of his heart, and that depends upon how much he has polished it. Whoever has polished it more sees more — more unseen forms become manifest to him.'[78] Just as a painter must train the eye, so a Sufi must train and purify their heart to see beyond appearances, and perceive the much vaster realities that lay beneath the surface. This is especially the case when it comes to scripture, which, Sufis would say, reflects our own depth back to us, whether we be a puddle, pond or ocean.

Sufism in Practice

Practically speaking, Sufi techniques are largely based on the Names of God given in the Qur'an. They include Names like *al-Hayy* (the Living), *al-Nur* (the Light), *al-'Alim* (the Knower) and *al-Rahman* (the Compassionate).[79] Alongside pointing to what we can actually know about God, these sacred Names are a powerful spiritual technology implanted throughout the scripture. Akin to mantras in Hindu and Buddhist traditions, the Divine Names have an outsized power and energy that activates within the heart the qualities they point to. Turkish Sufi teacher Taner Ansari describes the Names of God as 'word-forms which encode their essential nature', simultaneously acting on vibrational and symbolic levels.[80] In other words, the Names are mysteriously imbued with the power of the Named, and invoking

---

78   Jalal al-Din Rumi *Masnavi* IV.2909. As quoted in Chittick, *The Sufi Path of Love*, p.162.
79   The tradition of God having 99 names goes back to hadith literature relating statements of the Prophet Muhammad. In the *Sahih Muslim* and *Sahih Bukhari* collections of hadith (generally revered by Sunnis as some of the most authentic collections of prophetic sayings), we find references to Abu Hurayra's report that the Prophet stated that God has 99 names, 'one hundred minus one', and that 'whoever enumerates them will enter Paradise'. This promise of heavenly realms is also expressed in the more mystical hadith collection of *Sunan al-Tirmidhi*, in which it is related that Muhammad said, 'Allah most high has ninety-nine names. The one who knows them will enter paradise' (3507). This hadith continues to list 99 names of God. It is largely agreed upon within the Islamic tradition, however, that 99 is a symbolic number as the Qur'an itself names God by more than 99 names. Another Sufi tradition, as articulated by the famous Egyptian Sufi master of the Shadhili order, Ibn 'Ata Allah al-Iskandari (d. 1309), holds that the *Asma' al-Husna* are 1,000: 300 in the Torah, 300 in the Psalms, 300 in the Gospels, 1 in the religion of Abraham, and 99 in the Qur'an. Ibn 'Ata Allah al-Iskandari, *The Pure Intention: On Knowledge of the Unique Name*, translated by Khalid Williams (Cambridge, UK, 2018), p.18.
80   Taner Ansari, *The Sun Will Rise in the West: The Holy Trail* (Napa, CA, 2000), p.21.

them repeatedly initiates a transformative process in the self. Sufism's central practice is the invocation of these Names, a practice known as the remembrance of God (*dhikr Allah*), which we will discuss in more depth in this book's fourth chapter on Jonah. A Sufi master may assign a seeker different Names or combinations of them, to alchemically refine, balance, transform and ultimately dissolve the self.

Finally, another well-known definition of Sufism is that all of it is *adab*,[81] a term that means kind, respectful and conscientious behavior, or behaving with exquisite appropriateness in each moment. Sufis have long discussed the Muhammadan virtues that should accompany the path and suggest that, like the Prophet Muhammad, the Sufi is one who is cheerful and considerate, forgiving and generous, patient and reliable. In particular, Sufis have emphasized the ethic of service, to put others before oneself, to be a servant of God through those you encounter. In the Mevlevi Sufi order, based upon the teachings of Rumi, this ethic of service was formalized in a 1,001-day training program. Those seeking to become Mevlevi dervishes were first put to work in the lodge's kitchen, washing dishes, before being given other service-oriented tasks, including doing the laundry, cleaning floors and toilets, making beds and serving food.[82] Only when the adept proved pliable in service to others were they gradually taught the music, ritual and spiritual method of the Mevlevi order. In a play of cosmic proportions, we are all supporting actors, and an ethic of service helps align us with this reality.

Training the novice in service as the Mevlevis do, helps ensure that if some spiritual realization takes place within the seeker they will not become too full of themselves about it and end up abusing spiritual energy for their own ends. Rather, an orientation towards being of use to others, towards loving and serving those around you, helps ensure

---

81 In Arabic, the saying '*al-Tasawwuf kulluhu adab*' is attributed to Abu Hafs al-Nisaburi (d.880). For more on this, see Catherine Mayeur-Jaouen and Luca Patrizi's introduction, '*Ethics and Spirituality in Islam: Sufi adab*', in Ethics and Spirituality in Islam: Sufi Adab, edited by Francesco Chiabotti, Eve Fueillebois-Pierunek, Catherine Mayeur-Jaouen and Luca Patrizi (Leiden, 2017), pp.1–44.

82 See Buehler, 'The 1001-day Mevlevi Retreat: Intensive Sufi training in the lodge,' in *Recognizing Sufism*.

that spiritual energy is transmitted freely to those who need it most, without running aground on the rocks of ego, or employed for the purposes of self-aggrandizement. Put simply, service helps prevent the development of spiritual egomaniacs or religious narcissists.[83]

To summarize this brief overview, Sufism is best encountered in the silent depth of the present moment, with a wide-open heart, attuned to natural goodness and love. Drawing upon the depths of the Qur'an and the Prophetic example, Sufism is then expressed in a life of compassionate service, a way of being that is characterized by care, humility and kindly respect for all. Abu Yazid al-Bistami (d.c.875) summed this all up in saying that the Sufi is boundlessly generous like the ocean, unfailingly good like the sun and unassumingly humble like the earth. In Islamic terms this is what it means to be a servant of God, *'abd Allah* – the highest station on the spiritual journey, which Muslims believe to be most comprehensively embodied by the Prophet Muhammad.[84]

Who was Ibn 'Arabi?

Muhyi al-Din Muhammad bin 'Ali bin Muhammad al-'Arabi al-Hatimi al-Ta'i, more commonly known as Ibn al-'Arabi or Ibn 'Arabi, is 'possibly the most influential Sufi in history'.[85] Although mention of Sufis first appear in Iraq and Iran, in the Islamic East, Ibn 'Arabi hailed from Islam's far West, from *al-Andalus*, that region of Spain and Portugal that Muslims ruled between the 8th and 15th centuries.[86] He was born in Murcia in the month of Ramadan, 560 lunar years after

---

83 American Sufi teacher Kabir Helminski expresses this ethic well as follows: 'The fully ripened, spiritually mature human being is so non-defensive, so inwardly free of any need to impress, or to establish any sense of superiority for itself, that we experience that person as if they were our best friend. When we say the word "Sufi", what should come to mind is someone totally in service to life, asking nothing for themselves.' Kabir Helminski, *Holistic Islam: Sufism, Transformation, and the Needs of Our Time* (Ashland, OR, 2017), p.21.

84 This station of Muhammad will be discussed further in the last chapter.

85 Shahab Ahmed, *What is Islam? The Importance of Being Islamic* (Princeton, NJ, 2016), p.21.

86 Ibn 'Arabi was keenly aware that Sufis tended to see the East as the true center of gravity for Islamic spirituality. He wrote a book, *Ruh al-Qudus*, that attested to the accomplished Sufis and powerful saints that flourished in the Muslim West.

the founding of the Muslim community, or late July in the year 1165 of the Western calendar. His father served as a military advisor to the region's sultans (and Ibn 'Arabi himself may have briefly served in the military during his late teens).[87]

Historians continue to marvel at the cosmopolitan culture of Andalusia, where peoples of various religions and ethnicities lived together in (relative) conviviality, and where science and philosophy, literature and art, all flourished. It was also a hot bed of esoterica, including alchemy, Hermeticism and various forms of mysticism and magic. These cultural and intellectual riches of Andalusian society were only amplified by the beauty of its cities, with their fountains, mosques, libraries and markets, as well as the region's natural loveliness (it is truly stunning and well worth exploring), which quite understandably inspired a lot of Arabic poetry.[88]

While still a teenager in the bustling city of Seville, Ibn 'Arabi had a remarkable spiritual experience during his very first Sufi retreat (*khalwa*). He encountered the spiritual forms of Moses, Jesus, and Muhammad, the three great Abrahamic sages, who directly taught him the foundational lights of the Sufi path: receptivity, pure action and ecstatic love.[89] Following this intensive experience, he began studying with various Sufi teachers in his area, including a poor 90-year-old woman named Fatima bint Ibn al-Muthanna. She reportedly said of Ibn 'Arabi:

> Of those who come to see me, I admire none more than Ibn 'Arabi. The rest of you come to me with part of yourselves, leaving the other

---

[87] He first served in the army of Murcia's sultan, Ibn Mardanish, until the sultan's death in 1172, after which he moved his family to Seville, serving as a military advisor to the Almohad sultan Abu Ya'qub Yusuf (d.1199). Claude Addas, *Quest for the Red Sulphur: The Life of Ibn 'Arabi*, translated by Peter Kingsley (Cambridge, UK, 1993), p.18.

[88] For example, the poet Ibn Khafaja (d.1138) wrote:
You who live in Al-Andalus, with its waters, its shade, its rivers, trees – how blessed are you! The Garden of Bliss is nowhere else than in your country, and if it was possible for me to choose between them it would be your country I would choose.
Don't be afraid of going to Hell tomorrow; whoever has known Paradise will never enter Gehenna.
Cited in Addas, *Quest for the Red Sulphur*, p.11.

[89] Stephen Hirtenstein, *The Unlimited Mercifier: The Spiritual Life and Thought of Ibn 'Arabi* (Oxford, 1999), p.53.

part of you occupied with your other concerns, while Ibn ʿArabi is a consolation to me, for he comes to me with all of himself. When he rises up, it is with his whole self, and when he sits, it is with all of himself, leaving nothing of himself elsewhere. That is how it should be on the [Sufi] Way.[90]

Word spread about Ibn ʿArabi's precocious spiritual attainment, attracting interest from some of Andalusia's VIPs. Even the renowned judge, philosopher and theologian Ibn Rushd (d.1198), heard of this youth with insight far beyond his years, and was keen to meet him. Ibn Rushd would later become the most famous Muslim thinker in the Latin West, where he was known as Averroes. St. Thomas Aquinas (d.1274) in particular drew upon Ibn Rushd's commentaries on Aristotle to craft his hugely influential synthesis of Aristotelian philosophy and Catholic theology, which shapes much Catholic thought even to this day.

To encounter the young spiritual prodigy, Ibn Rushd set up a meeting in Cordoba through Ibn ʿArabi's father. Thankfully, Ibn ʿArabi wrote about this iconic meeting.[91] Upon entering Ibn Rushd's home, he was embraced by the elder philosopher and theologian, who looked intently at him and asked simply, 'Yes?' Ibn ʿArabi responded, 'Yes,' and observed him being pleased with his response. The youthful Ibn ʿArabi then exclaimed, 'No!' causing Ibn Rushd to appear confused and concerned. To clarify their exchange, Ibn Rushd asked Ibn ʿArabi if the truth he has found through spiritual experience is the same as what the philosophers like him find through rational thought. Ibn ʿArabi responded, 'Yes and no. Between the yes and the no spirits take flight from their matter and heads go flying off of bodies.' Ibn Rushd turned pale and began chanting a prayer of refuge in God, indicating to Ibn ʿArabi that he understood what he was alluding to. It seems as though Ibn ʿArabi was pointing to the profound difference between knowing something *intellectually*, and knowing it with *the entirety of one's being*. Although the scholar and the spiritual practitioner's knowledge may

---

90 Ibid., p.79.
91 See *Fut*.I.153 and II.372.

resemble one another in words, the reality of their understanding is in fact worlds apart.

As the Christian military campaign to take back Spain (known as the Reconquista) gained momentum in the late twelfth century, Ibn 'Arabi was drawn to the East. He traveled first to North Africa in 1200, where he stayed for some months before making the long journey to Egypt, and then the Arabian Peninsula, Turkey, Palestine and eventually Syria. After years on the road[92] he finally settled in Damascus, where he remained until his death on November 9, 1240, at the age of 75.[93] There he received the patronage of the Banu Zaki, a noble family who, for generations, had been judges in Damascus, and who provided a home for him in the Salihiyya neighborhood, at the base of Mount Qasiyun.[94] As a result, Ibn 'Arabi was able to write and teach in peace during his final years, finalizing and transmitting his two most important works, *The Meccan Revelations* and *The Gemstones of Wisdom*. By the time of his death, he was a renowned Sufi master, surrounded by disciples and students.[95]

Today, Ibn 'Arabi can be a figure of real controversy for some Muslims. If you want to test this, you can simply try name-dropping Ibn 'Arabi in Muslim company and see how it goes (it will quite possibly get interesting). On the one hand, Sufis consider him to be one of the greatest if not *the* greatest Sufi saint and master: the *shaykh al-akbar*, and even the 'seal', or last saint of those who inherit the fullness of the Muhammadan spiritual paradigm. In stark contrast,

---

92 An Ethiopian Sufi, 'Abd Allah Badr al-Habashi would become his closest travel companion and one of his best friends, and for more than 20 years they traveled together. Ibn 'Arabi described him as an 'unadulterated clarity, a pure light ... like a full moon (*badr*) without eclipse', one who 'acknowledges each person's right and renders it to him', one whose 'word is true, his promise sincere'. Fut.I.10, 72. As quoted in Hirtenstein, *The Unlimited Mercifier*, p.123.

93 An exception to his almost constant travelling was the several years he lived in Malatya, Anatolia with his family (likely between 1216 and 1222). Ibid., pp.188–90.

94 Mount Qasiyun was considered sacred as Abraham was said to have first experienced the oneness of God there, and it had long been a site of pilgrimage, associated in particular with Khidr (about whom more will be said in the sixth chapter on Moses). Ibid., p.220.

95 The Mosque of Ibn 'Arabi, where he is buried, is a truly beautiful place and well worth visiting. I was fortunate enough to spend some time there while visiting Damascus in 2010, and was impressed by the serenity and spiritual power of the place, and particularly the shrine room underneath, where Ibn 'Arabi is buried.

Ibn 'Arabi has also been vilified by his posthumous opponents as the greatest nonbeliever, the *shaykh al-akfar*. Some of his medieval haters were fond of saying that, if you do not consider Ibn 'Arabi to be an unbeliever, then *you yourself are one too* (how's that for emphasis). These medieval perspectives still resonate today among Muslims who know who Ibn 'Arabi is, and so we still tend to find strong opinions about him either way.

It's worth pointing out, however, that Ibn 'Arabi was basically the patron saint of the Ottoman Empire, one of history's longest lasting dynasties, and certainly Islamic history's most protracted. The Ottomans truly loved Ibn 'Arabi and the cultural memory of this love persists even today. As a notable recent example, we can point to *Ertuğrul* (2014–19), a Turkish television series about the forefather of the Ottoman dynasty, Ertuğrul Gazi (d.1281). During the pandemic the series became something of a global phenomenon, proving especially popular in South Asia, but gaining a widespread international (and largely Muslim) following. The series features Ibn 'Arabi prominently, as Ertuğrul's wise spiritual advisor and miraculous guide. He provides Ertuğrul with a deeper spiritual perspective and intervenes at critical points to aid him on the path, much as Sufis would have done for Ottoman rulers during the empire's heyday.

Although the relationship between Ertuğrul and Ibn 'Arabi is fictionalized and/or legendary, it is actually a good narrative representation of the relationship between Ibn 'Arabi and the Ottoman ruling elites more generally: there is an extensive historical record of Ottoman support of Ibn 'Arabi's teachings, from the very beginnings of the dynasty.[96] Ibn 'Arabi's place in Ottoman religious life was given official stamp in 1534 when the chief Islamic authority of the Ottoman

---

[96] For example, Orhan (d.1362), the second ruler of the Ottoman dynasty, established an Islamic university in Iznik, and appointed Dawud al-Qaysari (d.1350) as its director. Al-Qaysari was a 4th-generation disciple of Ibn 'Arabi and an author of one of the most influential commentaries on the *Gemstones*. Later, Mehmet II (d.1481), the conqueror of Constantinople, had an advisor who was schooled in Ibn 'Arabi's thought. The imperial library of his successor, Sultan Bayezid II (d.1512), included many works of commentary on the Qur'an by generations of students of Ibn 'Arabi. Hirtenstein, *The Unlimited Mercifier*, p.241; Mohsen Goudarzi, 'Inspiration, Intellect, and the Interpretation of Scripture in Post-Classical Islam', in *Treasuries of Knowledge: An Inventory of the Ottoman Palace Library* (1502/3–1503/4) (2 Volumes), edited by G. Necipoglu, C. Kafadar and C. Fleischer (Leiden, 2019), pp.267–308.

empire released a *fatwa* (religious decree) that 'henceforth the works of Ibn 'Arabi should be officially studied throughout Ottoman lands'.[97] With the aid of Ottoman official endorsement, Ibn 'Arabi's works were widely studied and commented upon throughout the 16th, 17th and 18th centuries, proving foundational to Islamic thought in the Ottoman realm.[98] Among his many, many works, however, the one that would receive the most (philosophical) attention was a relatively short book that he composed late in life, *The Gemstones of Wisdom*, to which we now turn.

What is The Gemstones of Wisdom?

Sufis have long venerated Ibn 'Arabi's *Gemstones* as the 'seal of his writings',[99] and the condensed essence of his entire body of work. The resulting density and profundity of such a text has inspired generations of commentary and elaboration.[100] Four in particular stand out as the most influential, all of which were written by a lineage of students traced back to Ibn 'Arabi himself, forming a living chain of masters and disciples, where commentary emerged out of a relationship of

---

97 The head Islamic authority at the time (or *shaykh al-Islam*) was Ibn Kamal Pasha (d.1536). Hirtenstein, *The Unlimited Mercifier*, p.242.

98 It is also worth noting that Ibn 'Arabi's total embrace by the Ottomans is contrasted by his total rejection by many modern Muslim networks. The shifting sands of orthodoxy are tied so often to power and politics, as *who* gets to define what the 'official' or 'authentic' version of Islam is changes over time.

99 'Abd al-Rahman Jami, *Naqd al-nusus*, as quoted in William C. Chittick, 'Ibn 'Arabi's Own Summary of the *Fusus*', *Journal of the Muhyiddin Ibn 'Arabi Society* 1 (1982), 31.
We should keep in mind here that Ibn 'Arabi's writings are *voluminous*, though deciphering precisely how many works he wrote has proven to be challenging. Ibn 'Arabi prepared his own list of his works, known as *al-Fihrist* or 'The Catalogue', which his stepson and successor Sadr al-Din al-Qunawi (d.1274) transcribed and confirmed by reading back to Ibn 'Arabi. Although this catalog indicates that Ibn 'Arabi wrote close to 300 works, we only have manuscripts of about 100 of them. For more on this see Pablo Beneito and Stephen Hirtenstein, 'Ibn 'Arabi's *Fihrist*: Books, Biographies and Bibliophanies. Part 1: Deciphering the *Abjad* Alpha-numeric Code', *Journal of the Muhyiddin Ibn 'Arabi Society*, 73 (2023), 1–34.

100 Osman Yahia lists more than 100 commentaries on the *Gemstones* in his catalog of Ibn 'Arabi's works. See his *Histoire et classification de l'oeuvre d'Ibn 'Arabi*, 2 vols (Damascus, 1964). His entry on the *Fusus* is found in Volume 1, 240–57 (*répertoire générale* no. 150).

spiritual pedagogy and practice.[101] These commentaries became the core of Ibn 'Arabi's school of philosophy, referred to in English as the 'Akbarian' school, after his title, *shaykh al-akbar*. This school – which Ibn 'Arabi himself titles the school of *tahqiq* or 'realization' – articulated Ibn 'Arabi's visionary Sufism in the language of Islamic philosophy, and soon became known as philosophical Sufism (or what I call Sufi philosophy). It basically translated the entire range of spiritual experience into an exacting technical vocabulary, and an overarching metaphysical paradigm. The comprehensive, precise nature of this approach, alongside its clear rootedness in the Qur'an, led to its prevalence among Sufis from the 13th century onward, and deeply shaped Islamic thought more broadly.[102]

Abu'l-'Ala Afifi (d.1966) published the first English-language study of the *Gemstones* in 1938, and later confessed that although each word of the Arabic text was clear in and of itself, the meaning of almost every sentence escaped him.[103] We might then imagine that reading the text with Ibn 'Arabi himself would almost *guarantee* our understanding of it, and yet Ibn 'Arabi's own closest disciple, Sadr al-Din al-Qunawi (d.1274), shared, 'If God had not displayed his bounty toward me by giving me a share in the root and origin of the Shaykh's [Ibn 'Arabi's] spiritual perceptions, I would not be able to discern his purpose from the sense of his words.'[104] Al-Qunawi's statement here suggests that even a sustained study of the text, under the guidance of the *author himself*, may not unlock its allusive language, unless assisted by serendipitous, spontaneous insight that reveals its real meaning. Keeping the text's well-known difficulty in mind, it is also worth pointing out that much of the *Gemstones* remains comprehensible, at least at a basic level, to someone with a background in Islamic philosophy and spirituality.

---

101 The first important commentary was composed by al-Qunawi, the second by al-Qunawi's own disciple, Mu'ayyid al-Din al-Jandi (d.c.1300), the third by his student, 'Abd al-Razzaq al-Qashani (d.1330), and the fourth by al-Qashani's student, Dawud al-Qaysari.

102 Chittick, 'Ibn 'Arabi's Own Summary of the *Fusus*', p.30.

103 As described in Michel Chodkiewicz, *An Ocean Without Shore: Ibn Arabi, The Book, and the Law*, translated by David Streight (Albany, NY, 1993), p.1.

104 William Chittick, 'The Chapter Headings of the *Fusus*', *Journal of the Muhyiddin Ibn 'Arabi Society 2* (1984), p.45.

Clearly, however, we are wise to approach the text with some humility, regardless of our qualifications.[105]

The *Fusus al-hikam* most literally translates as the *Jewel Settings of Wisdom*.[106] A *fass* is a setting or bezel, within which a jewel or gemstone is placed on a ring, though another rendering of *fass* could be, not the bezel, but the gemstone itself, such that the title can also be translated as *The Gemstones of Wisdom* (which is what I have opted for as it is more immediately intelligible in English, and, at least to my ears, sounds a bit better too). Ibn 'Arabi is using the idea of a jewel setting as a metaphor for a particular prophet. Each prophet's soul is a setting shaped according to the wisdom it receives from God, much like a bezel would correspond to the shape of a gemstone. This means that each prophet in human history has a distinct, innate nature (the bezel), which allows them to receive and embody a particular kind of wisdom (the gemstone).[107] Put differently, divine wisdom is always shaped according to the contours of its human vessel. Wisdom, coming from eternity, is one, and yet when it is embodied in human beings situated in particular times and spaces, it reflects the form of the beings it resides within, and the communities they are tasked with teaching, and hence this singular wisdom becomes multiple in expression – and this is why our various religious traditions can be understood to share an essence and origin, though differing in appearance and form.

Following a prologue, the *Gemstones* contains 27 chapters, each based on a particular prophet, beginning with Adam, and ending

---

105 Gerald Elmore observes that Ibn 'Arabi was 'as great a writer as he was a thinker'; being 'a master of late-classical Arabic prose, his language is actually very precise, albeit frequently complex and convoluted and always subtly allusive'. Gerald Elmore, Review of Ronald L. Nettler, 'Sufi Metaphysics and Qur'anic Prophets: Ibn 'Arabi's Thought and Method in the Fusus al-hikam', *Journal of Qur'anic Studies,* 7 (2005), 82.

106 Technically it would be 'wisdoms' but the pluralizing of wisdom that way in English doesn't quite work the same way as it does in Arabic, so I've left it as 'wisdom'. Gerald Elmore notes that the full title of the text is *Fusus al-hikam wa-khusus al-kalim*, which translates more literally as 'The Gemstones of the Wisdoms and the Specialness [i.e. distinct meaning] of the Words'. Gerald Elmore, 'Qur'anic Wisdom, Prophetology, and Ibn 'Arabi's *Fusus al-hikam*', *Journal of the Muhyiddin Ibn 'Arabi Society,* 42 (2007), 83.

107 Abrahamov, *Ibn al-'Arabi's Fusus al-hikam*, 25. Another reading of this is that the social-historical environment of each prophet is the bezel, while the prophet is the gemstone. Elmore, 'Qur'anic Wisdom', 78.

with Muhammad.[108] Each prophet represents the unfolding of the divine intelligence, or what Muslims call the Reality of Muhammad (*al-Haqiqa al-Muhammadiyya*), a concept we will explore at length in the final chapter of this book. Sufis understand Muhammad's reality to be the essence of all the prophets and of guidance in general (in a way that bears some resemblance to Christian understandings of Christ as the divine Word or *logos*). Each chapter in the book then illustrates the wisdom (*hikma*) of one of the prophets, a particularized form of the universal wisdom of the perfect or complete human, who comprehensively reflects God's reality.[109] For Ibn 'Arabi, Muhammad best represents the fullness of wisdom and human completion.[110] Although all prophets are believed by Muslims to be completely equal in one sense, in another sense each is thought to have their own perfection, with Muhammad's being a singular comprehensiveness.

The *Gemstones* is not a particularly long book, and yet, as the summation of Ibn 'Arabi's vast system of knowledge, it is a profoundly dense one, and writing a commentary on the whole text would be a giant undertaking, and one likely well beyond my capabilities. What I have chosen to do instead is to select an octave of chapters from Ibn 'Arabi's masterwork, each chapter discussing a prophet among the 27 he considers. The eight I have chosen are: Adam, Abraham, Shu'ayb, Jonah, Elijah–Enoch (we will see later why these two count as one), Moses, Jesus and Muhammad.[111]

I have chosen these particular chapters in the *Gemstones* as they allow me to explore some of the foundations of Sufi philosophy

---

108 The prophets in between, however, are not represented chronologically, with chapters on Moses, David and John coming after the chapter on Jesus.

109 Al-Qunawi defines wisdom as 'knowledge of the realities and things as they are in themselves and activity in keeping with that knowledge'. Elmore, Review.

110 Al-Qaysari writes, 'If we take *fass* to mean quintessence, the *fass* of each wisdom signifies the quintessence of the sciences actualized by the spirit of the prophet mentioned; these sciences are required by the Name that dominates over that prophet, for it effuses them into his spirit in keeping with his preparedness and receptivity. If we take *fass* to mean ringstone, then the *fass* of each wisdom is the heart (of the prophet), within which are imprinted the sciences specific to him.' Ibid.

111 Although I have generally maintained the ordering found in the *Gemstones*, I have moved the chapter on Jesus from where it occurs in the text (before Jonah) to occupy the penultimate chapter here, for thematic and historical flow.

(including the nature of God, love, human completion, religious diversity, and the relationship between prophethood and sainthood), and further to delve into some broader themes central to the Islamic-Sufi tradition (such as the nature of the human heart, knowledge, destiny, peace and conflict, spiritual practice, life after death, and the relationship between spirituality and sacred law). That being said, like 'Afīfī before me, there is a great deal of the text that is still *very* much beyond me, and I share here only the little that I hope to have at least approximately understood.[112] It is also worth pointing out, that, as some of the subjects dealt with in this book go far beyond mere conceptual comprehension, it may be that someone less well read in Sufi philosophy will understand these subjects much better than I and other scholars have. I also want to note that these chapters were revised *many* times before I realized that they will never really be finished, as the depth of these subjects means that there is always more to learn, and hence more to add and refine. I have come to appreciate that understanding a text like *The Gemstones of Wisdom* is more of a process than an endpoint – a journey, perhaps, without destination.[113]

---

112 The *Gemstones* itself has been translated into English several times. Binyamin Abrahamov, R. W. J. Austin, Aisha Bewley and Caner Dagli have all published complete translations of the work, while Titus Burckhardt's partial French translation of the book has been rendered into English by Angela Culme-Seymour. Although I have consulted these translations (particularly Abrahamov's, Austin's and Dagli's), I have used Ibn 'Arabī's original Arabic text to produce my own translation of the passages included, which I hope helps clarify the (often) dense prose of the original.

113 I would not compare this book to poetry, but I can certainly relate to W. H. Auden's (d.1973) paraphrase of Paul Valéry's (d.1945) saying, that 'a poem is never finished, only abandoned'. I must thank Patricia Robertson for bringing this wonderful saying to my attention.

1

What Does it Mean to be Human? Adam's Secret and the Wisdom of Divinity

O Oneness! You are the endless, rolling sea!
It is You who is seen among the many waves.
Though You have given Yourself a thousand names, a hundred thousand forms,
whatever is said – the sky, the stars, the spirit of the body –
is You, only You![114]

Our Strange Situation

Perhaps we all have those late-night conversations, as the earth exhales and hushed darkness draws out our deeper questions. We take leave of our 'nine to five' lives and discover a precious space to share our wonderings with a friend. The millions of stars in the night sky call us to reflect on the vastness of our universe, and together we fumble at the meaning of our existence. Such musings are almost inevitable. We find ourselves in an outlandish situation: hyperconscious mammals engaged in an incredible range of activities on a suspiciously ideal planet in some remote corner of the galaxy. We are impelled along by powerful instincts, unavoidable suffering and an unrelenting quest for satisfaction – which we all pursue in our own way (usually with mixed results). And then we leave this world entirely, forever, with no idea of where we are going, often just as we start to get the hang of it.

---

114 Ahmet Hilmi, *Awakened Dreams: Raji's Journey with the Mirror Dede*, translated by Refik Algan and Camille Helminski (Boston, 1993), p.53. (I've slightly modified the rendition for the sake of flow.)

Our situation could, of course, just be an elaborate accident of unconscious matter and energy, sort of bouncing around in improbably complex ways in an inexplicably gratuitous amount of space. And yet we cannot avoid encountering moments of meaning. A phrase of music elegantly falls together, touching off in us a profound sense of our human condition, with its poignant balance of pain and beauty. Or we feel the unmistakable, simple goodness of sharing a meal with those closest to us. The question follows: What is the nature of this meaning we encounter? Do we imagine it and then impose it upon an otherwise meaningless situation? Admittedly, when one is in the midst of a meaningful moment it may not matter that much. There are a whole host of things that are likely best left without overthinking them. I do not need to make much sense of watermelon on a hot afternoon, for example. I should probably just enjoy devouring it and move on. If you're like me, however, you can't quite resist the larger questions. Where do these experiences of meaning, goodness and pleasure come from? Why is this watermelon *so* good? This song *so* beautiful? Alternately, when things go wrong and we experience illness, accident, anxiety or loss – why must we suffer so terribly? Why are these experiences *so* bad? Put differently, why is our world so rich in a range of qualities, tastes and experiences? And who exactly are we who encounter them? Just what is going on here?

The Gemstones of Wisdom opens with a chapter on Adam, addressing these basic questions about what it means to be human. Abrahamic religions point to Adam as a symbol of our human condition, and so he is an appropriate figure through whom to consider what our human situation is all about. His story is first told in the Hebrew Torah, which names Adam as the original human being created by God (Genesis 1: 26–30), a sort of archetype of humanity. Not so much accounting for the mechanics of human origins, the Torah instead describes the *meaning* of being human through story. It tells us that Adam is made in the image of God, formed of a mixture of dust and spirit, and given dominion over the earth. He is first placed in a primordial paradise – the Garden of Eden – though warned not to eat from the tree of duality, of good and evil. God creates a companion for him, Eve, from his rib. A serpent ends up convincing Eve to try the forbidden fruit, which she does, and then gets Adam to do the same. God of course finds out and banishes the pair from the garden, to face the trials of earthly life. So begins the human saga.

The Qur'an tells the story of Adam's creation in seven places throughout the text, closely resembling the Torah narrative. Like the Torah, the Qur'an says Adam is a creature set apart from and over the rest of creation.[115] The Qur'an describes Adam as God's deputy (*khalifa*) on earth. It says God blew his spirit into Adam and, as a sign of his elevated status, commanded the heavenly hosts to bow before him (2:30–7; 38:71–2). They all do so, with the exception of a single *jinn*[116] named Iblis (from the Greek *diabolos*).[117] This is the Qur'an's satanic figure, banished from heaven as an open enemy of humanity, jealously seeking to prove to God that Adam is not so great after all, vowing to debase and misguide him and his descendants.

Interestingly, even the angels protest Adam's creation, asking how God can place on earth a creature who will *work corruption there and shed blood* (Q 2:30). God responds enigmatically, *Truly I know what you do not*, and then explains that He has taught Adam *all of the names*, which Muslim commentators have generally explained as referring to either the names of the essences of creation or the Divine names. In either case the names are considered to be a reference to the possibility of comprehensive knowledge, or enlightenment. The human being emerges then as a paradoxical figure, one who has an unparalleled potential for knowledge and wisdom, alongside a tendency towards misguidance, corruption and violence: the human condition is an inherently high-stakes situation.

The Qur'an also mentions Eve (or *Hawwa'* in Arabic), but, in an interesting divergence from the Torah, does not blame her for the fall

---

115 For more on this see 'Chapter Five: The Poetics and Politics of Adam and Eve', in Sa'diyya Shaikh, *Sufi Narratives of Intimacy: Ibn 'Arabi, Gender, and Sexuality* (Chapel Hill, 2012), pp.141–72.

116 Jinn are described both in the Qur'an and teachings of the Prophet Muhammad. Not so much demons (though some can be demonic), they are unseen beings (made of a sort of fire) that exist alongside us, with freewill like humans, meaning that some are genuinely good and can be allies to human beings and others quite the opposite.

117 Fitzroy Morrissey, *A Short History of Islamic Thought* (New York, 2022), p.14.

from the garden (Q 7:27). Instead, the Qur'an squarely blames either Adam or the primordial pair together.[118] Nor does the Qur'an include the Torah narrative of Eve's creation from Adam's rib, though this story did make its way into reports (hadith) of the Prophet Muhammad's teachings. Ibn 'Arabi basically subverts this story of Eve being created from Adam's rib, by first affirming it as true, but then suggesting that Eve is created from the best, choicest part of Adam, and hence woman represents 'humanity 2.0' in a sense, or the 'cream' of the human 'crop'.[119] In the seventh chapter on Jesus we will see that Ibn 'Arabi understands Jesus's creation through Mary without a human father as completing the circle that began with Eve's creation from Adam without a human mother, all four figures then intimately linked in our cosmic human drama.

Ibn 'Arabi opens his chapter on Adam with a bold commentary on the meaning of being human. In what could be seen as a radical act of anthropocentricity, he tells us that we humans – these sensitive, anxious mammals – are the whole *point* and *end* and *purpose* of the vast universe and its remarkably accommodating planet Earth. All of existence exists so that Adam can come into being. Human beings fulfill the purpose of the sun and the stars, the planets, plants and animals. As Hazrat Inayat Khan put it, 'the human personality is the end-product of the life process'.[120]

Now, before commencing a collective pat on the back for being so cosmically significant, we should qualify that, according to Ibn 'Arabi, humans fulfill the purpose of the universe *in principle*. Extrapolating from the Qur'an's description of Adam, Ibn 'Arabi suggests that we are born with a radical potential for enlightenment, though very few of us come anywhere close to actualizing it. Those who do succeed in realizing our Adamic nature have historically been venerated as prophets and saints, gurus and buddhas, sages and shamans, beloved

---

118 Amina Wadud, *Qur'an and Woman: Rereading the Sacred Text from a Woman's Perspective* (New York, 1999), pp.23–5.

119 Shaikh notes that, for Ibn 'Arabi, 'women are the choicest part of man', with 'a subtle level of relational priority and refinement over men and the "masculine," a position that is a continuous thread in his thought'. *Sufi Narratives of Intimacy*, p.159.

120 Inayat Khan, *Mastery through Accomplishment*, p. 13.

for the inestimably positive effect they have on those fortunate enough to encounter them. Despite the rarity of the full human flowering, our task is to actualize as much of our innate cosmic potential as we are able.[121] If the question of meaning is paramount, in the works of Ibn 'Arabi the answer couldn't be more clear: human life is inestimably meaningful, with the descendants of Adam having quite possibly the most meaningful sort of existence imaginable.

Like many medieval Jews, Christians and Muslims, Ibn 'Arabi utilized the language of alchemy to describe this process of fulfilling our human nature. We only need to eliminate the accidental defects that hamper the natural inclination of the soul, which seeks to reach its goal; to transform itself from base metal into the pure gold of its divine essence. Correspondingly, a spiritual guide is like a physician who intervenes to help rebalance the elements of the self, removing ailments and prescribing remedies, so that the soul's inherent gold can reveal itself. In his largest work, *al-Futuhat al-Makiyya*, or *The Meccan Revelations,* Ibn 'Arabi writes:

> Just as metallic bodies are graded in degrees because of the defects that befall them while they are being formed, and yet they [all] seek the rank of completion, for which their realities became manifest, likewise, the human being is created for perfection. Nothing can divert [them] from this completion except the defects and ailments that befall people, whether that is within the provenance of their own nature or due to accidental matters. So be aware of this![122]

In a profoundly positive vision of the human state, Ibn 'Arabi suggests here that despite whatever dysfunctional predispositions we may have – the maladaptive character traits, problematic personal proclivities or annoying neuroses that we all seem to carry to some

---

121 Rumi described this as though a king had sent us to a foreign land to carry out a single task, but rather than do this one thing, we do everything else beside it. If we do not accomplish this one task, Rumi continues, it's as though we've taken the finest sword and used it to hang wet clothes on (paraphrasing a bit here). For the actual discourse of his on this, see A. J. Arberry, translator, *The Discourses of Rumi (Or Fihi Ma Fihi)* (Ames, IA, 2000).

122 Ibn 'Arabi, *The Alchemy of Human Happiness (fi ma'rifat kimiya' al-sa'ada)*, introduced and translated by Stephen Hirtenstein (Oxford, 2017), 61–2.

degree – underlying all of these personal 'defects and ailments' is the pure gold of our deepest essence, the Adamic archetype seeking its natural wisdom, beauty and perfection.

To better understand this vast human potential and how it fits within Ibn 'Arabi's broader philosophy, we turn now to the three pillars of Ibn 'Arabi's thought: 1) *God*, 2) *the world* and 3) *the human being*, all of which are organically linked through the concept of being or *wujud* in Arabic.[123] This wonderful Arabic word *wujud* can mean both 'finding' and 'what is found to be'. The term then encapsulates both the subjective *experience* of being (finding all of this stuff going on) and its objective *facticity* (all of the stuff found). We will see that for Ibn 'Arabi the experience of the world and the world itself are ultimately one and the same, because both finding and what is found fall within being as such. Interestingly, the term *wujud* is derived from the same linguistic root as *wajd*, the Arabic word for ecstasy. The Arabic language itself then seems to suggest that being is both the finder and the found existing in ecstatic unity.

The Three Pillars of Sufi Philosophy: God, the World and the Human Being

Ibn 'Arabi begins the *Gemstones* by addressing that most basic of philosophical questions, what theologian John Wippel calls the 'ultimate why question', which can be put as follows: *why is there something rather than nothing*?[124] Although the very facticity of our world sort of begs an inquiry, we rarely pursue it. Why is there anything at all? Why is all of this stuff going on? Even if we can offer some explanation for why there is something rather than nothing, we are still left with the profound question of why what exists is so staggeringly *elaborate, complex, functional, beautiful, balanced* and

---

123 Mohammed Rustom states, 'The central concern of the school of Ibn al-'Arabi is with Being.' 'Philosophical Sufism', in *The Routledge Companion to Islamic Philosophy* (New York, 2016), p.400.

124 John F. Wippel, editor, *The Ultimate Why Question: Why Is There Anything at All Rather than Nothing Whatsoever?* (Washington, D.C., 2011).

diverse? Simply put, the very presence of our world, with all of its spectacular qualities and sophisticated order, exists as a giant question mark. Ibn 'Arabi opens his chapter on Adam with an elegant answer to this 'question of questions':

> The Real, sublime is He, willed to see the essences of His most Beautiful Names, which are countless. Or, if you like, to see His own Essence, in a comprehensive being encompassing the whole divine order, qualified by existence. Through itself this being reveals to God His own secret.[125]

We will unpack this rather dense passage by first considering 1) the nature of 'The Real' (God) and then exploring 2) the divine Names and their manifestation (the world) and finally 3) considering this 'comprehensive being' that reveals the Real's secret to Itself (the human being). Those less accustomed to philosophical reading may want to metaphorically 'buckle up' at this point, as we dive into Sufi philosophy's metaphysical foundations.[126]

God/The Real

To begin, the Real (*al-Haqq*) is one of Ibn 'Arabi's favored Names of God. The Arabic root of *haqq* means truth, reality and necessity.[127] *Al-Haqq* then is a name of God that points to that which exists by nature

---

125 In this book I am using Mahmud Erol Kilic and Abdurrahim Alkis's edition of Ibn 'Arabi's *Fusus al-hikam*, based on the facsimile of the Sadr al-Din Qunawi manuscript. Muhyi al-Din Ibn 'Arabi, *Fusus al-hikam* (Istanbul, 2016), p.17.

126 According to German philosopher Martin Heidegger (d.1976), the Western tradition of metaphysics goes back to the question of Being or essence, and within Christian thought, this essence 'in totality is divided into God, nature, and man', each of which has its own discipline of study: theology, cosmology and psychology. Martin Heidegger, *Kant and the Problem of Metaphysics*, translated by James S. Churchill (Bloomington, 1965), p.13.

127 It also has meanings of 'law' and 'right,' as in 'human rights,' the plural of *haqq* used for human rights in Arabic: *huquq al-insan*.

or that which is ultimately real: Absolute, Necessary Being.[128] We might call it a particularly philosophical as opposed to theological name of God, which certainly some are drawn to.[129] According to Ibn 'Arabi, the Real, in essence, is the ground of existence beyond all conception, attribute, name, quality, form or relationship. This is because the Real is not *a particular being*, but rather *being as such*. This means that it is not an existent thing among other existent things, but is the very *quality of existence* itself, what we might call is-ness or suchness. I will simply be calling this Being (with a capital 'b') going forward.

Whenever we speak of something and say that it *is*, for example – Montreal *is* beautiful in autumn, or this croissant *is* delicious – we are saying that it has being, that it exists. Now, on the one hand, to say that Montreal and croissants exist is totally obvious. We can encounter them and confirm their existence without too much trouble. In fact, we could go to Montreal in autumn and eat croissants there, which is probably the best way to verify their respective realities. However, once we try to grasp what exactly it is to exist, *what Being itself really is*, we are faced with a mystery. This is because unlike any particular being or existent thing, which is defined by certain qualities, colors, forms, locations, flavors, duration of existence and so forth Being itself is totally unlimited and unqualified – what philosophers like to call nondelimited – bereft of any possible reference point or descriptor.

Because Being can *only* be characterized when it takes on a particular form or limitation, there is really no way to characterize Being *as such*,

---

128 French scholar of Islam Louis Massignon argues that the usage of *al-Haqq* can be largely traced back to Ja'far al-Sadiq, the Sixth Imam of Shi'i Muslims, and a venerated scholar of Islamic law, mysticism, and science, for both Shi'i and Sunni Muslims. Al-Sadiq's favored usage of *al-Haqq* was transmitted to the emergent Sufi tradition via Dhu'l-Nun al-Misri, about whom more will be said in the last chapter on Muhammad. As described by Reza Shah-Kazemi in his article, 'The Notion and Significance of *Ma'rifa* in Sufism', *Journal of Islamic Studies*, 13:2 (2002), 160.

129 Irina Tweedie (d.1999), for example, was a British Sufi teacher who played a significant role in bringing Sufism to Europe and North America. After being widowed in her 50s she left Britain to travel through India, where she encountered a Sufi master of the Naqshbandi order, Radha Mohan Lal (d.1966) in Kanpur. When Mohan Lal asked why she had come to him, Tweedie replied, 'I want God,' but then clarified that she did not mean 'an anthropomorphic deity' – some sort of 'big guy in the sky' – but rather the 'Rootless Root' and 'Causeless Cause', the totally transcendent ground of all existence. Irina Tweedie, *The Chasm of Fire: A Woman's Experience of Liberation through the Teachings of a Sufi Master* (Dorset, 1979), p.12.

in its own essence. According to Ibn 'Arabi and his philosophical heirs, it follows that *to know Being is to know its unknowability.* As Being cannot be accurately characterized in any way whatsoever, we cannot say that Being is absolute or relative, general or particular in nature, and we do little better to declare Being to be somehow both or neither.[130] With no other conceptual option left to us we can only say that Being is an unfathomable mystery that is never solved, an 'eternally hidden treasure' that is never found.[131] A third-generation disciple of Ibn 'Arabi's, 'Abd al-Razzaq al-Qashani (d.1330), describes the essence of the Real as 'too sacred to be qualified by any property or any name': the wholly and holy transcendent, beyond all possible conception or knowledge.[132]

Interestingly, if we look at contemplative/mystical philosophies (that is, philosophies that are based upon a deep *experience* of Being through sustained meditation practice, as opposed to mere conceptual speculations about Being, which can only really scratch the surface), we find that they pretty much all agree with Sufi philosophers on this point, that the essence of the Real is totally unconditioned and hence escapes the various conceptual, linguistic nets we attempt to catch it with. This agreement even spans the divide between non-theistic religions (those without a creator-deity) and theistic ones (traditions premised on some notion of God).

In terms of non-theistic traditions, we can point to the great classic of Chinese philosophy, Laozi's *Dao De Jing,* an ancient text that was likely authored about five centuries before Jesus.[133] This short, subtle text, foundational to the Daoist tradition, begins by stating that

---

130 Hulya Kucuk and Stephen Hirtenstein, 'Sadr al-Din al-Qunawi's *al Nusus*: Considerations of *al-Haqq* and *tahqiq*,' *Muhyiddin Ibn Arabi Society*, https://ibnarabisociety.org/sadr-al-din-al-qunawi-al-nusus-hulya-kucuk/ (accessed November 28, 2022).

131 The Arabic term here is *al-ghayb al-mutlaq*, or the 'absolute unknown.' Shaikh, *Sufi Narratives of Intimacy*, 69.

132 Toshihiko Izutsu, *Sufism and Taoism: A Comparative Study of Key Philosophical Concepts* (Berkeley, 1984), p.25.

133 Throughout the book I will only be indicating dates that are prior to Christ/Common Era – BCE, while all other dates will be assumed as CE. Izutsu notes that 'we are left in utter darkness' as to whether or not there was actually a man called Laozi who actually wrote the *Daodejing*, or whether it is a work condensing a larger tradition with several authors. Ibid., p.287.

'the Dao that can be spoken is not the eternal Dao', the Dao being the mysterious 'Way' or nature of things.[134] Laozi then tells us that the Dao is 'shadowy and dark, prior to the existence of Heaven and Earth, unknown and unknowable', so much so that it can properly be called 'Non-Being' and yet it is pregnant with every possible being.[135] Similarly, if we look to the Nyingma school of Tibetan Buddhism – the oldest lineage of Buddhist teachings in Tibet (*c.* eighth-century), based squarely on yogic (meditation) practice as opposed to scholarly speculation – we find that ultimate reality is called *Rigpa,* a term that refers to the primordial nature of mind or 'self-born awareness'. *Rigpa* is defined as being 'beyond all concepts' and 'even beyond our imagination'.[136] Twentieth-century Nyingma master, yogi and scholar Dudjom Rinpoche (d.1987) poetically portrays its elusive nature:

> No words can describe it
> No example can point to it
> Samsara [delusion] does not make it worse
> Nirvana [enlightenment] does not make it better.[137]

Moving now to theistic traditions, we can point to one of the Hindu tradition's most pre-eminent philosophers, Adi Shankara (d.c.750). Hailing from Southern India, he is credited with systematizing the Advaita Vedanta (nondualist) school of Hindu philosophy – one of six schools generally accepted as 'orthodox', and one also premised on yogic practice. As evidence of Shankara's focus on practical spirituality, we can note that alongside his work as a philosopher he is credited with establishing a series of monasteries and monastic orders throughout India, many of which continue to this day.[138] Regarding

---

134 As Robert Cummings Neville puts it, 'The true Tao is that which gives rise to the horizontal tao of yin-yang process: Only the determinate tao is nameable, and the true Tao giving rise to it is not quite determinate and hence not nameable.' *Behind the Masks of God: An Essay toward Comparative Theology* (Albany, NY, 1991), p.55.

135 Izutsu, *Sufism and Taoism*, p.303.

136 Khenchen Palden Sherab and Khenpo Tsewang Dongyal, *Opening to Our Primordial Nature* (Ithaca, NY, 2006), pp.19–23.

137 Sogyal Rinpoche, *The Tibetan Book of Living and Dying* (New York, 2002), p.50.

138 For more on this, see Matthew Clark, *The Dasanami Samnyasis: The Integration of Ascetic Lineages into an Order* (Leiden, 2006).

his understanding of the Real, Shankara considers God or *Brahman* to be ultimately *nirguna,* beyond all distinction and attribute: 'absolutely One and unconditioned'.[139] For him, *Brahman* is totally bereft of characteristics and qualities, and is hence only understood by denying everything that could be associated with it. His philosophy is very much an exposition of Hindu scripture, and in particular the Upanishads, which are philosophical discourses found within the Vedas (the most ancient and revered of Hindu texts), and they suggest in several places that *Brahman* is 'object neither of mind nor speech' (2.9.1), totally beyond thought or word.[140]

Analogously, in the Western tradition, we can consider the Greco-Egyptian philosopher Plotinus (d.270), who understood philosophy not merely as intellectual activity but more importantly as a way of life and spiritual practice. Plotinus defines the Absolute, or what he calls 'the One', as follows: 'we can say nothing of it: we only try, as far as possible to make signs to ourselves about it'.[141] The spiritual philosophy that developed around Plotinus, later called Neoplatonism, continued to flow within Christianity through figures like Pseudo-Dionysius (early sixth century), and John Scotus (d.877), in a tradition known as negative theology. It was described as 'negative' simply because these theologians insisted that, beyond a theology of 'saying' God (*ketaphasis*), or describing God's attributes and qualities readily intelligible to humans, was a higher and more accurate theology of 'unsaying' (*apophasis*), negating all descriptions of God, to emphasize His total transcendence beyond all thought, name or form.[142] Gregory of Nyssa (d.395) nicely sums up this approach in stating, 'God's name

---

139 Devedatta Kali, 'Introduction', in *Svetasvataropanisad: The Knowledge That Liberates* (Lake Worth, FL, 2011), p.22.

140 J. G. Suthren Hirst, in *Samkara's Advaita Vedanta: A Way of Teaching* (New York, 2005), p.141.

141 Plotinus, *Enneads*, Volume 3: Treatise 49. As quoted in *Faces of the Infinite: Neoplatonism and Poetry at the Confluence of Africa, Asia, and Europe*, edited by Stefan Sperl and Yorgos Dedes (Oxford, 2022), p.7.

142 Michael A. Sells, *Mystical Languages of Unsaying* (Chicago, 1994), p.5. Sells points out that apophatic mysticism flowered simultaneously in Judaism, Christianity and Islam from 1150 to 1300 with figures like Ibn 'Arabi, Moses de Leon (d.1305) and Meister Eckhart (d.1328).

is not known: it is wondered at.'[143]

The World

Inherent within the unfathomable nature of Being is an infinite potentiality, a plenitude of qualities. In the Islamic tradition these qualities are known as God's Most Beautiful Names.[144] These manifold qualities can *only* be seen when they are expressed in particular forms, which inevitably limit the unlimited nature of Being, by individuating it into specific entities with their own defining features. Recall, in the examples given above: we noted that Montreal *is* – that it exists – but also that its existence has the *quality* of beauty in autumn, or that a particular croissant has the *quality* of deliciousness. As we can see in this world of beings, Being itself appears in a remarkable variety of forms, with a myriad range of qualities. It follows that Being is, in one sense, totally obvious, as all existent things we encounter, in their infinite variety, are Being and nothing else. And yet, none of these beings can encompass Being as such (as they are all limitations of it), and hence in and of itself Being remains forever hidden. We might say then that the *presence* of Being is the most obvious of all things while its *essence* remains the most hidden.[145] Being is paradoxically the most apparent and yet the most secret – simultaneously blatant and mysterious.

According to Ibn 'Arabi, this manifestation of Being into a vast qualitative multitude is not some sort of cosmic accident, but is rather a necessary consequence of its own nature: Being's absolute unlimitedness means that It is *not limited by unlimitedness*. Hence its unlimitedness *must* include every possible limitation: Being's infinite

---

143 Gregory of Nyssa, *Commentary on the Song of Songs*. As quoted in Kallistos Ware, *The Orthodox Way, Revised Edition* (Crestwood, NY, 1995 [1979]), p.14.

144 In *Fut*.II.122 Ibn 'Arabi explains this as follows: 'The names of the Real do not become plural except within the loci of their manifestation [creation]. But in respect of Him, the property of number does not rule over them.' As quoted in William C. Chittick, *The Sufi Path of Knowledge: Ibn al-'Arabi's Metaphysics of Imagination* (Albany, NY, 1989), p.57.

145 Ali, *Philosophical Sufism*, p.35.

nature by definition includes the finite.¹⁴⁶ As translator and Sufi scholar Laleh Bakhtiar (d. 2020) concisely puts it, 'the world exists because God is Infinite'.¹⁴⁷ In describing this basic idea within Platonic philosophy, philosopher Arthur Lovejoy (d.1962) calls it the 'principle of plenitude', whereby the Good in Its fecundity quite naturally expresses Itself in the multitude of forms that make up our world.¹⁴⁸

We can visualize the *process* of this manifestation using the analogy of light. Although light is invisible and colorless, it has the potential to become a rainbow of colors when shone through a prism. In one sense it already has all of these colors within itself *in potentia*, though their manifestation requires a catalyst. The prism is the catalyst, a limitation that reduces invisible light to visible colors, defining its inherently undefined nature according to a spectrum of hues. Physically speaking, a prism basically slows and separates the wave frequencies that make up light into their component colors, and so we see the prism turn light into red, orange, yellow, green, blue, indigo and violet. The prism is slowing and dividing light, and yet it is this *very limitation* that allows for light to be seen. In terms of our world, Being is the light, the prism is all possible existents considered as a whole (those things that are neither necessary nor impossible – in other words, everything that can and does exist), and the rainbow's many colors are the possible existents made manifest as the universe and everything within it.¹⁴⁹

This analogy further illustrates why Ibn 'Arabi says there is, in reality, only God. The spectrum of colors visible through a prism each

---

146 As al-Qaysari, the great Ottoman inheritor of Ibn 'Arabi's teachings, puts it, Being 'is not conditioned nor is it limited by either absoluteness or relativity ... It is neither a universal nor a particular', rather 'it becomes absolute, limited, universal, particular, general, specific, unitary or multiple, without experiencing any change in its Essence and reality'. Ali, *The Horizons of Being*, p.25.

147 Laleh Bakhtiar, *Sufi: Expressions of the Mystic Quest* (New York, 2004 [1976]), p.12.

148 Arthur O. Lovejoy, *The Great Chain of Being: A Study of the History of an Idea* (Cambridge, MA, 1971), p.52.

149 This is why Ibn 'Arabi describes God's desire or wish for creation: a longing to be known, and to know Himself through the mirror of the cosmos. The Upanishads include a quite similar notion. Monk and translator Devadatta Kali suggests, 'The divine impulse for self-expression, found in the Upanishads as the primal utterance 'let me be many' (*bahu syam*), is the initial volition necessary for cosmic evolution.' Devedatta Kali (translation and commentary), *Svetasvataropanisad: The Knowledge That Liberates* (Lake Worth, FL, 2011), p.338.

have their own property, distinguishing one color from another, each doing something slightly different with light. So, we are right to say that there are many colors when we look at the prism's rainbow, and on the level of perceptual reality their plurality is obviously the case. However, we also know that the colors have no reality *independent* of light itself, and in one sense they are simply a *single* light and nothing else. It follows that everything we encounter is real in *appearance only* but ultimately illusory in nature. Put a bit differently, the countless millions of entities that make up our world, all existent beings and things, are a vivid, lucid, hallucinatory rainbow, simultaneously revealing and hiding the only actual Reality: the sublime, singular light of Being – or in the Islamic tradition, *Allah*. The Persian Sufi poet Jami (d.1492) expresses this succinctly as follows:

The entities were all colored windows
upon which fell the rays of Being's sun
In every window – red, yellow, blue –
the light appeared in the window's color.[150]

So, how do we get from this pure, primordial Light to the beautiful spectrum of colors that make up our world? According to Ibn 'Arabi, the manifestation of the perceptual world is a kind of descent from Essence to expressions of increasing density and diminishing intensity. In medieval Europe monks and scholars called this grand emanative process the 'Great Chain of Being',[151] while Sufi philosophers in the Middle East, Africa and Asia described it as the descending Degrees of Being (*maratib al-wujud*).[152]

The process begins with God's own Essence, unmanifest Being, which then manifests its qualitative potentiality through various subtle, intelligible realms until we arrive at the solidity and multiplicity of our

---

150 As quoted in Sachiko Murata, *The Tao of Islam: A Sourcebook on Gender Relationships in Islamic Thought* (Albany, NY, 1992), p.33.

151 See Lovejoy, *The Great Chain of Being*.

152 It is important to qualify here that the degrees or gradation of Being apply only to its manifestations, and not to its Essence. Mukhtar H. Ali notes, 'The school of philosophical Sufism holds that Being is unitary and without differentiation with respect to the Essence but graded with respect to its manifestations.' *Philosophical Sufism*, p.40.

material world.¹⁵³ Each descending degree of God's self-manifestation (or *tajalli* in Arabic) represents an increasingly compounded limitation of Being, individuating it in ever more particular ways, dimming its intensity within layers of limitation, profusion and solidity, though Being itself in its Essence remains a pure singularity.¹⁵⁴ Each degree of Being then simultaneously a) reveals unlimited Being by allowing aspects of It to be seen, and b) obscures It, by reducing or limiting It through forms of intensifying opacity. The school of mystical philosophy that formed around Ibn 'Arabi's thought mapped this process of manifestation down into five primary planes or presences (*hadarat*) of Being, which I will briefly outline here:

1. The first plane is the presence of Essence (*dhat*), the unmanifest Mystery beyond all qualification or conception, also called the plane of *ahadiyya*, a word that means pure oneness without a trace of multiplicity. Whether we call it pure Being or pure Nonbeing, any descriptors here can only be provisional as the Essence is prior to any sort of manifestation whatsoever, a sublime ocean before a single wave or stirring. This is what the medieval Christian mystic Meister Eckhart (d.1328) called 'God beyond God', or the Godhead (*gotheit*) bereft of determinate properties (*eigenschaften*).¹⁵⁵ It is not only unknown but fundamentally unknowable and hence cannot be approached or worshipped. Within the Islamic tradition this plane is referred to using the sacred name of God's Essence, *Hu*. This name is drawn from the Qur'an, wherein God is frequently referred to as

---

153 This is succinctly summed up by Cyrus Ali Zargar in his *Sufi Aesthetics: Beauty, Love, and the Human Form in the Writings of Ibn al-'Arabi and 'Iraqi* (Columbia, SC, 2011), pp.4–5. We can also point out here that the Upanishads (G 1.19–20) themselves describe a quite similar emanative process: 'That name and form, being unmanifested, manifesting from that self, appeared in the name and form of ether ... From this, becoming more gross, name and form, manifesting, took the form of air. Then fire, from fire water, then earth.' As quoted by Suthren Hirst, in *Samkara's Advaita Vedanta*, pp.97–8.

154 Al-Qaysari writes that 'God's folk', 'hold that as Being descends in the degrees of existence, it becomes manifest in the enclosures of contingency, and the multiplicity of intermediaries – its hiddenness intensifies, its manifestations and perfections weaken.' Ali, *The Horizons of Being*, p.51.

155 Hugh Nicholson, *Comparative Theology and the Problem of Religious Rivalry* (New York, 2011), p.121.

'He', which in Arabic is *hu* or *huwa*. Ibn 'Arabi notes that when we say 'I' or 'you' we are referring to someone who is present, but when we say 'he' we mean someone who is *absent*. Hu is the eternally absent, as the Essence 'is neither manifest nor a place of manifestation, but He is the Sought which the tongue seeks to elucidate'.[156]

2. The first determination (or limitation) of Being occurs when Being is considered in terms of the sum total of the perfections and qualities inherent within It. This is still unity but a unity that includes a diversity of qualities, known as *wahidiyya* – which means the oneness of manyness. This first delimitation of Being is the Absolute manifesting as God at the level of divinity (*uluhiyya*): God *with* qualities and names, what, in the Hindu tradition, Shankara calls *Saguna Brahman*, or what we might call the personal God, the God that can be known, at least to some degree.[157] The qualities of Being's first determination are the means by which we know the 'hidden treasure' – the Ninety-Nine Beautiful Names of God, all of which are encompassed in the name Allah.

3. The plane of Divine Lordship (*rububiyya*) is the plane of relation between Names of God and the latent entities – those possibilities inherent within Being that are neither necessary nor impossible, and that thus have the potential to manifest. Each entity has its own relationship with Allah, and hence each knows Allah not in Himself, but only in relation to itself, as its own particular Lord (*Rabb*).[158] Before manifesting as the beings and objects of the world, however, entities are pre-existent archetypes in the knowledge of God, what Ibn 'Arabi calls the *a'yan al-thabita*, or

---

156 Beneito and Stephen Hirtenstein, 'Introduction', in Muhyiddin Ibn 'Arabi, *Prayers for the Week: The Seven Days of the Heart* (Oxford, 2021), p.7.

157 Shankara distinguishes between the higher *Brahman* without qualities (*nirguna*) and the lower *Brahman*, with qualities (*saguna*) who is the personal God, *Ishvara*. Kali, *Svetasvataropanisad*, p.338.

158 We will further consider this distinction between Allah and Lord in the seventh chapter on Jesus.

essential realities. These archetypes are a sort of bridge between the Divine Names and existent entities.

4. These essential realities or archetypes receive the qualities of the Divine Names, and then manifest as non-material entities, in the plane of spiritual forms (*amthal*), an intermediate realm between spirit and materiality, called the Imaginal Realm or the *'alam al-mithal* (we will discuss this plane further in the fifth chapter on Elijah–Enoch). Here the meanings and principles of the higher realms take form, but in a non-material way.

5. These immaterial forms condense on the plane of sensible experience or sensory witnessing (*mushahada*), as the material entities that make up the physical or perceptual world. Hence, this material realm we find ourselves in is an expression of a non-material world that itself is rooted in archetypes derived from the Divine Names that themselves reflect the unmanifest Essence. And it is only here in the material world where we find true multiplicity, whereas the closer we get to Essence, the more multiplicity becomes a metaphor rather than a reality.

Scholar of Islam Toshihiko Izutsu (d.1993) explains that these 'five planes constitute among themselves an organic whole, the things of a lower plane serving as symbols or images for the things of higher planes'.[159] It follows that the immeasurably diverse entities of our universe, ranging from black holes and spinning galaxies, to seaside sunsets, microorganisms, social media posts and that cactus your friend gave you as a housewarming gift, are all traces of the qualities inherent in the Real. Our world then is a sort of giant cypher, with everything in it a set of hieroglyphs symbolizing a reality that goes totally beyond them – beyond form, category or word – and yet they do communicate something of it, if we know how to decipher them.

As everything in existence has a singular reality, we can go from one end of the cosmos to the other, to any social context or culture, or to any dark or light corner of our mind, and all we will ever find

---
159 Izutsu, *Sufism and Taoism*, p.11.

are the infinitely varied traces of this one, sublime Essence. If you know this essential Reality (a kind of knowing that can also be called unknowing), then you are at home everywhere and with everyone. All that ever has or ever will exist, from time immemorial to future beyond conception, in every possible universe and state of living and dying, is a singular, intelligent, compassionate luminosity shone through the lens of possibility, expressing its qualities and perfections through them in ever new ways. Moroccan Sufi teacher Mohamed Faouzi al-Karkari describes this process of the Real's expression somewhat poetically as follows:

> For the ocean of the divine Essence is absolute stillness; it has no movement nor sound. But the waves of love caused movement in the midst of this fathomless and all-consuming stillness, and the ocean began to ripple with the motion of yearning that yielded the waves of existence.[160]

As we will explore further in the sixth chapter on Moses, the root of manifest existence, this rainbow spectrum of reality, is *love*: the Real's longing to know pure unity through radical diversity, to see Itself in the mirror of multiplicity. Although in one sense the universe itself is this mirror, Ibn 'Arabi describes it as 'unpolished', lacking pure reflectivity. It is only with Adam, the human being, that the mirror's reflective function is truly fulfilled. It is the human being who integrates and reflects the five planes of Being comprehensively, and it is to the nature of this being that we now turn.

The Human Being

Before the existence of humans, Ibn 'Arabi explains that the vast universe remained, in a sense, incomplete, like a body without a spirit, or an unpolished mirror that could not reflect the divine image in an integrated, comprehensive manner. Recall, in the above passage from the *Gemstones*, that the Real wanted to see Itself *comprehensively* or

---

160 Mohamed Faouzi al-Karkari, *Introduction to Islamic Metaphysics: A Contemporary Sufi Treatise on the Secrets of the Divine Name*, translated by Yousef Casewit and Khalid Williams (Brussels, 2021), p.20.

integrally reflected in a single being. At its pre-human stage, the universe was simply a 'preparedness' without that for which it was prepared. Although existing in this fashion, Ibn 'Arabi says that it is in the nature of God's order to only create a situation for the purpose of receiving a divine spirit. God would never create a sort of dead universe. Every aspect of existence has, rather, a profound purpose, all of which conspire to foster the emergence of the divine spirit of integral consciousness.[161] This consciousness is none other than the human being, symbolically represented by Adam, who is the principle of reflectivity within the mirror of the world. We could also say that the material universe evolved over billions of years such that a serendipitous place like Earth could emerge wherein a sophisticated, self-aware consciousness could be embodied. In other words, the awareness that is reading this right now is the end purpose of the Big Bang.

Unlike the visible universe, which expresses the Names of God in a kind of scattered way, the human being synthesizes all of the Real's qualities into a single form. It is a bit like capturing the entirety of one's favorite art museum into a single painting. Standing in front of this one painting, one can see, as if through a prism, all of the various exhibitions and collections. This is why Islamic, Jewish and Christian traditions all describe Adam as created in the image or form of God. Ibn 'Arabi explains this as follows: 'All of the Names contained within the Divine Image are manifest in the human formation, so that this formation has a rank such that it encompasses and integrates all existence.'[162]

The human being is a miraculous meeting place of all realities, bridging the seen and unseen worlds, the outer and inner cosmos, embodying the full spectrum of consciousness and matter. All other beings in the universe/multiverse, seen and unseen, manifest *some* of God's Names, some of the qualities of Reality. It is the human being, however, that is distinguished by having the potential to integrate them all in their totality.

Although we moderns have devoted immense energy to exploring

---

161 Ibn 'Arabi, *The Ringstones of Wisdom*, translated by Caner K. Dagli (Chicago, 2004), p.4.
162 Ibn 'Arabi, *Fusus*, p.18.

the nature and workings of the external, physical world, we often forget what our pre-modern predecessors seemed to know much better, that within the human self lies an entire universe as well. In his famous collection of letters concerning the spiritual path, the North African Sufi master Muhammad al-ʿArabi al-Darqawi (d.1823) explained this concisely:

> The self is a great matter. The self is the whole universe because it is a copy of it: everything that is in the universe is in the self, and everything in the self is in the universe. Whoever masters the self, masters the universe. Whoever is mastered by self is mastered by the universe. [163]

Because of the comprehensiveness of human consciousness, it can be described as a microcosm (small universe) that reflects the macrocosm (big universe) within itself. Ibn ʿArabi similarly describes the universe as a 'big human'.[164] Adam then is a synthesis of the form of the Real and the form of the world.[165] Hence why this chapter is titled the 'wisdom of divinity'. Divinity (*ilahiyya*) refers to the totality of Being as represented by the name Allah, which includes all of the Names of God and their manifestations. Besides Allah, the other Names refer to specific qualities or limited properties of Absolute Being, but Allah refers to all of their perfections as a whole. Adam reflects the name Allah in a comprehensive way. This is Adam's secret: the human drop contains the infinite ocean of the Real.[166]

Islam is not the only religion that connects the human essence

---

163 Muhammad al-ʿArabi al-Darqawi, *Majmuʿ Rasaʾil*, edited by Bassam Muhammad Barud (Abu Dhabi, 1999), p.84.

164 The twentieth-century Indian mystic Nisargadatta Maharaj (d.1981) expressed this by stating that we have two bodies: a) the personal, which 'comes and goes', and b) the universal body, which is the entirety of creation, which is 'always with you'. Hence, as he nicely put it, 'both anatomy and astronomy describe you'. Nisargadatta Maharaj, *I Am That: Talks with Nisargadatta Maharaj*, translated by Maurice Frydman (Durham, NC, 1973), pp.308–9.

165 Fitzroy Morrisey, *Sufism and the Perfect Human: From Ibn ʿArabi to al-Jili* (New York, 2020), p.54.

166 Hence Ibn ʿArabi confirms that 'my purpose in everything which I write is never that which appears in phenomenal existence (*al-kawn*), but rather, the knowledge of That which is found in this Human Essence and Adamic Individuality'. *ʿAnqaʾ Mughrib*, p.6. As quoted in Elmore, *Islamic Sainthood in the Fullness of Time*, p.11.

to a singular Ultimate Reality. It's probably fair to say that, in some form or another, *they all do*. Perhaps the central message of the Hindu Upanishads, for example, is that the individual self (*atman*) is, in essence, *Brahman*, for in fact there is only *Brahman*, all multiplicity being an appearance rather than a reality.[167] The Mahayana Buddhist doctrine that all beings have Buddha nature (*tathagatagarbha*), can be similarly interpreted as suggesting a singular Real that is found as the essence of all beings. In fact, this is precisely how the Shentong teachings of Tibetan Buddhism have understood Buddha nature.[168] Lama and scholar Shenpen Hookham explains this perspective as follows:

> The essential feature of a Shentong interpretation of Tathagatagarbha doctrine is that the Buddha is literally within all beings as their unchanging, permanent, non-conditioned nature. Shentongpas explain scriptural statements that the Buddha is present as a seed to be figurative only, because Buddha is by all accounts considered to be non-conditioned, eternal, unchanging, bliss, compassion, wisdom, power, and so on.[169]

It is interesting to note here that her description of Buddha nature – as non-conditioned and eternal, imbued with wisdom, compassion

---

167 With quite close parallels to Ibn 'Arabi's vision, the Upanishads distinguish between the multiplicity we encounter, the unity underlying multiplicity we discover, and finally the pure unity or non-duality of the One, Ultimate Reality, which we are. In the Mandukya Upanishad, for example, it describes the all-pervasiveness of the sacred syllable Om, which is believed to be the sound of God: 'This syllable *Om* is all of this [the universe], all that was, is and will be is only the syllable Om; whatever else is beyond threefold time, that too is surely *Om*. Therefore, all this universe is Brahman, this Self is Brahman.' Kali, *Svetasvataropanisad: The Knowledge That Liberates*, p.142.

168 Hookham shares that the fourteenth-century Tibetan master Dolpopa (d.1361) suggested that conventional reality, being conditioned, and including suffering and delusion is 'self-empty' (*rangtong*), meaning that it does not really exist. In contrast, Ultimate Reality is empty of what it is not (namely suffering, delusion and conditions), and hence this Reality is 'empty of other' (*shentong*). She later defines Shentong more explicitly as follows: 'Emptiness of Other (Shentong) refers to Ultimate Reality, which is said to truly Exist because it is empty of existence, non-existence, both and neither. It is none other than the Buddha Wisdom Mind (Buddhajnana), ineffable, mysterious, and beyond the reach of the ordinary conceptual consciousness (*vijnana*).' S. K. Hookham, *The Buddha Within: Tathagatagarbha Doctrine According to the Shentong Interpretation of the Ratnagotravibhaga* (Albany, NY, 1991), pp.1–2, and 15.

169 Ibid., pp.2–3.

and power – would comfortably fit with monotheistic notions of God, though of course Buddha nature is not an exactly equivalent idea. The fact that several traditions have strikingly similar perspectives on the nature of ultimate reality and its relationship to the human self has led some to suggest that there is a 'perennial philosophy', a singular truth that has been with us from the beginning, showing up in different times and places in different garbs, most often found in contemplative/ mystical/practice traditions, as opposed to those based on speculative thought.[170] English philosopher Aldous Huxley (d.1963) defined the perennial philosophy as

> the metaphysic that recognizes a divine Reality substantial to the world of things and lives and minds; the psychology that finds in the soul something similar to, or even identical with, divine Reality; the ethic that places man's final end in the knowledge of the immanent and transcendent Ground of all being – the thing is immemorial and universal.[171]

Although we are wise to appreciate the very real diversity of religions, with their disparate worldviews and practices, and not attempt to dissolve them into a sort of bland, featureless, unitary paste, we need not then overlook the remarkable shared elements found at the heart of so many of them. As we will see in Chapter Three on Shuʿayb, the Qur'an suggests something very much along the lines of a perennial

---

170 In contemporary Western contexts, perennialism can be largely traced back to the *Prisca Theologica* of the Renaissance, which first came to prominence at the Council of Ferrera (1438–9) in Florence, Italy. Here, Georgios Gemistos Plethon (d.1452), a Neoplatonist scholar among the Byzantine delegation, suggested to the Catholic scholars of Florence that a deep dive into the works of Plato could lead to the harmonization of divergent philosophical and religious views, with outward differences resolved in a transcendent unity. Plethon caught the attention of Cosimo de' Medici's (d.1464), a wealthy Florentine noble, who would become a patron of Neoplatonic and Hermetic thought during the Renaissance. He funded Marsilio Ficino's (d.1499) revived Platonic Academy, with Ficino an influential proponent of the *Prisca Theologica*. Ficino argued that all true religion and philosophy were diverse manifestations of a single truth, just as all visible forms shared a deeper ontological unity. The phrase *philosophia perennis* itself was later coined by the Italian humanist Agostino Steuco (1497–1548), who built upon Ficino's perennialism in his *De perenni philosophia* (1540). We will discuss both de' Medici and Ficino further in the fifth chapter on Elijah–Enoch, as Enoch in particular has long been associated with this perennial philosophy. C. B. Schmitt, 'Perennial Philosophy: From Agostino Steuco to Leibniz', *Journal of the History of Ideas*, 27:4 (1966), 505–6.

171 Aldous Huxley, *The Perennial Philosophy* (New York, 2009), p.vii.

philosophy, describing the teachings of all of humanity's prophets and guides as singular in nature, if quite different in expression.[172]

Ibn 'Arabi articulates a worldview that fits quite closely with Huxley's description of this (perpetually recurrent, because people keep discovering it) philosophy, especially with his account of the human soul's ultimate identity with the 'divine Reality'. The Perfect (or Universal) Human (*al-insan al-kamil*)[173] is, according to Ibn 'Arabi, God, in that what is reflected in a mirror is precisely that which it reflects, and yet in another respect what is reflected in a mirror is simply an *image* of the reflected entity, having nothing of its *reality*. So, in another sense the Perfect Human is categorically *not* God. Hence, just as we are correct, when viewing ourselves in a mirror, to understand the image we see to be simultaneously oneself and not oneself, so it is with all existent things. On the one hand, all things are simply the Real manifest – though to (very) varying degrees. Hence every entity or object that we encounter in our lives has no independent, distinct existence in and of itself, but rather it simply particularizes the singular being of the Real: the world is a singularity appearing as a lucid dance of multiplicity.[174]

In the *Gemstones* Ibn 'Arabi calls upon us, then, to 'Know your own essence! Who you are? What is your identity? And what is your relationship to the Real? Know in what sense you are the Real, and in

---

172 We will also discuss the perennial philosophy a bit more in the fifth chapter on Elijah–Enoch, as Enoch was believed by Jews, Christians and Muslims to be one of humanity's early progenitors of this ancient teaching.

173 As Stephen Hirtenstein pointed out to me, there has been some debate over whether *kamil* is best translated as 'perfect' or 'complete'. Ibn 'Arabi actually makes a distinction between *kamil* and completion (*tamam*), writing: 'Perfection (*kamal*) is that which is sought, not completion (*tamam*). For completion lies in the created world, whereas perfection lies in what the complete finds benefit in and acquires ... *God gives everything its created nature, so it is complete, and then He guides* (Q 20:50) to the attainment of perfection – whoever is guided has reached perfection and whoever stops with his completion has been deprived.' *Fut*.III.405 (as translated by Hirtenstein).

174 In the tradition of philosophy traced back to Plato, this is known as the distinction between 'that which partakes in *ousia* [essence or being]', and 'the *ousia* in which it partakes'. Lloyd P. Gerson, 'Goodness, Unity, and Creation in the Platonic Tradition', in *The Ultimate Why Question: Why Is There Anything at All Rather than Nothing Whatsoever?*, edited by John F. Wippel (Washington, D.C., 2011), p.31. Or, as Plotinus states, 'the first of first principles exists in the things and does not exist in them'. Plotinus, *Plotini Opera*, volume 2, edited by P. Henry and H.-R. Schwyzer, with English translation of the 'Plotiniana Arabica' by G. Lewis (Paris, 1959), p.353.

what sense you are the world, or "other than," or "unlike" the Real.'[175] He explains our situation here, combining the Real with the world in our very selves, by drawing upon the analogy of light shone through a piece of colored glass:

> It is like light in relation to a glass that comes between the light and the beholder: the light takes on the color of the glass and yet light itself remains colorless ... the light can only shine through the glass to the degree of the glass's purity. This is the case among those of us who realize the Real: in them the Real's Image is more manifest than in others.[176]

Like the color of the light in the analogy Ibn 'Arabi provides above, we as individual entities only *appear* to exist, but what *actually* exists is light itself.[177] And the more we purify our own self, the more it can act as a totally transparent lens through which shines the Real's sublime luminosity. Or, to put it a bit differently, the more we can allow ourselves to dissolve as self-referential beings, the more that God's Image, with all of its transcendently beautiful qualities and limitless compassion, can manifest through us, and we can fulfill our Adamic function as *al-insan al-kamil*, our very reason for existing.

In dissolving, we find that our own limited self, which we almost exclusively identify with, is basically non-existent in the first place. Ibn 'Arabi states this explicitly in suggesting, 'Being belongs to Him and non-existence belongs to you; He does not cease being and you do not

---

175 Ibn 'Arabi, *Fusus*, p.87.
176 Ibid.
177 Apparent entities like ourselves do not so much acquire being, but rather we become a location for the only Being to manifest. We are not then *independently existing* beings but rather different *modalities* of Being, our very selves the templates through which Being is particularized. However, these templates are ultimately non-existent, as Being is all there really is, while the templates function rather as possibilities of Being's expression. Put differently, Being encompasses everything, so any particularization of it cannot possibly be a result of something outside of it, because *there is no 'outside' of Being*. Anything you can think of or really anything at all, whether thought, object, etc. is within Being or a manifestation of it. Even the thought of non-being is a thought that exists within Being. Al-Qaysari frames this helpfully in noting that Being's 'individuation and distinction are through itself, not through individuation superadded to it, since there is nothing in existence contrary to it that shares with it in one thing and becomes distinct from it in another.' Ali, *The Horizons of Being*, p.35.

cease not being.'[178] However, the discovery of our own non-existence is followed by the discovery that there *is* something beyond this illusory self, which is not only our own deepest reality but the compassionate, intelligent, luminous Reality of all there is.

Although the human formation has this remarkable potential of realizing its essential, infinite nature, it is important to balance an awareness of our vast potentiality, with a keen sense of our own limitations and weakness. Ibn 'Arabi follows the Qur'an in noting the *fundamentally* weak nature of the human being. The Qur'an says that *God created you in a state of weakness* (Q 30:54), which Ibn 'Arabi holds to be the root or base of human nature: we are essentially weak, with any power or strength we find in ourselves being temporary and coincidental. As the Qur'an continues to point out in this verse, we begin with weakness in our infancy. If we are fortunate, we have some years of strength in youth and adulthood (even then ...), but we soon return to weakness as we age: from weakness we come and to weakness we go. Besides our physical weakness, in *The Meccan Revelations*, Ibn 'Arabi describes the human being as 'instinctively anxious', and even somewhat humorously notes that humans are the most anxiety-ridden of all the animals, with the exception of the cockroach, playing off of the old Arab saying, 'more frightened than a cockroach!'[179]

---

178 As quoted in Mohammed Rustom, 'Is Ibn al-'Arabi's Ontology Pantheistic?', *Journal of Islamic Philosophy*, 2 (2006), 53. In his Saturday evening litany, Ibn 'Arabi expresses this in prayer: 'O Lord, possibility is my attribute, non-existence my substance, and poverty my prize. Your Being is my cause, your Power my agent, and You my only goal!' My own translation of the original Arabic, from Muhyiddin Ibn 'Arabi, *Prayers for the Week: The Seven Days of the Heart*, translated by Pablo Beneito and Stephen Hirtenstein (Oxford, 2021), Arabic text, p.38.

179 In *Fut*.IV.32 Ibn 'Arabi traces our heightened anxiety directly to our powerful minds and imaginations, which are more sophisticated in humans than in other animals. Our advanced minds then are double-edged swords, both an immense strength and weakness, in that their ability for elaborate thinking and imagination can also create all kinds of terror for us. The sharp sword of the mind can effectively cut through much it needs to but, if mishandled, we end up cutting ourselves as well. We are thus weak in body and anxious in mind, with any strength we have being an added gift from God: as Muslims say: *la hawla wa la quwwata illa bi'llah* ('there is no strength or power except with God'), which is true, according to Ibn 'Arabi, because God is all there really is. Ibn 'Arabi, *The Openings Revealed in Makkah: al Futuhat al-Makkiyah*, Books 3 and 4, translated by Shu'ayb Eric Winkel (New York, 2020), p.511.

Sufis council that, as we deepen our realization of the expansive, shoreless ocean within, we must always maintain a carefulness of action reflecting our fraught human condition, and live with an awareness of our own drawbacks, faults and foibles, or, as my father, Kevin Dickson, likes to admonish, 'you need to shelter your weaknesses!' This dynamic of the path – opening to vastness while acting with scrupulous care – is exquisitely expressed by Malay poet and philosopher in the school of Ibn Arabi, Hamzah Fansuri (d.1590), who wrote:

> *Vacate your heart*
> *So as to become the Sublime Ocean*
> *When the wind dies down, the waves disappear*
> *You return to the sea of the Living One, the Eternal.*
> *The great sea is shoreless*
> *Majesty and Beauty are everywhere*
> *Do not plunge into it on the left*
> *Know perfectly how to conduct yourself.*[180]

At this point we have considered Ibn 'Arabi's basic view of reality, beginning with the Real's Essence beyond conception, which then, through the Names, manifests as the descending degrees of existence (that is, the world), with the human being playing the central role of integrating them all within a single form. What follows next is a consideration of what some of the implications of this view might be for our lives in a more practical, everyday sense: what might it mean to consciously live and express God's Names? How do we walk towards our own Adamic template, and work to perfect or complete our nature?

Living God's Names

Although we tend to think of ourselves as a basically static entity, it is probably more accurate to understand ourselves as a *process*, an ever-shifting pattern of awareness and action, idea and intention, emotion

---
180 Hamzah Fansuri, *The Poems of Hamzah Fansuri*, trans. and ed. by Gerardus W. J. Drewes and Lode F. Brakel (Dordrecht, 1986), p.133.

and relation. We are processes that idiosyncratically individuate Being over time, as living, dynamic filters of reality. We can simply consider the people we encounter, their various attitudes and acts, and the resulting ways they experience life, to see how this filtering process plays out. Although essentially there is one phenomenon that we are all a part of, we experience or relate to it quite differently, with a colorful variety of interesting results.

We can illustrate this with a somewhat banal example: if there are several people sitting in a café, we can agree that there is *one objective café* that they occupy, with verifiable objects and entities, chairs and tables and cups and people. However, there are as *many perspectives* on this café as there are people in it – each person in the café experiences it from a different angle and with different internal impressions, points of attention or opinions about how good the lattes are there. In a very real and precise sense then, there is in fact never *one café* or some kind of overarching perspective encompassing every possible take on the situation, but instead we only find the dynamic multiplicity of experiences of it, none of which is exactly like the other, and each changing from moment to moment. And yet despite the irreducibly many perspectives on the café, it is obviously and verifiably one. Singularity and multiplicity are always simultaneously present.

We all share one reality, but it is our own orientation that determines *how* we experience this reality at any point in time. Put into Sufi philosophical terms, we can say that our own predispositions (our attitudes and intentions) determine which of God's Names (which qualities of the Real) we encounter. This is because the Names of God are, in one sense, simply relationships between Being and beings.[181] Ibn 'Arabi specifies that the Names are *not* existent entities, but are, rather, relationships or correlations, as each of us in our existence 'demands a specific relationship with the Real', and that relationship is characterized by one of God's Names, which is an intelligible quality such as gentleness, love and attraction, or severity, distance and

---

181 It is also worth pointing out here that the Names are not simply the words we use to refer to them, but are rather qualities that such words point to and hence when we write or speak them we are using what Ibn 'Arabi calls 'the names of Names'. *Fut.*II.56. As quoted in Chittick, *Sufi Path of Knowledge*, p.34.

constriction.¹⁸²

When describing the destruction of an ancient people that rejected their prophet's call to truth and justice, for example, the Qur'an affirms that *it was not God who oppressed them, but rather they were the oppressors of their own selves* (Q 30:9). The way we think, what we intend and how we live all shape our self over time, coloring the lens through which we filter the light of Being, determining the degree to which we transmit or obscure its perfections. The various understandings of karma found within traditions like Buddhism and Hinduism offer another take on this situation, but are arguably describing very much the same phenomenon, namely the way in which *human attitudes, thoughts and actions condition our experience of existing* – the way in which we liberate or oppress our own souls.¹⁸³

One of the ways that our experience of reality can be understood within the Islamic tradition is through the traditional division of God's Names into two broad categories, representing the mysterious duality at the heart of universe. Sachiko Murata, a scholar of Islamic philosophy and spirituality, helpfully notes the similarity here between classical Islamic and Chinese thought. Just as Chinese sages have long seen the world in terms of Yin and Yang, a sort of dynamic polarity that manifests as day and night, winter and summer, masculine and feminine and so on, so Muslim sages have seen the world as a reflection of God's dual qualities, of *jalal* – majesty and transcendence and *jamal* – intimacy and beauty.

The Names of *jalal* include qualities that suggest power, justice and even wrath, and are sometimes described as the masculine Names of God. They include Names like *al-Mumit*, the one who gives death, *al-Qahhar*, the overwhelmingly powerful, and *al-'Adl*, the Just. The Names of *jamal* or those of intimacy, closeness, mercy and love, are also considered to be God's feminine Names (although it is worth

---

182 Ibn 'Arabi, *Fut*.III.441. As quoted in Chittick, *Sufi Path of Knowledge*, p.35.
183 The Upanishads define karma quite closely along these lines, suggesting: 'The dweller in the body, through its intentions, involvements, outlooks, and delusions, assumes a succession of forms and conditions according to its actions.' Kali, *Svetasvataropanisad: The Knowledge That Liberates*, p.342.

noting that they are not universally gendered in this way).[184] They include Names like *al-Halim*, the lovingly gentle and kind, and *al-'Afu*, the utterly forgiving. One way to understand our relationship with the Names would be to suggest that beautiful intentions and good actions lead to an experience of existence through God's *jamali* Names, whereas ugly intentions and harmful actions tend to lead to an experience of reality as *jalali*. However, Ibn 'Arabi also says that, in another sense, God's majestic qualities are the transcendent ones, and hence, 'He has prevented us from knowing Him through [them]', telling us instead that we *only* know God through His beautiful qualities, which allow us to encounter Him via the intimacy of 'revelations (*tanazzulat*), visions (*mushahadat*) and states (*ahwal*)'.[185]

The importance of our intentions and attitudes in shaping our experience of reality is also why the Qur'an repeatedly emphasizes gratitude as key to a good human life.[186] *Surah Luqman*, the 31st chapter of the Qur'an, describes Luqman as one who has been given wisdom by God. The *first* thing Luqman tells his son, his very first lesson in wisdom, is to be grateful to God. Interestingly, he explains that God does not need our gratitude, as God is *al-Ghani* – rich beyond need of the universe – and *al-Hamid* – inherently praiseworthy: the Sun neither needs us to shine upon, nor does it need to be told that it's bright. Rather, Luqman tells his son that being grateful is for his *own self* (Q 31:13).[187] Gratitude benefits the one who is grateful, not the

---

184 For more on the relationship between God's names and masculine and feminine qualities, see Murata, *The Tao of Islam*, pp.8–10.

185 Ibn 'Arabi, *Kitab al-Jalal wa'l-Jamal*. As quoted in Ali, *Philosophical Sufism*, p.58. Ibn 'Arabi further notes in this text that the *Jamali* qualities of God have two aspects that the practitioner can encounter, 1) the Majesty of God's Beauty (which he says some Sufis have mistaken for God's actual Majesty or *Jalali* qualities), and 2) what can be called the Beauty of God's Beauty. In either case one is experiencing God's *Jamali* qualities. For an English translation of this work, see Ibn 'Arabi, *On Majesty and Beauty: The Kitab al-Jalal wa'l-Jamal*, translated by Rabia Terri Harris, https://ibnarabisociety.org/wp-content/uploads/PDFs/Harris_On-majesty-and-beauty.pdf (accessed November 11, 2023).

186 Words derived from the root for shukr or gratitude (*shin-kaf-ra*) occur 75 times in the Qur'an. Atif Khalil, 'Ibn al-'Arabi on the Station of Gratitude', *Journal of the Muhyiddin Ibn 'Arabi Society*, 64 (2018), 30.

187 This notion that what God exhorts people to do is actually for their own benefit, for themselves, is repeated in several places in the Qur'an. For example, in verse 29:6, the Qur'an says that whoever strives (in God's path), does so only for their own self, as God is, again *al-Ghani*, rich beyond need of the worlds.

One to whom gratitude is given.

During my PhD research on Sufism in North America, I was staying for a few days in what was then the headquarters of the Sufi Order International (now known as the Inayatiyya). Their headquarters, called the Abode of the Message, was an old Shaker commune they had restored and renovated in the 1970s, in Upstate New York. After my first dinner there I went to the library and happened to meet an elderly woman who said she had lived at the Abode for some time. Among the many gems of wisdom she shared with me, one of the more memorable was that 'happiness is a synonym for gratitude'.[188] In the Qur'an the word *kufr* is often translated as 'unbelief' and yet it is probably, in many instances, better translated as *ingratitude*. The linguistic meaning of *kufr* is literally to cover up or hide a good that has been done for you: the opposite of gratitude (or *shukr* in Arabic). Just as *kufr* covers up or conceals the good that one has received, *shukr* also means to unveil, reveal or manifest the good that one experiences. The Qur'an condemns ingratitude, not because it affects God but because it deprives *us* of the abundant feast laid out before us. If we are grateful, we relate to the incredible richness of Being with appreciation and joy. As Izutsu observes, Islam as a whole is largely 'an exhortation to gratitude towards God'.[189]

According to Sufis, the more we cultivate qualities of heart like gratitude, the more our individual self can function as the Adamic archetype: a polished mirror reflecting Reality's sublime perfections in a dynamic balance, living God's Names, without getting in our own

---

188 Interestingly, the subfield of psychology that focuses on well-being has gathered a growing body of evidence to support her aphorism, finding that gratitude profoundly improves the quality of one's mood and relationships. For example, Laurie Santos, a psychology professor at Yale, has gained global recognition for her work on happiness, in part due to the immense popularity of her course on the subject. In her research she has found that gratitude is one of the qualities most consistently associated with happiness. Molly Oswaks, 'Over 3 Million People Took This Course on Happiness. Here's What Some Learned', The *New York Times*, March 13, 2021, https://www.nytimes.com/2021/03/13/style/happiness-course.html (accessed on November 1, 2021).

189 Toshihiko Izutsu, *God and Man in the Qur'an: Semantics of the Qur'anic Weltanschauung* (Kuala Lumpur, 2002), p.15.

way.¹⁹⁰ The Sufi path is not simply one of action, however. An old Sufi saying proposes that seeking does not lead to God, though only those who seek find Him.¹⁹¹ Like so many things in life, the fruits of the path are openings of grace, and the labors of the way merely make the seeker receptive to divine grace's operation. It is something like being a sailor and knowing that one cannot sail without a wind beyond one's control, but that only those who do the work of putting up and positioning the sail correctly catch the wind if and when it arrives. We must work, but the final outcome is ultimately not determined by our efforts.

On the Particularity of the Universal: Adam and the Angels

Each human being has the potential to dissolve the walls of self-orientation and open to the sky-like infinitude of Being. In other words, each human inherits a kind of spiritual genetics, a template through which to manifest the name Allah, which includes every sublime and beautiful perfection in the universe. In one sense then we have a profound capacity for universality, for manifesting the whole. However, Ibn 'Arabi notes in this chapter on Adam that there remains a distinct 'shape' to each human form that even when perfected expresses universal truth in a particularized fashion. As the title of Ibn 'Arabi's book indicates, each prophet's heart is a setting that shapes the wisdom-jewel they receive from God into particular insights and sciences. Each sage's own nature functions like a cup that receives the wine of wisdom according to its own shape, depth and color.

---

190 Of course, life is not always a joy, and when the Sufi practitioner encounters suffering, they shift from *shukr* to another quality the Qur'an extols: *sabr* or patience. We might think of *shukr* and *sabr* then as the Sufi's sword and shield, the first to cut through indifference when things are going well, and the second to protect them from flipping out when things go off the rails. Eventually, the goal is to reach a state of *rida*, a deep acceptance of and contentment with everything that life and death brings.

191 This saying (paraphrased here) is attributed to Abu Yazid al-Bistami. James Fadiman and Robert Frager, eds., *Essential Sufism* (San Francisco, 1997), p.37.

This explains both a) the inevitable diversity of our world's religions and philosophies (the many cups), as well as b) the profound unity of vision and purpose that underlies them (the single wine poured into them). Truth will always be expressed in particular ways reflecting the nature of the ones who express it. In addition, truth has many facets, with some prophets taught certain sciences that others are not (hence why we cannot simply equate religious and philosophical doctrines with each other) and yet these various truths are all expressions of one Reality, which is why their deepest teachings do in fact resemble one another quite closely.[192]

In short, within our world universality is always conditioned by particularity, oneness forever filtered through multiplicity. Hence the creed of Islam: *La ilaha illa Allah*, there is no god but God, no absolute but the Absolute. The Absolute is One, and when it manifests the world of appearances, it is always conditioned by the diverse limitations of these appearances. Ibn 'Arabi then simultaneously affirms a) the necessary oneness of all human religion (as it is ultimately rooted in this singular Source) and b) the inevitable diversity of its manifold, context-conditioned expressions. It follows that no person, perspective or religion can possibly represent unqualified, absolute truth.[193]

Ibn 'Arabi illustrates this paradox by drawing upon the Qur'an's description of God's creation of Adam. As we mentioned at the beginning of this chapter, when God announces that He is *placing a representative upon the earth*, the angels complain that Adam and his descendants will cause corruption and violence there while they praise God in heaven (Q 2:30). I think many of us probably sympathize with the angels' complaint here; their concern about the human propensity for negativity resonates all too often in our own lives. What is the purpose of humanity when we wreak so much havoc? We can look

---

192 Although the bezel, or prophetic self, shapes the jewel of wisdom received, it is perhaps better put that the bezel is itself determined by the jewel, which is the particular wisdom that God chooses to teach that individual (more will be said about this in the fourth chapter).

193 We should point out here that, even with this being the case, for Ibn 'Arabi, the Prophet Muhammad represents the most comprehensive embodiment of truth possible, with the Qur'an its most sublime expression in human language. The basic principle here remains, however, that God, Reality or Truth, is always conditioned by and yet always transcends Its various expressions and forms.

at the legacies of war, oppression, cruelty and bloodshed that leap from the pages of history (as well as current news headlines), and understandably wonder if there has been some sort of cosmic mistake.

The lesson that emerges in the Qur'anic narrative, however, is ultimately both a) knowing the limitations of one's own knowledge, and b) recognizing its unlimited potential. God responds to the protests of the angels, *Truly I know what you know not*, and continues, *and He taught Adam the names, all of them* (Q 2:31). God first of all affirms that the angels do not have the whole picture. They look at a mere fraction of it and complain of its absurdity, failing to see how the small part, which is all that they can perceive, fits within the image provided by the picture as a whole. Second, although humanity is a source of destruction and violence, God tells the angels that humans have a potential for knowledge that is not found anywhere else in the cosmos, including among themselves. In contrast to Adam's nature, which can comprehensively know all of God's Names, Ibn 'Arabi notes:

> The angels do not have the comprehensiveness of Adam and comprehend only those Divine Names particular to them ... nor are they aware that God has Names they do not know and by which they cannot glorify Him nor sanctify Him as Adam did.[194]

The angels in this story fail to appreciate that, as Ibn 'Arabi writes, *'no one knows a thing about the Real except that which their own essence gives them'*.[195] Our knowledge is always conditioned by our own self: you only look at reality through a 'you-shaped' window, and can only see as much as your own window permits. Understanding this leads to a perpetual intellectual humility, or what Ibn 'Arabi would call the essential servitude of all creation before God. The angels in this story protest the creation of Adam because they fail to appreciate the limited nature of their own knowledge. Ibn 'Arabi explains this further in noting:

> The Real explained this situation to us that we might learn how to act toward God, most high, accordingly. So, we cannot claim knowledge

---

194 Ibn 'Arabi, *Fusus*, p.18.
195 Ibid.

beyond what we have realized. How can we make unrestricted claims to knowledge of what we have no understanding of, without thereby becoming disgraced?[196]

At the social level, this insight accords with much in the way of cultural studies in recent decades, which highlights the irreducible difference between people and their life experiences: religion, race, gender, ability and appearance, culture and class, all profoundly shaping how we experience our collective reality. And yet, Ibn 'Arabi maintains that, whatever our identities and the perspectives they engender, we are all in fact simply One Being individuated in myriad forms. His thought then simultaneously affirms our absolute unity at the deepest level, while not then dissolving our real diversity as temporal beings, and the inevitably limited knowledge that our particularity prefigures.

In a sense, Ibn 'Arabi offers here a synthesis of modern and postmodern epistemologies. Whereas modern thought plowed forward under the assumption that objectivity was readily attainable and universal theories were possible, postmodern thinkers saw this as hopelessly naïve, as our own historically conditioned subjectivity (particularity) shapes our attempts to be objective (or universal). Although this is putting the matter a bit too simply, these broad tendencies find a sort of synthesis in Ibn 'Arabi's thought, where an ultimate objectivity is acknowledged, though one that in our world is inescapably shaped by our own subjectivity.[197] We might say then that the angels in the Qur'anic narrative fail to appreciate the basic postmodern insight that our own position and perspective condition our understanding: they fail to acknowledge the limitations of their own knowledge. As a result, they fall into something that Ibn 'Arabi calls the 'error of binding [*taqyid*]'.[198] This error is rooted in the belief that one's own understanding of reality, one's own perspective, sufficiently encompasses reality as such. It is the error of believing that

---

196 Ibid., p.19.

197 For more on these questions, see Peter Coates, *Ibn 'Arabi and Modern Thought: The History of Taking Metaphysics Seriously* (Oxford, 2002).

198 Michael A. Sells, *Mystical Languages of Unsaying* (Chicago, 1994), p.78.

one sees the entire sky through a skylight, that the part one perceives is in fact the whole. This error results from an attempt to *restrict*, *limit* or '*bind*' the Real with the ropes of one's own particular ideas about it. The problem here is that the Real by definition transcends any and all possible beliefs, and hence the true worshipper of God recognizes that dogma is a kind of idolatry, futilely attempting to 'freeze' God in an image, form or idea, when the Real is infinitely disclosing itself in new ways, none of which encompass its non-conditioned nature. The appropriate response of the true knower of God (*'arif*) is that one recognizes and venerates each form in which the Real expresses itself, without binding God to any one particular expression. All of the knots of belief are to be untied, every conceptual binding unbound, if Being is to be recognized anew each moment.

To conclude our discussion of Ibn 'Arabi's first chapter of the *Gemstones* on Adam, it is interesting to pause on the Qur'an's claim that, unlike the angels, Adam has been taught '*all the Names*'. This returns us to this chapter's main theme, the vastness of our human nature, and the call to perfect its immense potentiality. And yet even though the human being is uniquely formed to comprehensively reflect the totality of the Real, in its infinite vastness, the reflection is always at least partially conditioned by the mirror. An individual's self inevitably shapes the truth they are capable of reflecting, and hence the necessary diversity of our philosophies, ideologies and religions: even the fully enlightened human being comprehensively reflects Allah in way subtly conditioned by their own self, as only the Absolute is *truly* absolute. Our understanding of the world will always be filtered through the limitations of our own selves, which inevitably particularize a reality that, in its boundarylessness, ever escapes total comprehension or expression.

2

The Abrahamic Paradigm: the Wisdom of Love and the Mystery of Destiny

A thing can be explained only by something more subtle than itself. There is nothing more subtle than love – by what, then, shall love be explained?[199]

The Abrahamic Paradigm

Islam might just be the most Abrahamic of the three Abrahamic faiths, the other two of course being Judaism and Christianity. This is not to suggest that somehow Muslims have a stronger claim to Abraham than Jews and Christians do, or that his significance is any more or less in these respective traditions. Certainly, all three religions celebrate Abraham as their forefather, and it seems sort of silly to argue over which metaphorical child of Abraham's might be his favorite.[200] Rather, I think we can say that Islamic doctrine and daily practice are more *self-consciously* Abrahamic in orientation than either Jewish or Christian ones tend to be, even if they all value him equally.

Whereas Judaism crystalized as a tradition that situates monotheism within the sacred law, covenant and history of God's Chosen People,

---

[199] Sumnun al-Muhib (d.900), as quoted by Arthur F. Buehler (with some modification on my part), *Sufi Heirs of the Prophet: The Indian Naqshbandiyya and the Rise of the Mediating Shaykh* (Columbia, SC), p.7.

[200] The idea of Jews, Christians and Muslims being the 'children of Abraham' became popular in the West during the twentieth century, largely due to the efforts of Catholic scholar of Islam, and lover of Sufism, Louis Massignon (d.1962). He sought to reconcile the Catholic Church with Islam, through promoting a shared Abrahamic orientation. For more on this see Sidney Griffith, 'Sharing the Faith of Abraham: the "Credo" of Louis Massignon', *Islam and Christian–Muslim Relations*, 8 (1997), 193–210.

and Christianity grounds monotheism in the redemptive role of Christ's life, death and resurrection, the Qur'an suggests that Muhammad is a prophet who revives the universal monotheism of Abraham, prior to its being tied to a particular people or person. For Muslims, Abraham represents an original, unbounded, basic monotheism: the human being living compassionately, in accord with and devotion to God, without any qualifiers or particularizations. Muslims believe this primordial Abrahamic religion (which the Qur'an calls Islam) is the essence of every prophetic message, regardless of their permutations. This essential, basic religion is precisely what Muhammad is sent to re-establish. As such, we see that the Qur'an defines Islam as the 'religion of Abraham' (*millat Ibrahim*), and says, *Then We revealed unto you [Muhammad] that you follow the religion of Abraham* (Q 16:123).[201]

In the Torah, the Book of Genesis (12:1–25:18) tells us that Abraham was born along the Euphrates, in the ancient city of Ur, though his father Terah wanted to settle with his family in Canaan. They stop first in Haran where Terah dies after some years there. God then promises to make Abraham's descendants a great nation, and bids him to take his family to Canaan: 'Leave your country, your people, and your father's house, and go to the land I will show you' (12:1). In a sense, Abraham here represents each soul that first hears the call of the beyond, the unknown, the transcendent. It calls upon us to venture forth from the familiar, to eject ourselves from a zone of comfort, and journey forth without any clear sense of destination or even what the journey may entail. As Abraham's story indicates here, the spiritual path requires walking in the dark.

Abraham accepts the call of God, and sets out with Sarah and his nephew Lot, traveling to an unknown land. When he finally arrives in Canaan, he builds an altar to God. His wife Sarah is unable to have children so she gives Abraham her Egyptian maidservant, Hagar, who bears him a son, Ishmael (*Isma'il* in the Qur'an). Later Sarah herself bears Isaac (*Ishaq*), considered to be a miraculous birth as she was

---

201 In his commentary on the Qur'an, Sahl al-Tustari (d.896) defined this *millat Ibrahim* as a state of total openness and generosity, letting go of everything but God. Francesco Chiabotti, 'The Abrahamic Heritage in Medieval Sufism, Part 1: *Futuwwa* and *khulla*', *Journal of the Muhyiddin Ibn 'Arabi Society*, 65 (2019), 86.

unable to conceive prior, and was in her later years. All too human tensions arise between Sarah and Hagar, and consequently Sarah sends Hagar and Ishmael away. It is generally believed that Ishmael settles in Arabia, with Arabs descending from him, whereas the Hebrews trace their decent through Isaac. Abraham is then tested by God, being asked to sacrifice his son Isaac as an offering to God. Just before Abraham does so, an angel instructs Abraham to free Isaac and sacrifice a ram in his place. This story is also found in the Qur'an, though Muslim commentators have debated whether or not it was Isaac or Ishmael who was to be sacrificed.

Abraham is mentioned frequently in the Qur'an. In fact, he is mentioned more than any other figure in the text (with the exception of Moses), his story showing up in 240 verses in 25 of the Qur'an's 114 chapters.[202] The Qur'an situates Abraham as the quintessential Muslim, an archetype of Islam's core values. He is repeatedly described as a *hanif* (Q 4:125; Q 6:161; Q 16:120), a fascinating Qur'anic term that means something along the lines of a pure, upright, lover of God, without any particular religious affiliation.[203] The term is associated with *fitra*, the original human nature we come into this world with, naturally oriented toward truth and goodness. So, a *hanif* is someone with a natural, formless religion, based upon an experience of their own pure nature and its orientation toward the Good and the Real. Verse 2:135 of the Qur'an proclaims, *And they say, 'Be Jews or Christians and you shall be rightly guided.' Say, 'Rather ours is the creed of Abraham, a* hanif, *and he was not of the idolators.'* The verse suggests that, in contrast to the exclusive truth claims of any particularized creed, Abraham represents a more universal, formless truth beyond religious sectarianism.[204]

---

202 Gordon Nickel, 'Abraham', *Oxford Bibliographies*, 2012, https://www.oxfordbibliographies.com (accessed January 25, 2022).

203 As Stephen Hirtenstein shared with me, Ibn 'Arabi defines the *hunafa* as 'those who incline to the side of God', as the root meaning of *ha-nun-fa* is to incline or lean. *Fut*.IV.57.

204 Ibn 'Arabi associates the term *hanif* with the pure, unadulterated worship of God, in all states of being, with uprightness, humility and gratitude. *Fut*.I:722–3. For more on this see Francesco Chiabotti, 'The Abrahamic Heritage in Medieval Sufism, Part 2: The Station of Abraham', *Journal of the Muhyiddin Ibn 'Arabi Society*, 67 (2020), 21–38.

Besides his *hanifi* faith, the Qur'an describes Abraham as having a *sound heart* (Q 37:84) and a soft, compassionate nature (Q 11:75). The term that the Qur'an uses for Abraham in this verse is *halim*, which is also one of God's Names: *al-Halim*. The word *halim* is a beautiful one in Arabic, meaning one who is tender, mild, gentle, calm, compassionate and forgiving.[205] Abraham is gentle, but also remains steadfast through trial (Q 2:124). He is a relentless seeker of truth, who refuses to direct his worship to that which is made by human hands, or, like the sun and the moon, that which cycles and sets (Q 6:76–9). He debates idolators using reason (Q 37:90–6), and on one case is punished for his challenge to their gods, being thrown into a fire, which God makes cool and comfortable for him (more will be said on this in Chapter Four) (Q 21:52–70).[206] He is hospitable to guests, upright and devoted completely to God.

Alongside this doctrinal identification with Abraham, Islamic ritual life connects to Abraham at every turn. During the practice of the five-times daily prayers (*salat*), Muslims invoke prayers and peace upon not only Muhammad and his family, but also on Abraham and his family.[207] The pilgrimage to Mecca is also deeply Abrahamic, as Muslims believe that Abraham and his son Ishmael built an alter to God – the Ka'aba or 'cube' – there, as the first house of worship to the one true God. Just outside the door of the Ka'aba there is even a small square stone with two footprints, believed to be Abraham's, known as

---

205 For more on the meaning of this Name of God, see Wali Ali Meyer, Bilal Hyde, Faisal Muqaddam and Shabda Khan, *Physicians of the Heart: A Sufi View of the Ninety-Nine Names of Allah* (San Francisco, 2011), pp.86–90.

206 Several of these narratives of Abraham in the Qur'an have precedent in the Jewish Midrashic traditions. For the Midrashic account of Abraham smashing idols, and being thrown into the fire, see Midrash Rabbah 38:13.

207 Known as the Abrahamic Prayer (*al-salat al-Ibrahimiyya*), the earliest commentaries on the Qur'an and narratives about the Prophet Muhammad's life together suggest that this invocation of peace and blessing upon Abraham was included in the daily prayer (*salat*) during the Prophet's lifetime. See Franceso Chiabotti, 'The Abrahamic Heritage in Medieval Sufism, Part 3: Three Extracts from Ibn 'Arabi on the "Abrahamic Prayer" (*al-salat al-Ibrahimiyya*)', *Journal of the Muhyiddin Ibn 'Arabi Society*, 71 (2022), 63–86.

the *maqam Ibrahim*, or 'station of Abraham'.²⁰⁸ One of the two 'Eid holidays during the Islamic annual calendar ('Eid al-Adha) takes place at the end of the pilgrimage, when an animal is sacrificed as Abraham sacrificed one in the place of his son. Practicing Muslims then, invoke Abraham daily, identify their faith as quintessentially Abrahamic in orientation and further ritually connect with him on the pilgrimage to Mecca and the Festival of Sacrifice that follows it.

God's Intimate Friend

In this chapter Ibn 'Arabi focuses on the Qur'an's description of Abraham as *Khalil Allah*, a term that means God's close or intimate friend – *And God took Abraham as a friend* (Q 4:125). The Qur'an here reaffirms a Biblical precedent, with Abraham described as God's friend in Isaiah 41:8. Always paying close attention to the Arabic roots of terms, Ibn 'Arabi notes that the root of *khalil* is shared with *takhallul*, which means to 'pervade entirely', 'permeation' or 'interpenetration'.²⁰⁹ This interestingly implies that an intimate friendship is a state of mutual permeation, that love is an experience of being dyed in the color of the other. When we really love someone, they occupy our thoughts and emotions entirely, and if it is mutual, we occupy theirs. Our presences pervade each other, and we experience a profound connection of shared knowing in each other's company, which can actually feel like being one entity: we encounter the rapturous joy of being totally permeated by each other.

This is why this chapter is entitled the 'Wisdom of Rapturous Love'. The term for this love in Arabic is *muhayyamiyya* or *hiyam*.

---

208   The term 'station of Abraham' is derived from the Qur'an, which, in verse 2:125, relates that when Abraham and his son Ishmael built the Ka'aba as a sanctuary, God called people to *take for yourselves the station of Abraham as a place of prayer*. Verses 3:95–7 describe 'clear signs' of God to be found at the Ka'aba, with the *station of Abraham* named as an example of these. For more on this see Chiabotti, 'The Abrahamic Heritage in Medieval Sufism, Part 2: The Station of Abraham'.

209   Regarding *takhallul*'s connotation of interpenetration, in *Fut*.II.179 Ibn 'Arabi explains that the knower of God is totally penetrated by divine knowledge, and thereby becomes an 'intermediary through whom the divine commandments are realized' on various planes of being, both spiritual and physical. Chiabotti, 'The Abrahamic Heritage in Medieval Sufism, Part 1', 87.

It has connotations of ecstasy, enthusiasm, rapture, passion, getting lost, bafflement and enchantment. It is the kind of love where one transcends the mind, escaping the trap of constant self-reference by being overwhelmed with elation. In discussing this particular wisdom, Ibn 'Arabi unpacks the metaphysical implications of the linguistic meaning of *khalil*: describing Abraham as either completely pervaded by the qualities of God's Essence, or as encompassing the qualities of this Essence in his self: 'Truly, the Friend (al-Khalil) was only named "friend" due to his encompassment and pervasion of every quality of the divine Essence.'[210] There may be a rather obvious connection here between pervasion and ecstatic, rapturous love. To discover that one's own soul encompasses the totality of qualities of the entire universe, that it is pervaded by the fathomless subtlety and richness of God, would seem to lead quite naturally to falling into a sort of love that goes beyond conception. Hence the discovery of *takhalla* is the wisdom of *muhayyamiyya*.

Ibn 'Arabi says that this Abrahamic station of friendship with God is most fundamentally characterized by *universal love and mercy*, as the friend is totally permeated, in particular, by God's quality of *rahma* – this open, universal, motherly care for all creation. For the one who seeks this station, Ibn 'Arabi tells us that he 'must give what he has completely to the entirety of God's creation', indiscriminately sharing one's time, care and love with all (whether they be a believer or unbeliever, saint or sinner), and if the seeker does so to the total extent of their capabilities, they will then become 'the representative of the Real among the creatures with a mercy which encompasses everything'.[211]

Despite this total permeation of Abraham with the qualities of God, Ibn 'Arabi never equates creation and Creator, or suggests that a human being is somehow God incarnate. He elaborates on this by noting that Allah pervades Abraham in the same way that a color pervades a colored object. If we think of an orange, for example, it

---

210 Ibn 'Arabi, *Fusus*, p.61.
211 Ibn 'Arabi, *Fut*.II.363. As quoted in Chiabotti, 'The Abrahamic Heritage in Medieval Sufism, Part 1: *Futuwwa* and *khulla*', 88.

is not as though the fruit starts off as colorless (whatever that would look like – I'm guessing not entirely appetizing in appearance), and then the color orange is somehow *added on* to an orange. Rather, the fruit is *in itself* orange. Orangeness pervades it entirely (as the fruit's name suggests). Ibn 'Arabi also distinguishes this kind of pervasion, of a colored thing by its color, from the relationship between a particular space and the thing placed within that space.[212] Pervasion of color and the colored object is such that the color and its object are *perceptually* one, with the distinction between the two conceptual as opposed to actual. He then remarks that 'what permeates is veiled by what is permeated'.[213] This means that we can say that as God permeates Abraham, Abraham veils God. When our sight is based on what appears, we *see* Abraham, who is concealing what permeates him: God. Or, alternately if our sight is based on what actually is – Reality instead of appearance – we *see* Abraham's reality that is Being Itself, Allah, whose qualities then become the veil over Abraham:

> If the Real is apparent, then creation is veiled in Him; then creation is all the Names of God, His Hearing, His Vision, and all of His relations and perceptions. If creation is apparent, then God is veiled and hidden in it; and so, God is creation's hearing, sight, hands, legs, and all its powers.[214]

The perfect or complete human being (or *al-insan al-kamil*) is one 'who has actualized all the potentialities latent in the form of God', one who has become a pristine mirror reflecting the totality of divine qualities.[215] This is the final goal of human realization (if the word 'goal' can be used for a journey without end), integrating an awareness of all levels of reality with an ability to execute God's tasks for the sake of the world and all creation.

A later commentator of Ibn 'Arabi's, 'Abd al-Karim al-Jili (d.1424), phrases it a bit differently, stating that a fully realized human being like

---

212 Ibn 'Arabi, *Fusus*, p.61.
213 Ibid.
214 Ibid.
215 Chittick, *Imaginal Worlds*, p.23.

Abraham is a 'perfect copy' of God. In fact, such a person is the *only* way that God can be tangibly seen, as the perfect human being embodies God's qualities, thereby making these qualities perceptible.[216] The fully realized human being shows us what unmitigated love, transcendent wisdom and benevolent power look like in an immediate, perceptible way, and hence the complete human functions as a visible copy of God on earth. This is why those who have had the good fortune to encounter such beings tend to describe an experience of profound awe and overwhelming love in their presence, and why, historically, even great rulers have humbled themselves before such realized beings.[217]

We might think of this notion of 'copy' in a little more depth using the orange analogy again: although we can conceive of the color orange, the only way that we can actually *see* the color is in a particular orange-colored object, which, in a sense, is a physical 'copy' of the color itself. Note, however, that a copy is still something at least somewhat removed from, or limited in comparison to the original. The color orange itself is not somehow limited to the particular orange fruit you hold in your hand.

Regarding this difference between original and copy, Ibn 'Arabi and his students held that God's attributes, including lordship, can only be shared by humans to a *limited degree*, and that the 'humanness' of a human being forever remains a servant in need of its Lord.[218] Although Abraham is pervaded by God, he remains a servant of that which pervades him. Fakhr al-Din 'Iraqi (d.1289), a student of Ibn 'Arabi's successor, Sadr al-Din al-Qunawi, writes on this as follows: 'Know that between form and mirror no true unification, no "incarnation" can exist.'[219] He goes on to explain that this is because the idea of

---

216 Morrisey, *Sufism and the Perfect Human*, p.59.
217 Some of the best accounts I have come across of encounters with beings like this, include: Ram Dass's description of meeting his guru, Neem Karoli Baba (d.1973) in his classic *Be Here Now* (San Cristobal, NM, 1971); Sogyal Rinpoche's recounting of his early life with his master Jamyang Khyentse Chokyi Lodro (d.1959) in *The Tibetan Book of Living and Dying* (London, 1992); the account of Shaykh Ahmad al-'Alawi (d.1934) found in Martin Lings's *A Sufi Saint of the Twentieth Century: Shaikh Ahmad al-'Alawi* (Cambridge, UK, 1993); and Irina Tweedie's remarkable *Daughter of Fire: A Diary of a Spiritual Training with a Sufi Master* (Inverness, 2006), which offers a rich sense of her master Radha Mohan Lal (d.1966).
218 Morrisey, *Sufism and the Perfect Human*, p.61.
219 'Iraqi, *Divine Flashes*, p.93.

being unified with God, or God incarnating within a human being, implies two separate essences that somehow unite, when, according to 'contemplation's eye', we see that 'there exists in all existence but One object of contemplation'.[220]

In other words, there is no way for someone to be totally united with God, or for God to incarnate within someone, as there is, at the level of ultimate reality, no one besides God for Him to be united with, or to incarnate within. In our everyday life we encounter multiple beings and objects, so it certainly seems as though there are entities besides God. And indeed, on the perceptual level of reality we find ourselves functioning within, the diversity of entities is *obviously* the case: there are innumerable people, places and things we encounter on a day-to-day basis. And yet, as we discussed in the previous chapter on Adam, these many entities (and us who encounter them) are, in light of ultimate reality, ephemeral dream forms without their own independent existence – rather they and we all share one existence, or real essence, which is Being as such. Hence, we cannot say that someone becomes united with God's essence or that God's essence incarnates in someone, for God's is *the only essence there is*. This is also why Ibn 'Arabi refers to ourselves and our world as *huwa la huwa* or Him/not Him – we and all we see are simultaneously God and not God. This was succinctly expressed by the Prophet's cousin and son-in-law, and fourth successor, 'Ali, who said, 'God is in all things but not by being contained within them, and He is separate from all things but not by being isolated from them.'[221]

Keeping this important distinction between original and copy, or mirror and image, in mind, in this chapter in particular we find Ibn 'Arabi making explicit the way in which the phenomenal world we encounter, and ourselves as those who encounter it, are, altogether, none other than God's qualities manifest. He writes: 'Do you not see the Real manifest through the qualities of existent things – telling us about Himself – even with qualities of deficiency and qualities of

---

220 Ibid.
221 Mukhtar Ali, *Philosophical Sufism*, p.43.

blame?'²²² This can be a particularly challenging concept for those Islamic theologians (and similarly inclined Jewish and Christian theologians) who exclusively emphasize God's transcendence above and beyond the world. As we will see throughout the *Gemstones*, and will discuss in more depth in Chapter Five on Elijah–Enoch, Ibn 'Arabi suggests that God is only genuinely understood *both* in terms of transcendence (beyond likeness to anything whatsoever) *and* in terms of immanence (or likeness with literally everything found in existence – through image and form).

Perhaps a somewhat awkward fact for the 'transcendence only' theological crowd, this dual emphasis of Ibn 'Arabi's is actually rooted in the Qur'an, which describes God as *al-Batin* (the hidden or invisible) and *al-Zahir* (the obvious, apparent or visible) (Q 57:3). Throughout the text, the Qur'an maintains a careful balance of transcendence and immanence when describing God. Ibn 'Arabi comments on this:

> *How can I know You when You are the Inwardly Hidden [al-Batin] who is not known?*
> *How can I not know You when You are the outwardly Manifest [al-Zahir], making Yourself*
> *known to me in everything?*²²³

The entire phenomenal world is nothing but the hidden Essence of the Real expressed through His Names, the traces of which manifest as myriad invisible and visible realms. Hence, every quality of every existent thing, including those that appear to be negative, tell us about God, or are included among His signs. However, Ibn 'Arabi notes in *The Meccan Revelations* that the bad – or blameworthiness *itself* – is not traced back to God. This is because blameworthiness is always accidental, conditional or circumstantial.²²⁴

---

222   Ibn 'Arabi, *Fusus*, p.61.
223   Ibn 'Arabi, *Prayers for the Week: The Seven Days of the Heart*, translated by Pablo Beneito and Stephen Hirtenstein (Oxford, 2021), pp.35–6.
224   Ibn 'Arabi, *Fut*.III.472.

For example, let's consider a friend with a troubling character trait, perhaps one prone to bouts of white-hot anger, what we might call 'a bad temper'. Ibn 'Arabi would suggest that this trait of theirs is not in and of itself *bad*: their personality traits are ultimately rooted in Being, which is in one sense sheer good, or, in another sense, entirely beyond conventional notions of good and evil, a kind of transcendent neutrality. However, the trait then *becomes* bad through being improperly expressed or applied. It is the misapplication of the trait in particular contexts that leads it to be considered blameworthy. Our friend's personality trait that we experience as anger may in fact be, at root, a passionate care and concern, that, when frustrated by circumstance, lashes out. To get that upset one obviously cares quite a bit, and caring is in and of itself a good trait, but when misapplied it leads to a blameworthy manifestation.

Correspondingly, when a trait is applied positively, the very same quality we experience as negative becomes something we might celebrate. Let's say another one of our friends is an inordinately greedy person, never satisfied with what they have and always trying to accumulate more fancy stuff, add more lines on the resumé of their ego and bask in social media adoration – always attempting to 'one-up' those around them. We might, rightfully, consider this to be a blameworthy trait of theirs (or at least an exhausting one). And yet if this same friend decides to direct their considerable ambition toward becoming a surgeon, and commits to a lengthy process of medical training in their greed for rare, surgical skill, that same root trait is something that we would now likely celebrate as praiseworthy, as it will result in the relief of suffering that few can competently alleviate. As we can see in these examples, it is not the trait *itself* but rather *how* it is expressed that determines our judgment of it. In other words, it is at the intersection where trait and circumstance meet that the praiseworthy and blameworthy arise.

Ibn 'Arabi concludes from this that each human being is only subject to shari'a rulings in their relation to other subjects and objects, and that there is no divine judgement that can be applied to someone *in their own entity or essence,* and hence 'no ruling applies to [the essence] in respect of its reality'.²²⁵ A particular human soul is neither praiseworthy nor blameworthy in itself, as it is simply a unique expression of Being, just like every other soul.²²⁶ There is no such thing as a 'bad seed' among human souls; none of us, in our essential nature, are inherently problematic. Praise and blame pertain only to our self's expression, when we encounter various circumstances, and other beings, and in response develop *intentions* and pursue *actions*. The traits then, of any given personality, are always conditioned by their manifestation in particular circumstances, and hence only become 'good' or 'bad' through them. It follows that we need not fret over our own set of personal qualities and wish we could track down some cosmic market where we might trade them in for other very different ones, but rather ask ourselves how we can best, most creatively employ *our own qualities*, how we can use them to manifest the beneficial as opposed to the regrettable, in our own way.

As this very distinction between what is laudable and harmful only takes place in the relative realm we know as the world of circumstances, a realm of changing relations between entities in flux, it follows that there is nothing that is *absolutely* good or bad here. Ibn 'Arabi states this explicitly: 'there is nothing in the cosmos that is absolutely blameworthy or absolutely praiseworthy', because 'aspects and contexts delimit each thing'.²²⁷ The contextual, relative nature of our phenomenal world precludes any sort of absolute good or evil. The intergalactic Jedi master Obi-Wan Kenobi would agree, it seems, when he says in the *Star Wars* film *Revenge of the Sith* (2005) that 'only a Sith deals in absolutes'. In the *Star Wars* universe, Sith, those agents of the dark side, are fundamentally misguided in seeing the world through the lens of absolutes, as they simply do not exist here. As we see so vividly in history, those who traffic in absolutist ideologies, 'black and white' thinking, so often do violence to a world far more complex than their own limited thinking.

---

225 Ibn 'Arabi, *Fut*.III.390. As quoted in Chittick, *Imaginal Worlds*, p.48.

226 Chittick notes the situational nature of Ibn 'Arabi's ethics, as in *Fut*.III.390 he discusses how shari'a rulings apply exclusively to entities in relation to other entities and objects, but never to entities in and of themselves. Ibid., pp.47–8.

227 Ibid., p.47.

Although our world is one in which everything (blameworthy and praiseworthy) is conditioned by the contexts within which they manifest, every moment encountered by every being in existence, regardless of that moment's experiential tone and contextual limitation, is yet another note in the eternal music of the imperishable light of Being – the Song of God – though we so often fail to perceive the divine Musician behind it all. To draw upon Iraqi's poetic expressions of Ibn 'Arabi's teachings again, he writes:

> *Love plays its lute behind the screen –*
> *where is a lover to listen to its tune?*
>
> *With every breath a new song,*
> *each split second a new string plucked.*[228]

If each moment in our lives is another note in the universe's inexhaustible music, and this music is, ultimately, a symphony of genuine, profound love, the question follows: Why then must we experience songs of suffering? Why is it that our lives include not only the praiseworthy but the acutely (and often painfully) blameworthy? This takes us into Ibn 'Arabi's next discussion in this chapter on Abraham, on the perplexing question of how God's determination of everything can be reconciled with our own free will and choice. In other words, we turn now to the question of destiny.

The Mystery of Destiny

The basic questions of why people make the choices they do and why life happens to them in the way that it does, are generally considered by humanity's sages to be some of the most impenetrably mysterious. We might simply call this the mystery of *what we do and what happens to us*. This issue tends to be framed in the language of *destiny* in religions

---

228 'Iraqi represents the *madhhab-i 'ishq*, or 'way of love' or 'school of love'. Whereas Ibn 'Arabi and his more philosophically inclined disciples like Qunawi tend to describe God using the language of 'Being' (*wujud*), 'Iraqi describes very much the same view, but replaces 'Being' with 'Love'. Regardless of language, we see a shared understanding of reality's deep unity, a unity that is encountered through the doorway of our deepest heart. We will discuss this school of Sufism in greater detail in the sixth chapter on Moses. 'Iraqi, *Divine Flashes*, p.71.

originating in the Middle East (Judaism, Christianity and Islam), and discussed as *karma* in religions rooted in India (Hinduism, Jainism and Buddhism).

We can begin to appreciate the challenging nature of this issue by simply observing the precarity and unpredictability of our own lives. You can be humming along quite comfortably with everything seeming to fall into place without too much trouble, and then out of nowhere some accident, illness or shocking event turns your life upside down. Or you make a terrible decision with painful consequences and later agonize over why exactly you made it, wondering why you couldn't have just chosen differently. One can go from being someone people are jealous of and strive to emulate, to becoming a sort of cautionary tale whispered about with shaking heads and platitudes of pity, all quite rapidly. Alternately one can stumble upon an unexpected boon and find oneself in a situation of success and comfort not commensurate with one's own efforts (though unfortunately this seems to be the less likely of the two scenarios). The mystery of why things function this way begs for an explanation and yet the explanations on offer all tend to remain at least somewhat unsatisfactory.

Sages across the board suggest that that genuine knowledge of this aspect of life is *incredibly* rare, and that the conceptual frameworks religions have developed to account for destiny or karma can only approximate a reality that goes far beyond them. On this Ibn 'Arabi writes in the *Gemstones*: 'The mystery of destiny is one of the highest kinds of knowledge, and God only grants understanding of it to those whom He has singled out for perfect knowledge.'[229] Hypothetically, after decades of spiritual practice under the guidance of a realized teacher, one may, with grace from the side of the unseen, gain rarefied insight into the hidden depths of one's own self, develop beauty of character or have encounters with the spiritual forms of great beings, and maybe even come to directly know the Real in whatever way one is able to. However, even among this relatively small group of people blessed with such insight, virtue and experience, very, very few of them will come to gain a direct understanding of destiny. In what we might

---
229 Ibn 'Arabi, *Fusus*, p.122.

see as a sort of saintly braggadocio, one of Islam's most renowned saints, 'Abd al-Qadir al-Jilani (d.1166) (about whom more will be said in Chapter Six), claimed that 'when the saints reached destiny they all found it to be an impenetrable wall, except me: a window opened in it for me', suggesting that he was one of the very few who gained insight into this mystery.[230]

Lama Shenpen Hookham, a scholar and practitioner in the Tibetan Nyingma tradition of Buddhism, shares a quite similar Buddhist perspective on the impenetrable nature of this question of destiny/karma. She first observes that teachings on karma are by necessity 'incomplete and unsatisfactory', continuing,

> The Buddhist tradition is aware of this, but sees no way out of the problem, since how karma works is very mysterious (hidden). It can only really be understood by Buddhas themselves, when they come to understand the whole of the nature of reality.[231]

Along the same lines, Devadatta Kali offers a Hindu perspective in commenting on the Upanishads. He notes the magnitude of the context within which karma operates is such that only one with a 'bird's eye view' of reality as a whole would be remotely capable of making sense of it, observing that 'the web of human experience is far more subtle and infinitely complex' than physical causality, and hence it is 'impossible for us to take a big enough step backward to view the whole picture'.[232] In short, there seems to be a relatively broad agreement that, unless one has God's perspective on the totality of reality covering the entire continuum of time and space, one is not really in a position to understand fully how the events of human lives function within the Big Picture. It follows that knowledge of destiny/karma is reserved for those rare, *fully realized beings*, if anyone at all.

Ibn 'Arabi suggests that these rare, fully realized beings who have

---

230 As quoted in Bakri Aladdin, 'The Mystery of Destiny (*sir al-qadar*) in Ibn 'Arabi and al-Qunawi', translated by Abdul Rahim Hassan, *Muhyiddin Ibn Arabi Society,* https://ibnarabisociety.org/destiny-qadar-qunawi-aladdin-bakri/ (accessed November 27, 2022).
231 Lama Shenpen Hookham, *There's More to Dying than Death: A Buddhist Perspective* (Birmingham, 2006), p.65.
232 Kali, *Svetasvataropanisad: The Knowledge That Liberates*, p.347.

perfected knowledge indeed have *some* understanding of the mystery of *qadar*, and yet he also maintains that, in the final analysis, it is God alone who has full knowledge of destiny. Toshihiko Izutsu summarizes Ibn 'Arabi's perspective here as follows:

> The true reality of *qadar* in its entirety is the deepest of all secrets into which God alone can penetrate, because it concerns the very delicate ontological moments at which the Divine act of 'creation' comes into actual relation with its objects. And in this depth, 'There can be no "immediate tasting" (*dhawq*), no self-manifestation, no "unveiling" except for God alone.'[233]

The mystery of destiny lies beyond time and space, when an entity is brought into pre-existence, a 'moment' that we simply do not have any sort of experiential access to. Nor can we know the 'inner structure' of a latent entity, an archetype or possibility of being, which is 'an impenetrable mystery because it is part of Divine Consciousness'.[234] Hence the utter futility of judging others, whose inner origin, reality and trajectory we can literally *never know*. The only exception here is *our own archetype*. Ibn 'Arabi says that one particularly enlightened, of truly exceptional spiritual power, may get knowledge of the nature and contents of their own archetype (but only if that archetype itself includes this knowledge as part of its own contents). However, he maintains that this knowledge is not equivalent to God's, as God knows the archetype before its existence, while the enlightened sage can only be given insight into its existent states.[235]

If the fully realized human being cannot know this mystery of destiny in its fullness, the rest of us must make due with explanations that are merely suggestive in their explanatory power. Nevertheless, explanations we seek, and most religious traditions have histories of extensive discussion and debate around this issue. Islam is no exception, and has, since its earliest years, grappled with this question at length, most often framed in terms of destiny (*qadar*). The root

---

233 Izutsu, *Sufism and Taoism*, p.181.
234 Ibid. p.180.
235 Ibid., pp.180–1.

contains meanings of power, ability and determination. It refers to God's absolute and total power in determining the course of events. The question of *qadar* actually emerged as the first theological controversy or debate in Islam.[236]

We can trace this dispute all the way back to letters exchanged between the Caliph 'Abd al-Malik (d.705) and a famous Muslim scholar and ascetic, Hasan al-Basri (d.728), in the first century of Islamic history. Al-Basri was renowned for his piety, his asceticism and his knowledge, and would later be seen as a sort of proto-Sufi. As a revered religious authority, the Caliph wrote to al-Basri, asking him to confirm his views on the question of destiny, as the Caliph was a staunch proponent of it, believing that God predetermined all human action, good and bad. Author and journalist Mustafa Akyol interestingly suggests that the Caliph may have had good political reasons for favoring a strong view of God's determination of our actions: if God predetermines everything, then the actions of the Caliph, however mistaken or tyrannical, can be explained as part of God's plan. To assert the freedom of human action is also to suggest that human leaders like 'Abd al-Malik could have acted otherwise in their policies, opening their administration to critique and even rebellion.[237] Al-Basri responded by contradicting the Caliph, arguing instead that 'our Lord is too merciful and just and generous' to arbitrarily determine some for reward and others for torment.[238]

Regardless of political considerations, we can see why there is a problem here. There is an inherent tension between the proposition that a) there is an all-powerful Deity who determines every aspect of reality, and b) that humans freely choose their actions, and hence can be justly held accountable for them by this same Deity. Monotheistic traditions in general have struggled to reconcile these important premises of their respective faiths. It seems that if one gives full-throated support to free will, or the notion that we freely choose our actions,

---

236 Khalid Blankinship, '2. The Early Creed', in *The Cambridge Companion to Classical Islamic Theology*, edited by Tim Winter (New York, 2008), p.38.
237 Mustafa Akyol, *Reopening Muslim Minds: A Return to Reason, Freedom, and Tolerance* (New York, 2021), pp.16–17.
238 Ibid., p.15.

one thereby restricts God's determining power over us. Alternately, to suggest instead that our choices are predetermined by God, is to propose an inscrutable and seemingly arbitrary pre-programming that makes our reward and punishment by God seem distinctly unfair. It appears then that one must choose between declaring God to be all-powerful *or* God to be truly just, when monotheisms all agree that He is undoubtedly *both*.

What would become the most widely accepted Sunni solution to this dilemma was posited by the Ash'ari and Maturidi schools of thought, the two being the predominant schools of classical Islamic theology. They emerged as something of a synthesis of al-Basri's view of human freedom and the Caliph's belief in God's determination of our actions. The Ash'aris and Maturidis agreed with the Caliph that God is the omnipotent designer of the world, determining everything in the cosmos, including each person's actions. Medieval Maturidi scholar Nur al-Din al-Sabuni (d.1184) summarizes this position as follows: 'The People of Truth state that all actions, states, and words of creation – without exception – are based on God's eternal decree and predestination.'[239] However, Maturidis and Ash'aris also made room for al-Basri's point about free will, suggesting that people acquire (*kasb*) responsibility for the actions God predetermines and creates for them. They do this by freely *choosing* these actions. So, their overall position is that God totally determines and even creates our actions, but He does so only *in collaboration* with our 'own power, will, and choice'.[240] Some have suggested this is a sort of like a bubble of free will in a general sea of predestination.

Muslim theologians did not really see this attempt to synthesize free will and predestination as being entirely accurate or satisfactory, but rather believed it was the best possible framing of the problem within the constraints of Islamic theology, much in the way that Buddhist scholars have suggested that various theories of karma found within Buddhism do not quite cut it, in terms of explaining this rather

---

239 Nur al-Din al-Sabuni, *An Introduction to Islamic Theology (Al-Bidayah fi usul al-din)*, translated and annotated by Faraz A. Khan (Berkeley, 2020), p.290.

240 Ibid., p.238.

trenchant mystery, but at least go some of the way toward making sense of it. In theologian Asad Tarsin's primer on the basics of Islam for Sunnis, *Being Muslim* (2015), for example, he warns that 'it is important to recognize that completely reconciling these two realities (free will and divine predestination) is beyond the capacity of the human mind'.[241]

Essence and Existence: Which Comes First?

In this chapter on Abraham, Ibn 'Arabi offers his original account of destiny by suggesting (perhaps somewhat counterintuitively, at least from the perspective of a conventional monotheist), that *our own pre-existing, essential nature determines our destiny*: our lives unfold as they do based on who we ultimately are as individual entities. Our essence determines our existence. We cannot then blame God for creating us to be just the sort of people we are, for giving us *wujud* (being/existence) along the contours of our own self. The determiner determines, but only in accord with the determined. Ibn 'Arabi illustrates this with the analogy of knowledge, by observing, 'Knowledge has no effect on what is known. Rather what is known has an effect on knowledge. It bestows knowledge of itself – what it is, in its essence.'[242] It is the known thing that determines our knowledge of it. The known thing presents us with its qualities and our knowledge of it is shaped by those very qualities. Now, if a) God's determining will directly derives from His knowledge, and b) His knowledge itself is determined by what is known, it follows that c) God's determination of existence is constrained by what He knows of each possible thing – what each thing gives Him to know of its own self, in its pre-existent possibility. Ibn 'Arabi expresses this in *The Meccan Revelations* as follows: 'God wills only the actual situation. His will in the things is that they be what they are.'[243]

One of the keys to understanding Ibn 'Arabi's cosmology here is to recognize that, as we discussed in the last chapter, it is premised on the

---
241 Asad Tarsin, *Being Muslim: A Practical Guide* (Berkeley, 2015), p.34.
242 Ibn 'Arabi, *Fusus*, p.63.
243 *Fut*.III.356. As quoted in Chittick, *Imaginal Worlds*, p.143.

notion that lower realms of existence *derive* from higher realms, and yet the lower realms *determine* the form in which the higher realms manifest. This dialectical aspect of his cosmology can be particularly subtle, and quite challenging to more conventional versions of monotheism. Ibn 'Arabi emphasizes in various ways that a) from one perspective, God determines entities, and yet b) from another perspective, those same entities, in their latent essences, determine what God will determine them to be.

It's probably worth unpacking that a bit further (and we may want to put that philosophical seatbelt back on). A persistent point that Ibn 'Arabi makes in several ways throughout the *Gemstones* is that the various entities that derive from Being each have their own distinct nature, or essence, which determines the particular way in which they manifest when given existence. God creates entities, but the nature of the entities themselves, as inherent possibilities, determine what they will be created as.

We can illustrate this principle by using the example of shape. Before coming into existence, for example, a triangle by nature has already determined that it will have three sides. This is because a triangle is an inherent possibility within Being: among shapes, it is the possibility for shape to manifest in three-sidedness. This three-sidedness is what philosophers call a triangle's quiddity, or essential nature, its defining aspect, or essence. In Arabic this is known as something's *mahiyya* – which literally means 'what-it-is'. We can see that even if we do not encounter a physical triangle in existence, its defining aspect or *mahiyya* – three-sidedness – precedes it. Muslim philosophers would say than that the triangle's pre-existent essence is triangular before God gives it existence as an actual triangle.

Before existence, a triangle is merely an idea, or latent possibility, what Ibn 'Arabi terms an *'ayn thabita* or fixed entity. A fixed entity is one possibility inherent within Being that *can* exist, should God give it existence. Its own inherent definition/essence/form/nature determines how it will manifest when it does (and he suggests, further determines *if* it will manifest).²⁴⁴ God gives an entity existence, but God can only give it existence along the contours of its own self. In one sense then the triangle determines itself, and cannot legitimately accuse God of failing to make it four-sided: God can only create something to be what it is. In other words, the inherent nature of a possible thing is characterized by specific properties that qualify and quantify the measure (*qadar*) of being it can receive.²⁴⁵ Ibn 'Arabi expresses this as follows:

> The judge, in reality, complies with the subject of his judgment, ruling according to the requirements of its essential nature. The one judged then themselves determines how the judge will rule, in accord with their own essence.²⁴⁶

The word here translated as 'judge' is *hakim*, which is derived from the root *ha-ka-ma*, which includes meanings of one who passes judgment, determines, orders or controls. Although there is one sense in which the judge in a court case, for example, rules over the judged, there is another in which the judged themselves determine how the judge will rule, as the judge rules according to what they present. If someone is caught on camera strolling out of a store holding a new pair of Air Jordans they've failed to pay for, they leave a judge little choice but to find them guilty of theft – the judge's ruling is determined by the one who is on trial. The judged determines the judge's judgment.

On a deeper level, just as a judge (ideally) rules according to the nature of the judged, so the Determiner determines according to the nature of the determined. God's being infinitely emanates forth, though an entity only obtains from that emanation what its own essential nature allows it to – each one then gets a share of being based upon its own self, much like a pitcher pouring water, with the shape and size of the cup determining the amount of water that each one can contain.

---

244 Scholar of Islamic and Jewish studies Ronald L. Nettler explains that according to Ibn 'Arabi, although *logically* a possible thing (or contingent) may or may not exist, 'the nature of the contingent's latency *determines* whether or not it will be actualized'. 'The Figure and Truth of Abraham in Ibn 'Arabi's *Fusus al-hikam*', *Journal of the Muhyiddin ibn 'Arabi Society*, 24 (1998), 38.

245 Maria De Cillis, *Free Will and Predestination in Islamic Thought: Theoretical Compromises in the Work of Avicenna, Al-Ghazali, and Ibn 'Arabi* (New York, 2014), p.182.

246 Ibn 'Arabi, *Fusus*, p.121.

This is at the heart of the mystery of destiny: we are who we are, and our life unfolds as it does, not because God arbitrarily determines it, but because our own particularity demands it. Ibn 'Arabi states then, 'do not praise or blame any but yourself.'[247] Our experience of reality is a direct result of who we are, and hence we are, from one perspective, wholly responsible for it, and can only praise or blame ourselves.

This may seem to suggest that we are born with a fixed nature that predetermines our life, much like the triangle. Although in one sense this can be said to be the case, from another perspective the very opposite is true – we are born 'unfinished', open to a remarkable range of possibility. Ibn 'Arabi also affirms this. The Qur'an quotes the Angel Gabriel as saying, *And there is none among us but they have a known station (maqam ma'lum)* (Q 37:164). Ibn 'Arabi suggests that indeed all earthly creatures have a fixed station as well, with human beings the *only* exception to this.[248] As God Himself has no fixed station, being totally undetermined, and humans are created in the Divine image, they too are undetermined by nature. As William Chittick explains, whereas 'a pear tree enters this world as a pear tree and never leaves as a pumpkin', or 'a rhinoceros does not become a monkey or a mouse', a human being, in contrast, has a radical potential for transformation and degradation. Although we may not change our outward form very much (granted body modification can be rather extensive), our *inward form* can take on almost any shape.[249] In contrast to the pear tree and rhinoceros that Chittick mentions above, when we think of human lives we are struck by the sheer range of possibility: success and failure, compassion and violence, addiction and art, saint and sociopath, all of it.

This remarkable openness of the human state has historically been highlighted by the humanistic tradition in the West. Humanism is usually traced back to the fascinating Italian Renaissance philosopher Pico della Mirandola (d.1494). Influenced by various streams

---

247 Ibid., p.64.

248 That is, the only exception in this visible world – the other exception is generally held to be the *jinn*, unseen beings that also have free will, and hence lack a fixed station.

249 Chittick, *Sufi Path of Knowledge*, p.19.

of esoteric thought, including the Kabbalah (Judaism's mystical tradition) and Hermeticism, as well as by Muslim philosophers like Averroes, Mirandola sought to reconcile Aristotle and Plato, and really all philosophy and religion, producing 900 theses that attempted to show the singular truth underlying them all, publishing them as his *Conclusions* in 1486. Mirandola's theses, perhaps unsurprisingly, proved to be controversial among authorities, who generally wanted to preserve the Catholic Church's status as having a unique doctrinal superiority and salvific efficacy. Shortly after the publication of his *Conclusions* Pope Innocent VIII (d.1492) condemned and disputed many of them, eventually forcing Mirandola to flee from Rome to Paris, where the Pope had the French authorities imprison him for a time.[250]

Nevertheless, to make many of his *Conclusions* accessible to a wider audience, Mirandola then composed what would become his most famous work, seen as a kind of manifesto of the Renaissance, the *Oratio de Hominis Dignitate*. In his *Oratio*, he marvels at the wondrous nature of the human being. For Mirandola, we humans are almost miraculous as, unlike any other creature, we can actually appreciate the vastness of the cosmos and perceive (if not fully comprehend) its beauty and grandeur.[251] In addition, he praises humanity's undefined nature, with its wide-open possibilities. Mirandola describes God as saying to His human creation, 'We have given thee, Adam, no fixed seat, no form of thy own', such that 'thou mayest sculpt thyself into whatever shape thou dost prefer', lowering oneself to the level of 'brutes', or utilizing the soul's 'reason', to ascend to 'the higher natures which are divine'.[252]

Peter Berger, in his classic work on the sociology of religion, *The Sacred Canopy* (1967), suggests that this grand human freedom to sculpt ourselves, so celebrated by Mirandola, is a direct result

---

250 Brian Copenhaver, 'Giovanni Pico della Mirandola', *Stanford Encyolpedia of Philosophy* (2020), https://plato.stanford.edu/entries/pico-della-mirandola/ (accessed April 5, 2023).
251 Pico della Mirandola, *On the Dignity of Man*, translated by Charles Glenn Wallis (Indianapolis, 1998 [1965]), p.4.
252 Ibid., p.5.

of our biology, our being born instinctually 'unfinished'.[253] With the exception of humans, Berger notes, animals are born almost completely programmed by instinct – they tend to assume adult roles very shortly after birth, and, though having a range of possibilities in their expression of life, and some notable individual qualities, their primary choices are largely predetermined: when to mate, what sorts of food to eat, what kinds of shelter to pursue, making their lives almost entirely predictable. Generation after generation, we see that crows tend to lead quite similar lives, as do coyotes, bees, ants and so on. According to Berger, this is because an animal's world is 'completely determined by its instinctual structure'.[254] Again, this is not to deny the very real intelligence and disparate personalities of animals, or their ability to learn a great deal – anyone who has had pets knows well their diversity of orientation and nature. However, we might say that this diversity of nature and possibility for learning, though notable in many species, is found to a *categorically greater degree* in humans.

Our unfinished nature means that we must 'fill in the gaps' left by a lack of instinctual programming, which, Berger says, is why we create culture to finish the job, to tell us what or what not to eat, how to regulate sexuality, what are appropriate ways of living, etc. As we don't have a life-world given to us, we must make one for ourselves (and Jews, Christians and Muslims would suggest here that God sends prophets to help us with this, which we will discuss further in the next chapter). So, although in one sense we humans are, individually, like the triangle I described above, in that our own individual 'shape' determines the sort of life we will lead, as a species we are totally unlike the triangle, as we can become any number of shapes. Perhaps the paradox here is that (according to Ibn 'Arabi) whatever shape we *choose* to become, this shape of our eventual self, which emerges out of a stunning range of potentialities, ultimately accords with our own pre-existent nature. Our destiny is both a) our very open-ended undefined potentiality, and b) the way we ultimately choose to express and particularize it.

---

253 Peter L. Berger, *The Sacred Canopy: Elements of a Sociological Theory of Religion* (New York, 2011), p. 15.
254 Ibid., p.16.

It seems, then, that Ibn 'Arabi takes on the question of destiny by positing, in at least one sense, that each human being's essence (or essential nature) precedes their existence as an actual physical human on earth. It is this essence which determines the way in which the person will choose to experience life when they find themselves in it. It is interesting to note that this very idea – that a person's essence precedes their existence – is precisely why French existentialist philosopher Jean-Paul Sartre (d.1980) was an atheist. For Sartre, this idea that our essence as humans precedes our existence inevitably objectifies us as sort of preprogrammed machines, and that only a truly atheistic philosophy accurately accounts for human subjectivity and freedom, suggesting instead that our existence precedes our essence.

In a talk he gave in Paris in 1945, Sartre offered a defence of his philosophy – which he called existentialism – against the charges of its mid-century Christian and communist detractors. This talk was later recorded and published as an essay, 'Existentialism is a Humanism', perhaps one of his most read works, and one that echoes aspects of Mirandola's own humanism. Sartre begins by defining existentialism as, most fundamentally, the belief that 'existence precedes essence'.[255] According to Sartre, a manufactured object, say a pair of scissors, has an essence (its function of cutting) that exists in the mind of its inventor prior to its actual physical existence. Once a pair of scissors is manufactured it comes into physical existence, it does so with this essence preceding it. Simply put, the *idea* of scissors must exist before scissors themselves can manifest. For Sartre, if there is a God, then the human being can only be like the scissors, with an essence or purpose existing in the mind of God prior to the human being's creation in the world. If this is the case, our lives suffer from a kind of mechanical pre-programming. However, if there is no Creator, then the human being has no fixed function determining their nature. We simply find ourselves existing, with a huge range of possibility for what we may do with our existence. Sartre writes, 'There is no human nature for

---

255 Jean-Paul Sartre, *Existentialism is a Humanism,* translated by Carol Macomber, edited by John Kulka (New Haven, 2007), p.20.

there is no God to conceive of it.'[256] We begin as a proverbial blank slate, and only through our own concept and will do we craft our own self and determine our own nature. It follows that we determine our essence *after* the fact of existing, and we do this through our choices: we create ourselves through our ideas and the acts that follow them. This is the simultaneous thrill and burden, the joy and anguish, of human freedom. We can only find fulfilment in determining our own essence, yet doing so is often an uphill battle against the forces of family, culture and religion, among others, that try to predetermine our essence for us.

Ultimately, however, even if we allow others to shape us, we are responsible for the outcome, and hence Sartre thus holds that we can only 'praise and blame' ourselves, much as Ibn 'Arabi suggests. Although coming at the question from very different perspectives, both Sartre and Ibn 'Arabi agree that humans are fundamentally responsible for their own nature. They also agree with Mirandola that, unlike really anything else, a human being has no fixed station. Ibn 'Arabi, however, only points out that whatever essence a human being creates for themselves is *in fact what they already are*, as what is, is precisely what is meant to be. Each one of us is a distinct possibility of humanness – each one a particular manifestation of a more general type of being. Our particularity is our essence, and how we live and what we do among all possible choices is this essence manifest. So when someone lives a life characterized by say, repeated acts of harm and cruelty, and, as a result, they experience reality in a conflicted and ultimately tormented way, Ibn 'Arabi would say that it is not so much that God has arbitrarily chosen to create someone cruel who simply makes others suffer and then suffers themselves, but rather that this particularly challenging person is manifesting their own essence, which, like a triangle, is a latent entity with a particular nature that determines its own form, though God is the one who gives that form being or existence.

As people share God's quality of being undetermined, they come into the world with a range of possibilities, without any fixed station,

---
256 bid., p.22.

and yet what they ultimately do with this freedom is what they truly are, and what they are is what their latent possibility determines them to be, with God simply giving them existence according to the contours of their own self. Chittick illustrates this principle of Ibn 'Arabi's thought as follows: 'Thus, when God manifests *wujud* [existence] to the entity of the sun it shines, and when He manifests *wujud* to the entities of sinners, they sin,' and this is simply because these folks 'are loci of manifestation for delimited possibilities of outward existence possessed by nondelimited *wujud* in virtue of the fact that *wujud* allows for dispersion, deviation, error, suffering, and wretchedness'.[257] Being in its infinite nature includes possibilities of the negative, and hence these possibilities must manifest in some form or another.

It follows that people who, on the whole, create more suffering for themselves and others, are the natural outcome of Being's infinite possibilities of manifestation, and they are simply manifesting their own archetype, which is one of these possibilities. Ibn 'Arabi suggests that God cannot really be blamed for them causing harm and suffering as a result, as they are directly manifesting their own natures, or being what they are. God gives them *wujud*, but what they do with this follows from who they are in themselves. Chittick further explains, 'God can no more change the entities than He can change His own Essence, *wujud* Itself.'[258] Again, one can't blame God for making a triangle triangular. Ibn 'Arabi expresses this dialectic concisely in his chapter on Abraham as follows:

> So you nourish Him with your determinations and He nourishes you with existence. What can be said to be yours can be said to be His. The affair proceeds from Him to you and from you to Him. However, you are responsible, and He only makes you responsible due to your request, 'assign me responsibility,' which you spoke through the state of what you really are.[259]

---

257 Chittick, *Imaginal Worlds*, p.143.
258 Ibid.
259 Ibn 'Arabi, *Fusus*, p.64.

Drawing upon the Qur'an's characterization of Abraham as hospitable (Q 51:24–7), which of course includes offering nourishment to or feeding a guest, Ibn 'Arabi here shows how God nourishes humans with existence, while humans nourish God by providing the contours according to which existence manifests. Ibn 'Arabi maintains that we are responsible for these contours, and in fact request such responsibility. Although this request of ours may not seem apparent to us at this particular stage of existence, and we may even complain, during a particularly thorny time in life, that we never asked to exist in the first place, Ibn 'Arabi suggests that, if we do in fact find ourselves existing as a human being, our own essence has requested this very situation.

As we will see in the fourth chapter on Jonah, Ibn 'Arabi holds that, despite some asking for the intimidating responsibility of being human, and then dealing with it terribly, and suffering the natural consequences of this – all souls will, in the unfathomable field of eternity, eventually find felicity. Even those whose existence seems only to breed suffering – whom the Qur'an and Bible assure us will reap what they sow – even these will eventually find the peace that all souls seek (though it may take an incredibly long time). This is simply because negative qualities like suffering and hatred 'suffer' from a fundamental ontological lack. Simply put, they lack any real foundation in Being, and hence eventually disappear, as everything does, with the *exception* of the Essence, the Face of God. Now, in contrast, positive qualities like goodness and love are inherent to Being Itself, and hence can never die – they are deathless by nature. As we will see in the next chapter, it is in the human heart where we find the difference between each person's essential nature, and where the drama of manifesting our essence unfolds.

شعيب عليه السلام

3

What Does it Mean to Have a Heart? Shu'ayb and the Heart's Wisdom

> *Our pure hearts roam across the world.*
> *We get bewildered by all the idols we see,*
> *yet what we're trying to understand*
> *in everything is what we already are.*[260]

Why Do We Need Prophets?

Scattered throughout the Qur'an is a grand narrative of humanity's religious history. At its core we find the phenomenon of prophecy. Jews, Christians and Muslims believe that prophets are a natural outflow of the compassion of God, souls that God illuminates and then sends forth to provide us with insight into the nature of our reality and guidance on how we can live in accord with it, and hence find the happiness we all seek. The Qur'an is replete with stories of prophets familiar to Jews and Christians, including Moses (*Musa*), Jesus (*'Isa*), David (*Dawud*) and Solomon (*Sulayman*), Job (*Ayyub*) and Noah (*Nuh*). The story of

---

260 Jalal al-Din Rumi, *Divan* 549. As quoted in Kabir Helminski, in *The Knowing Heart: A Sufi Path of Transformation* (Boston, 1999), p.9.

Moses is recounted in many places throughout the Qur'an.[261] There is an entire chapter of Islam's scripture named after Mary (the 19th chapter, *Maryam*, relates her story in the chapter's first half), and another chapter devoted to Joseph (*Yusuf*).

The Qur'an also describes prophets not mentioned in Jewish and Christian scripture, like the ancient prophet Salih, sent to the northern Arabian tribe of Thamud. It further says that there are prophets sent to various peoples that are not named in the text: *Truly we have sent messengers before you [Muhammad]; of them there are some whose story We have told you, and some whose story We have not told you* (Q 40:78). The prophet Shu'ayb, whom Ibn 'Arabi bases this chapter on, is not mentioned by name in the Bible, though early commentators on the Qur'an tended to identify him with the Biblical figure Jethro, Moses' father-in-law.

Shu'ayb is sent to the people of Midian, calling upon them to worship God, and to repent from their deceptive and exploitative economic practices. He is characterized by his patience, modesty and gentleness. The people of Midian, who profit handsomely from their fraudulent business dealings, refuse his call, threaten and oppose him, and are eventually destroyed by God in a massive earthquake.[262] The Qur'an and the Bible both tell us that failing to heed prophetic warning, opposing truth, deceiving, exploiting and harming others, inevitably leads to divine retribution: we live in a fundamentally just universe, even if our immediate circumstances do not always reveal its workings.

---

261 There is some disagreement over precisely how many prophets are named in the Qur'an, as there are several figures named whose prophetic status remains unclear. Muslim authorities have suggested a prophetic list in the Qur'an ranging from 25 to 27. In verses 6:83–6 18 are mentioned as prophets: Abraham, Isaac, Jacob, Noah, David, Solomon, Job, Joseph, Moses, Aaron, Zachariah, John, Jesus, Elijah, Ishmael, Elisha, Jonah and Lot. In addition, Enoch (Idris) is mentioned as a prophet (19:56–7), as is Muhammad (7:157–8), for a total of 20, with a further three ancient Arab prophets mentioned: Hud, Shu'ayb and Salih, for a total of 23. Although Adam is not named as a prophet in the Qur'an, he is almost universally accepted as such in the Islamic tradition. Other Qur'anic figures that may or may not be included among the list of prophets in addition to these 24 include Ezra ('Uzayr), Luqman and Ezekiel (Dhu'l-Kifl). For more on Ibn 'Arabi's list of prophets, see Elmore, 'Qur'anic Wisdom', 96–107.

262 Nettler notes that Shu'ayb's story is told in the Qur'an in Q 7:85–93, Q 11:84–94, Q 26:177–90 and Q 29:36–7. Ronald L. Nettler, *Sufi Metaphysics and Qur'anic Prophets: Ibn 'Arabi's Thought and Method in the Fusus al-hikam* (Cambridge, UK, 2003), p.114.

I suppose one initial question might be: why do we need prophets at all? Can't we just figure stuff out on our own? There is certainly a strand of modern thinking that answers with a definitive 'yes', foregrounding intellectual self-reliance. This approach can be traced back to the early proponents of the European Enlightenment, an 18th-century philosophical movement that was premised on this very notion that we can figure out pretty much everything on our own. Enlightenment philosophers like Voltaire (d.1778), Jean D'Alembert (d.1783), Immanuel Kant (d.1804) and John Locke (d.1704) believed that if we free the rational intellect from the constraints of tradition and religion, we can solve almost any conceivable problem. Kant famously defined the Enlightenment as a maturation of the human being, whereby they are able 'to use one's own understanding without the guidance of another'.[263] Their views would prove foundational to much of modern culture, especially its more rationalistic and individualistic tendencies.

Ibn 'Arabi would not entirely disagree with Enlightenment philosophers, and affirms in many places that applying our own intellect can accomplish a great deal. However, he points out there is at least *one thing* that it cannot accomplish, writing that: 'If the intellect were able, on its own, to grasp what brings it happiness, it would have no need of prophets and the existence of prophets would be useless.'[264] Although we can independently figure out a great deal and human history shows that we have indeed discovered quite a lot, finding out what makes us *truly happy* requires an insight into the meaning of human life that goes beyond our calculative, problem-solving abilities. Our remarkable advances in science and technology have undoubtedly made many of our lives more comfortable and yet I don't think we can definitively say that they have made us *happier*. There is a good argument to be made that they may have unintentionally done the opposite. Interestingly, the Buddha is beloved precisely as someone who taught people insight into the nature of suffering and how to end

---

263 William Bristow, 'Enlightenment', *Stanford Encyclopedia of Philosophy* (2010, revised 2017), https://plato.stanford.edu/entries/enlightenment/ (accessed November 30, 2022).

264 Ibn 'Arabi, *Fut*.II.49. As quoted in Hirtenstein (with a slight rephrasing), *The Unlimited Mercifier*, p.63.

it (he even summarized his teachings as just that: suffering and its end). Although this might sound simple enough, it's not hard to see how few of us actually live joyously, making insight into what gives us happiness a rare, precious jewel.

In *The Meccan Revelations*, Ibn 'Arabi actually has a chapter on happiness, entitled 'The Alchemy of Happiness'.[265] Here he describes human happiness using a story of two individuals ascending through the heavenly spheres: a rationalist philosopher and a follower of the prophets. Together they ascend through the seven heavens, each of which is both a planetary realm and the spiritual abode of a particular prophet. They ascend first to the sphere of the Moon (and the abode of the prophet Adam), then to Mercury (Jesus and John), through the Sun (Enoch), Mars (Aaron), Jupiter (Moses) and Saturn (Abraham). As they rise through the spheres, we see that the prophetic disciple approaches reality through the holistic knowledge of the *heart*, while the rationalist represents the intellectual cognition of the mind. As a student of the heart, the disciple embraces each moment on its own terms, seeking to learn from it holistically, whereas the intellectual, following the mind, seeks to shape each moment in accord with *the knowledge they already have*.

Along the same lines, one of the first Zen teachers in America, Shunryu Suzuki (d.1971), taught his students to constantly return to the 'beginner's mind' (*shoshin*):

> The mind of the beginner is empty, free of the habits of the expert, ready to accept, to doubt, and open to all the possibilities. It is the kind of mind which can see things as they are, which step by step and in a flash can realise the original nature of everything.[266]

Suzuki's 'beginner's mind' corresponds to the disciple of the heart in Ibn 'Arabi's story, and is contrasted with the limitations of the mind of the 'expert', represented by the rationalist philosopher. As the two

---

265 In Arabic, this is *Kimiya' al-sa'ada*, perhaps a nod to an earlier book by al-Ghazali of the same title. For a full translation of this chapter, see Ibn 'Arabi, *The Alchemy of Human Happiness*, translated by Stephen Hirtenstein (Oxford, 2017).

266 Richard Baker, 'Introduction', in Shunryu Suzuki, *Zen Mind, Beginner's Mind*, Fortieth Anniversary Edition (Boston, 2010), p.xiv.

ascend, the rationalist only ever understands the surface appearance of things, learning 'how the planets affect the material realm' but failing to perceive and benefit from the prophetic sphere that encompasses it and the deeper reality it unveils.[267] Hence happiness is missed as the intellectual has failed to gain the transformative knowledge of 'the original nature of everything', a knowledge that plunges one 'into the supreme light, where love-ecstasy overcomes him'.[268]

This is not to suggest that, as disciples of the heart, we simply abandon critical thinking or analytical precision, but rather that we use these abilities of mind *within the context* of an open heart, which allows us to access and, ultimately, be transformed by reality's deeper dimensions. When I met with Professor Abdul Aziz Said during my doctoral research in Washington, D.C., he shared with me an ancient greeting used in Mesopotamia by tribal leaders and Sufi masters, a way of saying hello or goodbye that concisely expresses this principle: '*balak fi qalbak*'. This beautiful saying can mean something like 'mind your heart' or 'be mindful of your heart', but is more literally translated as '*keep your mind in your heart*'.

So, who exactly are these prophets of the heart? How is it that they know what makes us happy? In one sense prophets are regular human beings – they are certainly not any other sort of being. They are exceptional, however, in that their hearts are awakened to the full spectrum of reality. As they gain insight into life's deeper dimensions, which remain hidden to the vast majority of us, they have a rarefied understanding of the nature of humanity and its flourishing. Their awakened hearts not only allow them to understand much more of the whole than the rest of us, but such hearts open to the soul's innate goodness. This quality of natural goodness makes them suitable as vessels for guidance from the Source, as they ensure that this guidance can be received without egoic distortion, transmitted to others without the interference of ambition or narrow, self-oriented motives. In other words, prophets are rare vessels of truth. They appear in the time and space where they are most needed and where their impact can have

---

267 Stephen Hirtenstein, 'Introduction', in Ibn 'Arabi, *The Alchemy of Human Happiness*, p.27.
268 Ibid.

the greatest reach. The rarity of the prophet's open heart and natural goodness is precisely why they are celebrated and loved so much. They are clear channels through which guidance and grace can be transmitted, in a world where all too often the light is filtered darkly.[269]

According to Islamic tradition, Adam is the first prophet (*nabi*) and Muhammad the last. The Qur'an (Q 33:41) tells Muhammad that he is the 'Seal of the Prophets' (*khatm al-nabiyyin*), the final one sent to humanity before the end of our cosmic cycle. Between Adam and Muhammad, Islamic tradition suggests that 124,000 prophets were sent to the various tribes, nations and peoples of the world, affirming that no collectivity has been left without guidance in some form.[270] The guidance that God gives prophets has three basic dimensions: 1) *works*, or how to live and act; 2) *states*, ways of being that manifest beautiful character traits; and 3) *knowledge*, stabilizing an understanding of reality in its various modes.[271] Whether called sages, gurus, guides, shamans or awakened ones, prophets are tasked with sharing this three-fold guidance, teaching people beautiful ways of living, being and knowing. Each prophet shares this wisdom in a way that their people can understand, carefully tailoring it to their culture and mentality. As the Qur'an affirms, *We have sent no messenger but in the language of his people that he may make [the message] clear to them* (Q 14:4).

We can note here that some prophets are not simply enlightened guides and warners, but also messengers (*rasul*, plural *rusul*). Messengers are those who have a larger task of establishing a revelatory framework to shape and sustain whole cultures for centuries. According to Islamic tradition, Noah, Abraham, Moses, Jesus and Muhammad are all messengers with this greater mission of transmitting a scripture, a way of life and a sacred law. Some later Muslim authorities would

---

269 We can all probably think of authorities and guides who may have some genuine insight, wisdom or transformative spiritual power, but their own self, which is the vessel for this wisdom, is troubled by immaturities and flaws that can lead to various forms of distortion or abuse. This is also why contemplative traditions like Sufism emphasize things like moral development, ritual practice, companionship with a genuine teacher and service to others, as all of these things can help mature the self, such that it can be a healthy vessel for wisdom.

270 The tradition of there being 124,000 prophets between Adam and Muhammad is traced to a hadith, 21257 in *Musnad Ahmad*.

271 William C. Chittick, *Ibn 'Arabi: Heir to the Prophets* (Oxford, 2007), p.12.

include figures like Krishna and Buddha in this category as well.[272] It's worth noting that the Qur'an describes all of humanity's prophets as *muslim*. In the Arabic language a *muslim* is one who exists in a state of *islam*, a word that has connotations of peace, safety, soundness, health, surrender and submission. In the Qur'an God commands Abraham to '*aslim*', or submit, and Abraham responds, *aslimtu li-rab al-'alamin* or 'I have submitted to the Lord of the worlds' (Q 2:132). To be a small 'm' *muslim* then is not to have a particular identity, or to belong to a special club, or even to be the follower of one prophet exclusively, but rather to be in a state of harmony with reality as such.

According to Zia Inayat Khan, an American Sufi teacher and scholar who leads the Inayati Sufi order, the Qur'an uses the term Islam to describe 'the spiritual life of the human species' based on 'the whole spectrum of prophets and the revelations that flow from them'.[273] Islam then is this essential, perennial truth. It is what the Prophet Muhammad was sent to revive and affirm. Hence the Islam taught by Muhammad is meant to restate the essence of the Islam taught by Moses and Jesus, Noah and Abraham, and all of the other prophets. In other words, Islam is humanity's perennial philosophy, the timeless truth at the core of all genuine traditions of guidance. Authors Michael Green and Coleman Barks express this nicely, in describing how, when they were in the presence of their master Bawa Muhaiyaddeen, Islam 'didn't mean a religion or culture or even a belief system, but a bright burning state with a quicksilver universality too elusive and grand for anyone's ownership'.[274]

Another American Sufi teacher and scholar, Nur al-Jerrahi or Lex Hixon (d.1995), summed up the *content* of this essential Islam as 'the truly human experience of Oneness', alongside its practical implication, 'compassionate service'. Together, an experience of Oneness and a life of compassion form the core of 'universal Islam,

---

272 Dickson, 'The Golden Sufi Center: A Non-Islamic Branch of the Naqshbandiyya-Mujaddidiyya', 31.

273 Zia Inayat Khan, Interview with William Rory Dickson, April 22, 2010. New Lebanon, New York.

274 Coleman Barks and Michael Green, *The Illuminated Prayer: The Five-Times Prayer of the Sufis* (New York, 2000), p.14.

manifest in the heart of all traditions'.[275] In the Gospels, Jesus concisely expresses the essence of this perennial message when he says that the greatest commandment representing the whole of Biblical law is a) loving the one God with all of one's being, and b) loving one's neighbor as oneself (Mark 12:28–34).

In the Qur'an's usage then, a *muslim* is anyone who returns to their primordial nature (*fitra*), whose heart recognizes the singular Reality and basic Goodness underlying phenomena, and lives a life of genuine compassion for others.[276] The rest appears to be secondary. This also means that there are many Muslims who are not *muslim* in the Qur'anic sense, and many Jews, Christians, Buddhists and atheists who are *muslim* in the Qur'anic meaning of the term. This is, perhaps, a bit inconvenient for the gatekeepers of identitarian religiosity, as reality so often is. Regip al-Jerrahi is co-founder of the transpersonal psychology movement, and an American Sufi teacher based in California. He shared a wonderful story with me about his Sufi master, Muzzafer Ozak, that illustrates this Qur'anic truth quite well:

> As my *shaykh* said years ago, he said he met interesting Americans during his time here, many who call themselves atheists but he thinks they're Muslims. He said American scientists, for example, who love truth, they love Allah, because Allah is *al-Haqq*, Allah is truth. Even though they've labeled themselves incorrectly, they're still Muslims – they're still religious people.[277]

---

275 Lex Hixon, *Atom from the Sun of Knowledge* (Westport, CT, 1993), p.xiv.

276 The Qur'an describes the Covenant with the Children of Israel (*Bani Isra'il*) as consisting of the worship of God, kindness to parents and family, orphans and the poor, speaking compassionately, performing prayer and giving charity (Q 2:83).

277 Regip al-Jerrahi (Robert Frager), interview with the author. Redwood City, California. August 13, 2010.

Qur'anic Psychology: The Heart between Self and Spirit

Sufi psychology grew out of the Qur'an's mapping of the human self. The sacred text describes human consciousness using a variety of terms, and Sufis have tended to focus on three of them: spirit, heart and self, or *ruh*, *qalb*[278] and *nafs*. We will delve into each of these terms in some depth in what follows. Although they are at times used interchangeably by Muslim authors, I will describe how these terms are generally understood in Sufi psychology when used to refer to a particular dimension of the human being.

Linguistically, *ruh* derives from a root that can mean 'breeze' or 'wind', and like the wind, it is not seen in itself, but is rather witnessed only in terms of its effects.[279] W. O. Mitchell's great Canadian novel, *Who Has Seen the Wind?* (1947), refers to this phenomenon in its title. The book takes place on the Canadian prairie, in Saskatchewan, where the wind can be seen via its traces, as it courses through the prairie's vast fields of wheat and grass, something like waves in the ocean.[280] Mitchell's title is actually drawn from Christina Rossetti's short poem (with the same title):

> *Who has seen the wind?*
> *Neither you nor I:*
> *But when the trees bow down their heads,*
> *The wind is passing by.*[281]

Ibn 'Arabi similarly describes the spirit this way, as known by its traces, being 'nonmanifest in entity, manifest in property.'[282] The *ruh*

---

278 James Morris observes that the term for heart, *al-qalb* (in the singular and plural), appears in the Qur'an 132 times. James Winston Morris, *The Reflective Heart: Discovering Spiritual Intelligence in Ibn 'Arabi's Meccan Illuminations* (Louisville, KY, 2005), p.48.

279 As with many Arabic trilateral roots, *ra-waw-ha* has several core meanings, including not only breeze or wind, but also ease or relaxation, breath and scent, all of which suggest something quite subtle in nature.

280 I will also note, as someone whose parents both come from Saskatchewan, that the prairie is underrated for its stark beauty and vastness.

281 See: https://www.poetryfoundation.org/poems/43197/who-has-seen-the-wind.

282 Ibn 'Arabi, *Fut*.II.563. As quoted in William C. Chittick, *The Self-Disclosure of God: Principles of Ibn al-'Arabi's Cosmology* (Albany, NY, 1998), p.269.

or spirit is the mysterious unseen essence, a 'nondimensional point' that is the source of all life.[283] The Qur'an asserts that the spirit is of the affairs of God, and that humanity has been given only a little knowledge of it (Q 16:102). It is the breath of Divine Presence in the secret heart of our own being. We might also think of it as the ground of all consciousness, or the essence of all life. It is our deepest reality and mystery, beyond the world of forms and manifestation, beyond time and space, life and death.

In contrast to the *ruh*, the *nafs,* or ego-self, is found at the intersection of spirit and body: the combination of sensations, desires and thoughts that arises out of the embodied human experience. Helminski helpfully defines the *nafs* as 'the soul having an earthly experience'.[284] It is this earthly, embodied self that we identify with – largely analogous to contemporary psychological notions of the ego – and yet it is the furthest from what we really are. Just as *ruh* is derived from a root that can mean wind, *nafs* is related to the word for breath, *nafas*. Interestingly, an ancient Greek word for breath, *pneuma*, can also be used to mean soul or spirit. Again, like wind or breath, the human psyche, whether considered in terms of its transcendent essence (*ruh*) or embodied self (*nafs*), is something invisible, ethereal, but known clearly through its traces in the visible, material realm.

The heart (*qalb*) is the faculty within the human being that is the bridge between spirit and self.[285] When unobscured by desires for the entities and objects of the external, perceptual world, and allowed to fulfill its natural function, the heart acts as an open doorway to the *ruh*, and channels its primordial luminosity, through the vehicle provided by the *nafs*. For Sufis, then, the heart is clearly much more than simply an organ in your chest that circulates blood. They understand the heart closer to the way we use the English word when we say things like 'have a heart', 'heartfelt', or 'follow your heart'. Not so much a locus

---

283 Helminski, *The Knowing Heart*, p.64.

284 Kabir Helminski, *The Book of Language: Exploring the Spiritual Vocabulary of Islam* (Bristol, 2006), p.9.

285 Al-Qashani defines the heart as 'a luminous, disengaged substance halfway between the spirit and the soul [self or *nafs*]'. *Istilahat al-Sufiyya*, pp.167–8. As quoted in Murata, *The Tao of Islam*, p.299.

of emotion, the heart in Sufism is rather 'the center of consciousness, awareness, and intelligence'.[286] The heart is our true core, where our deepest qualities and intentions are found.[287] Although in English we tend to associate the heart with emotions and feelings (which it also includes), according to Sufi psychology the heart is better thought of as a *holistic faculty of knowing*, a means of perception, an organ of sight: one that synthesizes conscious and unconscious input, emotion and perception, to see beyond what the discursive mind can rationally comprehend.[288]

Although the senses perceive forms, and the mind can analyze their dimensions, it is the heart that perceives their *meaning*. And it is meaning that, though not quantifiable or empirically verifiable, is the most important thing in life. To illustrate, you can simply bring to mind one of your favorite people, a best friend, parent, child or deep heart connection, someone whom you truly love and are just so happy to have in your life. Their value to you is not really measurable in terms of centimeters, kilograms or liters, and there is no way that you can empirically prove how much they mean to you, or scientifically demonstrate the nature of your connection to them, and yet you *know* with a profound certainty in the very core of your being that your relationship with that person is meaningful, valuable and full of all kinds of wonderful intangible qualities that are not captured by equations and calculations. This certainty, this knowing, is the knowledge of the heart. The Qur'an hence describes real blindness not

---

286 Chittick, *Ibn 'Arabi*, p.15.

287 Murata notes that the Qur'an 'pictures the heart as the locus of that which makes a human being human, the center of the human personality', a 'place of vision, understanding, and remembrance (*dhikr*)'. *The Tao of Islam*, pp.289– 90.

288 The Arabic language offers a rich repertoire of words for the heart. Although *qalb* is the term that the Qur'an most frequently uses, it also uses other terms for the heart like *fu'ad* (drawn from a root meaning connect with 'flame', it suggests a heart when enflamed with emotion or passion), and *sadr* (with a root meaning the front/surface/face of something, usually referring to the breast or chest). Drawing upon this vocabulary, Sufis have developed several schemata for mapping the heart. An early Sufi figure, al-Hakim al-Tirmidhi (d.910), developed an influential model that begins outward and goes deeper within, starting with the *sadr*, which contains the *qalb*, itself containing the *fu'ad*, within which we find the core, or *lubb*. For more on this, see al-Timidhi's *A Treatise of the Heart (Bayan al-Farq bayn al-Sadr wa al-Qalb wa al-Fu'ad wa al-Lubb)*, in *Three Early Sufi Texts*, introduced and translated by Kenneth L. Honerkamp (Louisville, KY, 2003).

as a failure to see with the eyes, but rather a failure to see with the heart: *It is not the eyes that are blind, but blind are the hearts within their chests* (Q 22:46).

As the heart is a faculty of knowing, Muslim interpreters have associated it with another Qur'anic term for the human self, namely *'aql* or intellect. This faculty is sometimes thought to be *distinctly* human, a kind of reason or discriminating awareness that distinguishes humans from other animals. This is not always seen as such a boon, however, as the intellect can actually narrow possibilities of knowing rather than simply engender them, as we saw above with the rationalist philosopher ascending through the heavenly spheres. Generally speaking, however, in terms of Sufi psychology we can consider the intellect to be an aspect of the heart, which is a more encompassing term for human consciousness and intelligence. We should note here, however, that Sufi philosophers also use the term *'aql* to refer to a sort of original, universal intellect, akin to the Greek *logos*. As this *'aql* is understood to be coeval with the essential Reality or Light of Muhammad, we will discuss this concept in further depth in the last chapter on the Prophet Muhammad.

The Qur'an and the Bible both affirm, in many places, that hearts can either be soft or hard, open or closed, asleep or awake. A soft, intelligent and open heart is naturally attuned to the meaning of life's appearances, and when fully awakened, apprehends realities inaccessible to the physical senses. In our everyday lives, an intelligent heart can read the significance of emotions and body language; it is sensitive to gesture and expression; to timing, proportion and balance – all qualities key to communicative arts like music composition and performance, rhetoric and poetry, as well as sculpture and painting. An awakened heart is also compassionate, for in one sense compassion is simply a keen awareness of and sensitivity to the beings one encounters. In other words, *to be objective is to be loving*. The more we can awaken and open our hearts then, the more we can experience the profound meaning of reality, creatively express beauty, and love those we share embodied existence with for the short time we are here.

Existing in a sort of mid-point between a) the formless expanse of spirit and b) the demands and worries of the embodied self, the heart can be drawn in either direction; it can go way up and way down. We may think then that the heart is totally free to choose which direction it may like to go. However, according to Sufi psychology, the heart finds itself in a bit of a proverbial pickle. The lower *nafs*, with its desires and demands, its heedlessness and fear, tends to dominate the human being, and hence most people are dragged down by some level of ego tyranny. The problem for the heart is that, like gravity, the *nafs* seems to have momentum, and sort of automatically pulls us downward.[289]

This is why paths of spiritual transformation always include various forms of discipline – such as the regular practice of meditation and prayer – that counteract the gravitational pull of the commanding self. Discipline helps orient and re-orient the heart toward spirit. The more that the heart can open to the light of or our own essence, the more the pettiness, selfishness and oppressiveness of the self can be neutralized. Discipline is something done regularly, as the *nafs* is persistent in leading us to dispersion and distraction, and does not want to give up its position of authority. Hence, we require a constant effort to turn ourselves toward our true goal and ground of happiness.[290] Sufi practices, including remembering the Names of God (*dhikr*) and companionship with a Sufi teacher (*suhba*),[291] or the five-times daily prayer (*salat*) and fasting (*sawm*), are all meant to offer a regular discipline to awaken the heart's intelligence, and to draw its attention away from the fleeting distractions of the external world, which will inevitably fail to satisfy the self's endless demands, or provide the heart with genuine peace.

---

289 The Qur'an repeatedly describes humans as heedless or forgetful (*ghafla*), which Murata notes is understood within the Islamic tradition as a 'natural human tendency'. Murata, *The Tao of Islam*, p.249.

290 Interestingly, the Islamic notion of 'repentance' is *tawba*, which literally means to turn, away from distraction and dispersion, and toward what is Real. For more on this notion in early Sufism, see Atif Khalil's *Repentance and the Return to God: Tawba in Early Sufism* (Albany, NY, 2018).

291 Although the Sufi tradition as a whole emphasizes the critical importance of companionship with a realized teacher, *suhba* can also include companionship with fellow seekers, and even recognizing the ever-present Teacher within oneself and in all of one's experiences.

Discipline alone is not enough, however. Our practice must be animated by love, which is of course central to the Sufi path. Love brings joy to discipline. It is the power that awakens the intelligence of the heart and inspires us to transcend our selfishness, to leave our state of dispersion – that 'messy basement apartment with the bad lighting and broken thermostat' version of ourselves – and move toward centeredness and wholeness – the 'well-cared-for, charming villa on that beautiful seaside mountain' version of ourselves – which is not only a better place for us to live, but is a lot more comfortable for others as well.[292]

Despite the trials of ordering the self, there is a part of us that remains above the fray, a serene center ever ready to be accessed regardless of how far off we've wandered from it (and most of us wander quite far down the path of obsession, neurosis, fear and distraction). In *The Meccan Revelations*, Ibn 'Arabi describes the heart as a 'polished mirror' that is in fact never rusted or clouded over. He notes the saying of the Prophet Muhammad's that hearts are polished by the remembrance of God (*dhikr Allah*), and clarifies that this saying does not mean that the heart has a 'rust' that covers it, but rather that when the heart is occupied with 'understanding the secondary causes instead of understanding God' this preoccupation with surface appearances *functions* as an obscuration that prevents the heart from perceiving the sacred depth of each moment.[293] He explains:

> Since the Divine Presence is ever giving *tajalli* [self-disclosure or manifestation], one cannot imagine there being any curtain veiling us from Her, and from the *tajalli*. But when this heart cannot receive the *tajalli* from the Divine praiseworthy address – as the heart has accepted other than Her – then the receptivity to that 'other' is

---

[292] Sometimes people imagine spiritual discipline as a sort of pious ditch digging on a hot day without any water available, a sort of brutal labor that is *supposed* to be awful. I can't really see how that is a sustainable approach. In the teachings I've encountered, true discipline does in fact involve work, but there is always a joy and sweetness in it, and if there isn't any of that, I suspect one is just not relating to discipline in a healthy manner and will inevitably face a spiritual burnout at some point.

[293] Ibn 'Arabi, *The Openings Revealed in Makkah (al-Futuhat al-Makkiyah), Books 1 and 2*, translated by Shu'ayb Eric Winkel (New York, 2018), p.320.

expressed in the Revelation as 'becoming rusty,' covered, locked up, blind, possessed, and so on.[294]

The heart, in its essence, remains a pure, open faculty for receiving the perpetual gifts of Being. When the sun is obscured by clouds, it is not as though the sun has become cloudy; rather its natural light is being blocked by a temporary obscuration. So it is with the heart: it remains forever a doorway to inestimable forms of knowledge, meaning and quality, but when it is preoccupied with surface appearances, it fails to perceive the deeper realities that are continually manifest to it. In his chapter on Shu'ayb, Ibn 'Arabi makes a surprising claim about the human heart:

> Know that the heart – by which I mean the heart of the knower of God – is from the mercy of God, but it is vaster than it, since it encompasses the Real, exalted is He, whereas His mercy does not.[295]

He says here that, when awakened, the heart has an unfathomable depth and vastness, such that it can encompass the infinite plenitude of the Real. In contrast, God's mercy, although vast beyond conception, does not encompass God, because, Ibn 'Arabi affirms, God is the merciful one, not the object of mercy – and yet *the human heart* has this capacity. In other words, the more we awaken the heart's intelligence, and open to its vastness, the more it can encompass the boundless depth and beauty of the Real.

In saying that the heart encompasses the Real, Ibn 'Arabi is basically restating a well-known *hadith qudsi* or sacred hadith – given the name 'sacred' as it is a saying of God's shared by the Prophet Muhammad, though not considered to be a part of the Qur'an. The saying goes: 'Neither my earth nor my heavens can contain Me, only the heart of a believing servant can.'[296] It is probably useful to acknowledge at the beginning of this discussion how hard it is to convey the vastness

---

294 Ibid.
295 Ibn 'Arabi, *Fusus*, p.102.
296 For more on this, see Kautsar Azhari Noer, 'The Encompassing Heart: Unified Vision for a Unified World', The Muhyiddin Ibn 'Arabi Society, https://ibnarabisociety.org/the-encompassing-heart-kautsar-noer/ (accessed July 15, 2022).

of the heart when we know so little of it. There is a great deal more to ourselves than what we usually experience on a day-to-day basis. However, because so few have encountered the heart's hidden depths, most are skeptical that such depths even exist. It's a bit like spending one's life floating on the ocean's surface and, having never gone below, imagining it to be a puddle.

There is an ancient story about frogs I like telling in class that I think at least hints at this problem of communicating vastness beyond someone's experiential range.[297] It begins when one day a frog hops down into a well and encounters another frog, who lives there. The well frog greets his guest and asks where he is from. 'I am from the ocean,' the guest replies. Never having heard of this place, the well frog asks, 'what is the ocean like? Is it as big as my well?' The ocean frog replies, 'well, it is actually much, much larger.' Surprised (and perhaps a bit annoyed), the well frog clarifies, 'so it is *twice* the size of my well?' 'No, no, it's actually *much* larger than that.' 'Three times larger!?,' the well frog asks, with growing suspicion of this ocean frog's outlandish claims. 'Look,' says the ocean frog, 'there is really no way for me to convey to you just how big my home is unless I take you there.' So off they go hopping along, despite the well frog's suspicions. However, as they approach the ocean, the well frog crests a hill overlooking it, and finally sees its vastness; its roaring waves crashing on the beach; its end impossible to fathom. Then his head explodes. That's the end of the story as I tell it. It's a great analogy for why we have traditions of spiritual practice. Without actually seeing the vastness of the heart for oneself, no amount of explanation will do, and it will probably seem entirely implausible.

Ibn 'Arabi offers another take on the heart's vastness, this time quoting the famous ecstatic Sufi of the East, Abu Yazid al-Bistami (d.874). He writes, 'If the Throne' – and here he is referring to what the Qur'an calls the God's throne or *'arsh*, which is traditionally thought to encompass the entire cosmos – 'and all it contains' – which

---

297 From what I can tell the story is likely an elaboration of a saying of the Daoist sage Zhuangzi, that 'a frog in a well cannot conceive of the ocean'. It is also told in Hindu and Buddhist traditions in various forms. This version is likely a pastiche of those versions with some of my own idiosyncratic takes added on.

is literally everything – 'was multiplied a hundred million times and then placed within a corner among the corners of the knower of God's heart, he would not notice it.'[298] This is one of those sayings that, if we truly understood it, we may just end up like the well frog when he sees the ocean. According to the Sufis, when the heart is in its natural state of immensity, our world may not even register, even in its vast cosmic expanse, millions of times over.[299] Along these lines, Ibn 'Arabi rhetorically asks, 'When the heart encompasses the Eternal, how can it possibly notice the existence of the temporary?'[300]

Understandably, a heart contemplating the inestimable beauty and majesty of the Infinite can lose track of the finite, temporal (and often banal) particularities of our everyday lives and world of appearances. This was actually seen as a bit of a hazard on the spiritual path, with Sufis noting those 'mad ones' (*majdhub* or *majnun*) who get lost in the mind-blowing, boundaryless beauty of the Real, and forget to do things like brush their hair and pick up that salad on sale from the grocery store for dinner on Thursday. Although this is in one sense perfectly understandable, Sufis generally believed, following the early master Junayd al-Baghdadi (d.910), that being lost in ecstasy was a state of being that can be integrated into a higher station (*maqam*) of stability, one that balances inner drunkenness with an outward sobriety and functionality in the world.

On the one hand, there may not be anything inherently wrong with getting lost in the endless ocean of the Real. Even though (as quoted earlier) Ibn 'Arabi describes 'those who are gone (*al-waqifun*)' or 'have stopped' as 'of no use to anyone and no one is of any use to them'[301] – as they have hit the middle of the ocean and never return from it – this may not be a bad thing in and of itself, and presumably the lost ones

---

298 Ibn 'Arabi, *Fusus*, p.102.
299 The renowned Sufi of the Islamic West, Abu Madyan (d.1198), who is the founder of almost all North African Sufism, and someone whom Ibn 'Arabi wanted to meet in person, but was only able to meet in a spiritual form, said, *'idha dhahar al-haqq lam yabqa ma'ahu ghayruhu'*, which means, 'When the Real manifests, nothing else remains with it.' Abu Madyan Shu'ayb, *Uns al-wahid wa nuzhar al-murid*. As quoted in *The Way of Abu Madyan*, edited and translated by Vincent J. Cornell (Cambridge, UK, 1996), p.119.
300 Ibn 'Arabi, *Fusus*, p.102.
301 Ibn 'Arabi, *Fut*.I.76. As quoted in Kermani, *God is Beautiful*, p.316.

have little choice. As Ibn 'Arabi suggests, it's not so much that they've aimed for the very center of the ocean, but rather that *the very center of the ocean has aimed for them*. In various Buddhist traditions such folk are known as *pratyeka-buddhas* – private or solitary enlightened beings that do not teach others.[302] And yet, for most of us, who do not share that particular destiny, it seems we should certainly try to be useful to others, which we can only be when we're grounded in the practicalities of the material world and social life, when we've still got our feet firmly on the ocean's shore. For Sufis, the Prophet Muhammad's paradigm is uniquely comprehensive in that it fully integrates deep spirituality with effective action in the world, including commitment to family, friends and community building. This Muhammadan synthesis then represents for Sufis the most comprehensive model of human perfection, marrying heaven and earth, spirit and body, individual and community (a paradigm we further explore in the book's final chapter).

As Sufism crystalized over the centuries as a science of transformation, Sufis drew upon this Muhammadan synthesis as well as the teachings of the Qur'an to develop a sophisticated map of the self's maturation through seven stages or levels. As we consider the Sufi psychological paradigm here, we now shift from the *qalb* to the *nafs*, to look a bit closer at what this ladder of spiritual ascent looks like according to some of the more widely circulated Sufi teachings on the subject. The great Sufi master and saint of Baghdad, 'Abd al-Qadir al-Jilani, offers one of the more popular mappings of these levels of the self, which I will glean from in the following discussion of these stages.[303]

---

302 Reginald A. Ray defines them as 'meditators who dwell in remote places and aim at liberation', or as 'forest renunciants'. *Indestructible Truth: The Living Reality of Tibetan Buddhism* (Boston, 2002), pp.74, 355.

303 Isma'il Sa'id al-Qadiri, *Emanations of Lordly Grace (Al-Fuyudat al-Rabbaniyya)*, translated by Muhtar Holland (Oakland Park, FL, 2000), pp.56–61.

The Seven Storey Self

Before we begin, it is worth pointing out that the progression through the levels of the self is by no means *linear*. Spiritual development rarely takes place along a straight line of ascent, but much more commonly occurs more as a spiral, where we circle back around similar patterns and pitfalls, with some eventual progress usually followed by slips back into old patterns, and recoveries from these, followed by continual struggle and, with some blessing, eventual integration at a higher key or frequency. We can also note here that although several Sufi authors have situated the *nafs* as inherently defective, drawing us downward toward unfulfillable desire and distracting dispersion, its core redeeming quality is its receptivity or transformability: it is something that by nature can be purified of negativity.[304]

The Commanding Self

When we first set foot on the path, we start with the tail wagging the dog, so to speak, with our lower self ruling over us rather than the other way around. The Qur'an calls this self the *nafs al-ammara* (Q 12:53), the 'commanding self', as so often it commands and we obey. Now, at least for Ibn Arabi, this lower, commanding self is not inherently evil.[305] It is made up of our embodied instincts for food, sex and survival, all good and useful things in their own way. However, these instincts and desires are meant to be *servants* rather than lords, and when these self-oriented survival instincts and desires take the wheel all proverbial hell

---

304 Murata notes that the 'normal and normative condition of the soul is to be receptive to the lights that come down from the spirit', and it is through this receptivity that 'the soul becomes luminous and is transmuted into a spiritual substance'. *The Tao of Islam*, pp.260–1.

305 Several Sufis have had a generally quite negative view of the *nafs* and have framed spiritual development as not only a marginalization of *nafs* but even its annihilation. 'Abd al-Rahman al-Sulami (d.1021), for instance, describes the *nafs* as 'defective in all its attributes and is never empty of defects', while Abu al-Qasim al-Qushayri (d.1072) says that when Sufis refer to the *nafs* they refer only to 'those qualities of the servant that are defective'. As quoted in Murata, *The Tao of Islam*, pp.255–6. In contrast, Ibn 'Arabi says, 'I am one who believes in the positive existence of the soul, and I do not consider it correct to say that it can die in relation to its qualities because I know its realities and its place.' Ibn 'Arabi, *Risala Ruh al-Qudus*, as quoted in Roger Boase and Farid Sahnoun, 'Excerpts from the Epistle on the Spirt of Holiness (*Risalah Ruh al Quds*)', in *Muhyiddin Ibn 'Arabi: A Commemorative Volume*, edited by Stephen Hirtenstein and Michael Tiernan (Shaftesbury, 1993), p.54.

breaks loose. As ruler, the lowest self's instinct for self-preservation runs amok as self-aggrandisement, and its natural appetites can become full blown addictions. When in charge, this *nafs* bullies and harasses us with desires, demanding we constantly quench its endless thirst. It commands us to put ourselves first before others, and in some cases even lash out in aggression, and harm those who stand in the way of its satisfaction. As Rumi says: 'The light of Moses is here and now, inside you. Pharoah as well.'[306] The Pharoah within us is precisely this commanding self, whose despotic authority is challenged by the prophetic wisdom of our own inner Moses, or higher self. Al-Jilani suggests that the methodology for dealing with this self is the shari'a, which reigns it in, containing it within the boundaries of the sacred law. The commanding self requires *clear boundaries*, *discipline* and *regulation*, all represented by the shari'a guidelines in the Islamic tradition.

Obeying sacred laws like the Ten Commandments or core rules of the shari'a (or, more generally, striving to live a conscientious and ethical life) can certainly help us corral the commanding self's worst trajectories. On the other hand, we don't want to make the mistake of assuming that simply being a 'disciplined', 'religious' or 'spiritual' person automatically overthrows the commanding self's dictatorial regime, or offers a hard and fast solution to the problems it creates for us. This is because the *nafs al-ammara* is perfectly capable of coopting religion for its own purposes. A pious person operating under its command might embrace religion for the sake of feeling special and superior to others or to justify their anger against those they perceive to be enemies and heretics and such.[307] This produces a kind of 'bad faith' religion, characterized by things like self-righteous fundamentalism and self-serving sanctity. Alternately, we can think of some of the ways

---

306 Robert Frager, *Heart, Self, and Soul: The Sufi Psychology of Growth, Balance, and Harmony* (Wheaton, IL, 1999), p.57.

307 Interestingly, along these lines Bawa Muhaiyaddeen defined the four paths to hell as *religion, race, caste* and *class*, as these are the primary means, historically, by which humans have hierarchically separated themselves from others and then all too often abysmally treated those they perceive as somehow beneath them. This anecdote was shared with me by Bawa's long-time student, author and artist Michael Green, in an interview on June 26, 2010 in Coatesville, Pennsylvania.

folks have egotistically employed New Age teachings, fostering a flakey sort of spirituality that is utilized as a loophole to try to get out of being a basically reliable, responsible and considerate person.

The Blaming Self

Once we become sufficiently exasperated with the dictatorship of the commanding self and its oppression (both of ourselves and others that we negatively affect as a result of its bidding), we seek to organize a kind of psychological revolution: to rally our wits, paralyze its infrastructure, overthrow its dominance and mitigate its worst tendencies. It is at this moment that we have truly begun the path of transformation. This is the second stage of the self, the 'blaming self' (*nafs al-lawwama*), which is at least aware of the problem, willing to face it, and tries to do something about it. Unlike the commanding self, which is fundamentally ignorant (*jahil*), the blaming self is reflective (*fikri*) and has developed some basic awareness of the situation it finds itself in: we recognize that we are living in the aforementioned cold, messy and dysfunctional apartment, and attempt to fix it up and find a way out. We take on the burden of facing our negativities and destructive tendencies and commit to addressing them as best we can.

The method of this stage is the *tariqa* – an Arabic word that means literally a path or road, but in Sufi usage refers to the *spiritual path*. A path consists of a comprehensive methodology, a relatively coherent set of doctrines and practices that facilitate our ascent to higher realities, frequencies and ways of being. Every Sufi order or lineage of teachings has its own methodology, sharing much with others but each with their own emphases and techniques. These paths consist of precise practices that go beyond the basic moral restraints imposed by religion, offering a means to go further, to travel deeper within.

It is here, at this stage of the *nafs al-lawwama,* that people begin to *persistently* seek a way to get the tail to stop wagging the dog, to get the commanding self out of office, whether that be through something like therapy, yoga, meditation, regular prayer or some other form of discipline. This can be a particularly frustrating stage, as one is now keenly aware of the various problems caused by the lower self's dominance, but has yet to find or adequately implement the tools needed to address them. When we do finally make some progress here, and find that the lower self's power is at least somewhat constrained, we come across the danger of falling into *hypocrisy*, as we may feel that the little we have achieved is actually quite a lot, and end up projecting an ideal that we can't quite live up to.[308]

The Balanced Self

Once we have found some suitable tools for psychological 'home improvement', and apply them consistently enough over time, with some luck/grace we may achieve what Abraham Maslow (d. 1970) called self-actualization. Within the Sufi tradition the actualized self is known as the *nafs al-mulhama*, the balanced or inspired self. This is the self whose various instincts, desires and dimensions are reasonably well integrated into a functioning whole, with the *nafs al-ammara* removed from its preferred position as dictator-for-life. This lower self will still cause us problems, but they tend to be sufficiently reigned in, allowing for consistently creative, positive action in the world. Helminski suggests that this third level of the self, the stage of balance, is the goal of most conventional religion and psychology.[309]

When some balance is achieved among the elements of the self, we find that destructive habits fail to have the same hold over us, and the draw of external accolades, of status, fame and power, begin to lose their appeal. Correspondingly, as fascination with the outer world falls away the draw of the inner world increases: one is ever more led by the dictates of the heart, developing something of an intellectual and spiritual independence, identifying more and more with our own heart-core. At this stage we may find that prayer and meditation bear fruit, and the realities spoken of by religion can be tasted for oneself, not simply taken on faith. *We find that we can draw water from our own well.* It is thus at this stage that we move from the moral restraint

---

308 Frager, *Heart, Self, and Soul*, pp.68–9.
309 Helminski, *The Knowing Heart*, p.111.

imposed by shari'a, and the path of development offered by the *tariqa*, to experience directly what those are for: real insight into the nature of our own self and life's purpose. This kind of knowledge is generally referred to by Sufis as *ma'rifa* or *kashf* – a kind of direct, experiential knowing/unveiling that we will discuss further in the chapter on Elijah–Enoch.

Functioning at this level of the inspired self, someone might even be seen as a sort of a creative genius if they are able to express the insights the self allows for. Helminski notes that although this is only the third stage of Sufi psychology, it is in itself a major accomplishment that can take years of effort to achieve, and likely few truly do.[310] For many who connect with a spiritual path, this may be as far as they go, for the purpose they were after was simply this balancing of the self, so that their lives can proceed in a relatively creative, fruitful and satisfying way.

There remain dangers, however, as one is not yet totally free of ego, and its draw toward power, self-aggrandizement and deception. Sufis suggest that the stage of the inspired self is actually one of the most hazardous, as the spiritual practitioner, having made some real gains, is now vulnerable to believing she has already reached human perfection and need not travel any further. If the insight, creativity and visionary experience available to the inspired self are interpreted in an ego-oriented fashion, one may consider oneself to be an enlightened genius, or a great spiritual master or prophet. It is here, when the ship of spiritual development runs aground on the rocks of ego, that we find a plethora of half-baked spiritual teachers, self-appointed gurus or 'cult' leaders.[311]

This can be profoundly confusing for people, as these uncooked spiritual types will often have genuine insight and charisma, and in some cases even transformative spiritual power, and yet they may not be mature enough to transmit it without significant problems. Sufism's

---

310 Ibid.

311 Frager suggests, 'One of the important functions of the Sufi lineage is to prevent half-trained dervishes [students] from setting themselves up as teachers.' Frager, *Heart, Self, and Soul*, p.74.

system of lineages and orders is (ideally) meant to prevent this, by ensuring that one can only function as a teacher once their own teacher affirms that they have stabilized an ethical and spiritual maturity. A lineage or tradition further functions to remove the individual from the center of the show: it makes each individual teacher merely a link in a much larger chain. In contrast, if a spiritual teacher is not a part of some tradition or another, but functions rather as a sort of one-off enlightenment phenomenon, the teacher themself may become the entirety of the tradition, which can become a bit of a problem both for that teacher and for their students.

The Tranquil, Pleased and Pleasing Self

If the traveler on the path can maintain the necessary humility to recognize what progress has been made and what remains to be done, previous breakthroughs can be profoundly consolidated with the self's fourth stage, the *nafs al-mutma'inna*, the tranquil, or serene self. The Qur'an says about this self, *O self at peace. Return to your Lord* (Q 89:27–8). This is the stage at which spiritual development becomes genuinely stabilized, as opposed to spotty. Here the self is aligned with the heart, and they no longer function in a state of generalized conflict with each other. It is only at this stage that the danger of the ego hijacking the entire spiritual process begins to subside, and one is positioned to perpetually function in a state of awareness aligned with the Real. The method at this stage is *haqiqa*, reality itself.

The fifth level of the self is the fulfilled self, the *nafs al-radiyya* – the pleased or fulfilled self. It is when this shore of being is reached that the move toward the Real becomes irreversible. The fulfilled self is marked by total surrender and equanimity. Here the traveler accepts whatever befalls her, whether ease or hardship. Gain and loss become equal, as one is completely satisfied with whatever God chooses to bestow: poison can be tasted as honey. Every possible experience in life is welcomed as a guest sent by the Beloved. Such a welcoming, fulfilled self can face death as comfortably as life, a rare station that few appear to really function at. Here the aspirant is both aligned with the Infinite, and harmonized with the rhythms of our finite world, at peace with its cycles and fluctuations. Some suggest that it is at this stage that the power of healing, and other so-called miracles, may manifest, known as *karamat* (literally 'generosities') in the Sufi tradition. This is also described as the stage of *fana'*: the annihilation of the self in God. This self has gone beyond any method.

Following the pleased or fulfilled self, one enters into the self of complete submission to God, the *nafs al-mardiyya*, where one is not only pleased with God, but God becomes pleased with one as well. At this stage, the wayfarer descends from the bliss of annihilation in God, returning to the world with an individuality that subsists (*baqa'*) in God. This individuality is no longer ego-centered, but acts a vehicle through which the qualities of God, including protection, wisdom and compassion, can manifest in the world. This is the self as servant, the self that lives, 'not my will, but Thine' (Luke 22:42). It is at this stage that the Sufi becomes one of what the Qur'an describes as God's 'friends'. The method at this stage is again the shari'a, but this time not as something required to tame the self, but as the self's natural expression. Impeccable ethicality is one's very nature at this point.

The Perfected Self

The final, seventh level of the self is the *nafs al-kamila*, the complete or perfect self. The human being here is something of an absence, functioning as a totally spotless, clear mirror, reflecting God's qualities from the beyond into the here and now. One is in a state of pure unity or non-duality. This self has no method particular to it, but rather it integrates all of the previous methods. This is the Station of Muhammad, which is, in fact, the Station of No-Station – *maqam la maqam* (a notion we'll explore in more depth in the last chapter on Muhammad), where all stations are embodied, but the self (or perhaps, no-self) is limited by none of them. Although inwardly one's being is purified of any but God, outwardly one manifests a condition of 'exceptional ordinariness', integrating an inward ecstasy and realization of unity with an outward humility, maturity and simplicity.[312] One is available to whatever is required in each moment, giving the moment and its inhabitants their due, impeccably. In other words, one is functioning in complete harmony with existence, which is, according to the Qur'an, the state of being known as *islam*, and the station known as pure servanthood (*'ubudiyya*).

The Metaphysical Roots of Humanity's Many Religions

As we discussed in the chapter on Adam, even when the human being is perfected, and they can reflect the totality of reality, the reflection is always at least partially shaped by the mirror's contours. Ibn 'Arabi shifts in this chapter to consider the ambiguous nature of our world more broadly, and how this ambiguity ultimately relates to the diversity of human hearts (and the corresponding diversity of our philosophies and religions). To unpack his articulation of the world's inherent ambiguity, we can start by recalling, in the first chapter, that we discussed an important distinction that Ibn 'Arabi makes between God as Essence beyond all conception, and God as Lord known through his Names (a distinction that we will look at in even greater depth in the seventh chapter on Jesus). He elaborates upon that distinction here as follows:

> The Real, in its Essence, is rich beyond all need of the universe. Lordship, in contrast, does not have this position. The situation lies between the mutual dependency implicit in Lordship and the Essence's total independence from the world. Indeed, Lordship is, in its reality and qualification, none other than this Essence.[313]

God in Essence is totally beyond the universe and any need for it, which the Qur'an repeatedly asserts, describing God as *al-Ghani*, the 'rich-beyond-need-of-anything'. However, God as Lord is not in this situation, as lordship is a *relationship*, one with those whom one is lord of, and hence the interdependence between the Lord and servants.

---
312 Helminski, *Knowing Heart*, p.113.
313 Ibn 'Arabi, *Fusus*, p.102.

Simply put, with no servants there is no lord; with no creation there is no Creator. So, God and the world are, at least in one sense, co-constitutive of each other. Paradoxically, Ibn 'Arabi asserts here that the Lord is nothing besides the Essence, though the Essence qualified in relation to creation. God then is simultaneously *utterly independent* of the world as Essence and *mutually dependent* on it as Lord. This mutual dependence applies to all of the other Names of God as well, which are fundamentally relational in nature.

We can put this in more philosophical terms in considering the nature of God as *wujud* (existence/being). According to Ibn 'Arabi *wujud* has two aspects: 1) the absolute (*wujud mutlaq*) and 2) the conditioned or limited (*wujud muqayyad*). These two aspects correspond to God as *al-Batin,* the Essence totally transcendent to the relative existents that make up the universe (and nondelimited by form, quality, etc.), and God as *al-Zahir,* the apparent phenomena of the world, which are his Names manifest, or Being conditioned by limited forms.[314]

Philosopher and psychologist Peter Coates concisely sums up Ibn 'Arabi's perspective here: 'There is only One Unique Being which reveals itself in a multiplicity and infinity of its own forms, and which possesses two fundamental dimensions, transcendence and immanence.'[315] Similarly, though here expressed from the perspective of the experiencing subject, Buddhist teachings affirm that the 'primordial nature of the mind [the absolute] is not separate from the relative phenomena we perceive right now'.[316] Whether we use the language of *being, mind* or *deity*, those who have experienced the fullness of the Real suggest that in essence it goes totally beyond the forms of our world – and yet these forms are nothing but the Real manifest.

Describing the universe as God manifest is perhaps why some of the establishment theologians had such a problem with Ibn 'Arabi. Such folk have historically tended to prefer clearly defined borders

---
314 Nettler, *Sufi Metaphysics and Qur'anic Prophets*, p.117.
315 Coates, *Ibn 'Arabi and Modern Thought*, p.3.
316 Sherab and Dongyal, *Opening to Our Primordial Nature*, p.22.

between God and the world. Although Ibn 'Arabi certainly holds that God is *necessary, unconditioned* Being and hence totally distinct from the *possible, conditioned* beings of the world, he goes on to say that the world is in fact nothing besides this unconditioned Being filtered through the conditioned possibilities. The world then is fundamentally ambiguous, an 'in-between' zone, known in Arabic as a *barzakh*. A *barzakh* is also a limit – a limit being something that simultaneously separates and joins two things. A good example of a *barzakh*, and one drawn upon within Sufi writings to illustrate this, is an image in a mirror. An image in a mirror is simultaneously the very object it is an image of (and not some other object), and yet it is also definitely *not* the object itself, but merely its image or form. Also, we can say that the object in the mirror is not *separate* from the mirror, but rather is the very surface of the mirror. Then again, the mirror is not simply the image on its surface, but something else besides it. Hence, we must affirm and deny the nature of the mirror image: it both is and is not the mirror; it both is and is not the object it's reflecting.[317]

According to Ibn 'Arabi, the world is precisely like this image in a mirror. It is a sheer ambiguity that both exists and does not, depending on how we look at it. Scholar of Sufism Isobel Jeffery-Street notes simply that our world 'may be named "the Real" (*haqq*) when viewed as the Essence of all phenomena, or "creation" (*khalq*) when viewed from the angle of the manifestation of the phenomena of that Essence'.[318] This is also why Ibn 'Arabi frequently points out the limitations of reason or what he calls the 'power of thought' (*al-quwwa al-mufakkira*). As we will discuss more in the fifth chapter on Elijah–Enoch, he does not deny thought's utility, but simply points to its usefulness exclusively within its appropriate field of play. If you're trying to calculate the tip on a restaurant bill, for example, you will need to apply your basic mathematical abilities, and if you're trying to figure out 'whodunnit' in a murder mystery you will need to exercise your elementary powers of deduction, 'my dear Watson'. And yet, Ibn 'Arabi points out that,

---

317 Chittick, *Imaginal Worlds*, p.25.
318 Isobel Jeffery-Street, *Ibn 'Arabi and the Contemporary West: Beshara and the Ibn 'Arabi Society* (Sheffield, 2012), p.94.

when it comes to God, your intellectual abilities can only take you so far (and not very far at that).

It's probably not inaccurate to say that God begins where thought ends, simply because the paradoxical nature of the Real, 'which necessitates the harmony between opposites', is not comprehensible through thinking at all.[319] The famous riddles or paradoxes used by the Rinzai school of Zen Buddhism, known as *koans*, are employed for this very reason, to transcend the limitations of thinking. By having an aspirant spend a week or two meditating on the sound of one hand clapping, for example, and discovering that the only rational answers are bad ones, the Zen practitioner is eventually forced to go beyond the dualistic nature of rational thought, and gain direct insight into the nondual, post-rational nature of reality.[320] Paradoxically then, knowledge of the Real is a kind of perplexity; it is a knowing that can also be described as unknowing. This notion of perplexity or bewilderment (*hayra* in Arabic), is actually one that Ibn 'Arabi points to often, as a state of being necessitated by God's infinitely varied, ever-new manifestations, none of which can encompass His inexhaustible nature.[321]

One Tree, Many Branches

The remarkable diversity of human religions and philosophies is a necessary outcome of the fundamental ambiguity of existence, this simultaneous unity of Essence and multiplicity of manifestation. Although the Real is purely One in Essence, it can never be known directly, but only as it discloses itself to each heart: each heart experiences the Real through *itself*, and hence each person has a unique window

---

319 Ismail Lala, *Knowing God: Ibn 'Arabi and 'Abd al-Razzaq al-Qashani's Metaphysics of the Divine* (Leiden, 2020), p.12.

320 For more on the nature of *koan* practice in Rinzai Zen, see Victor Sogen Hori, 'Koan and Kensho in the Rinzai Zen Curriculum', in *The Koan: Texts and Contexts in Zen Buddhism*, edited by Steven Heine and Dale S. Wright (New York, 2000), pp.280–316.

321 Ibn 'Arabi writes, 'The bewilderment of the gnostic in the Divine Side is the most magnificent bewilderment, for he leaves behind all restricting and limiting ... He possesses every form, without any form restricting Him.' *Fut*.I.47 and I.218. As quoted in Hirtenstein, *The Unlimited Mercifier*, p.168.

onto reality that literally no one else has. This situation has long been illustrated in various Indian traditions with the story of the blind men and the elephant.[322] This story is also found in the Sufi tradition, though Rumi tells it as four men examining an elephant in the dark. In either case, the men cannot see the creature, and each grasp one of its parts. The man grasping its trunk proclaims the elephant to be like a snake, while the one who grasps its leg says it is rather like a pillar, while the one touching its tail says it's more like a rope. We can also imagine them beginning to argue over the nature of the elephant, when each is right, but only about the part he has encountered, while the whole remains beyond his ken.

Although in one sense we can say that our own heart forms or shapes what it receives from the Real, much like a cup would determine the amount of wine that can be poured into it (or where we stand next to the elephant determines which part we can grasp), in another sense, we can say that *the heart is shaped according to what it receives,* that each cup is *crafted* to receive a set serving of wine, and Ibn 'Arabi affirms this as well:

> As the forms of the Real's self-disclosures are differentiated, the heart is necessarily expansive or narrow in accord with the form of the divine self-disclosure, and the heart cannot go beyond the form in which the self-disclosure occurs. This is because the heart of the gnostic or the Perfect Human, is like the setting of a gemstone. The setting conforms to the dimensions and shape of the stone, be it circular, square, hexagonal, octagonal, or any other shape, as the setting conforms to the stone, and not any other. This is the opposite of what [the Sufis] say, that the Real manifests according to the measure of the servant's disposition. It is not like that, for truly the servant manifests to the Real according to the determination of the form in which the Real manifests Himself to the servant.[323]

In this rather subtle passage, Ibn 'Arabi says that the heart is just

---

322 One of the older versions of the story is found in the early Buddhist scripture known as the *Tittha Sutta*, though it can also be found in Hindu sources.
323 Ibn 'Arabi, *Fusus*, pp.102–3.

like the jewel-setting in a ring: it is 'shaped' according to the jewel of God's self-disclosure. We could also say here that each heart is shaped according to the share of Being that is disclosed to it, each cup crafted for a particular serving. Ibn 'Arabi then further notes that this way of putting it contradicts how the matter has been said by Sufis before him, namely that the Real manifests according to the heart's shape. Here he says that in fact the servant's heart manifests according to the Real's manifestation to it.

Ibn 'Arabi explains this apparent contradiction by going a bit deeper. He says that God has *two* self-disclosures. First, he gives each heart an essential predisposition or shape. This is the hidden (*ghayb*) self-manifestation of God to the heart, in the form of the heart's basic predisposition. This hidden self-manifestation is the *tajalli* of the Essence (*al-Dhat*), represented by God's Name of Essence: *Hu*.[324] The heart's resulting (hidden) shape then conditions what form of God the heart will encounter when, second, God manifests as the visible world (*shahada*). This relationship between hearts and God's self-disclosures is, according to Ibn 'Arabi, at the very root of religious and philosophical diversity, which is in fact a necessary outcome of this situation. There is one Reality, but as many understandings of Reality as there are hearts and their essential predispositions. It follows that you can't really blame someone for their basic worldview, as this is a direct result of their heart's own disposition, with all of its possibilities and limitations, its respective narrowness or expansiveness.

This brings us to a fascinating concept of Ibn 'Arabi's, the notion of the 'God created in beliefs' (*al-Haqq al-makhluq fi'l i'tiqadat*). Here he explains this as follows:

> Then He raised the veil between Him and His servant, and he [the servant] saw Him in the form of his own belief, for He is the essence of his belief. Hence the heart and the eye never see the Real except in the form of their belief. The heart encompasses the form of the Real delimited by belief.[325]

---
324 Ibid., p.103.
325 Ibid.

The Arabic word for belief is *i'tiqad*, which derives from the Arabic root meaning to knot or tie (recall our discussion of *taqyid* or binding in the first chapter). In terms of belief, *i'tiqad* can be translated as meaning 'a knot tied in the heart that determines a person's view of reality'.³²⁶ Although we sometimes limit beliefs to religion, Ibn 'Arabi appears to intend the term to apply to any relatively fixed conception of reality, which we all have. Our diverse impressions of and ideas about what is going on – about what existence, life and our world really is – are rooted in the underlying predisposition of our own entity, and the sorts of experiences it facilitates.

According to this predisposition, each human ties their own perspectival knot, attempting to bind the grand existential mystery within a conceptual framework of their own making, creating their own 'god'. This is especially the case with those who are convinced that only their religion, philosophy, ideology or what have you is true to the exclusion of all others. They fail to recognize that their own perspective cannot possibly exhaust the Real, and that the Real's dynamic plenitude transcends all of the conceptual knots we feebly attempt to bind it with. God's forms of self-manifestation are infinite and hence beliefs about God are as numerous as there are hearts to which He reveals Himself:

> It is no secret that beliefs are diverse. So, whoever restricts the Real to his own belief denies Him in other beliefs, affirming Him only when He discloses Himself in a way that conforms to his own belief. Whoever releases God from restriction, however, does not deny Him, affirming Him in every form that He transforms Himself into and worshipping all of the forms in which He is manifest, infinitely, for the forms of His self-manifestation have no end. So knowledge of God has no end where the knower stops. We are knowers at every moment, and yearn for increase: *'Oh my Lord, increase my knowledge'* (Qur'an 20:114). The situation is infinite, from both sides, whether you speak of the Real or creation.³²⁷

---

326 Chittick, *Imaginal Worlds*, p.138.
327 Ibn 'Arabi, *Fusus*, p.103.

In pointing to the infinite vastness of God, and His eternally creative self-manifestation, without end, Ibn 'Arabi sort of dwarfs religious exclusivism and philosophical narrowness, highlighting their profound naivety and conceit. They simply fail to account for the dynamic, infinitely new forms of God's manifestations, such that knowledge of God is as infinite as He is. Alternately, although no single belief about God can even remotely encompass Him, each one has at least a piece of the puzzle. So, just as we can say that all beliefs are by definition inadequate, we can also say that every belief is *accurate*, in its own limited fashion. Hence, Ibn 'Arabi actually counsels embracing every single perspective or form of belief:

> Beware of binding yourself to a specific belief and rejecting all others, for you will miss much good. Indeed, you will miss knowing reality as it is. Be within yourself a primal matter, receptive to all forms of belief, for God is too vast and too sublime to be confined to one belief to the exclusion of others.[328]

It may seem here that Ibn 'Arabi is saying then that *all beliefs are true*, and, in a sense, that is exactly what he is saying. In *The Meccan Revelations* he writes that, when one can appreciate where each person is coming from, the place from which they speak, one can see that their beliefs about reality are correct according to their own experience of it (their experience being determined by their own heart, which is shaped by God's hidden self-disclosure), such that 'there is absolutely no error in the cosmos'.[329] Everyone's belief corresponds in at least *some way* with what is Real, and hence each can be honored and respected, even if it otherwise limits That which goes beyond all conceivable limitation.

It follows that every imaginable worldview, ideology, belief, understanding or perspective *is simultaneously true and false* (though each in different ways and in varying degrees). Put differently, everyone's belief is *true* in that it accurately reflects a form of the Real's self-disclosure, and *false* in that this form is merely one of an

---

328 Ibid., pp.96–7.
329 Ibn 'Arabi, *Fut*.II.541. As quoted in Chittick, *Imaginal Worlds*, p.140.

infinite number of self-disclosures without end, which any one belief cannot possibly encompass. Hence, the more one can perceive the singular essence of all beliefs, and how each belief both reflects and obscures this essence, the more complete one's understanding of God's dynamic, infinitely multifaceted reality will be.

This situation was concisely articulated by the famous 19th-century Algerian Sufi 'Abd al-Qadir al-Jaza'iri (d.1883). He was not only an anti-colonial hero, in his remarkable and remarkably chivalrous resistance to the French invasion of Algeria, but also a close student of Ibn 'Arabi's works, and an inheritor of his spiritual way. He summed up this broader Akbarian perspective as follows:

> If you think and believe that [God] is what all the schools of Islam profess and believe – He is that, and He is other than that! If you think that He is what diverse communities believe ... Christians, Jews, Mazdeans, polytheists and others – He is that and He is other than that! And if you think and believe what is professed by the Knowers *par excellence* – prophets, saints, and angels – He is that! He is other than That![330]

God is both what every believer and knower believes and knows, and He is always and forever 'other than that'. Every belief is accurate and inadequate. Interestingly, Ibn 'Arabi holds that the study of various religious doctrines and beliefs is not something incumbent upon the average Muslim believer. However, he says that, for the 'folk of Allah' – those on the spiritual path or Sufis – the comparative study of religion is actually *required* of them so that 'they can know the doctrine of every sect and creed concerning God, in order to witness Him in every form'.[331] He notably does not recommend studying the variety of religious beliefs simply to catalog errors, as many theologians of his time would have suggested, but rather says Sufis should study them because these various beliefs are *sites through which to witness God in different forms*. As the only Real, God is the reality of the world and

---

330 'Abd al-Qadir al-Jaza'iri, as quoted in Michel Chodkiewicz, *The Spiritual Writings of Amir 'Abd al-Kader* (Albany, NY, 1995), pp.127–8.

331 Ibn 'Arabi, *Fut*.III.161. As quoted in Chittick, *Sufi Path of Knowledge*, p.110.

everything in it, including all religious beliefs, which are particularly pregnant places for witnessing Him. Hence the true followers of God witness God in every religious form, while one who limits their witnessing of God to one form only is 'not one of the Folk of Allah'.[332]

To conclude, Ibn 'Arabi appears to be suggesting in this chapter on Shu'ayb that the best way to start on the path toward realization is to 'release the Real from restriction', to 'untie the knots' in your mind and heart. Acknowledging that you're in the middle of something that goes well beyond your particular understanding may be the first step to *actually* understanding what it is that you're in the middle of. If you grasp onto the conceptual knot that you've tied into the dynamic fabric of reality, however, you are operating not through the heart, but via the thinking mind or intellect (*'aql*), which is something that 'restricts and seeks to define the situation within a particular paradigm, while in fact the Real rejects all limitations'.[333] When we operate at this level of restrictive intellect and dogmatic belief, Ibn 'Arabi calls us the 'people of beliefs' or those who set up a static doctrine that they hold as being right and true to the exclusion of others, whom the Qur'an describes as those *who deny and curse one another, and they have no helpers* (Q 3:22). As he points out in this chapter, the Qur'an describes itself not as a reminder for one with an intellect, but rather a *reminder for one with a heart* (Q 50:37), meaning one who knows the Real as totally *beyond* all forms of belief and *through* all forms of belief.

As we described at the beginning of this chapter, the intellectual aims for and misses happiness by getting stuck on surface concepts and appearances, where the heart-based human (the 'believer' or 'beginner') appreciates the deeper meaning underlying these and hence tastes the beauty of the Real. This is because the Real is radically dynamic, manifesting anew in each moment, transforming Itself into the forms of its self-disclosures indefinitely. Ibn 'Arabi writes on this:

> As for the people of unveiling, they hold that God discloses Himself in every breath and never repeats His self-disclosure. They also hold, through witnessing, that each self-disclosure gives a new creation

---
332 Ibid., p.111.
333 Ibn 'Arabi, *Fusus*, p.104.

and takes the previous one away.[334]

The heart, unlike the static conceptions of mind, is itself, in each moment, constantly changing and by nature receptive to the dynamic, ever-new, never-repeated self-manifestations of the Real. Interestingly, the word *qalb* in Arabic is connected to *taqallub*, which means to change or transform, and hence the word 'heart' in Arabic linguistically suggests its dynamic nature.[335]

When we are prostrate in prayer, we are in one of the few positions where our heart is higher than our head. So, when Muslims and other religious folk put their foreheads to the ground in worship and devotion, it is a symbolic representation of the heart's superiority as a means of knowing, an acknowledgment that the 'seat of our soul' offers a way of knowing that discursive thinking cannot even remotely hold a candle to. This is perhaps one of the reasons why Ibn 'Arabi associates Shu'ayb with the heart. Always a careful student of the Arabic language (a language that, like its linguistic sibling, Hebrew, seems to lend itself to a depth of interpretation), he points out that the Arabic root of Shu'ayb's name is the same one from which the word for branch, or branches (*shu'ab*), is derived. Ibn 'Arabi explains that Shu'ayb is associated with the wisdom of the heart, because humanity's varied beliefs are in fact so many branches of a single tree. Although the mind gets lost in the branches, the awakened heart sees the singular phenomenon of which they are all a part, and perceives the real meaning underlying their many expressions. In other words, the intelligent, illuminated heart does not miss the forest for the trees, nor the tree for the branches. As is so often the case, we find Rumi concisely expressing the very same insight here, only in poetry rather than prose:

---

334 Ibid., p.197.

335 *Taqallub* is an intransitive verbal noun derived from the root *qaf-lam-ba*. For more on this, see Meena Sharify-Funk and William Rory Dickson, 'Traces of Panentheism in Islam: Ibn al-'Arabi and the Kaleidoscope of Being', in *Panentheism Across the World's Religious Traditions,* edited by Loriliai Biernacki and Philip Clayton (New York, 2014), pp.153–4.

All the praises of all the prophets come together...
The object of praise is not more than One,
so religions are but one religion...
Each praises the moon reflected in his well,
though in truth they praise only the moon, and not the reflection.[336]

---

[336] Rumi, *Masnavi* III.2122–30. I have rendered here a somewhat condensed version of Nicholson's translation of these verses. See R. A. Nicholson, *The Mathnawi of Jalalu'ddin Rumi, Volume III* (Leiden, 1929).

4

Jonah and The Wisdom of Breath: Compassion, Remembrance and Life after Death

*The duration of your life is but a breath.
Take care that you master it,
And that it does not master you.*[337]

Jonah and Sacredness of Life

At least in North America, I imagine many people are only loosely familiar with Jonah as 'the guy who ended up in the belly of the whale'. The story comes to us from a collection of twelve chapters in the Hebrew Bible known as the *Nevi'im* or Prophets, with the Book of Jonah the fifth among them. Although the tenth chapter of the Qur'an is named after Jonah (*Yunus* in Arabic), he is only mentioned once in the chapter, whereas his story is briefly summarized in the Qur'an's 37th chapter, *al-Saffat* (Q 37:139–48). Jonah's is a richly symbolic story, touching on several profound social and psychological themes. We find the all-too-human struggle to face up to one's highest calling. We encounter the human tendency to wish for the destruction of one's enemies and to demonize the 'other'. Finally, the story points to deeper questions about death and the afterlife.

To summarize Jonah's Biblical narrative, he is first called by God to go to the booming imperial city of Nineveh and call them out for

---

337 Abu Madyan, *Uns al-wahid wa nuzhar al-murid*, as quoted in Cornell, *The Way of Abu Madyan*, p.116.

their exploitation of the poor, cruelty in war and for their idolatry and corruption. Likely anticipating the profound danger involved, or at least the sheer awkwardness of this task, Jonah attempts to flee from God's call and boards a ship to escape. When a great storm arises and threatens to sink the ship, the sailors seek the cause and draw lots, with Jonah losing. Jonah admits that he is the cause of the storm as he is attempting to flee from God, and suggests they save themselves by tossing him in the sea. The sailors prove more compassionate than one might anticipate in such circumstances: they try to row back to shore, not wanting to kill Jonah, despite his request they, in effect, do just that. However, as they try to sail back it becomes clear that there is little hope they will make it, so they decide to throw Jonah overboard despite their initial reluctance.

With his situation rapidly deteriorating from nightmarishly bad to even worse, Jonah finds himself swallowed by a whale (or giant fish), spending three days and nights inside it before he repents and promises to fulfill his task. God then orders the whale to cough him up, and Jonah somehow ends up alive and back on shore. God again commands Jonah to go to Nineveh and proclaim His message. Jonah's preaching (perhaps surprisingly) works, and the king and people of the city enter into a period of repentance to stave off the coming divine destruction. God relents and spares them. In an interesting commentary on human psychology, Jonah is not pleased with this turn of events, believing that the pagan Ninevites should have been destroyed by God, and forgetting the fact that earlier he himself required God's forgiveness, and now he is upset that *others* are getting it too. God responds to Jonah's anger by accounting for the thousands upon thousands of people and animals in Nineveh, and the loss of life that its destruction would entail.

Ibn 'Arabi's chapter on Jonah in the *Gemstones* elaborates upon some of the story's key themes, including a) God's compassion for life and desire that it be preserved, including the wisdom in forgoing vengeance, b) the remembrance of God and c) the nature of death and what follows. He opens this chapter with an account of the preciousness of each human being, represented by the fragility of breath: our lives are only so many of them, and when each of us breathes our last, our embodied existence comes to a close. He invokes themes from the Bible, the Qur'an and Islamic law to illustrate God's desire that human beings be protected and their lives honored, that their breath is preserved:

> Know that this human formation, with its perfection – in spirit, body, and mind – was created by God in His own image, and only He who created this formation can destroy it, whether by His hand (which is always the case), or by His command.[338]

The gravity of taking human life is emphasized as the human being is a delicate alignment of consciousness and matter, with a perfection in form reflecting the divine image. Each person is a finely tuned instrument for comprehensively reflecting God. As a result, taking human life can only be done by God (which is always the case, in that God is the ultimate cause of life and death), or done by those acting on God's command (only taking a life when it is absolutely necessary to prevent harm or fulfill the law). Even when life is taken lawfully, however, as in a legitimate war, the cost to the soul of the one taking life is inevitable: even when appropriate, violence is never something wholly holy; there is always a 'karmic' price to be paid for it. Ibn 'Arabi describes here the story of David, who, as someone who had shed blood in battle as a warrior for God, was unable to complete the building of the Temple:

> David wanted to build the Sacred House and tried to several times. However, each time he completed the building, it was destroyed. He complained of this to God, who revealed to him: 'My House shall not be built by the hands of those who have shed blood.' Then David said: 'O Lord, was this shedding of blood not carried out on Your path?' God said: 'Indeed, but were they not My servants?' David said: 'O Lord, may it be built by one of my family.' Then God revealed to him: 'Your son Solomon will build it.' The purpose of this story is to show the value of this human form, and that its

---

338 Ibn 'Arabi, *Fusus*, p.154.

protection is better than its destruction.³³⁹

I have always found this story to be a profound commentary on and critique of the concept of a just or virtuous war, a holy war, or any sort of killing that is perceived to be somehow justified or righteous. It is always better to care for God's servants. Preservation is better than destruction. Raising up is always preferred to breaking down. Of course, most of those involved in some manner of war tend to see their cause and their actions as righteous or at least just, or even blessed and supported by God. And it seems like at least in some circumstances fighting or killing may actually be the lesser of two evils (although I suspect these circumstances are far fewer than we might want to believe). Even when it is the better option, however, Ibn 'Arabi conveys here the inevitable price paid by those engaged in fighting and killing: David, one of God's own warriors, cannot build God's temple, for he has killed. Blood stains permanently and even the righteous cannot be cleansed of it.³⁴⁰

Striving and Fighting in the Path of God: Jihad and its Discontents

Ibn 'Arabi was not alone in holding that God always prefers preserving life over taking it. Muslim scholars more generally considered the protection of human life to be one of the five ends or goals (*maqasid*)

---

339 Ibid., pp.154–5.

340 If even the righteous remain stained by killing, how much more so those who kill conspiratorially, for ambition and power? This is famously illustrated by William Shakespeare in his play *Macbeth*, where Lady Macbeth initially suggests to her husband that mere water may cleanse them of their killing of King Duncan, but later, while sleep walking and rubbing her hands, she pleads, 'Out, damned spot,' futilely attempting to cleanse herself of the stain of murder, upon both her hands and her soul. Thanks to Bev Dickson for pointing out this reference to me.

of the entirety of the shari'a.³⁴¹ They held that the sacred law's overall objective was to benefit people (*maslaha*), to facilitate their lives and ensure the smooth and harmonious operation of society to the greatest possible degree. Correspondingly, at the international level Muslim jurists have generally held that peace is the preferential option, but accepted that fighting may be necessary to establish or protect it. Hence the Islamic concept of fighting for the sake of God. I've heard this described as 'picking up the sword to take the sword out of a tyrant's hand', and most cultures acknowledge that at times there are few other reasonable options. It's hard to fault partisans in Nazi-occupied Europe for engaging in acts of violence against the Nazi SS, for example. Regardless, it is probably worth considering just what jihad is all about, before moving on to consider some of the main themes of this chapter of the *Gemstones*.³⁴²

The first thing we need to get right if we want an accurate understanding of jihad is that, like any other religious value or concept, it is historically unstable, meaning that it is constantly being interpreted and reinterpreted based upon the needs of those doing the interpreting. For those familiar with the Christian tradition, we can see this clearly in how the meaning of 'crusade' has changed over time. Today, a politician might hold a news conference declaring a 'crusade' against corruption, and this, of course, no longer means suiting up in armor, picking up a broadsword, and cleansing their local government of infidels: the meaning of the word crusade is at least somewhat context dependent. Similarly, you will not find a single Muslim understanding of jihad persisting throughout the centuries,

---

341 As Mohammed Hashim Kamali notes, the *maqasid* of the law are drawn from the Qur'an, which, in various places, specifies God's intentions with His commands. Muhammad is described in the Qur'an as a mercy (*rahma*) to the world (Q 21:07), while the Qur'an describes itself as a healing for hearts, and says that God desires ease, not hardship for people (Q 5:6). It was not until the fourth century after the Prophet Muhammad, however, that Muslim jurists began to systematically define the *maqasid*. Al-Ghazali defined the shari'a's goals (*maqasid*) as the preservation of faith, life, intellect, lineage and property. Mohammed Hashim Kamali, '*Maqasid al-Shari'a*: The Objectives of Islamic Law', *Islamic Studies*, 38 (1999), 194–9.

342 We should note that getting an accurate take on jihad is no easy task, in part because the subject has become so politically charged in recent decades that accuracy basically finds itself cornered at knifepoint by partial, often-caricatured views who demand that accuracy keep quiet so their agenda-driven partiality can hold court.

but rather come across various interpretations and emphases, whether legal, moral or spiritual. All that being said, the many interpreters, with their own contexts and concerns, are still dealing with the same source material, the verses of the Qur'an and sayings of the Prophet Muhammad on the subject. So, what I'll offer here is a sort of flyover tour of both the source material and how this material has been interpreted by Muslims throughout history.

Forty-one verses of the Qur'an have words derived from *jim-ha-dal*. Linguistically, the root means to strive, struggle or exert oneself to the fullest. In several cases the Qur'an uses jihad to refer to exerting oneself for God, without any reference to fighting whatsoever (Q 22:78; Q 25:52; Q 29:69). In hadith literature, jihad is usually found phrased as *al-jihad fi sabil Allah*, or 'striving in the path of God'. Strenuous effort or exertion is a key aspect of the family of meanings associated with the Arabic root. We see this with the verb *jahida*, for example, which means to endure a state of hardship and difficulty.[343] The earliest Muslim commentators on the Qur'an (going back to the first century or so after the Prophet Muhammad) tended to define jihad broadly, essentially meaning to 'excel in the performance of good deeds', or to endure hardship in the process of trying to make the world a better place.[344] This can include smiling at people you meet on the street, setting up an animal shelter, helping to resolve a marital dispute or standing up for the truth when it's particularly difficult and controversial. From Islam's inception, jihad has been understood in a broad sense to mean struggling to do good, to uphold justice and to protect one's community.

That being said, Muslims have always considered fighting (*qital*) to be an important *aspect* of jihad. The first verses giving Muhammad and his followers permission to fight in the Qur'an are Q 22:39–40:

> *Permission is given to those who have been attacked, because they have been oppressed, and God is able to help them. They are those who have been expelled from their homes for saying 'God is our*

---

343 Asma Afsaruddin's *Striving in the Path of God: Jihad and Martyrdom in Islamic Thought* (New York, 2013), p.10.

344 Ibid., p.21.

Lord.' If God had not restrained some people by means of others, monasteries, churches, synagogues, and mosques in which God's name is mentioned would have been destroyed.

Fighting is allowed, but clearly in response to a) being attacked and oppressed, and b) with the express purpose of ensuring that people of various religions can engage in spiritual practice without interference. The goal (*maqsud*) then of fighting is to counteract oppression (*zulm*), establish justice and facilitate the free practice of religion. In other words, jihad is enjoined for the purpose of establishing benefit and preserving life, in both its material and spiritual aspects.

Fighting is a particularly virtuous form of jihad because of the hardship, struggle, loss and trauma it involves. If fighting is indeed something that needs to be done, it is work that is distinctly unenviable, and can require a courage and endurance that go beyond what most people are called upon to muster in their lives. This is why the concept of martyrdom (*shahada*) has a pride of place within Islam, as it does within Christianity. Simply put, suffering the pain and horror of fatal violence, giving one's own life for the sake of others, risking it all against manifest tyranny, all of this makes being a martyr one of the most noble sacrifices a human can make, and most cultures have their own celebrated martyrs.

A great example in my mind, of a *mujahida* (one who makes jihad) and a *shahida* (martyr), is Noor Inayat Khan (d.1944), the daughter of the first Sufi teacher to visit and teach in North America, Hazrat Inayat Khan. Born in Moscow, and having studied music and psychology in Paris, Noor was drawn to literature and the arts. She also inherited her father's teachings on non-violence. However, as the severity of Nazi aggression in Europe became apparent in the early 1940s, Noor and her siblings 'questioned their personal culpability in the disorder if they continued on the path of non-violent action and allowed the Nazis to carry on without meaningful resistance', and they eventually decided that it was ethically superior to join the military resistance against Nazism.[345] Abandoning their ostensibly cushy lives

---
345 William Rory Dickson and Meena Sharify-Funk, *Unveiling Sufism: From Manhattan to Mecca* (Sheffield, 2017), pp.44–5.

of cosmopolitan comfort and creativity, the siblings moved to London in 1940, where Noor signed up with the British Special Operations Executive. She was trained in radio operation and became the first female radio operator sent behind enemy lines in France in 1943. Her dangerous work led to the rescue of dozens of downed airmen and secured resources for the French resistance. After being captured by the Gestapo in France, she was isolated and tortured for months, and yet withheld any information. She was then sent to the Dachau concentration camp where she was executed in 1944, with her last word being 'liberté' or 'freedom.'[346] In 1949 the British government posthumously awarded Noor Inayat Khan the George Cross for her bravery fighting the Nazis during the Second World War. If fighting against tyranny is a component of jihad, and dying in that cause makes one a *shahid*, I can't help but think that Noor clearly fits the bill in both respects.

As we noted, Muslims have always seen fighting and dying in a just cause as a component of jihad, and yet Muslim scholars began to frame jihad exclusively in terms of fighting when they became affiliated with imperial authorities like the Umayyads and 'Abbasids in the eighth, ninth and tenth centuries. The Qur'an quite clearly prohibits Muslims from aggression (Q 2:190), and yet these scholars in centers of empire came to endorse offensive combat as a component of military jihad, even a collective duty for Muslims, arguing that the Qur'an's prohibition on this was overridden by other verses that commanded fighting unbelievers (Q 9:5). However, their opponents suggested rather the opposite, that the prohibition of aggression overrides verses that command fighting, though their opposition did not carry the day in the medieval era.[347] If you look at a classical Islamic book of law (*fiqh*) for instance, you'll see a chapter on jihad that deals with fighting to defend Muslim lands or to expand Muslim rule. For 21st-century readers, flipping through medieval manuals of Islamic jurisprudence on jihad can be a bit jarring. These texts seem to assume that a Muslim ruler should, at least annually, engage in some

---

346 Ibid., p.46.
347 Afsaruddin, *Striving in the Path of God*, p.4.

sort of military campaign to expand the borders of the *dar al-islam* or 'Abode of Islam', and thereby shrink the *dar al-harb* or 'Abode of War' (everywhere ruled by non-Muslims).

It is important to note that dividing the world into abodes of war and Islam has zero explicit precedent in the Qur'an and the teachings of the Prophet Muhammad. It was very much a legal concept developed by scholars of the law centuries after the Prophet. It has further been woefully misunderstood, in part due to the limitations of translation: the concept is actually not quite what it, at first glance, seems to be. The *dar al-harb*, for example, was a theoretical notion that Muslim jurists developed to describe the 'state of nature', where people existed without legal obligation. It was presumed to be the original human condition, that is only changed when someone enters into a legally binding contract. Calling this primordial state the *dar al-harb* is in line with Thomas Hobbes's (d.1679) suggestion that outside of contractual state or legal authority, sovereign individuals lived in a state of the 'war of all against all'. This state outside of legal obligation does not necessarily have to be put in such conflictive terms, of course, and Muslim scholars also titled this realm as the *dar al-ibaha*, or 'Abode of Permissibility'.[348]

The *dar al-harb* category was, as just described, largely based on an abstract notion of the 'state of nature', or living without any state-mandated legal obligations. However, it was also a term that, in many respects, reflected an international situation whereby war was assumed to be natural. It is useful to point out here that pre-modern legal concepts are only intelligible within their own context – to anachronistically interpret them in light of our current international framework inevitably distorts them. This is not to say that we cannot in any way judge the past by the present, but rather that, before we do so, we should at least *understand* the past on its own terms.

The period of late antiquity was one without any sort of international law, and rather than a presumed state of peace that could

---

348 Mohamed Fadel, Draft, 'International Law in General in the Medieval Islamic World', in *The Cambridge History of International Law, Volume III: International Law in the Islamic World* (forthcoming), p.21.

only be broken by a declaration of war (as we tend to assume today), there was something more akin to an assumed state of war that could only be halted by a peace agreement. This was the case not only within Arabia, but also in the broader Near Eastern world, Europe, Africa and Asia. People during the time that Islamic laws were being formulated were basically governed by competing tribes and warring dynasties, of various religious and ethnic persuasions, all of which tended to use force as diplomacy and see the expansion of their borders as a sign of divine favor.[349] As well, during this period of history, people were much less free to live their religions safely under the rule of others, and hence Muslims at this time tended to believe (not entirely inaccurately), that only under Muslim rule would they be safe to practice Islam. As such, Muslims 'continued to see *jihad* not only as a means of guaranteeing the security and freedom of Muslims but as virtually the only means of doing so'.[350]

It's also worth pointing out here that Muslims weren't the only ones joining imperial expansion to religious duty in late antiquity and the medieval period. In 554, just years before Muhammad's birth in Mecca, the Roman Emperor Justinian I (d.565) declared in an Edict to the people of Constantinople that the Christian faith was 'the first and greatest blessing for all mankind', and that, as Roman Emperor, his job was to ensure that Christianity be 'universally established', with the Emperor himself the faith's 'patron and protector'.[351] It was taken for granted by Roman Christians that uniting the world under Christian rule was an obvious good. This synthesis of imperialism and Christianity would prove to be a lasting one.

During the medieval period, Christian thinkers (very much like their Muslim counterparts), considered heresy, false doctrine and unbelief to suffice as justification for the use of force. Though neither Christian nor Muslim intellectual traditions ever reached a consensus on this point, both for a time largely embraced the notion

---

349 Sherman Jackson, 'Jihad and the Modern World', *Journal of Islamic Law and Culture*, 7:1 (2002), 6-7.
350 Ibid., 10.
351 Fred Donner, *Muhammad and the Believers: At the Origins of Islam* (Cambridge, MA, 2010), pp.5, 10.

that the wrong religious orientation can warrant the state's violence. For example, the twelfth-century canon lawyer, scholar and bishop Gratian was famous for his legal compilation, the *Decretum,* which became a sort of textbook of Christian law in that period. In exploring possible causes of just war, Gratian describes a situation whereby the Church, under imperial authority, wages war on a heretic bishop and his followers, killing them, taking their property, and imprisoning them. Such a war counts as a just one for Gratian, as the spiritual harm wrought by the heretics warrants redress. Such reasoning was further applied to non-Christians, such that, for Gratian and medieval Christian just war theorizing more generally, 'anyone seen as a threat to the Church on earth merited physical punishment even by war', with such war understood to be a 'positive moral duty'.[352] Later, the Catholic Church, with the 1494 Treaty of Tordesillas, went so far as to basically divide the known world between Spain and Portugal, essentially saying to those empires that the world was theirs for the taking, largely justified through the ostensible Christianization of conquered and colonized peoples.

Regardless of theoretical legal notions like *dar al-harb* and *dar al-Islam*, or medieval Christian notions of just war to protect the Church and Christianize the world, both Muslim and Christian rulers tended to see themselves and their empires as existing in a complex global system of imperial relations, where the enemies of one's enemies could become one's friends. Although theoretically they operated within a view of the world based upon religious community, in practice, they were rarely very puritan about this. Muslim and Christian rulers, like any others, appreciated the necessity of *realpolitik* in a world of complex, shifting interests, and frequently formed fruitful alliances across the borders of religion.

One particularly poignant example of this is found a bit later in history, with the 19th-century British–Ottoman alliance, which formed after the British backed the Ottomans against the Russians in the Crimean War (1853–6). Despite understanding themselves as

---

352 F. H. Russell, as quoted in David D. Corey and J. Daryl Charles, *The Just War Tradition: An Introduction* (Wilmington, DE, 2012), p.72.

representing the only Sunni Islamic caliphate, the Ottomans had no qualms about allying with the Christian British, but rather saw theirs as a shared fight among 'civilized' empires against the 'barbarous' Russians. The Ottomans saw the British not so much as recalcitrant unbelievers awaiting conquest, but as colleagues in global rule and civilization. Because of their alliance with the British, the Ottomans actually supported the British colonial authorities *against* the Muslims participating in the Indian Rebellion against British rule in India in 1857, despite these Muslims declaring their fight to be a jihad that (at least they believed) Muslims everywhere should back. Instead, the Ottomans, representing the Sunni Muslim caliphate, actually sent aid to British victims of the rebellion, and suggested that Muslims remain loyal to their British colonial rulers.[353] There was clearly no conception of the world at this point as somehow divided between 'the West' and 'Islam', a division so frequently invoked in recent decades.

Despite early theoretical notions of jihad as a military means to expand the rule of Islam (a theoretical notion that didn't always inform practical alliances, as we've just noted) Muslim scholars today increasingly return to the earliest Muslim understandings of jihad as a generalized struggle for the good. For their part, Sufis have often pointed out that the 'greater *jihad*' is the struggle against evil in one's own soul, based upon a saying of the Prophet Muhammad's, that, when returning from battle, he and his companions were leaving the 'lesser *jihad*' for the greater one, namely the struggle to live virtuously in everyday life.[354] This is the *jihad al-nafs* – the struggle against the self's own negative tendencies – the evil within. This is not to say that Sufis did not engage in the lesser jihad of battle; indeed Sufis formed the main organizing military force resisting European colonization in the 19th century, whether we think of the Naqshbandi Sufi leader Shamil Dagastani (d.1871), who resisted Russia's invasion of Dagestan

---

353 Cemil Aydin, *The Idea of the Muslim World: A Global Intellectual History* (Cambridge, 2017), pp.54–5.

354 David Cook suggests that this tradition did not really circulate until the post-formative period of Islam, with early Sufis not citing it, despite articulating its basic premise that the greatest human struggle is within the self. David Cook, *Understanding Jihad* (Berkeley, 2005), p.36.

and Chechnya, Tijani leader 'Umar Tall (d.1864) who fought French incursions into West Africa or, with the most global fanfare, Qadiri leader 'Abd al-Qadir al-Jaza'iri, who was a scholar of Ibn 'Arabi's thought leading the Algerian resistance against the French invasions of the 1830s and 1840s.

Taking the broad view of the Islamic tradition over time, we find that the various jurists and Sufis who defined jihad largely agreed that peace is the natural (and preferred) state of affairs, that fighting is not an end in itself and that it is to only be to be engaged in when peaceful means have been exhausted. The evidence for this in Islamic legal and moral literature is overwhelming. Of course, there are the un- or mis-educated young men in toxic extremist groups who basically fetishize jihad as a hypermasculine means to restore cultural and religious dignity and power, elevating it to a centrality it has never really had in Islam, abandoning totally the restrictions on fighting that guided Muslim teachings for centuries: sensible, humane things like not killing civilians, diplomats, journalists, religious clerics, etc. As many qualified Muslim scholars of the law have exhaustively shown, however, to the degree these groups engage in such brutality, they deviate markedly from the principles and rules of the shari'a.[355]

Ibn 'Arabi invokes the Qur'an, which commands Muslims to accept peace if an enemy inclines to it, and to place their trust in God (Q 8:61), highlighting the Qur'an's emphasis on the preferability of peace if possible. He further notes that Islamic law (following Biblical precedent, Leviticus 24: 19–21) allows for *lex talionis*, the law of retaliation, or an 'eye for an eye'. The Qur'an says *the recompense of evil is an evil like it*, which, Ibn 'Arabi wisely notes, means that the Qur'an is calling proportional retaliation an *evil*, even if it is a permissible one.[356] However, the Qur'an adds, *but whoever forgives and does good, his reward is with God* (Q 42:40). Hence Islamic legal norms

---

355 Muhammad Afifi al-Akiti's ruling (*fatwa*) against suicide bombing remains a masterclass in Islamic jurisprudence, showing clearly the various unequivocal principles of Islamic teachings violated by terrorism, including the targeting of non-combatants, military action undertaken without proper state authorization and the act of suicide itself. See his *Defending the Transgressed by Censuring the Reckless Against the Killing of Civilians* (UK, 2005).

356 Ibn 'Arabi, *The Ringstones of Wisdom*, trans. Dagli, p.202.

historically allowed for a family to ask that the one who killed one of their members is himself killed, and yet it encouraged the aggrieved family to forgive and accept a lesser penalty for the killer. Ibn 'Arabi drives the point home in noting that, according to the shari'a, if there is a disagreement in the family over whether or not the killer should be killed or pardoned, the lesser penalty or pardon is applied.[357] He sums up the takeaway here as follows:

> When you realize that God takes care of this human creation and protects it, you yourself should care for it all the more, which will bring you happiness. That is because, as long as a human being is alive, they have the opportunity to reach the perfection for which they were created. So, whoever tries to destroy a person is seeking to prevent their achieving that for which they were made.[358]

Regardless of how far we've fallen, human beings have a profound, delicate nature that is unique in the (known) cosmos, and hence preserving them is incumbent upon those who seek to be on right side of God, and hence to find happiness. The value of human life is incalculable, and the shedding of blood is never to be taken lightly. On the contrary, it is to be opposed and avoided if at all possible.

On the Remembrance of God and the Human Self

In discussing jihad, peacemaking and the question of retaliation, Ibn 'Arabi cites a saying of the Prophet Muhammad's, that what is even better than jihad on the battlefield, undergoing its difficulties and sacrifices, is the remembrance of God (*dhikr*). The hadith Ibn 'Arabi shares here is just one example among many that situates *dhikr* as the utmost deed, virtue and goal for Muslims. Another saying of Muhammad's situates *dhikr* even more starkly, 'this world and everything within it

---

357 Ibid.
358 Ibn 'Arabi, *Fusus*, p.106.

is cursed, except for the remembrance of God'.³⁵⁹ The Qur'an, after affirming the importance of the five-times daily prayer (*salat*), asserts that the remembrance of God is *greater* or the *greatest* (Q 29:45). If the remembrance of God is greater than jihad, *salat* and the entire world, then it is worth asking the question what exactly is it?

Ibn 'Arabi defines *dhikr* as 'presence with the One remembered'.³⁶⁰ It follows that *dhikr* is an existential state, the state of being present with the living reality of God in each moment, the state of presence with what is real, rather than being caught in the rather constant stream of illusions created by the mind. As Abdul Aziz Said writes, *dhikr* is 'remembering where we come from, remembering what we are, remembering what we are a part of'.³⁶¹ Sara Sviri notes that, paradoxically, at its highest pitch, remembrance is also a state of forgetfulness, 'of forgetting everything but God', such that a total absorption in awareness of God simultaneously leads to the disappearance of all else 'from the orbit of perception, imagination, or comprehension'.³⁶²

For Sufis, remembrance of God is usually embodied through reciting the Qur'an, performing the daily prayer, and most characteristically, in the repetition of God's Names. In all cases, *dhikr* is intimately connected to breath. Various Sufi orders have operationalized the remembrance of God in coordination with breathing. For instance, among some Naqhsbandi Sufis, the name Allah is said silently, with the first syllable of the name Allah, 'Al' said with the outbreath, while the second, 'Lah', is said with the inbreath. These practices all have the purpose of imprinting the heart, or creating a 'groove' within it, that allows consciousness to gravitate away from 'mechanical thinking' and

---

359 This hadith further adds, alongside *dhikr*, the seeking of knowledge. *Sunan Ibn Majah* 4112. William C. Chittick, in commenting on Ibn 'Arabi's view, observes that *dhikr* 'transmutes the accursed into the blessed', and, as everything in the world is a reminder or sign of God, when perceived accurately, all is actually *dhikr Allah* and hence all is blessed and nothing in the world is accursed. 'On the Cosmology of *Dhikr*', in *Paths to the Heart: Sufism and the Christian East*, edited by James S. Cutsinger (Bloomington, IN, 2002), p.49.

360 In Arabic this is '*al-hudur ma' al-madhkur*'. Ibn 'Arabi, *Fut*.IV.36. As Quoted in Chittick, 'On the Cosmology of *Dhikr*', 49.

361 Abdul Aziz Said, 'Tawhid: The Sufi Tradition of Unity', *Creation*, 4:4 (1988), 24.

362 Sviri, *The Taste of Hidden Things*, p.124.

ever-changing distractions, toward the more subtle and finer layers of consciousness found in the heart's deeper possibilities.[363]

We would not exaggerate in saying that being in a state of *dhikr* is the end point of every Islamic law, teaching, Qur'anic verse and hadith: *dhikr* is precisely what jihad and *salat* are for. The Qur'an as well as the Islamic legal tradition make this quite clear. As discussed above, the Qur'an justifies fighting by suggesting, *If God did not restrain people by means of others, many monasteries, synagogues, churches and mosques, where God's name is remembered, would have been destroyed* (Q 22:40). Muslims were allowed to fight to preserve the remembrance of God, regardless of which religious house this remembrance takes place within. The remembrance of God is so central to ritual prayer that, if one spends a significant amount of time during prayer not focused on God, but rather thinking about what to have for lunch, for example, Muslim jurists suggest that the prayer requires an additional prostration to make up for the lost time: prayer without *dhikr Allah* is invalid. In sum, the whole point of Islamic teaching and practice is to create a self and a society in which the remembrance of our transcendent Source, our true home and abode of peace, can be cultivated. It is as though the entirety of the tradition is oriented toward reintegrating manifestation and Essence, or harmonizing multiplicity according to a unifying key, whether this harmonization takes place within the human self or more broadly speaking, among communities and societies. Twentieth-century Sufi master Ahmad al-'Alawi (d.1934) sums this up in stating that 'the law was not enjoined upon us, neither were the rites of worship ordained but for the sake of establishing the remembrance of God'.[364]

Rumi drives home the superiority of *dhikr* in his *Fihi ma Fihi* ('In it is What's in it'), a collection of his talks given to disciples on the spiritual life. He relates a story about his father Baha' al-Din, who was, like his son Rumi, a mystic and theologian. His father is found by some of his students in a state of spiritual contemplation, *dhikr*, totally

---

363 I guess groove really is in the heart. (I tried and failed to resist a Deee-Lite reference here.) Ibid., pp.124–5.
364 Lings, *A Sufi Saint of the Twentieth Century*, p.96.

absorbed in the remembrance of God. The time of prayer arrives, and they call Baha' al-Din to come pray. He does not respond, so they leave to go perform the prayer, yet two stay with him, soaking in the very real, visceral energy of light and love that surround one in such a state. One of the students who went off to pray is given a spiritual vision, where he sees that he and those performing the required prayer are standing behind the Prophet, *but with their backs toward Mecca*. However, he sees that those who remained with Baha' al-Din are in fact *facing* Mecca. Rumi explains that this is because his father had 'passed away from any sense of personal identity', and became an empty vessel for the Light of God. As God's Light is the very essence of Mecca, anyone who is following a religious obligation but doing so in a way that takes them away from God's Light, is turning their backs on Mecca, whether they are physically facing it or not.[365] The students who stayed with Baha' al-Din were the ones who were truly engaged in prayer, even if, on the surface, they appeared to be missing it.

The story illustrates keenly the difference between the 'outward body' of prayer and its 'inner soul' of *dhikr*, and the superiority of the latter over the former. This is not to say that Rumi and other Sufis have disregarded outward forms of prayer – quite the contrary. Rumi praises formal prayer repeatedly in his works, describing it in his *Masnavi* as 'the shepherd who saves you from the wolves'.[366] For his part, Ibn 'Arabi counsels the Sufi seeker to perform not only the five obligatory daily prayers, but to ensure they complete the supplementary prayers practiced by the Prophet Muhammad (known as *sunnah* prayers), and further perform twenty extra cycles of prayer between the noon and afternoon prayer, and between the sunset and night prayer, alongside 13 extra cycles following the night prayer (altogether totaling a lot of formal prayer).[367] Exemplary of probably most Sufis, Ibn 'Arabi sees

---

365 Jalal al-Din Rumi, *The Discourses of Rumi (Or Fihi Ma Fihi)*, translated by A. J. Arberry (Ames, IA, 2000), pp.21–2.

366 Rumi, *Masnavi* VI.3575. As quoted in Gholamreza Aavani, *Rumi: A Philosophical Study* (Chicago, 2016), p.200.

367 Ibn 'Arabi, *Book of the Quintessence of What is Indispensable for the Spiritual Seeker*, translated by James Morris, https://ibnarabisociety.org/wp-content/uploads/PDFs/MorrisSpiritual-Practice.pdf (accessed July 21, 2021). See Morris, *Approaching Ibn 'Arabi* (Oxford, 2024).

salat as foundational to the Sufi path, and hence he engaged in a great deal of it. In fact, he understood each prescribed act of worship revealed to Muhammad (i.e. the Five Pillars of Islam) as having a particular spiritual function based upon which Name of God lay implicit within it. Each act of worship has a special connection with a specific Name of God, through which it connects with the human heart. According to Ibn 'Arabi, the *salat* connects to the human heart through God's Name *al-Nur* or the Light. The daily prayer is a light that, when carefully performed, drives away the heart's concern with anything other than God, much like light drives away darkness.[368]

As mentioned in this work's introductory chapter, however, this general Sufi orientation toward establishing a practice of ritual prayer based upon the form revealed to the Prophet Muhammad does not rule out the various expressions of Sufism that focus on other means of achieving the remembrance of God. The endpoint is a heart polished to a degree that it can reflect God's perpetual self-disclosures, attuned to both the dynamic, ephemeral nature of becoming as well as the eternal nature of Being it expresses. This paradoxical relationship between formal spiritual practice and the formless essence it is meant to open the human soul to, was brought home to me in an interview I conducted with a disciple of Bawa Muhaiyaddeen's,[369] artist and author Michael Green, who shared the following about his master's teachings:

> And finally, I got it, that what he [Bawa] was saying was that the real deal is this profound *dhikr* of dying with every breath. And if you're not dying with every breath, you're just 'playing house'. You know, it's just fun and games. He talked about rituals and those kinds of mechanical things that we use as crutches – he just dismissed them. He said, 'if you want to go stay in kindergarten that's what you do, but I am bringing you *dying with every breath*'. It was *heavy shit*, as we say. I once asked him, I said, 'Well you are talking to me, am

---

368 Morris, *The Reflective Heart*, p.77.
369 Interestingly, Bawa himself was a Sufi master and saint who did not practice the formal *salat*, even though he encouraged some (but not all) of his followers to do so. From my various interviews with his disciples I found that Bawa taught several approaches to the Sufi path, tailored to each individual's orientation. Green, interview with author, June 26, 2010, Coatesville, Pennsylvania.

I supposed to be doing *dhikr*?' He said 'yes'. Do you know what *dhikr* is? *La ilaha illa Allah* [There is no god but God]. His mystical translation of *la illaha illa Allahu* is, 'the "I" is an illusion. God alone is Real.' Which makes so much more sense than to simply say, 'there is no god but God.' But he said, 'Your identity is an illusion. God alone is Real,' with every breath. And then he builds a mosque![370]

Green concludes this particular reflection by noting that, despite Bawa's dismissal of outward forms of practice, he also built a mosque[371] to establish the practice of the outward form of Islamic prayer (*salat*) – which again we can link back to the dual ideas that 1) the point of any formal spiritual practice is not the practice itself, but rather a state of being (the awareness of what is Real) and 2) formal practice can be an important and even indispensable means of accessing this state of being that transcends it.

Regardless of the manner in which a state of *dhikr* is cultivated, whether more formal or formless in nature, Ibn 'Arabi suggests that *dhikr* is something that *unifies* the heart.[372] This suggests that the heart is not normally unified, but rather scattered in its foci, highlighting here the issue of the fragmentation and integration of the human self. Now for most of us, we would tend to think of ourselves as a unity, but actually, according to both Western and Sufi psychologies, we are generally fragmented into conflicting desires, ideas, bodily needs and intentions. A key part of not only psychological health but spiritual development is to *integrate* our psychological parts into a whole, to become one.[373] A great example of *not* being one is when we say things like, 'I don't know why I always do that [insert whatever pattern of behavior or reaction we wish we didn't do].' This implies that there

---

370 Green, interview with author, June 26, 2010, Coatesville, Pennsylvania.
371 Built in 1984, the lovely Bawa Muhaiyaddeen Fellowship mosque remains active in Philadelphia. For more information on it, see: https://www.bmf.org/mosque/ (accessed March 17, 2023).
372 Ibn 'Arabi, *Book of the Quintessence*.
373 In his *Toward a Psychology of Being* (1968) Abraham Maslow notes that 'one aspect of health is integration', and that in a peak-experience, 'the splits dissolve'. As quoted by Lauren Boni in 'The Sufi Journey Towards Nondual Self-realization' (MS Thesis, University of Lethbridge, 2010), p.19.

is a part of ourselves disconnected from our conscious awareness and understanding, one that we experience as an incomprehensible foreign entity doing things we wish it wouldn't. We also see this in people who live 'double lives', whereby their public persona and private modes can be quite shockingly different from each other.

In contrast, when we do things with our whole being, we experience not a sense of confusion and disconnect, but rather the doing is accompanied by a feeling of authenticity, integrity and even bliss. Any conceivable activity in life gains exponentially in meaning, richness and joy when it is done with your whole self. To try this out, you can simply engage in things with an effort to bring your whole self to bear, to be fully present. You can try listening to someone else with your whole being, eating with your whole self, speaking or walking with your head-to-toe self fully into it, with all of your attention brought to bear, to see what it might mean to live this way. Recall Ibn 'Arabi's teacher in Spain, Fatima bint ibn Muthanna, who loved him best because when he sat down or stood up or listened or spoke, he did so with *his whole self*, being 100 percent present.

Ibn 'Arabi asks in this chapter, which part of us is engaged in *dhikr*? If we chant God's Names with tongue only, he affirms, then God is with the tongue but not the rest. Similarly, he suggests that *salat* is really only performed properly when the heart is holistically in a state of remembrance: when the receptive heart in is a state of correspondence with God,[374] and hence is empty of any else. We must first ourselves become a unity before we can do anything holistically, and to remember God with our whole being is in fact to witness God's self-manifestations in every state of existence. When we ourselves become one, we see oneness all around us. Rumi expresses this beautifully in the metaphor of a broken mirror, noting that the world appears many to us, as, like a shattered mirror, each piece of our self reflects a different image. However, if we heal the divisions within ourselves, and restore the self as a single mirror, it reflects a single image: unity within and unity without.[375]

---

374 Morris, *The Reflective Heart*, p.78.
375 As quoted in Frager, *Heart, Self, and Soul*, p.84.

What about Death?

After discussing the sanctity of human life and the nature of the remembrance of God, Ibn 'Arabi turns in this chapter on Jonah to address the meaning of death, and the nature of the afterlife. If Jonah's experience in the belly of the whale can be read as a metaphor for death, it seems fitting that Ibn 'Arabi considers it here. Now, death is not an easy topic to broach. If we were to consult an etiquette manual for a list of subjects best avoided during a dinner party, I would imagine that death would be close to the top. After commenting on the salad dressing, one is well advised to avoid sharing a reflection on how we're all going to die and yet we don't know when or how or what comes next. And yet for some of us, a preoccupation with this basic fact of life is hard to avoid. Science and religion author John Horgan shares what his own obsession with mortality was like as a child, following a classmate's death:

> My parents, siblings, friends, all were doomed, and yet they blithely went on with their lives as if they had all the time in the world. My horror of mortality was most acute in the most cheerful, chattering contexts – in a classroom or at a party. I wanted to scream out to the oblivious fools around me, 'You're all going to die!'[376]

Despite its ubiquitous inevitability, death is a difficult subject for us to broach for all sorts of generally obvious reasons, including the various kinds of suffering and loss it entails, the separation of our self from every familiar comfort, companion and reference point we have, and the mystery of what if anything we will encounter after we die. Dainin Katagiri Roshi (d.1990), founder of the Minnesota Zen Meditation Center, shares a poignant story about a Zen master on his deathbed who was asked by his disciples, 'what do you think about death?' He responded simply, 'I don't want to die.'[377] His disciples were hoping for something perhaps a little more inspiring from their

---

376 John Horgan, *Rational Mysticism: Spirituality Meets Science in the Search for Enlightenment* (New York, 2003), p.12.
377 Katagiri Roshi, 'Dying Together', *Windbell*, 34 (1990), 3.

master, but he simply shared his very human desire to not have to go through it: death is a daunting prospect.

Ibn 'Arabi affirms, first of all, that death is not what we think it is: 'The Real does not destroy this [human] constitution through so-called "death." It is not a bringing to non-existence but rather a separation.'[378] It is worth pausing to note that Ibn 'Arabi refers not to death but rather to 'so-called' death. There is a subtle but profound indication here that the name does not fit the reality, that death is something other than what it appears to be. This is because while alive we only know death from the *outside*, as an external observer, and hence it looks to be a destruction and end. However, when we know it from the *inside* we discover its true meaning as opposed to its apparent nature. Despite what *appears* to be happening with death, Ibn 'Arabi maintains what religions as a rule hold to be the case, and what the Qur'an repeatedly, even exhaustively emphasizes: death is not a total destruction of the self or its final end, but rather death is a separation of soul from the body, with both body and soul returning to their origins, the body to the earth, and the soul to its luminous origin in what we might call the spiritual world, or perhaps the world of unbounded consciousness. As a return to origins, death is the closing of a circle, and hence, in a sense, a completion of the human being.[379]

Regardless of our precise perception of it, death is a profoundly meaningful moment, in that an embodied human journey comes to an end, and yet as we noted above, the human soul itself is not destroyed by death. Hazrat Inayat Khan writes that 'mortality exists in conception rather than in reality' and that death only appears to be an end due to the 'lack of the soul's understanding of its own self'.[380] In a very real sense then, death is an illusion, a mistaken concept, a wrong idea. It is a bit like waking up from a dream and thinking that you have died and become someone else. And, as Inayat Khan points out here, the way to avoid this mistaken conception and to genuinely know death, is

---

378 Ibn 'Arabi, *Fusus*, p.157.
379 Ibn 'Arabi, however, distinguishes between perfection (*kamal*) and completion (*tamam*), writing that 'perfection is that which is sought, not completion'. *Fut*.III.405.
380 Hazrat Inayat Khan, *Mastery through Accomplishment*, edited by Donald A. Graham (New Lebanon, NY, 2011), p.72.

to *truly know the nature of one's own self*. The deeper we go within, the further we can see beyond the borders of this life.

A genuine experience of the depth and reality of our own being leads to the profound discovery that it is in no way dependent on the temporary material constitution it experiences itself as. Rather, it is quite the other way around. It is more accurate to say that it is our soul or consciousness that is currently dreaming that it has a body. The dream is dependent on the dreamer, and not the reverse. To truly know the soul, or to realize the nature of consciousness, is to transcend death altogether – to not die at all, as the essence of the soul is indestructible and hence deathless by substance. Direct knowledge of this reality brings a profound liberation from fear of death and the trials of life, allowing one to embrace life fully knowing that what is called 'death' is a change of state. In other words, like life, death too occurs within consciousness.

Meena Sharify-Funk shared with me that, when she was studying with Asad Ali in Damascus some years ago, his first assignment for her was to write a paper explaining her questions for him, outlining why she had come to study with him. Her biggest question then was based upon a celebrated saying of the Prophet Muhammad's, calling on his followers to learn to 'die before you die'. She asked Professor Ali in her paper how this is to be done, how one is to die before their death? Some months passed without receiving an answer. Then, at the conclusion of a meeting with students, just prior to exiting the room, he approached her and simply stated: 'We don't die. Goodbye.'

American spiritual teacher Ram Dass (d.2019) offers a helpful explanation of how it is possible not to die, using the metaphor of television. He notes that our perception is something like a television antenna (televisions used to have these, for those born after the 1980s), and that we generally use that antenna to receive two channels only: the channel of the physical body and the channel of mental states and psychological drama. When our perception is attuned to the first channel, he explains, we see and judge bodies, based on size, attractiveness, threat, etc. When we switch to channel two, however, we perceive psychological and social data, focusing on things like personality qualities, status and human drama: this person is a professional, that person appears to be upset, this other person is really creative, 'I've been really working on my anxiety lately', etc. This TV channel basically consists of stories we narrate about who we and others are.

Ram Dass points out that there are actually many more channels available to us, but we don't know how to adjust our antennas to receive them. This is precisely where the fear of death comes in. As both channels one and two shut off when we die – we die as bodies and embodied personalities – if we are tuned into these channels only, death will appear to be a destruction and end, and the prospect of it will cause some understandable concern and anxiety. However, if we tune in to the channel of the soul, which exists beyond time and space, we are able to watch the drama of life and death unfold with significantly more equanimity, as we are seeing from the perspective of that which continues throughout the entire process of birth, life, death and what follows.[381]

If death is not what it appears to be, and, as a soul, we continue to exist after it takes place, what is the state of affairs like after our so-called death? Ibn 'Arabi's basic take on this is that *the next life is an externalization of your soul*. Your inner motivations, intentions and states – the qualities of soul you've cultivated while embodied – are revealed and externalized in the realm your consciousness finds itself in following separation from the body. This notion is drawn from the Qur'an, which suggests that the afterlife is one where *the hidden secrets are made manifest and tested* (Q 86:9). Ibn 'Arabi sums this up concisely in stating: 'the nonmanifest dimension of the human being in this world is the manifest dimension in the next world.'[382] So, if one has cultivated an interiority of self that is oriented toward things like enviously plotting against 'those people who don't deserve what they have', bitterly fomenting discord, fueling hatred, lashing out in anger and breaking hearts, the soul becomes a nexus of malice, that, following the death of the body, is externalized in a realm of tormented images

---

381 Ram Dass, as quoted in the documentary *Becoming Nobody*, directed by Jamie Catto (2019).
382 Ibn 'Arabi, *Fut*.III.441. As quoted in Chittick, *Imaginal Worlds*, p.107.

and sensations. In contrast, if one has cultivated a soul of care and compassion, generosity and openness, this loving soul is externalized after death in a realm of luminous beauty, joy and meaning.

The Qur'an communicates the nature of these realms vividly, using the imagery of fire and torment for hell, and gardens, rivers and companionship for heaven. Historically, there has been some disagreement among Sufis and other Muslim interpreters, over just how literally to take these descriptions. Perhaps the most famous of Muslim philosophers was Ibn Sina (d.1037), or Avicenna as he was known in Latin Europe, and he argued that the fully realized soul (*nafs kamila*) was no longer concerned with sensory matters, and when the body dies, such a soul exists in true felicity in a realm of pure intelligibility, contemplating the One.[383] For those souls that remain unperfected, however, Ibn Sina argued that the faculty of imagination within the soul (a faculty that we will discuss at greater length in the next chapter), allows people to experience a sort of imaginary (but not unreal) realm of torment or joy, based upon the nature of their own soul.[384] Although most Sufis would not have followed Ibn Sina in interpreting the afterlife in such a way, there are some interesting exceptions: Badr al-Din of Simawna (d.1420), for example, was an Ottoman scholar and Sufi, and he totally rejected a literal understanding of the hereafter, flatly declaring there to be no fires or gardens, asserting rather that what follows after death is beyond space, time and material images, being the realm of spirit surpassing our earth-based abilities of conception.[385]

Similarly, Hazrat Inayat Khan refused to say, definitively, much about the afterlife, seemingly accepting notions of reincarnation at times and rejecting them at others. Finally, when pressed by his students on the question, he suggested that he answered 'yes' at times and 'no' at times, based upon the needs of the person who asked him the question. He elaborated that there is no use holding a rigid belief about the afterlife, as it concerns 'things of the finest nature which

---

383 L.W. C. van Lit, *The World of Image in Islamic Philosophy: Ibn Sina, Suhrawardi, Shahrazuri, and Beyond* (Edinburgh, 2017), p.22.

384 Ibid., p.25.

385 Tosun Bayrak, *Inspirations on the Path of Blame: Shaikh Badruddin of Simawna* (Putney, VT, 1993), pp.77–82.

words cannot explain', and further said that trying to describe the hereafter is like attempting to 'photograph the spirit'. In contrast, he suggested to his students that they have the patience to practice the path sufficiently so that they can realize for themselves what life after death consists of, and until they do, to realize that doctrines are a sort of temporary substitute, mere 'pills given to ill people for their cure'.[386] More recently, Nur al-Jerrahi described the Qur'anic imagery of paradise somewhat metaphorically as follows:

> The abundant fruits of Paradise are simply love. The rivers of Paradise – clear waters of awareness, pure milk of knowledge, strong wine of ecstasy, and clarified honey of mystic union – are rivers only of love. The companions of Paradise are companions of love. The perpetual springtime shade of Paradise is the incomparable refreshment of love. The goblets of Paradise are composed of the crystal of peaceful love and the silver of brilliantly flashing love in harmonious conjunction.[387]

Correspondingly if heaven is simply love manifest, we might understand hell as the manifestation of love's lack, or perhaps opposition to it. In contrast to these more interpretive understandings of the hereafter, Ibn 'Arabi assumes as fact the accounts of the afterlife found in the Qur'an and hadith, on the death, resurrection and judgment of human beings, and their end in a place of bliss (*jannah* or paradise) or torment (*jahanam* or hell), an end determined by the kinds of lives they lived and deeds they did. In fact, he explicitly rejects any rationalistic interpretation or abstraction of the scriptural accounts of the afterlife.[388] However, he (controversially for some Muslim theologians) suggests that, unlike the joys of paradise, the torments of hell do not last forever. This is connected with his view that, as we discussed in the third chapter on Shu'ayb, all beliefs are, from at least one perspective, right:

---

[386] Hazrat Inayat Khan, *Social Gathekas*, '9. Reincarnation' (2021), https://www.hazrat-inayat-khan.org (accessed March 7, 2023).
[387] Lex Hixon, *Atom from the Sun of Knowledge* (Westport, CT, 1993), p.168.
[388] Chittick, *Imaginal Worlds*, pp.97–8.

There is nothing but beliefs, and all are correct, and the correct one is rewarded, and the one rewarded is happy, and the happy one is satisfied because of it, though he may suffer for a time in the Abode of the Hereafter.[389]

Although you may live in an ignorant, misguided and even egregiously harmful way, such that your state after death is unpleasant, the realm of suffering you've essentially created for yourself, the house of pain you've built brick by brick, will at some point come to an end and collapse, and you will find happiness and satisfaction beyond its walls. In this chapter on Jonah Ibn 'Arabi writes that the final end of those in the hell 'is enjoyment, but enjoyment in the fire.'[390] He cleverly notes that the Qur'an describes the fire as eternal, but not the punishment therein. After those in hell have fulfilled their obligations there, have paid their dues and had their malice burned away, the fire calms and becomes for them a realm of comfort and joy. This perspective of Ibn 'Arabi's, though surprising to hear for many Muslims (and probably for many Christians as well, who might similarly believe in an eternal damnation), is in fact deeply rooted in Islamic text and cosmology.[391]

For instance, it is a well-established principle within the Islamic tradition that God's mercy is greater than His wrath. In fact, there is a famous hadith, where the Prophet Muhammad shared that, upon completing creation, God inscribed his Throne with, 'My Mercy is Greater Than My Wrath' – a symbolic way of affirming just how central mercy is to God's nature.[392] Ibn 'Arabi further clarifies that, symbolically speaking, the Throne of God (*'arsh*), which exists above all creation, is pure mercy.[393] It is only when we descend to a lower

---

389 Ibn 'Arabi, *Fusus*, p.97.

390 Ibid., p.295.

391 Ibn 'Arabi's approach here may have been influenced by one of his first masters in Seville, Abu Ja'far al-'Uraybi, who said, 'God has told me that in every soul weighed in the balance on the Last Day there is something worth saving from the fire.' R. W. J. Austin, *Sufis of Andalusia: The Ruh al-Quds and al-Durrat al-Fakhirah* (Chisholme House, 2002 [1971]), p.64.

392 *Sahih al-Bukhari*, 7453.

393 For Ibn 'Arabi, mercy or *rahma* is not simply an orientation toward compassion, care and love, but, quintessentially for God, it is 'primarily the act of making things exist'. Izutsu, *Sufism and Taoism*, p.116.

level of existence, represented by God's Footstool (*kursi*), which is said to encompass the heavens and the earth, that we first find wrath.

God's two feet rest upon this Footstool, one foot consisting of pure mercy, and the other consisting of mercy mixed with wrath.[394] Ibn 'Arabi notes that wrath is not an *essential* quality of God's, but is simply the result of the evil wrought by creatures: 'Were it not for the creatures, the Real would not have become wrathful.'[395] That foot with a bit of wrath only has this wrath in it due to the evil wrought by human hands and hearts. In contrast, mercy is inherent to the very nature of God.[396] The Sovereign Good, the Eternal Beauty, is just total mercy and love. Hence whoever is close to God encounters only compassion, gentleness and bliss. It is only when one exists a great distance from the Source that experiences of wrath occur. We may think of this as something like, being in the center of the wheel of life, one experiences perfect stillness and peace, and yet if we gravitate to its outer most circumference, a kind of motion sickness occurs. Even when beings do experience wrath, it is not so much a result of divine anger as it is the result of their own non-receptivity to God's ever-emanating love and mercy. One of Ibn 'Arabi's commentators, al-Qashani, explains this as follows:

---

394 Chittick, *Imaginal Worlds*, p.111.

395 Ibn 'Arabi, *Fut*.III.386. As quoted in Chittick, *Imaginal Worlds*, p.111.

396 It is worth pointing out here that Ibn 'Arabi did not even remotely think of God as a 'big guy in the sky' sitting on an actual chair with giant feet. The previous discussions of his ontological understanding of deity should sufficiently rule that out. However, he makes this point explicit in his *Book of the Quintessence of What is Indispensable for the Spiritual Seeker* (translated by James Morris), https://ibnarabisociety.org/wp-content/uploads/PDFs/MorrisSpiritual-Practice.pdf (accessed July 21, 2021):
As for realizing His transcendence (of any likeness to creation), which is urgent for you because of the literalist (*zahiri*) anthropomorphists and 'corporealists' in this age, just hold to His saying: There is no thing like Him/like His Likeness (42:11), and that is sufficient for you: whatever description (of God) contradicts this verse is to be rejected, and do not add to or go beyond this 'homeland'. This is why it has come down in the tradition (of the Prophet, his saying): 'God was, and there was no thing with Him' – may God be far exalted above what the wrongdoers/darkeners say! So every (scriptural) verse or hadith which makes us imagine a likening (of God to the creatures), whether that expression has come in the language of the Arabs, or in the language of anyone else upon whom God has sent down some revelation or information, you must simply have faith in it to the extent of what God has taught and sent down through that – but not like those who falsely imagine something (about God) and then ascribe their 'knowledge' of that (imagination) to God.

The absence of receptivity in some of the things for Mercy entails the non-appearance of Mercy (in those things), whether in this world or the Hereafter. And the fact that Divine Mercy is prevented from overflowing into a thing of this kind because of its non-receptivity is called Wrath in relation to that particular thing.[397]

This means for Ibn 'Arabi that mercy and love are absolute and eternal, but wrath is incidental and temporal: pure, absolute or perpetual wrath is totally impossible. In *The Meccan Revelations* Ibn 'Arabi explains why this is so:

God made [human] hearts receptacles for the real and the unreal, faith and unbelief, knowledge and ignorance. The eventual outcome of unreality, unbelief, and ignorance will be dissolution and disappearance, because these are properties that have no entity in *wujud*. They are a nonexistence that has a manifest property and a known form. This property and form seek an existential something by which they can be supported, but they do not find it, so they dissolve and become nothing. Hence the final end of all will be felicity.[398]

Alongside the fact that negativity lacks any grounding in Being and hence cannot last, Ibn 'Arabi further cites the Qur'an's (Q 78:26) affirmation that divine punishment is always 'an appropriate recompense', so 'a limited sin cannot warrant an unlimited punishment'.[399] Hell then is a place in which those who have cultivated a soul of malice, deception and hatred are purified of these until only their pure, original nature (*fitra*) remains, after which they are restored to the natural felicity of their being, to the love that is their genuine core. To believe in eternal punishment then is to totally misunderstand the nature of God and our world (which of course for Ibn 'Arabi are, at the deepest level, one and the same). In *The Meccan Revelations* Ibn 'Arabi describes meeting Adam in the realm of spiritual forms. Adam

---

397 Izutsu, *Sufism and Taoism*, p.117.
398 Ibn 'Arabi, *Fut*.III.417. As quoted in Chittick, *Imaginal Worlds*, p.113 (with slight modification).
399 Ibid.

informs him that if God's anger was continuous then suffering would be, but this is not the case:

> However, it is felicity that continues forever, even though the dwellings are different. God has placed in each abode (of Heaven and Hell) that which constitutes the pleasure and enjoyment of the people who live there, and that is why both abodes must necessarily be inhabited.[400]

Ibn 'Arabi elaborates on how exactly it is that even hell can become pleasant, considering its unimaginably unpleasant nature. He notes that our experience of really any conceivable realm is deeply conditioned by our own perspective, and hence, the same situation can be experienced in various ways, even hell notwithstanding. The scriptural precedent for this is found in the Qur'anic narrative of Abraham, where the idolators persecute him and attempt to execute him by burning him alive. However, God protects Abraham, and he experiences the fire not as a burning torment but rather as *peace and coolness* (Q 21:69). From the perspective of the bystanders watching Abraham, the fire is exceedingly hot. However, from his perspective, the fire feels like a comfortable evening breeze. This means that, according to Ibn 'Arabi *a single thing is varied in the eyes of its observers.*[401] This is of course all too obvious in more pedestrian ways in our everyday lives, which provide endless examples of a single situation experienced differently. That medium-rare ribeye steak just off the grill causes a meat eater to experience a sort of anticipatory joy, while their vegan companion experiences repulsion and perhaps nausea: the steak can be experienced as a little piece of heaven or hell, though it remains the same object regardless of one's perspective on it.

This simultaneous a) singularity of situation and b) diversity of experience of said situation, is fundamental to the world, a world that for Ibn 'Arabi is nothing else but God's eternal self-disclosure. Although God is One, His self-disclosure becomes multiple through the

---

400 Stephen Hirtenstein, 'Lunar View, Air-glow Blue: Ibn 'Arabi's Conversations with the Prophet Adam', *Journal of the Muhyiddin Ibn 'Arabi Society*, 16 (1994), 62.

401 Ibn 'Arabi, *Fusus*, p.157.

experience of observers based upon the diversity of their perspectives. As this is the nature of reality in general, it follows that, in whatever corner of the universe you happen to find yourself, in whatever state, mood, world or condition, among the myriad realms that beings may end up, that realm can be experienced in radically different ways.

As we will see in the sixth chapter of this book, on Moses, the various realms of manifestation we may encounter are themselves rooted in love, and hence love is the ultimate reality of them all. As Meena Sharify-Funk shared with me, Abdul Aziz Said liked to say that 'every moment of fear has the potential to be turned into a moment of love', and this is because love is real, or is a quality of real *wujud*, whereas fear is not. Ibn 'Arabi concludes this chapter by affirming that if death truly was a total destruction and final end of the human being, then God 'would neither bring about the death of anyone nor command their execution'.[402] The fundamentally benevolent nature of God (and, as a result, our universe) precludes a nihilistic destruction of the human being. Death is a return to the Real, and hence, ultimately, is not a destruction or loss but rather a change of state. The dreamer simply awakens and finds that what is hidden has become manifest.

---

402 Ibid., pp.157–8.

5

What do you Really Know? The Transcendent Wisdom of Elijah–Enoch

And tell me about Hermes: is he Enoch?[403]

The Ancient Roots of Transcendent Wisdom

In this chapter we explore one of life's most basic questions, namely: *What do we really know*? What kinds of knowledge are there? What *can* we know? In his chapter on Elijah in the *Gemstones*, Ibn 'Arabi considers some of the varieties of knowledge we *may* be able to access through our human form – some rather obvious, and some distinctly less so. To explore the spectrum of knowledge that Ibn 'Arabi points to, we will end up taking a proverbial 'long and winding road', through various centuries, cultures and planes of reality. He starts us off on this journey with a rather strange, enigmatic statement: 'Elijah is Enoch, a prophet before Noah. God raised him to a high station. He lives in the heart of the celestial spheres, within the sphere of the sun.'[404]

What can this possibly mean? How is Elijah Enoch? And what does it mean to live in the sun? The answers will require the intellectual equivalent of an archeological excavation, delving into an underground history of immortals, giants and angels, with roots in the ancient Near East and influence on the foundation of the modern West. Although little known outside of scholarly circles today, this stream

---

[403] Al-Jahiz (d.868), *Kitab al-taribi' wa'l-tadwir*. As quoted in John C. Reeves and Annette Yoshiko Reed, *Enoch from Antiquity to the Middle Ages, Volume 1: Sources from Judaism, Christianity, and Islam* (New York, 2018), p.275.
[404] Ibn 'Arabi, *Fusus*, p.170.

of esoterica, traced back to ancient centers of civilization like Egypt and Mesopotamia, would prove to have immense influence on later Jewish, Christian and Islamic traditions, and even play an important role in the Renaissance. Ibn 'Arabi's opening statement here can only be made sense of in light of this fascinating subterranean tradition.

To begin, the Biblical prophet popularly known as Elijah in English, is actually Eliyyahu[405] in Hebrew, which literally means 'Yahweh is my God'.[406] Eliyyahu was later known as Elias in Greek, and perhaps that is why we find him named Ilyas in the Qur'an. In Islam's sacred text he is described as a messenger and servant of God, sent to call his people away from worshipping the idol Baal (Q 37:123-32). In the Bible (1 Kings 17-19 and 2 Kings 1-2), his story is narrated at greater length, with God sending Elijah to confront Israel's wayward king Ahab, who has set up an alter to Baal in the Temple.

In the Biblical narrative, Elijah warns Ahab that there will be no rain in the land until he says otherwise, earning the king's fury. To escape certain death, Elijah takes off and hides in a ravine, where the local ravens bring him food in the mornings and evenings. He later stays with a widow, miraculously provides her with food and successfully calls upon God to restore her son to life after his death. Later, in a showdown on Mount Carmel with Ahab and the prophets of Baal, Elijah calls down the fire of God upon his altar, proving God's power over Baal, whose priests fail to get any fiery response from their deity. Finally, he is taken up to God in a whirlwind, without dying, and is hence considered to be an immortal. Although Elijah is clearly very much human, he also has characteristics we would normally associate with divinity: miraculous powers, the ability to raise the dead to life and immortality.

Elijah's immortality connects him with Enoch, who is the first Biblical figure that God took to Himself: the first immortal. Within the Islamic tradition, Enoch and Elijah are *one immortal being*, but a being whom God gave two forms: first as Enoch before the great Flood,

---

405 This is also transliterated as 'Eliahu' and 'Eliyahu'.
406 Diarmaid MacCulloch, *Christianity: The First Three Thousand Years* (New York, 2010), p.58.

and second, as Elijah descending to earth much later.[407] Although we first find the story of Enoch in the Hebrew Torah, it actually says very little about him. He is briefly accounted for in Genesis 5:18–24, as the seventh in the line of Adam, making him Noah's great-great-grandfather. These verses in Genesis tell us only that Enoch 'walked with God', that he lived 365 years (the same number as the days of the solar calendar) and that 'God took him away'. As we will see in what follows, Enoch's ancientness, as a sage before the Great Flood, quite naturally lends itself to his association with what Renaissance thinkers called the *Prisca Theologica,* humanity's original religion, a holistic system of knowledge covering the entire spectrum of science, philosophy and spirituality, which would later be known as the perennial philosophy.

Muslims believed quite early on that Enoch is also mentioned in the Qur'an, though he is not visibly named therein. The Qur'an does, however, twice refer to a prophet named *Idris*, describing him as one who was raised to a 'high' or 'sublime' place, and who was sincere, righteous and patient (19:56–7 and 21:85–6). Although the exact origins of the name Idris are unknown, Muslims associated Idris with the biblical Enoch within about a hundred years of the Prophet Muhammad's death.[408] The influential commentator on the Qur'an, Muqatil bin Sulayman (d.767), states that Idris was Noah's great-grandfather and that his name was Enoch, while the famous author of the Prophet Muhammad's biography, Ibn Hisham (d.833), simply affirms that Idris is Enoch 'according to what they claim'.[409] As these early authorities carry significant weight in the Islamic tradition, their assertion of Idris's identity as Enoch has been largely accepted by Muslims of later generations. It is also worth pointing out that, by the time of Islam's rise in the seventh century, Enoch was already a very well-known figure in the Near East.

---

407 In the *Sahih al-Bukhari* hadith collection, it is reported that the Prophet Muhammad's close companions Ibn Mas'ud and Ibn 'Abbas 'said that Ilyas was Idris' (4/335). Also see Ali Hussain, 'Jesus and Enoch in the *Barzakh* of Muhyi al-Din Ibn al-'Arabi', *Journal of the Muhyiddin Ibn 'Arabi Society*, 60 (2016), 59 for more on Ibn 'Arabi's understanding of their conjunction.

408 Reeves and Reed, *Enoch from Antiquity to the Middle Ages*, pp.284–5.

409 Ibid.

Considering the briefness of his description in the Bible, Enoch's fame may come as a bit of a surprise. Nevertheless, by the Hellenistic period he had become a full-blown 'cultural hero'.[410] Immensely popular, Enoch was venerated in antiquity as humanity's first great teacher, an ancient sage to whom knowledge of mathematics, medicine and magic can be traced. He is the subject of the two oldest Jewish texts outside of the Hebrew Bible, *The Book of the Watchers* and the *Astronomical Book*.[411] These texts would become part of the most famous of apocryphal books: *1 Enoch* or simply the *Book of Enoch*.[412]

The first Christians quite liked the *Book of Enoch*, and early Church authorities including Irenaeus (d.200), Tertullian (d.220) and Origen (d.253) considered it to be authentic. However, Augustine (d.430) denounced the text as 'too ancient to be trusted', which appears to have shut down any possibility of its acceptance in the later Western Church.[413] Various Jewish authorities shared Augustine's suspicion and discouraged engagement with them. Despite these condemnations, Enochian materials remained popular, 'travelling across creedal and community boundaries in the Near East and beyond'.[414] The *Book of Enoch*, for example, survived in Africa and is included as a part of the Bible of the Ethiopian Orthodox Church. Christian monks and scribes in the Middle East more broadly continued to engage with Enochian texts throughout the medieval period. Although long available only in Ethiopic and Greek, multiple copies of the original Aramaic version of the *Book of Enoch* were found among the Dead Sea Scrolls, confirming both the text's antiquity and popularity during the Second Temple period.

The text claims to record Enoch's own words, a recounting of what he saw in his visionary journey across the ends of the earth

---

410 Ibid., p.53.

411 Although copies of these texts can be traced to the second century BCE, they were likely composed much earlier.

412 R. E. Kaske, 'Beowulf and the Book of Enoch', *Speculum: A Journal of Medieval Studies*, 3 (1971), 422.

413 Helge S. Kvanvig, *Primeval History: Babylonian, Biblical, and Enochic* (Leiden, 2011), pp.319-20.

414 Reeves and Reed, *Enoch from Antiquity to the Middle Ages*, p.6.

and throughout the entire cosmos, making him a repository of rare knowledge beyond the ken of those less cosmically well-traveled.[415] Enoch describes a group of angels tasked with overseeing the universe, known as 'the Watchers'. These angels were struck by the beauty of the first human women, and took some as lovers. They ended up sharing with their human lovers forbidden secrets regarding the production of magic and jewelry. The resulting angel-human offspring were giants (the Nephilim of Genesis 6:1–2), that then roamed about the earth, with appetites commensurate with their size. In reproducing with humans, the angels violated the divine order, and their giant, hungry children wreaked havoc on the earth, as one could imagine they would. When humans complained to God about this, He decided to wipe the slate clean in a great flood destroying the giants and their human allies, with only Noah and his family surviving.[416]

Another early Hebrew text on Enoch is the *Book of Jubilees*, which was also considered to be apocryphal by most Jewish and Christian authorities, though it was, like the *Book of Enoch*, accepted as part of the Ethiopian Orthodox Bible. *Jubilees* was believed to have been dictated to Moses by the 'Angel of the Presence' during his 40-day stay on Sinai, an angel that some would later associate with Metatron, whom we will discuss shortly. *Jubilees* characterizes Enoch as a sort of primordial purveyor of knowledge. He is the first human to learn to write, and to establish a calendar based on the movement of the sun, moon and stars.[417] Interestingly, we also find early commentaries on the Qur'an describing Idris/Enoch as the first writer, the first to have knowledge of astronomy and astrology (*'ilm al-nujum*), medicine and mathematics, and even the first to have made sewn clothing.[418] As the Enochian tradition grew in antiquity, we find him playing an outsized role in the history of knowledge, as humanity's original scribe, astrologer, mathematician, doctor and even tailor – in all cases an ancient repository of science, craft and learning. It is worth noting

---

415 Ibid., p.1.
416 Kvanvig, *Primeval History*, pp.324–5.
417 Ibid., pp.56–7.
418 *The Study Qur'an*, p.779.

that the name Idris is itself an intensive form of the Arabic root *da-ra-sa* meaning to study or learn.

Alongside the *Book of Enoch* (*1 Enoch*), two further books on Enoch were composed in the centuries following. *2 Enoch* dates from the first century CE, and has only survived in old Slavonic and Coptic translations. It describes Enoch's ascent through the many heavens above the earth. In the first heaven he is shown the 200 angels who govern the stars, and above them he finds realms of fiery torment for those who reject God's commandments and verdant paradise for the righteous who keep them. In the fourth heaven he is shown the realm of the sun, in the fifth he sees fallen angels and in the sixth Enoch encounters the Archangels who oversee the divine order and maintain cosmic harmony. He eventually reaches the Throne of God, where he loses consciousness. He is aided by the archangels Gabriel and Michael, and then God assigns an angel to initiate Enoch into the hidden knowledge of the celestial archive.[419]

With Enoch's ascent through the heavens we have a wonderful symbolic illustration of the levels of knowledge beyond those most readily available to us in our earthly existence. A heavenly ascent acutely points to kinds of knowledge that go *far* beyond what we are accustomed to in our embodied existence here on earth. Interestingly, Islamic traditions that describe the Prophet Muhammad's (quite similar) ascent (*isra'*) through the heavens suggest that he encountered Enoch in the fourth heaven,[420] and hence Ibn 'Arabi understands the fourth heaven, of the sun, to be where Enoch resides. The Sun is also the center of the solar system, around which the planets revolve, and hence Enoch residing there conveys his elevated cosmic status, a sort of pole of knowledge and enlightenment around which the other spheres revolve.

If Enoch's ascent through the heavens and angelic initiation into celestial mysteries seem fantastical, perhaps even more so is the claim

---

419 For bibliographic information on 2 Enoch, and for English and Latin translations of the text (2009), see: https://www.marquette.edu/maqom/2enoch.html (accessed November 3, 2023).

420 See *Sahih Muslim* 162a: https://sunnah.com/muslim:162a (accessed November 3, 2023).

in *3 Enoch* that Enoch was eventually transformed into Metatron, 'the most important of postbiblical Jewish angels'.[421] In various Jewish traditions, Metatron is something like the head of the angels, with his own throne akin to God's. He is described as God's own delegate, fulfilling a 'mediating, prime-ministerial function'.[422] He oversees God's kingdom and is even assigned 70 angels to help him manage the 70 nations of the earth. Metatron blurs every border of being, having begun as the human prophet Enoch, become the highest of angels and even at times described as a 'lesser YHWH' or 'lesser God'. He is also called the 'Prince of the Divine Presence', the 'Prince of the World', the 'Prince of the Torah', 'the great scribe' and more enigmatically, simply the 'Youth'.[423] Perhaps as a result of his eminent position in the heavenly hierarchy, Metatron would become important in Jewish and Muslim traditions of magic. Jewish magicians called upon Metatron to facilitate the memorization and understanding of the Torah, and later Muslim magicians would call upon him as well, seeing Metatron or *Mitatrush* as the 'chief of the angels' much like their Jewish counterparts.[424]

Scholars suggest that this whole Enochian tradition that developed in antiquity has even *more* ancient origins in Mesopotamia, particularly with the tradition surrounding pre-Flood king Enmeduranki. There are some striking parallels here. First, Enmeduranki is the seventh king, and Enoch is the seventh in the line of Adam. Second, Enmedruanki is king of Sippar, city of the Sun god, while Enoch is associated with the solar calendar in the Bible, with his 365 year life span (and of course we see Ibn 'Arabi situating Enoch in the sphere of the sun).[425] More substantively, their roles are closely aligned: Like Enoch, Enmeduranki undergoes a heavenly ascension, where he is initiated into various forms of secret knowledge. Also, like Enoch, he experiences a

---

421 Reeves and Reed, *Enoch from Antiquity to the Middle Ages*, p.255.
422 Steven M. Wasserstrom, *Between Muslim and Jew: The Problem of Symbiosis under Early Islam* (Princeton, NJ, 1995), p.188.
423 Andrei A. Orlov, *The Enoch-Metatron Tradition* (Tübingen, 2005), p.89.
424 Wasserstrom, *Between Muslim and Jew*, p.198.
425 Orlov, *The Enoch-Metatron Tradition*, pp.22–38.

'metamorphosis into a new angelic or semi-divine body'.[426] Now as an immortal, Enmeduranki shares this knowledge of hidden things with humans. Enmeduranki and Enoch are both mediators between the celestial and terrestrial realms; having been initiated into mysteries by gods or angels, they are now tasked with recording this knowledge (in a shared scribal role) and transmitting it to humans.

Despite remaining unsanctioned by the Western Church, Enochian lore would go on to have a wide-ranging influence, informing early medieval traditions ranging from Anglo-Saxon literature in the British Isles to Ethiopian Christianity in East Africa. The legends of Enoch would shape later Jewish mysticism or Kabbalah, and we even find Enoch emerging as a key figure in Renaissance-era traditions of magic. John Dee (d.1609), for example, was Queen Elizabeth I's (d.1603) court astronomer and a well-known mathematician and natural scientist. (Apparently even Ivan the Terrible (d.1584) sought to entice Dee to join his court in Moscow, though he remained in England.) Dee was said to possess 'Elizabethan England's Greatest Library'.[427] He was also an alchemist and magician. With his long white beard, vast library and magical laboratories, Dee would become the archetype for more recent, pop-culture portrayals of wizards, including J. K. Rowling's Albus Dumbledore of *Harry Potter* fame.

Dee drew upon the *Book of Enoch* to develop a means of contacting angels, in a system generally known as Enochian magic, which for him was an integral aspect of a universal knowledge that encompassed all forms of understanding, ranging from the natural to the supernatural. Although we tend to think of things like science, on the one hand, and magic, on the other, as two *very* different things, for Dee, science and magic existed along a shared spectrum, within a singular paradigm that encompassed both internal and external realities, sense and spirit. He ambitiously sought to express the core principles underlying this universal paradigm in his fascinating book *Monas Hieroglyphica*

---

426 Michael Muhammad Knight, *Magic in Islam* (New York, 2016), p.117.
427 Nicholas Goodrick-Clarke, *The Western Esoteric Traditions: A Historical Introduction* (New York, 2008), p.60.

(1564), or *The Hieroglyphic Monad* (what a title!).[428] In fact, the Oxford Science Museum still displays Dee's Enochian tablet, as representing the genesis of British science.[429] Islamic studies scholar and author Michael Muhamad Knight aptly summarizes this fantastically wide-ranging Enochian influence:

> As textual resources and traditions flowed between Persia, Mesopotamia, Egypt, Palestine, Greece, and Rome, Enoch traveled between various characters, literatures, and meanings. At whatever arbitrary border divides two cultures or bodies of knowledge, we can often find an Enoch-shaped hole in the fence.[430]

Is Hermes Enoch?

If we combine the blurring of divine–angel–human boundaries in the stories of Enoch, with his role as a mediating scribe between heaven and earth, we find ourselves with someone very much resembling Hermes Trismegistus, easily one of history's most mysterious figures. As scholar of Islamic thought John Walbridge aptly (and humorously) observes, 'the problem of Hermes Trismegistus is a scholarly swamp of substantial acreage, muddiness, and gloom'.[431] Regarding al-Jahiz's question at the beginning of this chapter, as to whether Hermes is Enoch, Muslims tended to answer '*yes*', though the association of Enoch with Hermes is much older, and can be traced back at least as far as the fifth century BCE. [432]

In the Hellenistic period Hermes was venerated (much like Enoch) as humanity's most ancient repository of wisdom, the 'ancestor of the

---

428 For the original Latin version of Dee's Moas Hieroglyphica (1564), see: http://ldysinger.stjohnsem.edu/@texts2/1537_john-dee/monad/monad.htm (accessed February 13, 2023).
429 Vladimir Vladimirovich Weidemann, 'Geopolitics and John Dee', *E-International Relations*, April 18, 2020, https://www.e-ir.info/2020/04/18/geopolitics-and-john-dee/ (accessed February 13, 2023).
430 Knight, *Magic in Islam*, p.117.
431 John Walbridge, *The Wisdom of the Mystic East: Suhrawardi and Platonic Orientalism* (Albany, NY, 2000), p.17.
432 Reeves and Reed, *Enoch from Antiquity to the Middle Ages*, pp.270–1.

Sages', 'the scribe of the gods' and 'the prophet of the philosophers'.[433] Works attributed to him would go on to have a huge influence on Jewish, Christian and Islamic traditions, among others. Egyptologist Jan Assman even makes a case that Hermes should be placed next to Moses and Plato as one of the three pillars of Western thought.[434] If a) Western religion is rooted in the Hebrew prophetic tradition (paradigmatically represented by Moses) and b) Western philosophy goes back to the Greeks (Alfred North Whitehead famously described the European philosophical tradition as 'a series of footnotes to Plato') then c) Western mysticism and magic can be traced back to Egypt, and particularly to Hermes.[435]

Hermes is, of course, far less well-known than either Moses or Plato, but it seems he would have wanted it that way. The Hermetic tradition is characterized not only by its antiquity, but also by its legendary secrecy. Hence our idiomatic use of 'Hermetic' in saying that something is 'hermetically sealed', locked in secrecy except for those initiated and given the necessary keys to unlock what is hidden. This is also why Hermes has long been associated with symbols and hieroglyphs, as his teachings were thought unfit for the uninitiated, and hence encrypted in a symbolic language to protect them from those who would misunderstand, abuse, or be damaged by them.

To begin to understand Hermes, we need to go back to Alexandria, about two thousand years ago. When Alexander the Great founded the city following his conquest of Egypt in 332 BCE, he opened up the Graeco-Roman world to ancient Egyptian mysticism and magic.[436] The Hellenistic Greeks were understandably enchanted with Egypt, with its rich history going back millennia. When Greek historian Hecataeus (d.476 BCE) made the mistake of bragging to Egyptian priests

---

[433] Corbin, *Alone with the Alone*, p.36.

[434] Jan Assman, 'Foreword', in Florian Ebeling, *The Secret History of Hermes Trismegistus: Hermeticism from Ancient to Modern Times*, translated by David Lorton (Ithaca, NY, 2005), p.vii.

[435] We could and probably should include Islam here as a Western religion (at least in terms of what Assman describes above), and we can accurately, I think, conceive of Sufi philosophy as a kind of Islamic synthesis of these three pillars: the prophetic, philosophical and mystical.

[436] Nicholas Goodrick-Clarke, *The Western Esoteric Traditions: A Historical Introduction* (New York, 2008), p.16.

that he could trace his lineage back through 16 generations, they responded with one of Antiquity's greatest 'mic drops,' and showed him family trees that went back 345 generations.[437] Ancientness is a sort of currency, and the Greeks tended to respect Egyptian religion as representing something closer to the holistic wisdom of early humanity.

Emerging out of this Greek fascination with Egyptian religion was the *Hermetica* or *Corpus Hermeticum,* a collection of Greek texts likely produced by a group of Egyptian priests, transmitting much older Egyptian teachings on the nature of the soul, the cosmos and God, said to unveil 'the secrets of creation' and 'the hidden workings of the universe'.[438] Hermetic texts generally take the form of dialogs between Egyptian gods like Tat, Ammon and Asclepius, and their teacher Thoth, 'one of the most important and ancient gods of Egypt'.[439] Thoth's original Egyptian name was Djehuty, represented as an ibis-headed man. Knight offers a helpful summary of Thoth's character:

> Having invented hieroglyphics, Thoth was a god of writing and education, and was venerated as a patron god for various sciences. He served as the scribe of the gods, author of priestly ritual, and an attendant of Osiris. For his privileged access to the transcendent knowledge of the gods and association with human education and technology, Thoth was seen as a mediator between divine and human realm, a point of contact through whom humans could potentially obtain divine secrets.[440]

In the *Hermetica* Thoth/Djehuty is given the Greek name Hermes, with Trismegistus or 'thrice greatest' added as Thoth was also known by this title. 'Trismegistus' may have further functioned to distinguish him from the Greek Hermes, who was the mischievous messenger of the gods.[441] However, Egyptologist Florian Ebeling suggests instead that

---

437 Knight, *Magic in Islam*, p.109.
438 Kevin van Bladel, *The Arabic Hermes: From Pagan Sage to Prophet of Science* (New York, 2009), p.3.
439 Ebeling, *The Secret History of Hermes Trismegistus,* p.3.
440 Knight, *Magic in Islam*, p.110.
441 Bladel, *The Arabic Hermes*, p.4.

Hermes Trismegistus 'arose from a merging of Thoth and Hermes'.[442] The boundaries defining Hermes were fuzzy quite early on, and he was seen to take on several forms, divine and human, all for the purposes of preserving and transmitting ancient wisdom. Hermes has been depicted as a god, sage and prophet, making him equally comfortable in pagan and prophetic traditions alike.

Coming out of Hellenistic Egypt, the *Hermetica* proved enormously influential far beyond their place of origin, being studied and transmitted by pretty much everyone in the larger Mediterranean and Middle Eastern regions, including pagan Greek philosophers, Christian priests and Zoroastrian scholars.[443] Considering the notable proliferation of Hermetic works, it makes sense that as early as the eighth century Arabic scientific works cite Hermes as an authority, and by the ninth century he is considered to be an ancient prophet close to humanity's origin, 'a primordial Egyptian sage, who founded human religion before the Flood', and whose teachings were passed down through later philosophers like Pythagoras and Plato. An early Islamic astrologer, Abu Ma'shar al-Balkhi (d.886), wrote the most influential account of Hermes, suggesting there were actually many Hermai, with three being the most important: 1) the first Hermes was Enoch, before the Flood, originator of astrology, poetry, medicine and the builder of the great pyramids; 2) the second Hermes lived much later in Babylon, reviving the knowledge lost in the great Flood, teacher of Pythagoras; 3) while the third traveled widely, taught alchemy and built smaller pyramids in Egypt.[444]

In the twelfth century, we even encounter what might be called a 'Hermetic Sufism',[445] founded by Shihab al-Din Suhrawardi (d.1191). Hailing from northwestern Iran, Suhrawardi came to Aleppo as a wandering dervish, with his ragged appearance leading to the impression that he was more of a donkey driver than a philosopher.[446]

---

442 Ebeling, *The Secret History of Hermes Trismegistus*, p.6.
443 Bladel, *The Arabic Hermes*, p.13.
444 Walbridge, *The Wisdom of the Mystic East*, pp.21-2.
445 Knight, *Magic in Islam*, p.129.
446 John Walbridge and Hossein Ziai, 'Translators' Introduction', in Suhrawardi, *The Philosophy of Illumination*, translated by John Walbridge and Hossein Ziai (Provo, UT, 1999), p.xv.

However his unmistakable brilliance soon drew a circle of devoted students. He gained a reputation for charismatic teaching, profound philosophical insights and even magical abilities. The prince of Aleppo, Malik Zahir (d.1226), became one of his followers, after Suhrawardi, reportedly, magically produced a gemstone. The prince was the son of Salah al-Din al-Ayyubi (d.1193) or Saladin, the famed opponent of the Crusaders, respected for his chivalry on the battlefield. Although Saladin was an early supporter of Sufism, he favored Sufis that fell within the bounds of (the recently crystalized) establishment Sunnism. Suhrawardi's more Hermetic sort of Sufism inspired concerns among Aleppo's Sunni clerics, and perhaps jealousy over his influence on the prince. Their complaints about him would eventually reach Saladin, who likely had his own worries about his son being brought under the sway of a controversial spiritualist. As a result, he had Suhrwardi put to death in 1191, at the age of 36, earning Suhrawardi the title *al-shaykh al-maqtul*, or 'the Executed Master'. Despite his early death, Suhrawardi's philosophy would go on to have real influence, especially in eastern Islamic lands, with his almost 50 written works (he wrote in both Arabic and Persian) not only celebrated for their profound insight, but also seen as literary masterpieces in their own right.[447]

Suhrawardi conceived of his school of thought as a revival of the 'philosophy of the Ancients', who utilized 'mystical intuition as a philosophical tool' and expressed their insights through symbols.[448] He believed that not only Sufis, but the ancient Egyptians, Greeks and Persians, all had systems of thought premised on 'knowledge by presence', or mystical experience and direct tasting of higher realities. He called his particular form of mystical philosophy 'Illuminationism', or the *Ishraqi* school. He conceived of being as light, with God as the Light of lights, emanating lesser lights, which the human soul can

---

447 Ibid., pp.xvi–xvii. Seyyed Hossein Nasr observes that Suhrwardi's Illuminationist school would come to be integrated with Avicenna's philosophy and Ibn 'Arabi's 'gnostic doctrines', within a broader Shi'i matrix. We can also point out here that whereas Sufism (or Islamic esotericism) has come to be seen as a somewhat separate aspect or science within Sunnism, in Shi'i traditions the esoteric or Sufi elements have been, arguably, more seamlessly integrated into the overall Islamic paradigm. Seyyed Hossein Nasr, *Three Muslim Sages* (Cambridge, MA, 1969), pp.56–8.

448 Walbridge, *The Wisdom of the Mystic East*, p.ix.

open itself to. As Zia Inayat Khan nicely summarizes his approach: 'at the heart of [Suhrawardi's] mystical science is the recognition that the "I" of every self-aware entity is pure, immaterial light'.[449]

Suhrawardi claimed that the true originator of Illuminationism was actually Hermes/Enoch, whose ancient wisdom was transmitted in two separate lines: 1) a Greek-Egyptian line going through Pythagoras and Plato and 2) a Persian line going through the ancient kings in Persia. Suhrawardi held that both of these lines of ancient Enochian/Hermetic wisdom coalesced in Sufism. He traced the Persian line into Islam through Mansur al-Hallaj (d.922) in Iraq (whom we will discuss further in the seventh chapter on Jesus), while the Greek-Egyptian line was transmitted via Dhu'l-Nun al-Misri (d.862) in Egypt (whom we discuss more in the last chapter on Muhammad).[450] We find in Suhrawardi a precursor to the Italian Renaissance fascination with Hermes, and a belief in a perennial philosophy percolating just beneath the surface of human history, one based on mystical insight rather than deductive reasoning.

Whether we refer to Enoch, Thoth or Hermes, we are dealing with a figure associated with the ancient wisdom of earliest humanity, the first repository of the perennial philosophy – a more complete and holistic knowledge that was believed to have been fragmented and lost over time. This belief would prove especially important to the Renaissance, with its grand quest to revive the wisdom of the ancients. Florence's 'leading merchant-prince' Cosimo de' Medici (d.1464), for example, acquired the Greek *Hermetica* from a monk in his employ in 1460. Thrilled to finally have the legendary (and reputedly ancient) texts in his possession, Medici asked his scholarly protégé Marsilio Ficino (d.1499) to drop what he was doing and immediately start work on translating the texts into Latin. Medici and Ficino believed that the *Hermetica* were as old as the earliest works of the Bible, and that Hermes was likely a contemporary of Moses. For Medici and

---

449 Zia Inayat Khan, 'Preface', in Henry Corbin, *The Man of Light in Iranian Sufism* (New Lebanon, NY, 1994), p.i.

450 A secret, gnostic line of wisdom from al-Misri through Sahl al-Tustari (d.896) – about whom more will be said in the book's last chapter – is said to continue in the lineage of Ahmad al-Rifa'i (d.1182). Bowering, *The Mystical Vision of Existence in Classical Islam*, pp.52–4.

Ficino, the *Hermetica* represented this *Prisca Theologica*, or 'original religion' of humankind, of which later religions and philosophies are so many fragments. Once Ficino's translation of the *Hermetica* into Latin was complete in 1471, the texts would prove deeply influential on Renaissance science, spirituality and poetry, though this influence would decline a century later when evidence suggested that the texts were more likely traced to the early Christian centuries rather than to the time of Noah or Moses.[451] Regardless of when they were written, it appears as though the teachings they represent can be fairly considered to represent a much older Egyptian tradition, though expressed in Greek idiom.

So, what is this ancient, original religion represented by Hermes'/Thoth's teachings, that so enchanted medieval mystics and Renaissance princes? The worldview found in the *Hermetica* can be summarized as follows:

> God is one, and the creator of all things, which continue to depend on God as elements in a hierarchy of beings. Second in this hierarchy after God himself comes the intelligible world, and then the sensible world. The creative and beneficent powers of God flow through the intelligible and sensible realms to the sun, which is the demiurge around which revolve the eight spheres of the fixed stars, the planets and the earth. From these spheres depend the daemons, and from the daemons Man, who is a microcosm of creation. Thus everything is part of God, and God is in everything, his creative activity continuing unceasingly. All things are one and the pleroma of being is indestructible.[452]

As we can see in this passage here, the Hermetic account of reality has some striking parallels with Jewish, Christian and Islamic mystical-philosophical teachings (and Sufism in particular). In the *Hermetica* we find an understanding of God as One, which is of course foundational to the Abrahamic monotheisms, but we also see a descending hierarchy

---

451 Bladel, *The Arabic Hermes*, p.6.
452 Garth Fowden, *The Egyptian Hermes: A Historical Approach to the Late Pagan Mind* (Princeton, NJ, 1993 [1986]), p.77.

of beings derived from this God (much like the 'Great Chain of Being' in Christian mystical philosophy or the 'Degrees of Being' found in Sufi philosophy), and hence the cosmos is characterized itself by a unity (akin to Ibn 'Arabi's articulation of what would later be called the 'oneness of being' or *wahdat al-wujud*),[453] with the human functioning as the microcosm of creation (*al-insan al-kamil*), and the visible world functioning as a set of signs and symbols of, or correspondences with, higher realms (as the Qur'an and Bible exhaustively suggest). We can also note in this passage here the centrality of the Sun in Hermetic texts, and hence Ibn 'Arabi's association of Enoch with the Sun.

To break down the teachings of Hermes a bit further, they have been classified into two broad categories: 1) *technical*, in that they offer techniques for interpreting astrological signs for predicting the future, or for working with plants and other earthly elements in terms of their correspondences with various planetary and astral powers (and hence the long association of Hermes and magic) and 2) *philosophical*, with teachings on 'how to transcend their bodily circumstances and to overcome fate … leading to a true knowledge of God'.[454] In short, Hermetic teachings concern both *magic*, or the technical manipulation of correspondences for prediction and healing, and *mysticism*: the transcendence of self and realization of divine knowledge.

It is with the philosophical Hermetic teachings that we find further parallels with Neoplatonism, perhaps not surprising considering their shared origin in Alexandria.[455] Both of these ancient Greek systems would play a huge role in shaping Sufi philosophy, though we can also find several fascinating ways in which the Qur'an itself shares some key Neoplatonic and Hermetic emphases.

---

453 It's worth emphasizing that, although Ibn 'Arabi's philosophy was later characterized by this term *wahdat al-wujud* (both by proponents and opponents, beginning with Ibn Taymiyya), Chittick observes that 'this is misleading, for he never uses the expression'. Although the term has been misused and can certainly be misleading if it is understood in an overly simplistic fashion, there remain significant grounds suggesting its general suitability as a term for his view. 'Ibn 'Arabi', *Stanford Encyclopedia of Philosophy (Spring 2020 Edition)*, edited by Edward N. Zalta, https://plato.stanford.edu/archives/spr2020/entries/ibn-arabi/ (accessed October 28, 2023).

454 Bladel, *The Arabic Hermes*, p.5.

455 As Nicholas Goodrick-Clarke notes, the *Hermetica* 'have their origin in Alexandria', and Plotinus, the 'leading figure' of Neoplatonism, studied under Ammonius Saccas in Alexandria. *The Western Esoteric Traditions*, pp.16–21.

Sufism, the Qur'an and Ancient Greek Philosophy

Before considering the Greek philosophical resonances found within, not only Sufism, but even the Qur'an itself, it's probably useful to at least briefly discuss Neoplatonism here. First, what we now call 'Neoplatonism' is something that its proponents would have understood as Platonism proper, and there is some debate over whether or not the prefix 'neo' is an appropriate one. Regardless of whether it was a new trajectory of Plato's thought or simply its continuous living expression, we can trace Neoplatonism back to Plotinus (d.270) and his most famous disciple Porphyry (d.305).

Porphyry fortuitously wrote a detailed biography of his master, and hence we know a great deal more about Plotinus than we do about most of his contemporaries. Born in Egypt, Plotinus studied philosophy in Alexandria, before joining a Roman military expedition in the hopes of seeking wisdom as far afield as Persia and India, though the expedition would ultimately be called off when the emperor leading it, Gordian III (d.244), proved so unpopular with his troops that they killed him. Plotinus appears to have abandoned hopes of studying philosophy in the East and settled in Rome.[456] From Porphyry's account we see that Plotinus was something of a philosopher-mystic, which for him was simply what a true philosopher was: one who lived their life in such a way that higher levels of wisdom and spiritual insight could be sustainably accessed. For Plotinus this lifestyle included vegetarianism, celibacy and rigorous ethical standards, all things that he believed would facilitate the discovery of wisdom, which is of course what philosophy means as a word: the love (*philo*) of wisdom (*sophia*).

In one sense Neoplatonism was the last great gasp of pagan philosophy in the face of Christianity's growing momentum in the first centuries. This final flowering of pagan Greek thought is generally believed to have come to a close when Emperor Justinian (d.565) shut down the Platonic Academy in Athens in 529 (the last hotbed of pagan Neoplatonism). And yet Platonism would prove to have a remarkably

---

[456] Lloyd Gerson, 'Plotinus', *Stanford Encyclopedia of Philosophy (Fall 2018 Edition)*, edited by Edward N. Zalta, https://plato.stanford.edu/entries/plotinus/ (accessed February 9, 2023).

vibrant afterlife, permeating not only the spiritual philosophies of Judaism, Christianity and Islam, but also their cultural and artistic practices. The Neoplatonic worldview is summarized by Nicholas Goodrick-Clarke as follows:

> Plotinus posited an absolute, transcendent One or Good, defined in Aristotle's phrase as 'that to which all things aspire'. Its existence was inferred from the necessity of unity in everything that exists. Below the One, Plotinus described a cosmology of continuous creative emanation, whereby the higher level of reality is imparted to the lower without being diminished. However, each new level of emanation is necessarily less perfect than its begetter, to which it longs to return.[457]

Neoplatonic texts were available in Arabic translation as early as the ninth century, with elements of Plotinus's *Enneads* translated into an Arabic volume entitled *The Theology of Aristotle*, and known in the West as the *Plotiniana Arabica*. And yet for Sufis this Neoplatonic influence (which becomes readily apparent in some later Sufi poetry and philosophy) is not so much seen as an *infusion* of the classical philosophical heritage into Islam, but rather as the Islamic revelation *confirming* the truth of classical philosophical teachings to which it corresponds.

Stefan Sperl, a scholar of Arabic and Middle Eastern studies, suggests that the Qur'an itself can be seen as something quite close to a Neoplatonic text.[458] Very much like Neoplatonic philosophy, the Qur'an describes the human soul as originating with God, but falling into the material world, before counseling a path of return to God, through remembrance and contemplation. The Qur'an also repeatedly describes God as both transcendent beyond likeness to any created thing (*Not a thing is like Him*, Q 42:11), and immanently present (*Wherever you turn there is the Face of God*, Q 2:115). This simultaneous

---

457 Goodrick-Clarke, *The Western Esoteric Traditions*, p.21.
458 He suggests that the Qur'an is 'a veritable repository of significant parallels with Neoplatonism'. Stefan Sperl, 'Stages of Ascent: Neoplatonic Affinities in Classical Arabic Poetry', in *Faces of the Infinite: Neoplatonism and Poetry at the Confluence of Africa, Asia, and Europe,* edited by Stefan Sperl and Yorgos Dedes (Oxford, 2022), p.100.

transcendence and immanence of the One is central to Neoplatonic metaphysics. Perhaps more fundamentally, Sperl notes that the Qur'an veritably revolves around a distinction between the *visible world* and the *unseen world* or the afterlife. The Qur'an repeatedly describes the visible world as temporary, ultimately unsatisfying and deceptive in what it appears to offer. In contrast, the Qur'an suggests, it is with the unseen, with God and the hereafter, that what is real, permanent and truly satisfying can be found.

At a basic level, this Qur'anic division of reality corresponds with the Neoplatonic distinction between the *sensible world*, the world of material forms that we access through our senses, and the *intelligible world*, the world of ideas perceptible only to the intellect. Although we could take a massive detour into the precise meaning of these worlds (and we will indeed explore them a bit further below), I hope it suffices here to give just a few brief examples to illustrate.

For Plato, and his Neoplatonic followers, the intellect perceives the pure ideas of which the objects of this world are but traces, or imperfect manifestations. For example, the mind perceives 'blueness' while the eyes perceive blue objects. No blue object encompasses the totality of blueness, and even after a blue object is destroyed, blueness (as an idea, ideal or possibility) persists. We may even say that blueness is eternal, whereas blue things are temporary manifestations of the principle of blueness, which is clearly not bound by time (or space for that matter). Similarly, we can define a perfect triangle mathematically, but cannot find an *actual* physical triangle that is as perfectly triangular, down to the millionth of a millimeter, in the sensible realm. And even if we destroy every single triangle that we can get our hands on (perhaps in fanatical fealty to Team Square), triangularity remains as a geometric ideal. Other examples of Platonic ideas or forms we could point to include things that may be even more difficult to contemplate, such as beauty. What is it that each beautiful thing shares, we may ask? What is beauty itself? Although all beautiful things apparent to the senses will pass, beauty itself remains something that the intellect can contemplate the meaning of, as an idea, quality or essential reality.[459]

Like the Qur'an, the Neoplatonists suggest that the sensible world of material forms is not what is ultimately real. Rather, it is a mere shadow of the *intelligible world*, the higher, more profound and meaningful world of ideas and forms, which culminates in the One, the form of the Good, Beautiful and True: the Absolute. Simply put, Neoplatonists believe that 'the intelligible realm of Being is more real than the sensible realm of becoming', the latter a realm of transitory forms, temporarily expressing the intelligible, all traced back to the eternal One.[460] As the Qur'an says, in a verse favored by Sufis (Q 55:26): *All that dwells upon the earth is perishing, yet abides the Face of your Lord, majestic, splendid.*

For Muslims these parallels between Hermetic and Neoplatonic philosophy and Islam are not necessarily controversial, as the Qur'an states that the wisdom of all the prophets is, ultimately, drawn from the same well, and hence the esoteric teachings of the Greeks or Egyptians or Mesopotamians, if traced back to a prophetic figure like Enoch-Hermes, would naturally correspond with those revealed to Muhammad. The whole question of historical influence rather breaks down then, since if a Sufi metaphysician articulates the nature of God, the world and the human soul in terms that sound Neoplatonic or Hermetic, this is not necessarily because ancient Egyptian-Greek philosophies are somehow *added onto* Islam: it may rather be because Islam itself originates from the same well as they did, and hence there are a whole series of natural correspondences that can be utilized by the Muslim interpreter.

From this perspective, we can say that the basic worldview of the Islamic tradition is Hermetic and Neoplatonic in several important

---

459 Chittick notes that, in the *Futuhat*, Ibn 'Arabi 'uses presence [*hadra*] to designate a name's realm of influence and then describes various ways in which the properties and traces of the name are displayed in the cosmos and human beings', and hence 'one might say that he is describing how things participate in Platonic idea' (Chittick, 'Ibn 'Arabi', *Stanford Encyclopedia of Philosophy*). And yet, Ibn Arabi's articulation of what universals are is not identical to Platonic thinking on this. In the chapter on Adam in the *Fusus*, for example, Ibn 'Arabi states that 'universal realities, although intelligible, do not have concrete existence, but exist only when determined by a relationship with a concrete entity'. Ibn 'Arabi, *Fusus*, p.30.

460 Walbridge, *The Wisdom of the Mystic East*, p.8.

respects, just as we could say that Hermeticism and Neoplatonism are essentially Islamic in some key ways. Or put differently, all of these traditions communicate something fundamentally accurate about reality, and as it is singular in nature, they by definition resemble one another. Although these traditions utilize different languages, symbolic references and conceptual frameworks, if reality is indeed One in essence, then it necessarily follows that even in their notable diversity, true religions and philosophies will reflect that singularity to some degree, and underlying their diverse conceptions, names and theories we can detect shared themes and emphases.

The Spectrum of Knowledge

Ibn 'Arabi articulates the overall value of knowledge within the Islamic tradition as follows: 'God never commanded His Prophet to seek increase of anything except knowledge, since all good lies therein. It is the greatest miracle.'[461] He even goes so far as to suggest, 'Idleness with knowledge is better than ignorance with good works.'[462] An ignorant activist is a much bigger problem than a wise slacker, for pretty obvious reasons: doing very little good is to be greatly preferred over doing a great deal of harm. When it comes to the *nature* of knowledge, one of the hallmarks of the Sufi tradition is what we might call an *epistemological pluralism*: Sufis have long emphasized that there are different ways of knowing, and hence different kinds of knowledge.[463] We find repeatedly in Ibn 'Arabi's works a critique of Muslim philosophers, jurists and theologians – not for their pursuit of knowledge through the rational

---

461 Ibn 'Arabi, *Fut*.II.370, as quoted in Chittick, *Sufi Path of Knowledge*, p.148.
462 Ibid.
463 In the century before Ibn 'Arabi, influential Sufi luminaries made extended cases for epistemological pluralism, and, in particular, drew attention to the rational intellect's inability to understand matters transcendent. The famous Persian Sufi 'Ayn al-Qudat al-Hamadani, for example, was executed by the Seljuks in 1131, ostensibly for heresy, but in actuality for his critique of their brutal policies and land seizures. Mohammed Rustom notes that, prior to his untimely death, al-Hamadani wrote 'the first fully developed, mystically informed rational case concerning the limitations of the intellect in the Islamic tradition'. 'Ayn al-Qudat, *The Essence of Reality: A Defense of Philosophical Sufism*, edited and translated by Mohammed Rustom (New York, 2022), p.xx.

intellect or through inherited tradition – but for their belief that these are the *only* means by which knowledge is gained, or for elevating these means beyond their appropriate place within the broader spectrum of knowing. On this, in *The Meccan Revelations* he writes:

> Each human faculty has a playing field in which it roams and beyond which it should not step. If it goes beyond its field, it falls into error and makes mistakes and is described as having deviated from its straight way. For example, visual observation may discover things where rational arguments stumble, because the arguments have left their proper domain.[464]

Now the basic way we gain knowledge, regardless of faculty, is by *paying attention*, and this basic act of attention, viewing or observing is known in Arabic as *nazar* (literally 'to look'). According to Ibn 'Arabi we look through three faculties we have within our human formation, and each gives access to a different dimension of reality: 1) the bodily senses, 2) the rational mind and 3) the heart.[465] These distinct faculties function as metaphorical eyes that allow us to *see* different aspects of existence, and we err when we attempt to use one of these faculties of knowing outside of its appropriate domain.

Within the Latin Christian tradition, we find an almost identical breakdown of the human faculties, notably articulated in the works of St. Bonaventure (d.1274), a Franciscan friar, professor at the University of Paris and Cardinal of the Catholic Church. A historical contemporary of Ibn 'Arabi's, Bonaventure similarly describes three ways of knowing or three 'eyes' through which we see different dimensions of reality. He traces this tripartite division of knowledge back to Hugh of St. Victor (d.1141), a foundational mystical theologian in medieval Latin Christianity:

> For this triple vision, man was endowed with a triple eye, as explained by Hugh of St. Victor: the eye of flesh, of reason, and of contemplation; the eye of flesh, to see the world and what it

---

[464] Ibn 'Arabi, *Fut*.II.281. I've slightly modified Chittick's translation here. *Sufi Path of Knowledge*, p.165.

[465] Chittick, *Sufi Path of Knowledge*, pp.159–60.

contains; the eye of reason, to see the soul and what it contains; the eye of contemplation, to see God and that which is within Him.[466]

Bonaventure describes here three 'eyes' by which we see the world: the *eye of the flesh*, consisting of our five bodily senses, with which we perceive the external world of space, time and material objects, the *eye of reason*, consisting of our faculty of mental reflection, through which we perceive logic, mathematics, thought and symbolic meaning – the world of the mind or soul, and finally the *eye of contemplation*, through which we perceive transcendent realities inaccessible to either sense or reason.[467] Regardless of terminology, there is a broad agreement here between Latin and Arabic-speaking mystics on the basic outlines of how we look upon the worlds, both outer and inner, visible and invisible.

Ibn 'Arabi highlights, in the passage quoted above, the mistakes we make when we attempt to use one eye to see something that properly belongs to the domain of another eye, what American philosopher Ken Wilber calls a 'category error'. This is a pretty straightforward error to appreciate, as Ibn 'Arabi indicates. He describes the mistake of using rational arguments where visual observation can give us concrete results. We could, for example, attempt to reason out whether or not a heavier object will fall faster when dropped than a lighter one, and conclude that indeed it will, based on the rational principle that as a material object increases in one respect, it increases in others, and hence an increased weight will undoubtedly lead to an increased speed of fall. However – and this was exactly the revolution inaugurated by modern science – our best way to *know* whether or not this is the case is to use the eye best equipped to get this knowledge. Instead of applying rational principles (the eye of the mind), we could gather several objects that are the same size but different weights, and drop them from the same height, and then observe (using the eye of the flesh) what happens. Galileo (d.1642) did just this and discovered that in fact heavier objects fall at the same speed as lighter ones.[468]

---

466 St. Bonaventure, *Breviloquium* II: 12.5.
467 Ken Wilber, *Eye to Eye: The Quest for the New Paradigm* (Boston, 2001), pp.2–3.
468 Ibid., pp.12–13.

Now, just as we are wrong to try to reason out things with the mind that are best observed with the senses, we are equally mistaken to try to observe things with our senses, or reason them out with the mind, when they are by nature perceptible only to the eye of contemplation, or the heart. There is no use looking outside for what lies within, or trying to calculate the nature of the incalculable. And yet this is precisely the category error of *scientism*, to presume that the eyes of the flesh and mind can be used to answer questions of meaning. According to Bertrand Russell (d.1970), 'the sphere of values lies outside science',[469] simply because empirical science is descriptive rather than prescriptive in nature – it can *describe* how life works but is not equipped to *prescribe* what a good life is, or determine what it really means. The exercise of external observation and application of measurement and calculation are simply not methodologies that provide knowledge of everything. They are of course perfectly valid means of understanding how the material world operates, but they utterly fail to answer questions about what we can broadly refer to as interiority: what the experience of sadness is like, what a Shakespeare play is really all about, what makes for a good jazz improvisation or whether or not you really love someone. This is simply because these sorts of knowledge are ultimately unavailable to the eyes of flesh and reason, even if they can get at some of their material and conceptual correlates.

Whereas the vast majority of people are capable of confirming the knowledge of things we access via the eye of the flesh (sensory data, like whether something is bright, cold, wet or loud) and the eye of the mind (mathematical equations, logic, language, philosophical concepts and such), at least to some degree, once we shift to the third eye, the knowledge of contemplation – or the knowing of the heart – we find truths of another magnitude more subtle. The heavenly ascension stories of Enoch illustrate this quite well, metaphorically showing how certain kinds of knowledge go far beyond earthly sorts. It is precisely these trans-sensory and trans-rational kinds of knowledge that the eye

---

[469] Bertrand Russell, as quoted in Huston Smith, *Forgotten Truth: The Common Vision of the World's Religions* (San Francisco, 1992), p.14.

of contemplation is for. This is because the depth dimension of reality, or God, cannot be understood via either the eyes of the flesh or the mind. Early Christian theologian and ascetic Evagrius Ponticus (d.399 CE) states this nicely: 'God cannot be grasped by the mind. If he could be grasped, he would not be God.'[470]

Although we all have at least some taste of the knowledge given by the heart, a much smaller minority take the time to truly cultivate this faculty and develop its full potential. As a result, very few of us have *direct, experiential* knowledge of the transcendent realities that our heart is capable of accessing. Because of its rather rarefied nature, Sufi philosophers developed a unique terminology for this higher kind of heart-knowledge, generally referring to it using the Arabic term *ma'rifa* rather than the more conventional word for knowledge, *'ilm*. For Sufis, *ma'rifa* refers to 'the highest knowledge to which the individual has access', that which our opened eye of contemplation, through the faculty of the heart, reveals to us. Paradoxically, such knowledge is also a kind of unknowing. It is a light so dazzling that it blinds.[471] This is why Ibn 'Arabi always held that the spiritual states and sublime realizations given by *ma'rifa* can really only be communicated symbolically, and even then, only to those who have had at least some taste of these subtle realities.[472]

For the Sufis, attempting to know God by study alone is akin to looking at maps of great canyons and mountains, but not doing any real hiking, or scrutinizing the menus of the best restaurants in town without ever ordering any food: the difference between these

---

470 Evagrius Ponticus, *Patrologia Graeca* 40.1275C. As quoted in Ware, *The Orthodox Way*, p.11.

471 Dhu'l-Nun is reported to have said, 'Those who know God best are the most bewildered regarding him.' Shah-Kazemi, 'The Notion and Significance of *Ma'rifa* in Sufism', pp.155, 164.

472 It's worth noting that the term *ma'rifa* is not found in the Qur'an itself, and hence Ibn 'Arabi at times prefers the term *'ilm* for the highest spiritual knowledge, as this term *is* found in many places and forms in the Qur'an, with one of God's Names being 'the Knower' or *al-'Alim*. However, Chittick notes that although Ibn 'Arabi does sometimes distinguish *'ilm* from *ma'rifa* in this way, 'for the most part he does not'. Chittick, *Sufi Path of Knowledge*, p.148. Shah-Kazemi argues that, over time, *'ilm* lost its original 'suppleness' and 'polyvalence' in the Islamic tradition, and hence the need would emerge for a 'separate word to designate a specifically spiritual kind of knowledge'. 'The Notion and Significance of *Ma'rifa* in Sufism', p.157.

being, experientially, rather stark. Sadly, too few of us get to know religion much beyond the map or menu, and the claims regarding its deeper realities made by those who have genuinely opened the eye of contemplation – those of *ma'rifa*, or the *'arifun* – tend to be rejected outright or at least approached with skepticism by those many more whose contemplative eye remains largely closed. As al-Ghazali wisely pointed out, however, just because you yourself have not had an experience of something is not solid intellectual grounds to dismiss the claims of those who have.[473]

Plato's famous Allegory of the Cave, found in his *Republic* (Book VII), brilliantly illustrates this situation. He describes a group of people who live their lives chained to a cave wall, with a fire behind them. Between them and this fire, various objects are paraded past – wooden horses and statues of people, each casting a different shadow on the wall across from the chained ones, which they witness and discuss. Their whole world is a shadow-play, with the shadows of statues of things taken to be the real things themselves (an analogy for those who merely know appearances, or the world as it presents itself to the senses). In their discussions of these shadows, the cave folk celebrate the genius of those renowned experts who can most carefully describe the shadows and recount their histories or predict their trajectories.

Plato then observes how shocking and even intolerable it would be for one of these people if they were to be unchained, shown the fire behind them and made to appreciate what their entire life has consisted of so far. In philosophical terms, this would be to see how the sensible, which is all they have known to this point, is a mere trace of the intelligible, a 'shadow' of the real world. Even more unbearable for these folk would be to climb up straight out of the cave (presumably with sore joints and eyes, neither accustomed to this sort of usage), and once finding themselves outside of it, to behold the shocking richness and vibrancy of the real world. Finally, after some acclimatization, they may be able look up at the sun, and get a sense of what real light truly is (contemplating the Good/True/Beautiful, or as Plotinus would call

---

473 See Abu Hamid al-Ghazali, *Al-Ghazali's Path to Sufism: His Deliverance from Error*, translated and edited by R. J. McCarthy (Louisville, KY, 2000).

it, the One), in contradistinction to the fire-cast shadow play they've known all their lives.[474]

It is not hard to see how challenging it would be for such an escapee, after having these mind-blowing experiences beyond the world they've known, to *go back into* the cave, and attempt to inform their cave-compatriots of the real nature of their situation, and the reality of the sun, which would sound impossibly outlandish and unconvincing, and probably a little insulting, if not completely insane. They might even end up in danger, as their cave compatriots lash out in hostility against this annoying prophet relativizing their world, and making claims to knowledge beyond what they can fathom. In what follows, we take a closer look at some of the ways in which Ibn 'Arabi illustrates this full spectrum of knowledge, both within the cave and without.

Knowledge between Elijah and Enoch: Sense, Intellect and Imagination

The animal or the number? This is the cross of metaphysics.[475]

In the pithy quote above, French philosopher Alain Badiou describes the line or 'cross' dividing philosophy, as the question of whether reality is fundamentally *conceptual* or *sensual* in nature. Do mathematics or biology best account for our world? Do we choose axiom or existence, rationalism or empiricism? Badiou traces this division throughout the entirety of Western philosophy, all the way back to Plato and Aristotle, with the former generally associated with the pure contemplation of transcendent forms, while the latter being perceived as more of an empiricist, studying and cataloging the things and beings of this world.

In this chapter on Elijah in the *Gemstones*, Ibn 'Arabi suggests that together, Elijah and Enoch represent a *synthesis* of both intellect and

---

474 Nicholas Denyer remarks that, in the *Republic,* 'the Good has the privileged position of being what accounts for the existence and intelligibility of Forms, much as the Sun has the privileged position of being what accounts for the growth and visibility of plants (508b–e, 509b)'. 'Sun and Line: The Role of the Good', in *The Cambridge Companion to Plato's Republic*, edited by G. R. F. Ferrari (Cambridge, 2007), p.284.
475 Alain Badiou, *The Adventure of French Philosophy* (New York, 2022 [2012]), p.xiv.

sense, or number and animal. Echoing the various Hermetic traditions that suggest the transcendence of the body through a purified intellect, Ibn 'Arabi says that Enoch was one who went beyond bodily limitations entirely, becoming totally spiritualized, a completely pure, uninhibited intellect (akin to those Enochian traditions that said he became the angel Metatron). In this state Enoch is freed from the desires and distortions of the lower, animal self, and can perceive the transcendent in a direct way.

> The Real, in him, was transcendent and so he had half of the knowledge of God. For when the intellect is isolated in itself, it acquires the speculative sciences, and it knows God as transcendent only and not immanent.[476]

In commenting on Ibn 'Arabi's discussion of Enoch here, al-Qashani seems to be aware of the Jewish and Christian Enochian lore, suggesting that Enoch went to a sort of extreme in transcendence, subtracting from himself materiality, becoming totally spiritualized (*tarawwuh*), 'so much so that in the end he himself was turned into a pure spirit', casting off his body, mixing with the angels and ultimately residing in the heavenly sphere of the sun.[477] As himself a pure spirit or intellect, Enoch was one who could perceive the fundamental ideas or meanings underlying the appearances of the world, contemplating the transcendent forms of which the world is so many traces, and even contemplate Plato's metaphorical Sun – the One, their ultimate principle and source. This kind of pure intellectual/spiritual contemplation, applying the eyes of reason and contemplation, unencumbered by materiality, remains for Ibn 'Arabi only *half* of knowledge: Enoch's transcendence requires Elijah's immanence for knowledge to be complete.[478]

> Whoever wants to discover this wisdom of Elijah and Enoch, for whom God willed to give two forms, first as a prophet before Noah, then raised and descended as a messenger after that – God joining

---
476 Ibn 'Arabi, *Fusus*, p.170.
477 Izutsu, *Sufism and Taoism*, p.52.
478 Hussain, 'Jesus and Enoch', p.59.

these two stations for him – then let him descend from the ruling of his intellect, to his desires, and be an animal, absolutely, so that he may discover what every creature knows.[479]

In a fascinating passage, Ibn ʿArabi suggests that the combined wisdom of Elijah and Enoch includes both the objective contemplation of the intellect *as well as* the totally embodied knowledge of the animal self. Although we may associate animality exclusively with sensory or empirical experience, Ibn ʿArabi suggests that pure animality actually includes a keen awareness of the ways in which the spirit world interacts with our own, and hence he uses a derivative of the term *kashf* here, which literally means 'unveiling' but is generally used by Sufis to refer to spiritual experience.

Ibn ʿArabi interestingly shares two indications that one has in fact achieved absolute animality in their station, namely that 1) they can see the dead as if they are living, able to perceive what sort of state the souls of those passed are in, and 2) that they become totally unable to speak, like animals. Islamic studies scholar Pasha M. Khan observes that this state of animality then, is a 'non-intellective unveiling', one that combines an immediate, we may even say 'pre-intellective' perception of this world, with a simultaneous awareness of the non-material world and its interaction with our own, including the state and presence of those who have passed from material existence.[480]

Interestingly, Khan notes that, for Ibn ʿArabi, one of the reasons why the knowledge of animality is so valuable is that the intellect suffers from the deficiency of needing to 'pin down' a situation of perplexity, paradox or mystery: the intellect has a hard time living with what it cannot grasp, define or map out.[481] The intellect, although celebrated by humans as something that distinguishes them from animals, can also be something of a defect or drawback, *narrowing* our ability to accurately perceive reality's transrational nature. Interestingly we find cross-cultural anecdotal accounts that 'pre-intellective' beings like

---

479 Ibn ʿArabi, *Fusus*, p.174.
480 Pasha M. Khan, 'Nothing but Animals: The Hierarchy of Creatures in the *Ringstones of Wisdom*', *Journal of the Muhyiddin Ibn ʿArabi Society*, 43 (2008), 45.
481 Ibid., 25–6.

animals and small children tend to be sensitive to the unseen in ways adult human are often not, being aware of the spirits of those passed, or other unseen beings.

Although in this book's first chapter on Adam we saw Ibn 'Arabi situate the human as uniquely capable of reflecting all of God's Names, and in that sense standing 'above' or apart from the rest of creation, he notably, in some of his other writings, situates the human being as *below* animals, with plants and finally rocks above everything else. Medieval Jewish, Christian and Muslim philosophers, following Aristotle, tended to situate the human, rational soul at the top of a hierarchy, underneath which we find the animal and finally plant souls. Ibn 'Arabi (uniquely among his peers) reverses this hierarchy, in the chapter on Isaac (Arabic *Ishaq*) in the *Gemstones,* stating that 'no creation is higher than the rock, and after it a plant, followed by sentient animals', suggesting that all of these creatures know God directly, through immediate perception, but only the human being limits the possibilities of immediate witnessing of reality via the delimiting of the intellect.[482]

The World of Imagination

Alongside the knowledge we gain through applying the faculty of intellect, and the knowledge given to us by our bodies, or animality, in this chapter Ibn 'Arabi focuses on the knowledge we access *in between* these two faculties, through the *imagination.* The terms 'imagination' and 'imaginary' are usually thought to refer to something unreal – mere subjective images formulated in the mind's eye – and hence it may be surprising that Ibn 'Arabi considers imagination to be a way of knowing. As French scholar of Islam Henry Corbin (d.1978) notes, for Ibn 'Arabi the world of imagination is a realm unto itself, found between the world of material objects perceptible to the senses, and the world of ideas perceptible to the intellect. Existing at this mysterious borderland between the material and intellectual, the Imaginal World is a *barzakh* – an isthmus, or intermediary realm – meaning that it both separates and

---

482   Ibn 'Arabi, *Fusus*, as quoted in Khan, 'Nothing but Animals', pp.26–7.

joins the world of material form and the world of pure idea or meaning, having characteristics of both, but being wholly determined by neither.

This in-between world is 'a world of Idea-Images, of archetypal figures, of subtle substances, of "immaterial matter".'[483] In Arabic, this world is known as the *'alam al-mithal,* which literally translates as the world of 'likenesses' or 'images'. Recall from the first chapter on Adam that the Imaginal Realm exists as the fourth of the five planes of Being, in between the world of Lordship or essential, unmanifest realities, and the material world we currently find ourselves in. Like the material world, the Imaginal World is populated by forms, images and entities. However, like the world of pure idea and meaning, these entities are *non-material* in nature, and hence not subject to the same spatial and temporal constraints of concrete, material entities and objects. The Imaginal World is 'as real and objective, as consistent and subsistent' as both the material world and ideational world.[484] Perhaps to sidestep the negative connotations of 'imaginary' Corbin called this world the *imaginatrix,* or in Latin, the *mundus imaginalis.*[485]

This *imaginatrix* consists of two aspects, an objective reality *independent of us* and a subjective reality *within us.*[486] And it is with the subjective faculty of imagination that we access the objective world of images. In an interview with the *Saturday Evening Post* in 1929, Albert Einstein (d.1955) shared that 'imagination is more important than knowledge. Knowledge is limited. Imagination circles the world.'[487]

---

483 Corbin, *Alone with the Alone*, p.4.

484 Ibid.

485 In some respects, this notion of an imaginatrix, a world of disembodied images or spiritual forms, can be traced to Suhrawardi, the Hermetic Sufi we briefly mentioned earlier in this chapter. He situated the *'alam al-mithal* between the world of sense (*'alam al-hiss*) and the world of intellect (*'alam al-'aql*), but in his writings described it as the 'world of suspended images' (*'alam al-muthul al-mu'allaqa*). Van Lit, *The World of Image in Islamic Philosophy*, pp.51–6.

486 Mukhtar Ali notes that within Sufi philosophy the objective aspect of the Imaginal Realm is called the *'alam al-mithal al-munfasil*, meaning 'disconnected' from our own subjectivity – this is the objective spiritual world where the *a'yan al-thabita* take form. The subjective aspect of this realm is the *'alam al-mithal al-muttasil*, the aspect of this realm that connects to our own perception and experience. *Philosophical Sufism*, p.110.

487 Jeff Nilson, 'Albert Einstein: "Imagination is More Important than Knowledge"', *Saturday Evening Post*, March 20, 2010, https://www.saturdayeveningpost.com/2010/03/imagination-important-knowledge/ (accessed February 13, 2023).

Ibn 'Arabi would agree with Einstein here, and says that the Imaginal World is the vastest of all worlds, combining both the unseen and visible, and hence the imagination is the most expansive faculty of perception.[488] William Chittick defines the imagination as 'a specific faculty in the soul that brings together sensory things, which have shapes and forms, and consciousness, which has no shape or form'.[489]

Dreams are a wonderful example illustrating the nature of imagination, as 'the dreamer sees meanings in the form of sensory objects', and Ibn 'Arabi suggests that this is the primary way that most people access this realm.[490] So, how exactly do meanings take form in objects? We actually know this quite well, as almost all of us dream, and in many cases at least, dreams are quite explicit examples of meaning taking form. A woman in the midst of realizing that her marriage is beyond rescue, for instance, may dream that her wedding ring has somehow fallen down a drain as she struggles in vain to retrieve it. Her wedding ring has not *actually* fallen down the drain, but the dream concretizes the *meaning* of what she is going through. Her marriage is symbolized by the ring, and the loss of the marriage is represented by its irretrievability in the drain. Dreams offer a rich repository of symbolic expressions of our mind and consciousness.

The broader principle here is that meanings are expressed in image and form, and hence we perceive meaning through concrete entities. It follows that, through the awakened imagination, we can a) perceive the deeper meaning of the material forms and entities we encounter in this realm, and b) further perceive *spiritual forms* in the Imaginal Realm. Ibn 'Arabi explains in this chapter on Elijah that the human imagination is more powerful than the intellect, as we inevitably think *through* images, objects and forms.

> Imagination, in this [human] formation, has a stronger ruling power than intellect, for whatever an intellectual attains through intellect, cannot be attained but with the determining power of imagination over it, as one cannot think except through form.[491]

---

488 *Philosophical Sufism*, p.110.
489 Chittick, *Imaginal Worlds*, p.54.
490 Ibn 'Arabi, *Fut*.II.379. As quoted in Chittick, *Imaginal Worlds*, p.54.
491 Ibn 'Arabi, *Fusus*, p.170.

For Ibn 'Arabi, all genuine religion then has traditionally affirmed both transcendence and immanence, neither divorcing Being from its transcendent principle nor from its immanent expression, or what Bishop Kallistos Ware describes as 'the *otherness* and yet the *nearness* of the Eternal', God being both 'wholly Other' and personally present.[492] Hence revelation engages all of the various human faculties, including the senses, the rational intellect and the imagination, through various traditions of philosophy, mythology and ritual embodiment, to express these contrasting facts and facets of the Real.

One of Ibn 'Arabi's key arguments in this chapter is that the symbolism, imagery and mythology of religion is necessary for a full or complete understanding of reality. This stands in stark contrast to some contemporary spiritual trends that lean toward a sort of purist, rational mysticism. For many of those attempting to foster a more scientific approach to consciousness exploration (certainly a worthwhile task), religion is seen as at best secondary to the contemplative life, and at worst, a distasteful carryover of a superstitious past, that will progressively dissolve in the light of scientific, rational forms of spirituality.[493] This understanding of religion is especially well-illustrated by Sam Harris, a popular author, lecturer and podcaster, who has written on a range of philosophical and religious questions. After his bestselling *End of Faith* (2004), which made an extended, if amateurish, case against religion,[494] Harris has been associated with the so-called 'New Atheists', though his perspective includes what may be understood as a modernist form of mysticism. In his *Waking Up: A Guide to Spirituality without Religion* (2014), Harris, perhaps surprisingly, suggests that the contemplatives and mystics of every culture throughout all ages of history *have actually been correct* in their acknowledgment of the many deeper states of consciousness available

---

492 Ware, *The Orthodox Way*, pp.11-12.
493 See, for example, Ken Wilber, *A Sociable God: Toward a New Understanding of Religion* (Boston, 2005).
494 Harris unfortunately offers up a sophomoric and even harmful take on Islam in this book, which I have critiqued at length in William Rory Dickson, 'Religion as Phantasmagoria: Islam in Sam Harris's *End of Faith*', in *Religion and the New Atheism*, edited by Amarnath Amarasingam (Leiden, 2010).

to people. However, their insights 'have been discussed entirely in the context of religion and, therefore, have been shrouded in fallacy and superstition for all of human history'.[495] Harris sees the various rituals, visions, mythology, sacred narrative and reports of unseen beings offered by religions as a series of superstitious fallacies that the genuine pursuit of inner knowledge needs to be purified of, so a kind of direct apprehension of consciousness in all of its states can be experienced and cataloged, for the first time ever. Much like alchemy was replaced by chemistry, so religion should be replaced by a scientific spirituality.

If one has not encountered the spiritual forms of the Imaginal Realm in a relatively sustained way, Harris's view may seem almost obvious. For Ibn 'Arabi, however, a scientific form of spirituality is precisely one in which the symbols and stories of religion have a necessary place. This is simply because reality is known *both* a) through rational understanding and abstract spiritual contemplation, and b) through the rich images, forms and beings (angels, *jinn*, the spiritual forms of prophets and saints, etc.) that make up the intermediate realm of imagination, visions and dreams.

The metaphysical root of this state of affairs is that God, being totally unlimited, is not therefore limited by absoluteness – God transcends both absoluteness and relativity, meaning that His reality includes both truth beyond form, and the various forms of the imaginal and material realms: God's transcendence is such that it transcends both transcendence and immanence, including both but limited by neither. Ibn 'Arabi writes, 'All religions descend according to imagination ... all religions have a message determined by imagination, as the Real is never free of a quality when He manifests.'[496] In other words, religions offer a system of 'Idea-Images', or 'archetypal figures', as God never reveals Himself except through various forms or qualities. For Sufis God is ultimately transcendent beyond all form and quality, as we discussed in the first chapter, but again He is never known except *through* them. Hence revelation offers humans a way of understanding God *both* as absolute Essence beyond image, name or form (we may also say as pure

---

495 Sam Harris, *Waking Up: A Guide to Spirituality without Religion* (New York, 2014), p.15.
496 Ibn 'Arabi, *Fusus*, p.171.

Being or consciousness), and as qualified by form, quality and name. In other words, religion offers knowledge through both intellect and imagination, communicating both the Real's transcendence beyond all possible things, as well as affirming its similarity to them. Simply put, true religion reflects all five planes of Being, ranging from the unmanifest Essence, through divinity, archetypes, imaginal forms and entities, and material realities.

This is why religions never simply communicate a 'philosopher's God', a sort of abstract principle to be coolly contemplated. Although the transcendent Essence of the Real is always acknowledged, genuine revelations give people access to this Essence through a particular Self-manifestation of It. Hence, we have the God of the Bible and the Qur'an, who is not simply pure transcendence (though He is that, too), but also Lord, Father, Creator, Protector and Beloved, who sees and hears us, and hence whom we can call upon, and experience intimacy with. These various qualities and attributes of God's self-manifestation are nothing but the Essence in relation to creation, and yet they are the only means by which the Essence of the Real can be known. Again, according to Ibn 'Arabi, knowledge of God *always* includes the imagination: image, form and quality.

The true sage then gives each faculty its due, and when God reveals Himself, acknowledges both the contours of the form through which God is revealed, whether in dream, image, experience or idea, and the way in which God totally goes beyond any conceivable form, image, experience or notion. In contrast, we usually either find a) philosophers and theologians attempting to rationalize or 'explain away' all of the stuff in revelation that sounds mythological or anthropomorphic (such as Jacob wrestling with God in the Bible, or the Qur'an's description of God's hands, face and throne), or, on the other hand, we find b) the basic believer assuming that revelation is true because 'God says so', taking the anthropomorphic stuff a bit too literally with no larger perspective.[497] Chittick notes that neither of these approaches 'give intelligence its full credit, since there are modes of gaining knowledge of the true situation through the power of imagination, which can

---
497 Chittick, *Sufi Path of Knowledge*, p.113.

perceive the divine self-disclosures for what they are'.[498] That is, the true knower recognizes that God appearing in a dream-form, or spiritual experience, or describing Himself using human-like qualities in scripture, is *really* God, but that God is not thereby *limited* to these forms and images, and hence both the form and what is beyond it are given their due.

For some contemporary philosophers of consciousness and contemplation, not only the anthropomorphic accounts of God in scripture, but also the esoterica of the past – the angels, immortals and revelations associated with Elijah and Enoch, for example – should simply be dismissed as fantastical mythologies of simpler times and minds. However, according to Ibn 'Arabi, these entities and experiences are *a factual part of our world*, that no holistic paradigm of reality can afford to neglect, lest it fail to account for an aspect of knowledge critical to an adequate picture of the whole, and hence of the ways in which Being manifests Itself at all levels of reality, whether within material, spiritual, imaginal or intellectual realms.

Ibn 'Arabi further notes in this chapter that not only the intermediate realm between pure meaning and form can be considered to be imaginary, but in fact our own material world can be accurately understood as imaginary too. In one sense, the *whole universe* is imagination, as it delicately hangs between 'sheer Reality and utter nonbeing'.[499] It is a constant dance of display and disappearance, a remarkable intertwining of reality and illusion. Ibn 'Arabi illustrates this in commenting on a verse in the Qur'an (Q 8:17), in which God tells the Prophet Muhammad that, during a battle in which he threw a handful of sand or pebbles: *It was not you who threw, but God threw*. Although this may be read as a sort of metaphor, Ibn 'Arabi tends to read the Qur'an quite literally, and sees here a clear statement of the cosmos' imaginal nature:

> The eye perceived none other than the Muhammadan form, with sight affirming the act of throwing in the physical domain. God first

---
498 Ibid.
499 Ibid., p.54.

denies this form's act of shooting, and then secondly affirms it, as God's throwing in the Muhammadan form.[500]

Here we find the imaginal nature of our world expressed in the Qur'an, in that clearly Muhammad was a physical human being, who in the midst of this battle threw a spear, and yet from another perspective, that of what is ultimately real, only God exists and hence only God acts: Muhammad only appears to be the thrower here. Our world then is more like a dream than we tend to appreciate, a place where meanings take forms, forms without independent existence of their own.[501] It also follows then that our own subjective experience of this world is a *dream within a dream*, or as Ibn 'Arabi puts it towards the end of his chapter on Joseph in the *Gemstones*, 'imagination within imagination'.

> The world is illusory. It has no real existence. And this is the meaning of imagination. For you simply imagine that the world is an autonomous reality existing independently of the Real, while in actuality this is not the case. ... Know that you yourself are imagination, and everything you perceive and say 'this is not me,' is also imagination. All of existence is imagination within imagination.[502]

---

500 I've modified the passage slightly from its original Arabic here for clarity. Ibn 'Arabi, *Fusus*, p.173.

501 In Chapter 188 of his *Futuhat* Ibn 'Arabi discusses dreams, noting that 'when man ascends in the degrees of gnosis, he will come to know through both faith and unveiling that he is a dreamer in the state of ordinary wakefulness and that the situation in which he dwells is a dream'. As quoted in Chittick, *Sufi Path of Knowledge*, p.120.

502 Ibn 'Arabi, *Fusus*, p.88.

6

Things are Even Stranger Than You Think: Moses and the Wisdom of Sublimity

> *You are nothing*
> *when you are wed [to] the One;*
> *but you are everything*
> *when you become nothing.*[503]

Embracing the Mystery

The central theme of this chapter – eminence, exaltation or sublimity (*'uluwiyya*) – suggests the need for intellectual humility in the face of a world that goes way beyond our ideas about it. We are wise, to quote Pulitzer Prize-winning artist Kendrick Lamar, to 'sit down' and 'be humble' in a cosmos far stranger and more exalted in scale than we can know. In just the *observable* universe there are somewhere between two hundred billion and two trillion galaxies. Sufis tell us that our inner universe is even vaster than this. It follows that, if we do not even have a *tiny fraction* of the variables needed to solve the cosmic equation (and cannot fathom how many more we may need), how can we possibly solve it? We need only think of the great scientists, philosophers and mystics throughout history who have taken human knowledge to its outermost limit, where they encounter the ever-expanding horizons of what we do not and even cannot know, rendering them in a state of increasingly muted awe. Einstein famously traced the 'source of all true art and science' to this encounter with mystery, and considered 'the

---

503 'Iraqi, *Divine Flashes*, p.112.

mysterious' to be the most beautiful experience we can have.[504]

A great illustration of this theme of exaltation can be found in a story about ants by Ahmet Hilmi (d.1914). Hilmi was an interesting mix of traditional Sufi and revolutionary modernist who lived during the twilight of the Ottoman Empire. He was a wide-ranging author of philosophy, history, fiction and poetry. In his autobiographical short novel, *Awakened Dreams: Raji's Journey with the Mirror Dede*, he shares a story that keenly illustrates the limitations of our ability to comprehend the cosmos. The main character, Raji, is a troubled young guy, haunted by existential questions and a gnawing skepticism, losing himself in drink to distract from his emptiness and anxiety.

In one of his walks in Istanbul, he happens upon an eccentric old man living in an abandoned cemetery, known as the Mirror Dede. People call him the Mirror as he wears mirrored glass pieces on his hat. Raji is initially off put by the strangeness of his appearance, and respectfully asks Dede about his mirrored hat. Dede responds that people wear things they enjoy, and in some cases spend a great deal of money on what they wear, and yet he enjoys the simple mirrors on his hat. He continues to suggest that his mirrored hat is no stranger than wearing a halter and calling it a necktie, and that even if both indicate the nonsensical nature of humanity, at least his choice is more luminous and beautiful. Raji can't help but appreciate the surprisingly sensible nature of the Mirror's answer. He is intrigued by his unassuming depth, and decides to spend time with the elderly man.[505]

Each day while drinking tea with the Mirror Dede, Raji experiences a prolonged lucid dream, whereby he finds himself in another life and world, perhaps a metaphor for the deeper dimensions of consciousness that can open up when one spends time with a Sufi master. One day, after tea with the Mirror, Raji awakens as an ant, in a meticulously organized colony of hundreds of thousands, with a complex division of labor, and sophisticated legal and education systems. Raji finds that he is the son of a master ant, and receives the best training available under top ant scholars. He cannot help but reflect on how much

---

504 Albert Einstein, *Living Philosophies* (New York, 1931), p.5.
505 Hilmi, *Awakened Dreams*, p.9.

more efficient and polite his newfound ant society is than its human counterparts tend to be.

Raji soon discovers that he is able to switch perspectives at will, and can see the world both as an ant and as a human. While attending an academic conference held by the ants, on the renowned 'strange field' outside their colony – whose angular borders have long mystified ant scientists – *tragedy strikes*. From the sky rains an unexpected deluge, with an intensity never seen before in the colony's history. Many among the thousands of conference attendees are washed away, including Raji. Before he drowns, however, Raji switches to the human perspective to try to see what is happening, and finds himself equal parts shocked and amused by what he sees. He recognizes the 'strange field' as one of the cobble stones on a wide avenue lined with pleasant shops. A small carriage has stopped on the avenue while the driver takes a nap. The carriage's two horses take the pause as an opportunity to relieve themselves, unaware that they are washing away thousands of ants in the process. One of the more famous ant scientists who survived the catastrophe later formulates an explanation for the great flood: electromagnetism that periodically caused sudden, dangerous cloud bursts.[506]

Raji bemusedly sees that there is no way for the ants to realize how much is going on beyond their experience of the world. Whereas he can, at will, switch to the perspective of a human being and perceive the larger world that the colony exists within, there is no way for the ants to know that their world is itself existing within other worlds beyond their ken, on a scale beyond what they can fathom. As such, their scientific theories fall humorously short of accounting for what is actually going on. One may know a tiny fraction of existence, and may know it quite well, but this offers little ground for extrapolating what might be the nature of the whole. Furthermore, some kinds of knowledge may be exceedingly subtle and hence quite rare, requiring a perspectival shift unavailable to most (as we discussed in the previous chapter).

---

506 Ibid., pp.92–5.

We can recall here the story of the frogs meeting in the well, from the chapter on Shu'ayb. Until the well frog sees for himself just how vast the ocean frog's home is, he has no way of gauging how much more there is to reality than what he knows of his little well. This notion, that beyond the appearances of our world, lay realities far vaster and stranger than we can fathom, is actually central to one of the key stories of Moses in the Qur'an, and hence Ibn 'Arabi's chapter on him in the *Gemstones*. After all, Ibn 'Arabi always maintained that his works were something along the lines of an extended commentary on the Qur'an, which we see quite clearly here.

Moses and the Green Man

Moses is likely one the most recognizable names in humanity's collective history. He is a paradigmatic prophet for not only Jews, but also for Christians and Muslims, who altogether make up about half of the world's population. Moses is believed by members of all three religions to have received the word of God, transmitted God's commandments and led his people from oppression to freedom. The Ten Commandments are foundational to not only Jewish but also Christian notions of law and morality. Muslims further see Moses as the quintessential predecessor of Muhammad, who also functioned as a law-giving, community-leading prophet. The Qur'an actually mentions Moses (or *Musa* in Arabic) more than any other person in the text, and excerpts of his story are shared throughout Muslim scripture.

Like the Bible, the Qur'an tells of Moses' mother placing him as an infant in a basket, and sending him down the Nile to avoid being killed by Pharoah. Baby Moses is discovered by Pharoah's wife, eventually, serendipitously given back to his mother for nursing, then coming of age in Pharoah's palace (Q 28:3–14). Although things initially look good for Moses in Pharoah's court, he ends up having to go on the run for killing an Egyptian, who Moses found beating a fellow Hebrew (Q 28:15–20). The Qur'an continues to narrate his work as a shepherd and his marriage (Q 28:23–8). It details Moses' eventual encounter with God at the burning bush, his call to prophecy and help from his brother Aaron (*Harun*), and return to Pharoah to free his people from slavery, who obstinately refuses to acknowledge Moses and his God or free the Hebrews. Pharoah later dies when the Red Sea that opened for Moses and the Hebrews closes in on him and his army pursuing them (Q 20:9–80). The Qur'an further narrates Moses leading his people through the desert, where they are given sustenance by God. However, during his 40-day retreat on Mt. Sinai, they fall into the worship of the golden calf, and Moses returns to rebuke them, and shares the tablets of the Torah (Q 7:148–54).

There is one particularly mysterious story of Moses that is found nowhere in the Bible. The story lies at the heart of the Qur'an (in the book's actual middle), in the 18th chapter, known as 'the Cave', or *Surah al-Kahf*. Islamic studies scholar Bruce Lawrence calls this chapter the Qur'an's 'centerpiece'.[507] The chapter contains three strange narratives that have interesting parallels with more ancient legends in the Middle East,[508] particularly those that deal with questions of death and immortality.[509] This particular story about Moses narrates his encounter with an inscrutable guide who has been given knowledge directly from God's presence, one who knows the unseen realities behind what transpires in the world of appearances.

From records of Muhammad's explanations of the story, we find this mysterious one's name: *al-Khadir* (literally 'the Green One' or 'Green Man'), or more commonly Khidr or Khizr.[510] For Muslims, the

---

507 Bruce Lawrence, 'Foreword', in Hugh Talat Halman, *Where the Two Seas Meet: The Qur'anic Story of al-Khidr and Moses in Sufi Commentaries as a Model of Spiritual Guidance* (Louisville, KY, 2013), p.vii.

508 The narrative on Dhu'l-Qarnayn (18:83–102) has some remarkable similarities to an earlier Syriac text, *Neshana dileh d-Alexandros* or the *Alexander Legend*, as pointed to by van Bladel, though he probably overstates these similarities in places. See Kevin van Bladel, 'The Alexander Legend in the Qur'an 18:83–102', in *The Qur'an in its Historical Context*, edited by Gabriel Said Reynolds (New York, 2008), pp.175–203.

509 The *surah* is named after one of these three narratives, the one known as the 'Companions of the Cave' (*ashab al-kahf*), which retells elements of a widely circulated Christian story – the Seven Sleepers of Ephesus. For more on this, see Sidney Griffith, 'Christian Lore and the Arabic Qur'an: The "Companions of the Cave" in *Surat al-Kahf* and in Syriac Christian Tradition', in *The Qur'an in its Historical Context*, edited by Gabriel Said Reynolds (New York, 2008), pp.109–37.

510 Talat Halman, *Where the Two Seas Meet*, p.1.

Green Man became something of a patron saint of the lost and alone, God's emissary of hidden grace to those without a living master, and the one who intervenes when most needed by those lost in the seas of life's trials. Some suggest that Khidr has drank from the water of life and transcended the constrictions of time and space. Like Elijah–Enoch, he is an immortal, a being that can show up anywhere. He is named the Green One as wherever he steps greenery grows, overflowing with life and verdancy.[511]

The narrative of Moses' encounter with Khidr occurs in verses 60 to 82 of *Surah al-Kahf*. It begins with Moses and his servant seeking the 'meeting place of the two seas' (*majma' al-bahrayn*) (18:60), a pregnant metaphor that suggests a liminal space, a space in-between the 'seas' of the seen and unseen worlds, a place 'that is in the world, yet beyond it; it is both-and / neither-nor at the same time'.[512] Hence it remains unclear whether his encounter with Khidr that follows takes place in a vision, dream or the material realm. Some have drawn parallels here to the ancient Mesopotamian Epic of Gilgamesh. In the Epic's ninth book, Gilgamesh, struggling with the loss of his friend and his own mortality, seeks out an immortal, Utnapishtim, who can be found at the 'mouth of the rivers'.[513] Whether the mouth of rivers or the meeting of seas, the confluence of waters suggests a place of power, possibility and immortality.

In the Qur'anic narrative, Moses vows to keep seeking this meeting place of the seas, even if it takes *years of travelling* (Q 18:60). Already he is modeling how the seeker of hidden knowledge should proceed: for knowledge precious and rare, one should be single-minded in their dedication to find it, embracing the possibility of a lengthy journey. For Sufis, the story of Moses' encounter with Khidr is seen as an iconic illustration of the master–disciple relationship on the spiritual path. Rumi's teacher, Shams-i Tabrizi, reportedly said, 'Blessed is the one who finds such a servant [like Khidr] and who holds the story of

---

511 The Prophet Muhammad reportedly described Khidr as one who 'would sit on a felt mat and underneath him would sprout greenery (*khadra*')'. Quoted by Ibn Arabi in *Fut*.II.15.
512 Halman, *Where the Two Seas Meet*, p.ix.
513 Brannon Wheeler, 'Moses or Alexander? Early Islamic Exegesis of Qur'an 18:60-65', *Journal of Near Eastern Studies*, 57:3 (1998), 192.

Moses and al-Khidr in his heart, and makes it his *imam* (guide).'[514] We will see that Moses' tolerance for what escapes his understanding is repeatedly tested, tests that anyone who embarks on such a journey must undergo.

After seeking for some time, Moses and his servant finally rest on a rock where the seas meet. He asks his servant to prepare the fish they brought for their meal (Q 18:62). The servant replies that he forgot to mention that the fish escaped into the water, in a strange and wondrous way (Q 18:63). Moses recognizes this as a sign that they have reached their sought-after destination. This particular episode of the story, where the fish miraculously escapes into the water, has some interesting parallels with an episode from *Alexander Romance*, a beloved saga of Alexander the Great that circulated widely in the Mediterranean and Middle East of late antiquity, based on a third century CE Greek work. Accurately referred to as 'antiquity's most successful novel', *Alexander Romance* became immensely popular in the centuries before Islam, being translated into Latin, Coptic, Syriac and later Hebrew, Arabic, Persian and Turkish (among other languages), undergoing several variations.[515] In every case, however, *Romance* is chock-full of tales of Alexander's cleverness, magnanimity and heroism, and his encounters with fantastical peoples and creatures beyond the known world. According to these legends, Alexander explores the ends of the earth with his army, and comes across 'a translucent spring, whose water flashed like lightning'.[516] He calls for his cook Andreas to prepare a meal. Andreas takes some salt fish and washes it in the spring, whereupon it miraculously comes to life and swims away. He is afraid to report this to Alexander, and in some version of the tale, Andreas instead drinks some of the water, becoming immortal.[517]

---

514 Talat Halman, *Where the Two Seas Meet*, p.1.

515 The story has 80 recorded versions in 24 languages. B. P. Reardon, 'The Alexander Romance', translated by Ken Dowden, *Collected Ancient Greek Novels* (Berkeley, 1989), p.650.

516 Ibid., p.710.

517 This element of the *Alexander Romance* narrative is, interestingly, also found within Islamic traditions. Ibn 'Arabi, for instance, reports that Khidr was initially a soldier sent by his commander to find water, and he discovered a well that turned out to be the Source of Life, drinking from it and becoming immortal. *Fut*.I. See Addas, *Quest for the Red Sulphur*, p.63.

Just as Moses suspects, the fish's strange escape indicates they have arrived, and he soon finds Khidr, whom the Qur'an characterizes as *one of Our servants* whom God has given mercy and knowledge directly from His own presence (Q 18:65). Moses asks Khidr to teach him some of his knowledge, but Khidr cautions Moses that he will not be able to bear with him, for *how can you have patience with that which is beyond your understanding?* (Q 18:68). Khidr here points to our tendency to react negatively to that which we do not understand: we tend to be instinctive enemies of that which escapes our comprehension. We much prefer our comfortable zones of 'ah yes, that makes perfect sense and accords well with my expectations and prepackaged ideas of what things should be like'. We generally find people or experiences that challenge our preconceptions disturbing. Mystical or esoteric traditions have historically faced persecution at various times, in some cases for precisely this reason, and hence the frequent need for some manner of discretion and even secrecy. This need was well understood by the Prophet Muhammad and his closest companions, several of whom hinted at an inner teaching given to them that was not shared with the entire community. For example, Abu Hurayra (who was also a frequent narrator of reports about Muhammad's teachings), said: 'I have committed to memory two vessels (of teachings) from the Messenger of God: One of them I have widely disseminated; but as for the other, if I had disseminated it this throat of mine would have been cut!'[518]

Despite Khidr's warning to Moses, Moses affirms that he will do his best to be patient with Khidr and follow his direction, again modeling how the seeker should be with a spiritual guide: if someone is going to lead you beyond all of your familiar reference points, you will have little choice but to go along for the ride, because you're not going to have much of an idea of where you're going or how to get there. As the spiritual path takes one far beyond the familiar terrain of everyday consciousness, it requires a profound degree of trust. This is

---

518 *Sahih al-Bukhari* Vol. 1, Book 3, No. 121. As quoted by James Winston Morris, 'How to Study the *Futuhat*: Ibn 'Arabi's Own Advice', *Muhyiddin Ibn 'Arabi: A Commemorative Volume*, edited by Stephen Hirtenstein and Michael Tiernan, p.78.

also why various contemplative traditions emphasize the importance of choosing your teacher wisely, of ensuring that they are a mature guide whom you have a genuine relationship with and who clearly has your best interests at heart.

Khidr accepts Moses as his student on the condition that Moses not question him about anything until he first mentions it. Their time together, however, proves to be totally unbearable for Moses, and he is unable to abide by Khidr's condition. During their travels together Khidr inexplicably sinks a boat, later kills a boy they randomly come across and then repairs a wall in a town they have just been kicked out of. Each time he engages in a shocking and outrageous act, Moses vehemently (and understandably) protests. In a way, Moses is the archetypal representative of the law, of moral guidelines, of fair and reasonable ways of being, which Khidr appears to be exploding. The third time Moses challenges him, Khidr announces their parting, and proceeds to explain his actions:

> *As for the boat, it belonged to poor people who worked at sea. I wished to damage it, as there was a king after them who seized every ship by force. As for the boy, his parents were believers, and we feared that he would oppress them by rebellion and disbelief. So we intended that their Lord should give them one better in righteousness and nearer to mercy. And as for the wall, it belonged to two orphan boys in the town; and there was under it a treasure belonging to them; and their father was a righteous man, and your Lord intended that they should attain their age of full strength and take out their treasure as a mercy from your Lord. And I did it not of my own accord. That is the interpretation of what you could not bear with patience. (18: 79–82)*

During his time with Khidr, Moses is shocked when he does things that appear to be outrageous and even morally egregious. Khidr then explains the *reality* behind the actions, a reality that, when understood, makes the actions comprehensible as having a larger purpose not immediately intelligible, namely the purpose of *mercy*.

We might think of this story in light of Raji's experience as an ant – from the ant's perspective there are a whole host of things that seem bizarre and inexplicable, but when seen from a much grander perspective, they are comprehensible, at least to a much greater degree than when perceived in a more limited fashion. In this case, the surface appearances of Khidr's actions *appear* to be either destructive or absurd, though, with a knowledge of the unseen, of what lies beneath, behind or above our daily experiential reality, his actions prove to be ultimately creative in nature. Carl Jung (d.1961) interprets this story psychologically, with Moses representing 'ego-consciousness' and its reactions to the deeper wisdom of the 'higher consciousness' or 'self' (Khidr), 'through the twists and turns of fate'.[519] The ego struggles to follow the self's own higher wisdom, as it is in accord with the deeper nature of things, which transcends reason.

This paradoxical contrast between appearance and reality, or the ego-self and higher consciousness, is, for Ibn 'Arabi, definitive of our world, as much of it seems so inexplicable, and yet when understood from a more encompassing vantage point its wisdom and mercy become apparent. This contrast between appearance and reality further explains why someone who is operating in the world with an awareness of the bigger picture will seem at times inexplicable, for their actions reflect a far larger scale of awareness than those whose ego-consciousness remains fixated on surface appearances. This phenomenon sometimes appears in folk tales about the 'holy fool'[520] or traditions of 'crazy wisdom'.[521] Simply put, people who live with

---

519 Carl G. Jung, *The Archetypes and the Collective Unconscious*, Second Edition, translated by R.F. C. Hull (Princeton, NJ, 1969), p.141.

520 The idea of the 'holy fool' in Christianity can be traced back to early Christian ascetic traditions and later monastic contexts in Byzantium and Russia. The holy fool is one who is immersed in God, and in a sense goes beyond convention, often behaving in shocking, incomprehensible or blameworthy ways. St. Symeon of Emesa, for example (also known as Symeon the Holy Fool), apparently entered the town of Emesa dressed in rags and dragging a dead dog behind him. He was known to disturb church services, and generally treated like a madman, but later venerated as one of the first 'fools for Christ'. Priscilla Hunt, 'Holy Foolishness as a Key to Russian Culture', in *Holy Foolishness in Russia: New Perspectives*, edited by Priscilla Hunt and Svitlana Kobets (Bloomington, IN, 2011), pp.1–2.

521 Chogyam Trungpa (d.1987) translated the Tibetan *yeshe chowla* as 'crazy wisdom', referring both to a style of sainthood in Vajrayana, and a state of being without reference point or goal. See Chogyam Trungpa, *Crazy Wisdom*, edited by Sherab Chodzin (Boston, 2001).

a much larger awareness, one that dwarfs conventional perspectives, can at times seem entirely strange and surprising.[522] Jung concludes his observation of this story by suggesting, 'To the initiate capable of transformation it is a comforting tale; to the obedient believer, an exhortation not to murmur against Allah's incomprehensible omnipotence.'[523]

The Prophet and the Saint

This story in the Qur'an raises an interesting question about the relationship between prophethood, sainthood and knowledge. Moses is the *paradigmatic* prophet and yet Khidr, who is not named as a prophet in the Qur'an, is given knowledge directly from God that Moses does not have, and therefore seeks to learn. Within Jewish, Christian and Muslim theologies, prophets are generally assumed to be the *only* people who are given knowledge directly from God, with some concession that saintly figures may have such knowledge, but in a more limited way. What then can be the meaning of this? How is it that a non-prophet has knowledge from God that a prophet does not? Is Khidr a sort of singular being in this regard, or is he representative of a broader phenomenon? Or, alternately, is Khidr a sort of unofficial, unaffiliated prophet? Is the border between a prophet and a non-prophet getting blurred here?

We can explore this issue in a bit further depth through one of the most famous saints in Islamic history, 'Abd al-Qadir al-Jilani. He was a committed Hanbali, meaning he was an exponent of the juristic-theological school known for its adherence to the literal meaning of the Qur'an and hadith. Al-Jilani was renowned during his life as a no-

---

522 Ibn 'Arabi devotes the 44th chapter of his *Futuhat* to the Bahalil: people who appear to be 'crazy' or *majnun* to observers, but are actually 'intelligent people with no intellects', as the intensity of God's self-disclosure to them simply erases their rationality (but not their intelligence, and it's worth noting the distinction between the two here). He further shares that saintly ones respond in a variety of ways to such intense inrush of God's presence – some are dominated completely by it and appear to be among the mad ones for their whole life; others experience a kind of divine madness for a period of time only; and others are able to integrate such intense spiritual awareness within an everyday functioning self. See 'The Bahalil', in Ibn 'Arabi, *The Openings Revealed in Makkah, Books 3 & 4*, translated by Winkel, pp.398–406.

523 Jung, *The Archetypes and the Collective Unconscious*, p.141.

nonsense, even 'fire-and-brimstone' kind of preacher in Baghdad, calling people to repentance, prayer and obeying God's laws before they die and face divine judgment. It was, interestingly, only over time that the spread of his spiritual way by his disciples led to al-Jilani's global fame as one of the very pillars of Sufism, and his celebration as one of Islam's highest, most realized saints.[524] To this day the Qadiri Sufi order remains one of the most globally widespread, and al-Jilani is celebrated in song and festival by Muslims the world over.

In *The Meccan Revelations* Ibn 'Arabi shares that al-Jilani proclaimed: 'Assemblies of the prophets! You have been given the title, but we have been given what you were not given.'[525] Now, al-Jilani was an especially devout follower of the Prophet Muhammad. For such a dedicated follower of the Prophet, and one of Islam's most beloved saints, his saying seems to fly in the face of his own religious sensibilities. Happily, many of al-Jilani's sermons were written down and collected by his students. In one of his talks found in a quite beautiful collection known as *al-Fath al-Rabbani* or *The Sublime Revelation*, he addresses this issue of the relationship between prophethood and sainthood:

> The Prophets receive their training from the Lord of Truth (Almighty and Glorious is He) through his direct speech [*kalam*], while the saints [*awliya'*] are trained by Him through His indirect speech [*hadith*]. This indirect speech is an inspiration [*ilham*] within their hearts, because they are the caretakers [*awsiya'*], the deputies [*khulafa'*] and the servants [*ghilman*] of the Prophets.[526]

Al-Jilani clearly distinguishes prophets as receiving *direct* communication from God, whereas saints receive it only indirectly as inspiration in their hearts, and hence they remain the servants of

---

524 Hamza Malik convincingly shows that J. Spencer Trimingham's contention that 'there is not the slightest indication that [al-Jilani] was a Sufi at all' fails to take into account the larger picture provided by al-Jilani's works and biographies, arguing instead that 'he was [a Sufi] and that his reputation as the greatest saint amongst the Muslims is not an incomprehensible phenomenon'. *The Grey Falcon: The Life and Teaching of Shaykh 'Abd al-Qadir al-Jilani* (Leiden, 2018), pp.21, 25.

525 Ibn 'Arabi, *Fut*.II.90. As quoted in Chittick, *The Self-Disclosure of God*, p.378.

526 'Abd al-Qadir al-Jilani, *The Sublime Revelation: A Collection of Sixty-Two Discourses*, translated by Muhtar Holland (Houston, 1992), p.29.

the prophets. In light of this statement of his, what can he mean by saying that saints have received something that prophets have not? Ibn 'Arabi relates that his words can be traced directly back to the Qur'an, particularly with this story of Khidr, who was given what Moses was not, even though Moses has the title 'prophet'. The question follows, however, what exactly is it that Khidr and al-Jilani have that the prophets do not? Does this mean that the saints are somehow higher or more realized than prophets? Quite the contrary, as we will see. To elaborate, we must enter into a fascinating discussion of Ibn 'Arabi's on the precise nature of prophecy, sainthood and the relationship between the two.

As we have previously discussed, the word for 'saint' in the Islamic tradition (though not an exact equivalent in meaning) is *wali*. The Qur'an says that *truly the friends of God (awliya li-llahi) shall neither fear nor sorrow* (Q 10:62). A *wali* or 'friend' is one who is both an *intimate* and a *deputy* of God. One of the meanings of the root *waw-lam-ya* is proximity and love, and hence a friend of God is one brought near to God's presence in a relationship of mutual love. Another meaning of the root is guardianship, and hence a *wali* is also tasked by God with being a guardian for those in his or her community or region, caring for them and transmitting the life-giving energy of blessing to them. Mukhtar Ali notes that when *waw-lam-ya* is in the form *walaya*, it means 'proximity, contiguity, love and friendship', and when in the form *wilaya*, it means 'governance, authority and sainthood'.[527] To keep things simple I have simply opted to use *walaya* as a term referring to both meanings of proximity and guardianship.

The Islamic doctrine of *walaya* really comes to maturity in the works of Ibn 'Arabi (at least for Sunnis), and Muslims after him have tended to understand sainthood within the framework he solidified. His doctrine on saints was not without controversy, however, and his opponents focused on it with particular opprobrium. And, I suppose, we can't really blame them. Saints tend to be controversial, and most religious traditions have accounts of saintly figures facing condemnation by religious clerics and scholars, for the living spirit

---

527 Ali, *The Horizons of Being*, p.13.

of religion so often disturbs its solidified scaffolding. Ibn 'Arabi says on this, 'The religious scholars of every age have been, and remain, in relation to those who have realized truth [saints], like pharaohs in relation to prophets.'[528] People grounded exclusively in the doctrines, rules and regulations of religion tend to be disturbed by those who have realized the spiritual intention and meaning of these things, and, as a result, can target them for persecution.

We see this vividly within the history of Christianity as well: early Protestants were totally opposed to the Catholic notion of sainthood, and even the Catholic Church only accepted a saint as genuine after they had been given an official stamp of approval by the Vatican. Broadly speaking, religions are largely stabilized by canonizing whose religious experiences count as authentic (usually the founder's and some key early figures). Someone coming along claiming to have similar insight as the founder can be seen as rocking the proverbial boat. It is often easier to acknowledge that one person many centuries ago had a profound experience of God or truth or enlightenment – that's one thing. But now someone down the street is talking about having those experiences too? Does that mean that they also deserve some of our veneration and devotion? What if they're a quack? It's not really that difficult to see why this idea, that there might actually be *living* holy folks, is a tough pill to swallow for those concerned with maintaining a hyper-coherent religious tradition with clearly defined borders. This is doubly so if you are among the scholarly clerical class whose own commitment and livelihood is premised on a mastery of this clearly mapped religious terrain.

In Islam, sainthood is a doctrine that can be traced, in an interesting way, to Khidr himself. Although it is of course in the Qur'an where we find the origin of *walaya*, the subject receives its first full treatment by al-Hakim al-Tirmidhi (d.c.932), a sage from Islam's eastern lands. Hailing from the border zone between eastern Iran and Afghanistan, known as Khorasan, al-Tirmidhi was a prolific early Sufi author. As a young adult he focused on studying hadith and law but after a pilgrimage to Mecca in his late twenties he thereafter switched

---

528 Muhyi al-Din Ibn 'Arabi, *Ruh al-qudus fi munasahat al-nafs* (Tunis, 2004), p.181.

his focus to spiritual practice and memorizing the Qur'an.[529] In terms of his spiritual training, al-Tirmidhi was a disciple of Khidr's, the mysterious Green One apparently visiting him every Sunday to impart esoteric teachings.[530] This might seem incredibly strange, but a great many Sufi orders are premised on teachings given from non-material beings, whether immortals like Khidr, or from the spiritual form of a Sufi master long since passed from the earth.[531] Recall that the *Gemstones* itself is a text Ibn 'Arabi received directly from the spiritual form of the Prophet Muhammad. As we discussed in the last chapter, the intermediate world of spiritual beings is as objectively real as the world of material ones, and as the world of pure ideas, it's just that very few have had access to it historically and so it seems quite strange to those unaccustomed to such encounters as al-Tirmidhi's.[532]

Generally speaking, Sufi teachings suggest that the border between our world and the unseen/realm of spirit is not as stark as we imagine, and that genuine communication is possible between them, especially for those who have opened the 'doors of perception' that lay within. One of the particular ways in which spiritual transmission can occur across the border of the seen and unseen, is known as an Uwaysi connection. This phenomenon is named after Uways al-Qarani (d.657), a Yemeni who lived during the time of the Prophet Muhammad.[533] It is said that he never met the Prophet, but still believed in him through a spiritual intuition, sensing his presence and reality. And the Prophet was also

---

529 Although we gain some of these details from his autobiography, he actually spends much of it recounting symbolic dreams, ones he had, as well as those of his wife, dreams that facilitated both of their spiritual wayfaring. Bernd Radtke and John O'Kane, *The Concept of Sainthood in Early Islamic Mysticism: Two Works by al-Hakim al-Tirmidhi* (New York, 1996), pp.1–2.

530 Chodkiewicz, *Seal of the Saints*, p.29.

531 Ibn 'Arabi himself reports encountering Khidr several times in his life, beginning in his youth, and culminating in his receiving the *khirqa khadiriyya*, or symbolic, initiatic cloak from Khidr, meaning that he could thenceforth transmit the particular *baraka* or blessing energy of Khidr. Addas, *Quest for the Red Sulphur*, p.62.

532 It's worth mentioning here that Ibn 'Arabi had a close spiritual relationship with al-Tirmidhi. In addition to citing him several times in his works, he also wrote a treatise on al-Tirmidhi, and in the 73rd chapter of his *Futuhat*, provided a full set of answers to al-Tirmidhi's famous questionnaire.

533 For more on the Uwaysi phenomenon in Sufism, see Julian Baldick, *Imaginary Muslims: The Uwaysi Sufis of Central Asia* (New York, 1993).

aware of Uways. He reportedly said, regarding him, 'The Breath of the Merciful comes to me from Yemen'.[534] For Sufis, al-Qarani is an icon of those who receive initiation or teaching from one not physically present.[535] In Sufi practice this occurs when 'the imaginal form (*ruhaniyat*) of deceased shaykhs appear during a visionary experience'.[536] Hence, those Sufis who were trained by a shaykh no longer in the body are referred to as Uwaysi in reference to al-Qarani. In some orders, like the Naqshbandiyya, this is a built-in element of their training. Because the deep reality of the heart transcends time and space, if one has a heart connection with a being, that connection need not be restricted by the borders of life and death. Many more of us encounter this kind of connection with loved ones who have moved on to the next world, whether in dream, vision, sign or intuition.

Al-Tirmidhi begins his discussion of sainthood with some consternation, as so few genuinely know anything of the phenomenon. He laments that 'those who talk of sainthood know nothing about it whatsoever', evaluating the question of sainthood with a surface-level analysis, drawing upon their own uninformed opinion to make sense of it, and as a result 'they have no conception of the way in which Allah operates'.[537] Saints are in fact integral to how the world works, though their nature is little understood. Very few people know about this aspect of life, because exceedingly few have a genuine experience of a saint and even fewer are saints themselves.

---

534 Schimmel, *Mystical Dimensions of Islam*, p.28.

535 In his *Ruh al-Qudus*, Ibn 'Arabi refers to al-Qarani as 'the best of disciples' despite never having met Muhammad in person, and one whose nights were spent bowing in prayer, and days giving everything he had away in charity. See Roger Boase and Farid Sahnoun, 'Excerpts from the Epistle on the Spirit of Holiness (*Risala Ruh al-Quds*)', in *Muhyiddin Ibn 'Arabi: A Commemorative Volume*, edited by Stephen Hirtenstein and Michael Tiernan, pp.55–6.

536 Buehler, *Sufi Heirs of the Prophet*, p.88. As we discussed in the first chapter, Sufi cosmology, especially following Ibn 'Arabi, tends to divide reality into three realms: one of formless spirit (God), one of material forms (the cosmos) and an intermediate realm between the two, a realm of spiritual forms (angels, saints, *jinn*). For more on this, see Chittick's *Imaginal Worlds* (1994).

537 Al-Tirmidhi, *Kitab khatm al-awliya'*. As quoted by Chodkiewicz, *Seal of the Saints*, pp.28–9.

This is, in part, why so many clerics have historically had their doctrinal feathers ruffled by the question of saints. The existence and workings of saints is a part of the exalted strangeness that goes beyond appearances, but is in fact integral to the world's functioning. Al-Tirmidhi gives us a clue on how to find them, however, sharing that the guarantee of genuine sainthood is that God's peace and presence (*sakina*) is found with them. In other words, spending time with them brings a palpable serenity and organically inspires recollection of the sacred, of life's preciousness and rich meaning, of love. The Prophet Muhammad said that 'the Saints among you are those who you cannot see without remembering God'.[538] Jesus said, 'you shall know them by their fruits' (Matthew 7:16) and indeed the fruits of visceral peace, love, healing and remembrance are precisely how one knows a saint.

One of the most important points that al-Tirmidhi makes in his work on this subject is also one that disturbed some of the jurists and clerics of his time, who would persecute him for years because of it. Al-Tirmidhi pointed out that *nubuwwa*, the phenomenon of prophecy, clearly comes to an end, while sainthood, *walaya*, does not. First, he observes that the highest rank among the prophets are messengers (those who bring scripture and law), and their line ends with the last messenger, Muhammad. So, Muslim belief unquestionably affirms that the line of messengers (*risala*) comes to an end. Second, al-Tirmidhi points out that the sacred laws and communal teachings brought by prophets are *historically contingent*. They simply do not last forever, as divine legislation ceases to be relevant when the world ends and there aren't any human societies to govern anymore. However, in contrast to this situation, *walaya*, the phenomenon of sainthood, is eternal. God Himself is named *al-Wali*, the eternal Friend and Guardian, though He is not named *nabi* or *rasul*, also indicating their contingent nature. Furthermore, spiritual realization has no historical limit – it neither comes to an endpoint somewhere in human history, nor does it cease with the world's end.[539]

---

538 Ibid., p.29.
539 Ibid., p.30.

Before concluding, incorrectly, that this means that saints are somehow superior to prophets (and this is exactly the incorrect conclusion that the opponents of al-Tirmidhi, and later the opponents of Ibn 'Arabi, came to), it is important to add to this that both al-Tirmidhi and Ibn 'Arabi believed that *walaya* encompassed *nubuwwa*, or put differently, that prophecy is a special *kind* of sainthood. Every prophet is first and foremost a saint or *wali*, namely one who has actualized the fullness of their human nature (a nature we discussed in the first chapter), and who has knowledge of the reality of things.[540] However, a prophet is a special kind of saint, one who has been tasked with communication – whether that be warning, teaching, reforming, guiding and so forth. Among prophets, the special group of them called to be messengers is even smaller in number, rarely occurring in human history, as they are called to transmit a scripture, law and path, shaping the trajectory of whole cultures over centuries.

In other words, sainthood (*walaya*) is the largest possible category in the Islamic tradition for describing human spiritual realization. It can also function as an umbrella term for all of the great sages and realized souls of our world's various traditions. Although the line of messengers comes to an end with Muhammad, Ibn 'Arabi holds that a sort of 'general prophethood' continues, which is simply the persistence of sainthood: human realization, spiritual power, knowledge of the unseen, and guidance, all occurring without the advent of a new scripture or sacred law.

Ibn 'Arabi interprets al-Jilani's claim, that he has something that prophets do not, as meaning that he has a higher rank of knowledge among saints, who constitute this 'general prophethood'. Perhaps another way to interpret his saying is to suggest that prophets do not have what al-Jilani has, *in their social role as prophets*, though what they have in terms of spiritual realization, *as saints*, is greater than what he or any other follower of a prophet has in terms of knowledge. In this regard, sainthood is superior to prophethood, but prophets, and above them messengers, by definition have the greatest degree of sainthood, making them a rank higher than their various saintly

---

540 Chittick, *Heir to the Prophets*, p.13.

followers.⁵⁴¹ Ibn ʿArabi sums this up by saying that prophethood is the shadow of God's function, and sainthood is the shadow of the prophetic function, clearly affirming the superiority of prophets over saints, much as al-Jilani does in the passage from the *Sublime Revelation* quoted above.⁵⁴² Prophets then are the highest rank of saint, as their knowledge (as saints) is more comprehensive than that of non-prophet saints, while their prophetic mission is actually something secondary to their spiritual level.

Regardless of how we illustrate this relationship, we may still ask what then is it that distinguishes these various degrees of sainthood? Ibn ʿArabi says simply that sainthood is defined by nothing else besides knowledge. He suggests that a *wali* is at base one who has genuinely realized the nature of reality, namely Oneness. A saint lives with the existential awareness that *the appearances that constitute ourselves and our world are none other than God's self-manifestation in the space–time continuum*. Reality goes infinitely beyond these appearances, which can only ever gesture toward the ocean underlying them, and the saint lives with an awareness of this oceanic spectrum of reality at all times, and hence can operate on various levels simultaneously. Prophets are themselves saints with this knowledge and ability, only with the addition that they are given knowledge of revelation and law that other saints follow.⁵⁴³

Ibn ʿArabi draws this out in his discussion of the Qur'anic narrative of Moses and Khidr, holding that Khidr respected Moses' rank as a messenger, and hence his parting from Moses was not simply out of

---

541 Izutsu, *Sufism and Taoism*, p.267.
542 Chodkiewicz, *Seal of the Saints*, p.41.
543 Ibn ʿArabi elaborated upon this notion of degrees of *walaya*, describing a hidden hierarchy of perfected humans, with select numbers living on earth at any particular time, tasked by God with preserving the world. Some among this select group of perfected humans have a privileged relationship with a particular Name of God. For example, Ibn ʿArabi discusses the *abdal* (literally the 'replacements' or 'substitutes', as they are always being replaced by another to take over their position when they die). The *abdal* are among the highest levels of perfected humans, a sort of Jedi knight high council, with seven of them living on earth at any point in time, tasked with preserving the seven geographical regions of the world. He notes that each of them is a servant of a particular Name of God, including 'The Living' (*al-Hayy*), 'The Loving,' (*al-Wadud*), 'The Grateful' (*al-Shakur*) and 'The Seer' (*al-Basir*). Ibid.

a lack of patience, but rather, Khidr leaves Moses also out of respect for him, acknowledging that although he had knowledge of the unseen that Moses did not, Moses, as a prophet, also had knowledge unavailable to Khidr, and a rank with God beyond what Khidr could achieve. Hence Khidr was manifesting the core Sufi virtue of *adab* or etiquette here, in respectfully acknowledging the rights due to Moses based on his rank with God.

The Nature of Moses and the Meaning of Embodiment

Ibn 'Arabi next considers the origin story of Moses, drawing attention to how this story illustrates just how starkly appearances can be at odds with their deeper reality. He starts with elaborating the divine wisdom underlying Pharaoh's slaying of Hebrew boys, something Pharaoh ordered as his astrologer predicted that a male among them would lead the Hebrews in rebellion (this male being Moses). On the surface this appears to be an unmitigated atrocity, and of course, on one level, that is exactly what it is. And yet Ibn 'Arabi points to the greater significance of Pharoah's actions, totally unbeknownst to him as the doer of them. Pharoah's killings in fact have the opposite effect of his intent to prevent Moses:

> The wisdom of killing the sons because of Moses was that the life of every slain boy would revert to Moses, being killed as if he were Moses. And there was no ignorance in this, for the life of every slain boy was necessarily returned to Moses. Each life was pure, because its inborn nature of the primordial covenant was unimpaired by selfish aims. So Moses was an amalgam of all of the lives taken as if they were him. Hence, every spiritual predisposition of each slain boy inhered in Moses.[544]

The souls of the slain were pure as they retained their original nature that they had before coming into this world, uncorrupted by the fear-based selfishness that distorts the human condition. The Qur'an

---
544 Ibn 'Arabi, *Fusus*, p.185.

portrays all human souls, before their manifestation in the world of appearances, standing in the presence of their Creator (Q 7:173). God asks them, 'Am I not your Lord' (*alastu bi-Rabbikum*) and they answer in the affirmative – establishing the primordial covenant, whereby each soul innately aligns with ultimate reality, and recognizes beauty, goodness and truth. The souls of all of the male children slaughtered by Pharaoh, all these pure souls with their unsullied primordial orientation to truth, revert to Moses in strength, infusing Moses as it were, with the spiritual vitality of hundreds of pure human potentialities, because each was killed as if he were Moses. Moses is born then as an amalgam of many spirits, with a rare potentiality for spiritual potency, power and wisdom. Hence, we have, on the surface, an act of brutality: a tragedy, an atrocity. In actuality, what is happening is a part of a much larger, complex, long-term plan totally unbeknownst to those involved: the killing of children, unambiguously awful, undertaken by an oppressive tyrant, engendering untold suffering, turns out to be simultaneously integral to the formation of a rare being that will liberate thousands of people, and act as a vehicle of grace, light and guidance for millions. Destruction turns out to be liberation. Death turns out to be the very condition for life. A tyrant's terrible act to protect his power turns out to be the very thing that undoes it.

Next, Ibn 'Arabi describes the exceptional power of these infant souls infusing Moses by noting the power of the younger over the older, of children over adults, in contrast to the general assumption that they are in fact the weaker.

> Do you not see how the child acts on the adult in a particular way so that the adult descends from his position of authority and plays with the child, holding him and appearing before the child as his equal in mentality? Thus, the adult becomes dominated by the child without being aware of it. Further, the child occupies the adult with his care, protection, and the meeting of his needs, such that the adult sacrifices his own ease to ensure the child does not become disturbed. All of this pertains to the power of the younger over the older.[545]

---

545 Ibid.

Normally adults *appear* to have power and authority over children, and in one sense, of course, they do. However, Ibn 'Arabi observes here that, in another sense, adults are *completely dominated* by children: a small child can reduce a powerful adult to becoming themselves child-like, making child-like noises, and being completely at the child's disposal. Even if you roll your eyes and shake your head at others when you see them do this with babies, you will very likely end up doing the very same thing at some point. Whether you're a hardened outlaw biker, aloof avant-garde artiste or CEO of a giant multinational corporation, no one can avoid baby-talking around a baby for very long. The reason for youth's power over age Ibn 'Arabi tells us is that *those closer to God have power over those further*, and infants and children have more recently come from the primordial Source and hence exert this magnetic power. We might also say that it is their very powerlessness that itself exerts a tremendous power over us, as we are compelled to care for them as a result of it.

Ibn 'Arabi further alludes here to the fact that, as we discussed in the second chapter on Abraham, God directs the cosmos, but does so based on the cosmos's own inherent form/nature. The higher realm manifests the lower, though the lower determines the form of its manifestation. Again, here the child (cosmos) directs the father (God), as God can only create a world based on its form, much in the way that knowledge can only consist of that which the objects of knowledge provide, or possibility can only manifest based on the possible. Just as the objects of knowledge determine knowledge's contours, so the essential forms of the cosmos determine their expression when given existence by God. In all cases, we find a sort of counterintuitive reality hidden beneath appearances, where the greater acts according to the parameters of the lesser.

Ibn 'Arabi continues with the story of Moses after his birth (as described in both the Bible and the Qur'an) with his mother placing him in a basket and sending him adrift down the river Nile, to protect him from Pharaoh's orders to kill Hebrew boys.

As for the wisdom of placing Moses in the basket and casting it into the water: the basket is his human body, and the water is the knowledge he obtains through the body, with its speculative thought, sensory perception and imagination. The soul can only access these faculties through the mediation of a physical human body.[546]

He shifts to interpreting this next part of the story of Moses metaphorically, suggesting that the basket that Moses is placed within represents the material human body, with its various faculties (the various 'eyes' we discussed in the previous chapter), while the river represents the knowledge gained through these faculties. It is the faculties supplied by the physical human body that allow the soul to 'float' down the river of the world, to accrue knowledge through the eyes, nose, tongue and hands, through the human brain with its complex capability for thought, analysis and imagination. This complex relationship between mind and body is something we will consider further in the following chapter.

We see here that, paradoxically, materiality is required for the immaterial soul to gain knowledge. Souls are embodied, as embodiment provides the conditions for kinds of knowledge that are unavailable elsewhere. We also see here that the body exists as a *vehicle* or servant of the soul. However, as we discussed in the chapter on Shu'ayb, it is usually the body and its desires that rule the soul. Spiritual practice is a sustained attempt to reverse this disorder, and center the soul as one's core and organizing principle. The reason we find ourselves in this material world, then, is that there are things that can *only* be learned through this physical form of existence.

It follows that the very purpose of our embodied life is knowledge, which Muslims believe that the Qur'an affirms. In the sacred book, it is stated that God created humanity only to worship Him (Q 51:56). One of the first explanations of this verse among Muhammad's companions

---

546 Ibid., p.186.

is that 'to worship' here actually means 'to know'.⁵⁴⁷ The purpose of our existence then is to *know* God, through the world and ourselves, which, Ibn 'Arabi suggests, are simply His forms, or Names, shone through the prism of relativity. In other words, we exist as temporary, finite beings, to discover the infinite richness of Being within our own selves and within our world. Correspondingly, the world exists so that God can know His own infinite nature through the mirror of the temporal and finite forms of existence. At the very heart of this knowledge – both our knowledge of God through the forms of the world and God's knowledge of His own being through them – is *love*. And in this chapter on Moses Ibn 'Arabi shifts here to discussing love and its foundational function in the appearance of the world.

Islam and Romanticism: Love, Beauty and the World's Origin

Perhaps one of the more surprising claims that Ibn 'Arabi makes in this chapter on the strange, exalted nature of our world, is that its origin is due to love. Love is the motivating force, the substrate undergirding our entire phenomenal world. Ibn 'Arabi's view here reflects a broader orientation in the Islamic-Sufi tradition. For non-Muslim readers (and even for some Muslims) it can be similarly surprising to learn that Islam, as a whole, is a deeply *romantic* tradition. William Chittick helpfully notes:

> Those familiar with the histories and literatures of the Islamic peoples know that love ... is so central to the overall ethos of the religion that if any word can sum up Islamic spirituality – by which I mean the very heart of the Qur'anic message – it should surely be *love*.⁵⁴⁸

---

547 Ibn 'Abbas says that 'to worship' in this verse of the Qur'an means 'to know'. *The Study Qur'an: A New Translation and Commentary*, edited by Seyyed Hossein Nasr et al. (New York, 2015), p.1280.

548 William C. Chittick, *Divine Love: Islamic Literature and the Path to God* (New Haven, 2013), p.xi.

In the West, Romanticism is a term used to describe an intellectual and artistic movement in late 18th- and early 19th-century Europe. This movement was something of a reaction to the cool rationalism of the Enlightenment, and the 'disenchantment of the world' fostered by industrialization and modern science. Famous European romantics include Johann Wolfgang von Goethe (d.1832), Ludwig van Beethoven (d.1827), John Keats (d.1821) and William Blake (d.1827). In the face of reason's expanding sovereignty, these romantics planted the flags of *emotion*, *imagination* and, above all, *beauty*. The romantic movement's 'main commitment was to the idea that the character of art and beauty and our engagement with them should shape all aspects of human life'.[549] We might also call this the 'primacy of the aesthetic'.[550] Romanticism is a sort of spiritual mood oriented toward beauty as the highest truth.

It makes sense then that the romantics were great lovers of poetry. They considered it to be more effective at communicating truth than prose, and even saw poetry as a model for all endeavors in life. For the romantics, a life well lived is one lived *poetically*. They were also somewhat mystically inclined, often seeking the Absolute, but holding that its nature was ungraspable, and hence could not be caught by any conceptual net. Rather, this mysterious Absolute could only be known through its beautiful traces in nature and art.

Here in North America, when many think of Islam, it is unlikely that 'romantic' is the first descriptor that comes to mind. The images that proliferate in film and news media tend more toward the stern, serious and even menacing. The 'Islamophobia industry' is of course built on disseminating these images and centering them as representative of the phenomenon of Islam as a whole. And yet Islam is a profoundly romantic tradition. Muslims have likely produced more love poetry *than any other group in human history*. Whether we think of Africa, the Middle East, Central or Southeast Asia, we find Muslim cultures

---

549 Keren Gorodeisky, '19th Century Romantic Aesthetics', *The Stanford Encyclopedia of Philosophy* (Fall 2016 Edition), edited by Edward N. Zalta, https://plato.stanford.edu/archives/fall2016/entries/aesthetics-19th-romantic/ (accessed April 29, 2022).

550 Ibid.

with long and prolific traditions of exquisite love poetry. So where does this romanticism come from? Why this emphasis on beauty, love and the poetic in so much of the Islamic humanities? To answer, we need to go to back to Mecca, the sacred site of Islam's origin, where all roads eventually lead in Islamic history. In going back to Mecca to try to answer this question of why Islam is so romantic, we do well to note that the uncontested foremost cultural artifact of the ancient Meccans was poetry. Eloquent odes to romance, longing and the corresponding suffering it brings, to courage, heroism and adventure, were the highest cultural currency that the pre-Islamic Arabs had. The Prophet Muhammad was hence born into a culture steeped in romantic poetry. We need only think of the famous *Mu'allaqat*, the seven poems hung from the Ka'aba, the ancient shrine in Mecca traced back to Abraham.

Here we find Imru al-Qays's (d.544) famous poem, where he describes himself crying at the abandoned campsite of his lover. Their passionate affair was all too short lived, and now she and her tribe have returned to their territory, leaving him a broken man lost without his love, clinging to the traces of her presence, inconsolable despite his friends' best efforts to calm him down. The theme of lost or unrequited love produced its own subgenre of Arab poetry, known as *'udhri* love poetry. Its peak of expression is credited to Qays Ibn al-Mulawwah (d.688), a Bedouin poet who was nicknamed 'Majnun', which means one possessed or crazy[551] – in this case possessed by or crazy in love for a woman who was betrothed to another man, a woman named Layla, which means 'night' in Arabic, but can also have connotations of wine or intoxication. Majnun writes of Layla:

> *If I had two hearts I would live with one*
> *And let the other be tortured by your love.*
> *But I only have one heart owned by love.*
> *Neither pleased by living nor that death is near.*

He is another inconsolable one, so tortured by love that neither life nor death offer any consolation. If you fancy yourself to be something of a romantic and love hasn't yet possessed you and left you destitute,

---

551 The Arabic term *majnun* literally means to be '*jinned*' or possessed by a *jinn*.

equally unhappy with life or death, we can safely say that you've not quite reached Majnun's level of romance.

It is important for us to note then that the Qur'an emerges out of this cultural matrix of romantic poetry. It interestingly declares that it is not itself poetry, nor is Muhammad a poet (Q 36:69). However, the Qur'an is undoubtedly poetic, marked by a rhythm and rhyme throughout. Asad Ali hints at this paradoxical nature of the Qur'an, as a sort of poetic non-poetry, in his poem inspired by the 26th chapter of the Qur'an, *Surah al-Shu'ara*, where he writes:

> *You, Compassionate One,*
> *Have revealed Yourself*
> *and distinguished poetry from revelation;*
> *and so, poetry has been distinguished from poetry.*[552]

The Qur'an's deeply poetic nature has led to a unique Islamic doctrine. This doctrine suggests that the proof of the Qur'an's divine origin is its *beauty*. We might call this an aesthetic argument for divine origin. And, indeed, for centuries Muslims have argued that the Qur'an is a miracle of beauty, that the perfection of its language goes beyond human possibilities of composition.[553] It is said that the greatest living Arab poet of the Prophet Muhammad's time was Labid ibn Rabi'a (d.661), whose poems hung on the Ka'aba. When Muhammad's followers hung an excerpt of the Qur'an on the Ka'aba and challenged him to recite it, he initially laughed at their presumption. However, upon reading the Qur'an he was overwhelmed by its beauty and became a follower of Muhammad's.[554] Being Islam's great miracle of beauty, it is no surprise then that the Qur'an's words have been further beautified in Islamic arts like calligraphy and Qur'an recitation, where the divine word is celebrated as visual art or music – though again it would not be classified as music or art by Muslims, but rather as the sacred communicated in artistic or musical ways. Regardless of terminology, celebrating the sensual, beautiful nature of scripture is a

---

552 Ali, *Civilization of Paradise*, p.91.
553 For an extensive study of the aesthetics of the Qur'an, see Kermani, *God is Beautiful*.
554 Ibid., p.1.

central fact of the Islamic tradition, and is likely one of the major roots of its prolific romanticism.

This romanticism would take shape over the centuries among Sufis as an approach to the spiritual path premised on love as the highest truth, known as the *madhhab-i 'ishq*, or 'school of love' in Persian. For Sufis of this school, love is the ultimate reality. This view was expressed most concisely by Farid al-Din Attar (d.1221), who boldly said *la ilaha illa 'ishq* or 'there is no god but Love', replacing the name Allah with Love in the Islamic creed.[555] The great poets and philosophers who followed this path saw romantic love and passionate desire as metaphorical expressions of a vaster Reality. In fact, everything that we love is but a metaphor for God, a temporary trace of God's qualities, and hence all anyone ever loves is God. Ibn 'Arabi articulates this as follows:

> None but God is loved in the existent things. It is He who is manifest within every beloved to the eye of every lover – and there is nothing that is not a lover. The universe is all lover and beloved, and all of it goes back to Him. . . . Although they all love only their own Creator, they are veiled from Him by the love for Zaynab, Su'âd, Hind, Layla, this world, money, position, and everything loved in the world.[556]

Although in one sense the beings and forms of this world are veils over the true Beloved, they can also be appreciated from a perspective that sees the greater truth they express in their own limited ways; they can also be celebrated as expressions of God. Hence those Sufi poets of the *madhhab-i 'ishq* developed a method and program premised on love and beauty, as opposed to the staid speculations of scholastics, a love and beauty for both of the things of this world, and the Reality of which they are metaphors. For Ibn 'Arabi, this emphasis on love in Sufism goes back to an oft-quoted tradition, a report from the Prophet Muhammad regarding a saying of God's. Ibn 'Arabi begins his discussion of this subject here as follows:

---

555 Joseph E. B. Lumbard, 'From *Hubb* to *'Ishq*: The Development of Love in Early Sufism', *Journal of Islamic Studies*, 18 (2007), 347.
556 Ibn 'Arabi, Fut.II.326. As quoted in Chittick, *Sufi Path of Knowledge*, p.181.

> The Messenger of God, may God bless him and give him peace, called our attention to this, saying, 'I was a hidden treasure and loved to be known.' If not for this love, the world would not have appeared. Its movement from non-existence to existence results from its Creator's love for it. The world too loves to see itself in existence as it saw itself in its latency. In every respect then its movement from non-existence into existence is a movement of love, from both the side of the Real and the world.[557]

He first invokes the famous saying of God's shared by Muhammad, that God made the world so that His hidden perfections could be known. The key word here in Arabic is *ahbabtu* or 'I loved' to be known. Hence the movement of every existent thing from the state of potentiality to the state of manifest existence is a result of this love to be known, to manifest. The world itself also loves to manifest, to witness its own existence, and hence the world's origin is love from the side of both the Creator and creation. Much like the exuberance of spring, the joyful bursting forth into color, movement and sound, life longs for itself to be expressed.

> Perfection is loved in itself. His knowledge of Himself, as being rich beyond need of the worlds, is for Him in his Essence. Nothing remains but to complete the degree of knowledge through knowing the temporal, which comes from the entities of the world when they manifest in existence. The form of perfection is manifest through knowledge of both the ephemeral and the eternal. The degree of knowledge is perfected by means of these two aspects.[558]

In a beautiful passage here, Ibn 'Arabi articulates existence from a slightly different angle: the world exists so that God can perfect his knowledge of Himself, both as He is in his Essence, eternal beyond need of the temporal, and as He manifests through his Names, in the temporal forms of the world. Perfection is constituted by the fullness or completeness provided by the coexistence of the eternal and

---

557 Ibn 'Arabi, *Fusus*, p.191.
558 Ibid.

ephemeral, by being and becoming. As perfection is loved in and of itself, God's motivation to complete this knowledge is love:

> For the eternal is God's being in Himself, whereas the ephemeral is God's being in the latent forms of the world. It is called ephemeral because one part of it manifests to another. He is manifest to Himself in the forms of the world, and thus is existence perfected. And so the motion of the world is that of the love for perfection, so understand.[559]

For the fullness of perfection to manifest, the world must exist – in other words, the world is the completion of the perfection of God. This is precisely why Ibn 'Arabi can maintain that God as Essence is beyond all need of the world, and yet God as Lord is in fact dependent on the world, for the Lord can only be a lord, can only fulfill that aspect of the Essence's potential, *in relationship* to created, phenomenal existence. This is why, as Ian Almond notes, that Ibn 'Arabi understands God as 'in some way dependent upon us'.[560] And yet this aspect of God that is dependent on the ephemeral does not define God as such, an addendum that is often missed by Ibn 'Arabi's critics.

> Do you not see how He relieves the divine Names of the nonexistence of their effects' manifestation in the identity called the world? For ease is loved by Him, and He only reaches it through formal existence, both high and low. So it is established that motion belongs to love, there being no movement in existence except because of love.[561]

One of the hallmarks of Ibn 'Arabi's thought is a valuation of the world as an expression of God, in contrast to a condemnation of the world as an obstacle to or distraction from God, that needs to be simply abandoned. Ibn 'Arabi's positive valuation of the world notably contrasts with several historical expressions of spirituality that

---

559 Ibid.
560 Ian Almond, 'Divine Needs, Divine Illusions: Preliminary Remarks Towards a Comparative Study of Meister Eckhart and Ibn 'Arabi', *Medieval Philosophy and Theology*, 10/12 (2001), 11.
561 Ibn 'Arabi, *Fusus*, p.191.

tend to situate the world as something that one condemns, flees from and abandons. Monastic traditions in Christianity, Hinduism and Buddhism have tended to take this approach, and some early Sufis also took a dim view of earthly existence, drawing upon the more ascetic verses in the Qur'an or sayings of the Prophet Muhammad, to counsel an abandonment of worldly pleasures, and condemnation of worldly life. In contrast, for later Sufis like Ibn 'Arabi and certainly for the representatives of the School of Love, worldly existence is *the very means* by which God is known. In fact, Ibn 'Arabi takes a somewhat critical stance on renunciation:

> 'Renunciation' of things can occur only through the ignorance and lack of knowledge of the one who renounces and through the veil which covers his eyes, that is, the lack of unveiling and witnessing ... If he only knew or witnessed the fact that the whole cosmos speaks by glorifying and lauding its Creator.[562]

If one is able to see that the entire world and everything in it celebrates the perfections of the Real of which they are but the surface expressions, then the world becomes the very means by which deeper realities are known, the very path to God. The world then is itself beloved as a manifold expression of the real Beloved. Ibn 'Arabi continues on this point, critiquing the renunciant:

> His ignorance makes him imagine that the cosmos is far removed from God and that God is far removed from the cosmos. Hence he seeks to 'flee' (*farar*) to God. But this is an imaginary flight, and its cause is the lack of tasting (*dhawq*) of the things.[563]

If one truly 'tastes' the entities of this world, there is no need to flee from them to God, as one tastes God *through* them. Ibn 'Arabi notes, however, that some initial abandonment of the world, in the form of isolating oneself in spiritual retreat (*khalwa*), may be necessary, before one is able to taste God in the forms of the world. In *The Meccan Revelations* he suggests that the seeker 'must be alone with himself

---

562 Ibn 'Arabi, *Fut*.III.263. As quoted in Chittick, *Sufi Path of Knowledge*, p.157.
563 Ibid., p.158.

with his Lord in his inmost consciousness', so that 'after having gazed upon Him in his inward dimension', the seeker then 'may discern Him within the midst of the secondary causes'.[564] And indeed we find that Ibn 'Arabi himself took this approach when he first began on the Sufi way, as a young man in Seville, Spain. He relates that one of his first masters, Abu Ja'far al-'Uraybi, advised him at this stage to 'shut out the world, sever all ties, and take God alone as your companion, He will speak to you directly without any intermediary.' Ibn 'Arabi shares that he 'pursued this course until I succeeded.'[565]

This nature of the world as the 'completion' of God's Names, so to speak, is why God and the world both love for the world to manifest into concrete existence. God loves the world's existence as He can perfect knowledge of Himself through the ephemeral, and the world loves to exist simply for the 'pleasure of existence' itself. Here we also see that ease is something that God loves, and hence something inherent to existence, despite the various difficulties our lives will inevitably entail. In the Sufi master's work, we find terms like 'love', 'ease' and 'pleasure' undergirding our reality, a reality that is simultaneously sensual and spiritual, with no great dichotomy formed between the two. Rather we find that the former is the perfection of the latter. In the following two (and final) chapters, we see Ibn 'Arabi explore the question of the relationship between the sensual and spiritual, divinity and materiality, much further, in his discussion of Jesus and Muhammad.

---

564 *Fut*.III.265, cited by Cecilia Twinch, 'The Beauty of Oneness Witnessed in the Emptiness of the Heart', *Muhyiddin Ibn Arabi Society*, 25 (1999), p.38.

565 I've slightly altered the translation of the quote from al-'Uraybi for clarity's sake. Austin, *Sufis of Andalusia*, p.63.

عيسى عليه السلام

7

Between Divinity and Humanity: Jesus and the Wisdom of Prophecy

The wind blows where it wishes, and you hear its sound, but you do not know where it comes from or where it goes.[566]

The Mind–Body Mystery

As human beings we find ourselves existing as a rather curious cocktail of consciousness and matter; a subtle presence of awareness somehow encapsulated within a fleshy mammalian form. Despite a flurry of research in recent decades on how exactly our mind and body interact with each other,[567] we have yet to solve what philosophers and scientists have long referred to as the 'mind–body problem'. This problem arises from the fact that our world seems to consist of two very different kinds of things: 1) those that have extension in space, meaning that they can be observed and measured, weighed and touched, what Descartes called *res extensa*, and 2) those that do not – and are subject to no such measurements or physical confirmation – what he called *res cogitans*.[568]

---

[566] John 3:8.

[567] In the United States, at least, a focus on neuroscience was given a sort of political 'stamp', when President George H. W. Bush declared, in 1989, that the 1990s were to be the 'Decade of the Brain'. See the Library of Congress: https://www.loc.gov/loc/brain/ (accessed February 3, 2023). This decade, and the ones following it, have seen the growth of several sub-disciplines of brain study, almost too numerous to list, including affective neuroscience, behavioral neuroscience, cognitive, computational, cultural and evolutionary neuroscience, neuroanatomy, neurotheology, neurophysics and psychobiology. David Lag Tomasi, *Critical Neuroscience and Philosophy* (New York, 2020), p.6.

[568] See Descartes's *Principia Philosophiae* (1644), and Jean-Luc Marion, 'Cartesian Metaphysics and the Role of the Simple Natures', in *The Cambridge Companion to Descartes*, edited by John Cottingham (Cambridge: Cambridge University Press, 1992), p.126.

As the famous Anglican bishop and philosopher George Berkeley (d.1753) is said to have phrased it: 'What is mind? No matter. What is matter? Never mind.'[569]

To illustrate, we *can* measure how much coffee you pour in a cup on Sunday morning (matter), but we *cannot* measure how badly you desire said cup upon waking (mind). Your thought: 'Wow I so need that cup of coffee right now,' combined with a warm feeling of yearning, and maybe an imaginary, anticipatory picture of the softly steaming brew, simply do not *in themselves* have extension in space, though they may have some correlates in the body that do. The question quite naturally follows: how exactly is it that these physical and non-physical phenomena interact with each other? Is one set simply an epiphenomenon of the other? Is the mind an illusion produced by the body? Or, on the other hand, is the body an illusion produced by the mind? Then again, perhaps neither mind nor body are reducible to each other, existing rather as two distinct realities, a sort of interactive dualism? The more one reflects on this problem, the more intractable it appears to be, as none of these views prove evidentially satisfying. This is perhaps why solving the mind–body problem has been one of the most persistent philosophical and scientific failures in human history.

Poet and philosopher Michael Robbins, reflecting on the last two decades of research on consciousness, concludes that, when it comes to the question of the precise relationship between mind and body, 'the main thing I've learned is that no one has the slightest idea'.[570] There is even an extensive debate over whether or not anyone *will ever* have the slightest idea: the mind–body problem may not be solvable at

---

569 Tomasi, *Critical Neuroscience and Philosophy*, p.55.
570 Michael Robbins, 'I Me Mind: On the Unending Quest to Explain Consciousness', *Bookforum* (December/January 2020), https://www.bookforum.com/print/2604/the-unending-quest-to-explain-consciousness-23772 (accessed January 20, 2023).

all.[571] As Buddhist studies scholar Robert Sharf observes:

> [But] despite the wealth of new empirical data and the profusion of increasingly sophisticated philosophical arguments, the underlying quandaries – quandaries related to the 'hard problem' of consciousness and how our percepts relate to the mind-independent world – go back to the dawn of philosophical reflection, and the verdict is still out on whether the spate of new work bespeaks progress.[572]

Referring to the 'dawn of philosophical speculation', here we can, at least in the Western tradition, point all the way back to Plotinus. In his *Enneads* he reflects on the challenge of making sense of soul and body, noting that 'a living being is either a certain kind of living body, or the sum of body and soul, or some other third thing that arises from both of these'.[573] He continues to consider the various possible relations between soul and body (asking whether it is something like the soul piloting the body as a ship, or how it is that what affects the body affects the soul, but not always, etc.), in ways that seem surprisingly contemporary considering the state of modern science and philosophy on this issue.

Although the challenge of making sense of the relationship between consciousness/mind/soul and body is quite clearly an ancient one, in 1994 philosopher David Chalmers famously focused analysis on the 'hard problem' at the heart of it. He aptly noted the general

---

571 This problem's insolubility may be, in part, traced to issues intrinsic to the materialistic conception of reality. Philosopher Laurence BonJour articulates this here as follows: 'Materialism presumably says that everything that exists is material and physical in character, but the precise boundaries of the material or physical are rendered seriously obscure by the expectation of continued progress in physics and related sciences: if some radically new kind of entity or process is discovered in the future, one that stands to physical reality as presently conceived in something like the way that electromagnetic waves stood to the seventeenth-century corpuscular conception of physical reality, what exactly will decide whether or not an acceptance of these new items is compatible with materialism?' Laurence BonJour, *In Defense of Pure Reason: A Rationalist Account of A Priori Justification* (Cambridge, UK, 1998), p.154.

572 Robert H. Sharf, 'Knowing Blue: Early Buddhist Accounts of Non-Conceptual Sense Perception', *Philosophy East and West*, 68 (2018), 827.

573 Plotinus, *Enneads*, as quoted in John Dillon and Lloyd P. Gerson, *Neoplatonic Philosophy: Introductory Readings* (Indianapolis, IN, 2004), p.5.

issue, namely that despite knowing conscious experience more intimately than anything else, 'there is nothing harder to explain'.[574] He then honed in on the *particular* issue that makes accounting for consciousness so difficult: although we can increasingly explain (at least to some degree) how brain activity leads to the processing of sensory input and how it facilitates appropriate responses, we cannot explain *why* these input/output processes include the *subjective experience of being a person*. In isolating this 'hard problem', Chalmers was simply pointing out that all the science can tell us is that we should be high-functioning zombies, effectively responding to sensory information without any subjective experience of doing so. However, quite unlike zombies, we inexplicably have a rich subjective experience of being alive, one that is neither a necessary outcome of brain processes nor germane to the demands of biological survival.[575]

In short, despite our various advances in brain science,[576] we still have no satisfactory answer to Chalmer's basic question, on why neuronal activity and cognitive information-processing are accompanied by distinct (and distinctly deep) subjective experience.[577] We've learned a great deal about *how* our brain functions, but cannot seem to explain *why* these functions are accompanied by the ridiculously rich experience of consciousness. Italian philosopher Riccardo Manzotti illustrates this elegantly in his conversation with novelist Tim Parks in *The New York Review of Books*:

---

[574] David J. Chalmers, 'Facing up to the Problem of Consciousness', *Journal of Consciousness Studies*, 2 (1995), 200.

[575] Chalmers explains, 'What makes the hard problem hard and almost unique is that it goes beyond problems about the performance of functions. To see this, note that even when we have explained the performance of all the cognitive and behavioral functions in the vicinity of experience – perceptual discrimination, categorization, internal access, verbal report – there may still remain a further unanswered question: *Why is the performance of these functions accompanied by experience?*' Ibid., 202.

[576] Much of which is due to relatively recent technologies / methodologies including, 'brain imaging (MRI, fMRI, EEG, PET, SPECT, CAT/CT, MEG, etc.), manipulation (including inhibition and psychopharmacological interventions), and stimulation (as in TMS), as well as via measuring methods like electrode-based monitoring (single-unit or multi-electrode recordings), sensitive dye-based optical techniques (examples include voltage-sensitive dyes and voltage-sensitive fluorescent proteins that have been genetically encoded), as well as functional neuroanatomy and genetic (sequential) mapping and engineering.' Tomasi, *Critical Neuroscience and Philosophy*, 58–9.

[577] Chalmers, 'Facing up to the Problem of Consciousness,' 202.

There is nothing about the behavior of neurons to suggest that they are any different with respect to consciousness than, say, liver cells or red blood cells. They are cells doing what cells do best, namely, keeping entropy low by generating flows of ions such as sodium, potassium, chloride, and calcium and releasing neurotransmitters as a consequence. All of that is wonderful but far removed from the fact that I experience a light blue color when I watch the morning sky. That is, it's not easy to see how the physical activity of the neurons explains my experience of the sky, let alone a process like thinking.[578]

This inherently mysterious presence of consciousness within a brain that is in many respects indistinct from the rest of the body, is analogous, in several ways, to what Christians have claimed for centuries about Jesus, namely that his *very being* is a fundamental mystery, an inscrutable joining of divinity and humanity, spirit and flesh. In this sense Jesus is an archetype for the curious constitution of humans more generally. Although we will see that Muslims differ notably from Christians in defining who exactly Jesus is, we will also find that there is significant overlap in their conceptions of him, much of which concerns the nature of consciousness/soul/spirit, and its relationship to the physical body. It is to Jesus and his nature, then, that we now turn.

Jesus the Christ and the Prophet

After a poem about Jesus as the son of Mary, Ibn 'Arabi opens this chapter of *The Gemstones of Wisdom* with a discussion of this mysterious relationship between mind and body, or what he calls the intersection of *lahut,* literally meaning 'godliness' or 'divinity', and *nasut*, which means 'humanity' or 'human nature'.

> Know that one of the qualities particular to spirits is that everything they come into contact with becomes alive, and life permeates it ... The measure of life that permeates things is called *lahut,* and *nasut*

---

578 Riccardo Manzotti, as quoted in Robbins, 'I Me Mind.'

is the vessel in which this spirit resides. *Nasut* is only called spirit [or alive] because of what resides within it.[579]

Spirit (or consciousness) is situated by Ibn 'Arabi here as the active agent, with matter being that which is acted upon – rather than the reverse, which physicalist models suggest.[580] The *nasut*, or physical body, only appears to be alive when it is imbued with the presence of consciousness or spirit. It is also worth noting here that, for Ibn 'Arabi, 'life', 'consciousness/spirit' and 'divinity' have overlapping meanings, all contained within the term *lahut* – an Arabic word indicating the enlivening spirit present within a bodily vessel. Interestingly Jesus describes himself in the Gospel of John (14:6) as not only 'the way and the truth', but also *'the life'*. Like other immortals in the Abrahamic traditions, such as Elijah and Khidr, Jesus is associated with an abundance of life. When we think of such figures, we find examples of life exponentially magnified: Khidr's steps produce greenery wherever he goes; both Jesus and Elijah raise the dead; all exist beyond mortality, as beings so alive they have transcended death entirely.

Besides this association of *lahut* with life, and life abundantly, Ibn 'Arabi's consideration of the relationship between *lahut* and *nasut* is especially apropos in this chapter, in light of the centuries of debate over the precise relationship of divinity and humanity in the person of Jesus. Before further exploring this question of spirit and form in the person of Jesus, it is worth first considering just who Jesus was.

To begin, Jesus would not have been known as 'Jesus' during his life but rather as Joshua or Yeshua, 'Jesus' being a later Greek version of his Hebrew name.[581] Outside of the Gospels we have very little in the way of historical sources about who Jesus was, but we do know that he lived during a time of great religious ferment. Palestine under Roman rule was pulsing with various movements and mystics, reformers and revolutionaries, and Jesus was a part of this vibrant Jewish spiritual

---

579 Ibn 'Arabi, *Fusus*, pp.127-8.
580 The materialist or physicalist model is fraught with the question of how exactly it is that something unaware could itself produce awareness, or: How is it that awareness arises out of what is unaware? We may frame the question more facetiously in asking how is it that meat generates consciousness?
581 Diarmaid MacCulloch, *Christianity: The First Three Thousand Years* (New York, 2010), p.19.

scene.[582] Although he would become the central figure in Christianity, it is important to point out that Jesus 'saw himself as a Jew, spent his life amid other Jews in the Galilee and Judea, and drew on earlier Jewish tradition in what he taught and how he behaved'.[583] Jesus' critique of legalistic clerics, for example, is just as much an expression of first-century Judaism as that of his pharisaical opponents.

After pointing out just how limited the historical record on Yeshua/Jesus really is, Huston Smith summarizes what we do know, namely that he was 'a Jewish carpenter' who was 'executed as a criminal at age thirty-three, never travelled more than ninety miles from his birthplace, owned nothing, attended no college, marshaled no army, and instead of producing books did his only writing in the sand'.[584] And yet his teachings and personality would prove to be some of the most influential in human history. The poverty of event makes the profundity of impact all the more striking.

Although the Gospel narratives include some detail of Jesus' birth and infancy, almost nothing is said about him as a child and young adult, picking up the story at about the age of thirty, following his baptism in the River Jordan by John the Baptist (*Yahya* in the Qur'an), and his public preaching shortly thereafter. Smith traces some of Jesus' immense impact to his astonishing teachings. Although in almost every case they are paralleled in the Torah (and later the Talmud), they stand out for their remarkable urgency, vividness and passion: 'If your hand offends you, cut it off. If your eye stands between you and the best, gouge it out.' Smith noting that such 'gigantesque' language 'is part of the message itself'.[585] By all accounts he was not a conventionally religious man, and yet Einstein stated on multiple occasions that he was particularly impressed with the singular personality of Jesus. In an interview with the *Saturday Evening Post*, he shared that 'no one

---

582 The three best-known Jewish movements of this period are the Pharisees, Sadducees and Essenes, described by Roman-Jewish historian Flavius Josephus (d.100), but likely originating a few centuries prior to his writing. John Efron, Matthias Lehmann and Steven Weitzman, *The Jews: A History, Third Edition* (New York, 2019), p.81.

583 Ibid., p.110.

584 Smith, *The World's Religions*, pp.319–20.

585 Ibid., pp.326–7.

can read the Gospels without feeling the actual presence of Jesus. His personality pulsates in every word', and further affirmed that the spiritual magnitude of Jesus simply cannot be captured by modern writing, as he 'is too colossal for the pen of phrasemongers, however artful'.[586]

In Christianity's core texts about him, we find Jesus a relentless critic of what we might call 'religion for religion's sake', with its performative piety, self-serving spirituality and pedantic legalism. The Gospels (likely with more than a pinch of polemic) depict his religious opponents, the Pharisees, as representing just this type of religion, the kind that misses the 'forest for the trees', forgoing what really counts in life in favor of what should really be a sidebar. In the Gospel of Mark, for example, the Pharisees accuse Jesus and his disciples of breaking the prohibition on doing work (in this case harvesting) during the Sabbath, when they find them snacking on grain they pick as they walk through a field. Jesus responds, 'The sabbath was made for man, not man for the sabbath' (Mark 2:27), articulating here what we might call a humanistic understanding of religion, as something that facilitates rather than restricts human flourishing: God makes religion for people, not people for religion.

Alongside his critique of religious hypocrisy and legalism, Jesus drew upon some of the earliest teachings of the Torah in teaching a transcendent morality that emphasized love, mercy and 'turning the other cheek'. Going way beyond the instinctive human orientation toward survival, struggle, retaliation and the like, Jesus taught his followers to trust in God so completely that they even stop worrying about food and shelter:

> So, I say to you, do not worry about your life – what you will eat or drink, or about your body, what you will wear. Isn't life more than food and the body more than clothing? Look at the birds of the air. They do not sow or reap or gather into barns; yet your Father in heaven feeds them. Are you not of more value than they?[587]

---

586 Albert Einstein, as quoted by Nilson, 'Albert Einstein', *Saturday Evening Post*.

587 In this passage, Jesus continues: 'And which of you by worrying can add a single hour to his life? And why do you worry about clothing? Consider the lilies of the field, how they grow. They neither toil nor spin. Yet I tell you that not even Solomon in all his glory clothed himself like one of these.' Matthew 6:25-9.

Jesus further called upon his followers to do the opposite of seeking redress when wronged, advising them, 'If someone takes your coat, give him your shirt as well' (Luke 6:29). Smith summarizes his teachings as 'a burning glass to focus human awareness on the two most important facts about life: God's overwhelming love for humanity, and the need for people to accept that love and let it flow through to others'.[588] In addition to this uncompromising ethic of love and trust, Jesus taught that 'the Kingdom of God' was nigh, that the end of the world was close, perhaps a factor in the urgency we encounter in his teachings. The Gospels further suggest that he was the Messiah, a term that literally means 'the Anointed One', and in Jewish tradition, a term that referred to a long-awaited redeemer-king, one who would liberate and lead the Jewish people. Whether prompted by the Pharisees or acting more in their own interests, the Romans deemed Jesus to be a destabilizing threat to their governance, and he was arrested in Jerusalem and crucified outside the city shortly after.[589]

Jesus' remarkable power as a short-lived spiritual teacher and healer in Roman-ruled Palestine would evolve in the century following his death into a doctrine at the heart of the Christian faith, namely that he was not only Jesus the historical human being who lived and taught as a Jewish mystic and healer, but he was also Christ, the resurrected Savior of humanity, the Son of God, and even God Himself. The Church's first Councils sought to clarify precisely how these various aspects of Christ cohered in a single person, particularly in terms of his divine and human natures. Whereas some theologians emphasized Christ's humanity and others his divinity, the compromise position that would come to dominate the largest Christian churches over time was formulated by a church council in Chalcedon, near Constantinople, in the year 451, as follows:

> Christ: the same perfect in divinity and perfect in humanity, the same truly God and truly man, of a rational soul and a body; consubstantial with the Father as regards his divinity, and the same consubstantial with us as regards his humanity.[590]

---

588 Smith, *The World's Religions*, pp.328-9.
589 MacCulloch, *Christianity*, pp.91-2.
590 Ibid., p.226.

This doctrine of Jesus declared him to be a single (and singular) being, yet with two natures, one divine and the other human. It follows that Christ also had two wills, both divine and human, though they coincided perfectly as Christ's human will was in complete harmony with his divine will.[591] Christ's full inclusion in the nature and definition of God led to the Christian articulation of a unique theology, notably distinct from both Jewish and Islamic unitarianism, a theology known as the Trinity. A 'tri-unity', or threefold oneness, is an approach that defines God as 'one in essence', though eternally existing as three separate persons: the Father, Son and Holy Spirit, each a 'distinct centre of conscious selfhood', and yet singular in reality, will and being.[592] Hence, 'there is in God genuine diversity as well as specific unity'.[593]

In the Islamic tradition, Jesus is known as *'Isa ibn Maryam*, or Jesus, son of Mary. This close association of Jesus with Mary is based on the Qur'an itself, where most references to Jesus occur 'within a context where Mary is the dominant figure'.[594] We find Jesus described in a Qur'anic chapter named after Mary (the 19th chapter), and in a chapter named after her father, Imran (the third chapter). Overall, Jesus is mentioned in 15 chapters and 93 verses of the Qur'an, where he is described as a 'sign', 'mercy', 'witness' and 'example'.[595] Now, it is generally well known that the primary difference between Christian and Muslim understandings of Jesus is that Christian doctrine defines Jesus as the Son of God, the second Person of the Trinity and as the Lord and Savior of humanity, while in the Islamic tradition he is simply a holy prophet (*nabi*) or messenger (*rasul*). And, indeed, the Qur'an makes this distinction quite clear, and in several places clearly repudiates Christian notions including the Incarnation, God begetting a Son or God being thought of as in some way fundamentally three in

---

591 Ware, *The Orthodox Way*, p.72.
592 Ibid., p.30.
593 Ibid.
594 As Stephen Hirtenstein pointed out to me, the larger norm of the male child referred to as the son of the father (*ibn* in Arabic) is not possible in the case of Jesus as he has no human father. Oddbjorn Leirvik, *Images of Jesus Christ in Islam*, 2nd Edition (New York, 2010), p.19.
595 Geoffrey Parinder, *Jesus in the Qur'an* (Oxford, 1995 [1965]), p.16.

nature:

> Truly the Messiah, Jesus son of Mary, was only a messenger of God, and His Word, which He gave to Mary, and a Spirit from Him. So believe in God and His messengers, and say not 'Three'. Refrain! It is better for you. God is only one God; Glory be to Him that He should have a child. (4: 171)

> Say: He is God, the One. God the Eternal. He begets not, nor is begotten. And there is nothing like Him. (112: 1–4)

We can see here an explicit rejection of the Triune doctrine of God. And yet the Qur'anic view of Jesus tends to place him a little closer to Christian ones than is usually appreciated. Jesus is described above as a Spirit (*Ruh*) from God and as God's Word (*Kalam Allah*), invoking Christian notions of Christ as the divine Word or *logos*. He is also affirmed to be the Messiah (*Masih* in Arabic), the 'anointed' one, which in the Jewish tradition was believed to be a future redeemer king of the Davidic line.[596]

In his writings we find that Ibn 'Arabi actually considers Trinitarianism somewhat positively, as he sees it reflecting an aspect of *tawhid* or the Islamic doctrine of God's oneness, and hence sees Christians as quite possibly included in the Islamic conception of salvation:

> As for people of the Trinity, salvation is hoped for them. This is because of what the Trinity contains of oddness of number. Since oddness is one of the traits of the One, they are those who affirm oneness compositely. Therefore, it is hoped that they will be encompassed by composite mercy.[597]

---

596 Translator and scholar Ralph W. J. Austin suggests a possibility here as to why Ibn 'Arabi titled his chapter on Jesus as 'the Wisdom of Prophecy', or *nubuwwa*. Each prophet is 'a particular and special receptacle for the divine Word', much like the whole cosmos represents a set of receptacles for the *lahut*.' R. W. J. Austin, translator, Ibn 'Arabi, *Bezels of Wisdom* (New Jersey, 1980), p.173. However, some commentators, including al-Qunawi, have interpreted this chapter's title as 'elevation'.

597 Ibn 'Arabi, *Fut*.III.172.

As three is the first odd prime number, it shares the quality of oddness with the number one, and hence triplicity is a kind of composite oneness. Ibn 'Arabi reasons that Christians then fulfill the Islamic doctrine of God's oneness (*tawhid*) compositely, and hence can be hoped to receive God's mercy in a composite way.

Interestingly, although Muslims and Christians differ over the ultimately unitarian or trinitarian nature of God, they do agree that Jesus was born miraculously. The Qur'an states that Jesus was born of a virgin (Q 19:16–22), and even narrates his conception and birth in some detail. It relates an encounter between Mary and a Spirit (whom Muslim commentators identify as the Angel of Revelation, Gabriel) that appears in the form of a man. She initially responds in fear, seeking God's protection and asking the man to leave her alone, if he is God-fearing (Q 19:18). Ibn 'Arabi comments on the significance of the mother's state of being during conception, suggesting that it can have a profound impact on the one conceived: 'For if [the Angel Gabriel] had breathed into her at that moment, in this state, Jesus would have emerged with an unbearable personality resulting from his mother's state.'[598] Instead, however, Gabriel announces that he is a messenger from God, to give Mary a 'pure son', and Ibn 'Arabi describes her as relaxing, releasing her fear, and experiencing a sort of spiritualized passion as a result.[599]

> Desire flowed through Mary and the body of Jesus was created from the real water of Mary, and the imaginal water of Gabriel. ... Thus, the body of Jesus was formed from imaginal and real waters. Then, he emerged in the human form as a result of his mother and due to the human form in which Gabriel appeared, so that his birth occurred in a normal manner.[600]

He pays particularly close attention to Jesus' unique physiological constitution – a synthesis of material and spiritual natures – resulting

---

598 Ibn 'Arabi, *Fusus*, p.128.
599 Islamic tradition further suggests that all human souls are touched by Satan, with the exception of Jesus and Mary, both of whom are born pure of this touch of evil.
600 Ibn 'Arabi, *Fusus*, p.128.

from Mary's physical and Gabriel's spiritual formation. Ibn 'Arabi, like many religious writers in medieval Muslim contexts, was not shy of speaking about matters related to sex and reproduction. He uses the term *shahwa* here for Mary's desire, a term usually associated with sensual passion or sexual yearning. Scholar and translator Caner Dagli notes that such desire was not seen as something negative in the classical Islamic tradition, as long as it occurred within a context spiritualized by divine permission (whether by law, or in this case, divine intervention).[601] Hence, for Ibn 'Arabi, Mary's spiritual purity is not compromised by sensual desire. We can also note that, during his time, reproduction was believed to be the result of the joining of male and female sexual fluids, a theory drawn both from the Qur'an and hadith, as well as Greek (Galenic) medical thought.[602] Ibn 'Arabi hence describes Jesus as a result of Mary's physical water and the angel Gabriel's spiritual water, transmitted through metaphorical breath.

Although it's undoubtedly a bit anachronistic to phrase it this way, it's also somewhat correct to say that, within the Islamic tradition, Jesus represents a unique embodiment of the 'mind-body' mystery, as this combination of spiritual (from Gabriel) and physical (from Mary) natures. Scholar of Sufi philosophy Ali Hussein suggests that Jesus, with his special, synthetic nature, actually represents 'the human soul, itself a *barzakh* between a natural bodily mother and ethereal spiritual father'.[603] Here we see Christ as an archetype of the mystery of human existence, with its strange marriage of physical body and spiritual consciousness. We can also note a parallel to Christian notions of

---

601 Dagli, *The Ringstones of Wisdom*, p.159.

602 The translation of Greek medical texts into Syriac and Arabic occurred quite early in Islamic history, beginning in the mid-eighth century (just a hundred years after Muhammad's death), with what is now referred to as the Graeco-Arabic translation movement. Seminal here is Hunayn ibn Ishaq (d.873), a Christian physician and translator, appointed by the Caliph al-Mutawakkil (d.861) as his court physician, also known for his Arabic translation of Galen's (d.216) work. For more on Ibn Ishaq's translations, see Uwe Vagelpohl, 'The User-friendly Galen: Hunayn ibn Ishaq and the Adaptation of Greek Medicine for a New Audience', in *Greek Medical Literature and its Readers: From Hippocrates to Islam and Byzantium,* edited by Petros Bouras-Vallianatos and Sophia Xenophontos (New York, 2018), pp.113–30.

603 Ali Hussain, 'Sainthood between the Ineffable and Social Practice: Jesus Christ in the Writings of Muhyi al-Din Ibn al-'Arabi and later Sufism' (PhD Dissertation, the University of Michigan, 2019), p.82.

Christ as a synthesis of divinity and humanity; only here his father is not so much God as the Angel Gabriel. Ibn 'Arabi interestingly connects Jesus' synthesis of spiritual and human natures to the Christian veneration of icons:

> In fact, Jesus was not born of a male belonging to the human species, but of a Spirit [the Angel Gabriel] who manifested himself in a human form; that is why, in the community of Jesus the son of Mary more than in any other, the doctrine of the legitimacy of images predominates. Christians fashion representations of the divinity and turn towards them in order to worship, because the very existence of their prophet proceeded from a Spirit who clothed himself in a form; and so it is to this day in his community.[604]

Perhaps the most famous proponent of icons in Christianity, St. John of Damascus (d.749), makes a quite similar argument, that, as God became clothed in flesh in the person of Jesus, and could be seen, 'I make an image of the God whom I see.'[605]

The Qur'an, besides having its own account of Jesus' conception, further describes his birth. Whereas the Gospels of Matthew and Luke relate that Jesus was born in a stable in Bethlehem, the Qur'an offers a somewhat different account:

> *Mary withdrew to a remote place, and during the pains of child birth drove her to cling to a palm tree she cried, 'I wish I was dead and forgotten long before this.' But a voice called from below, 'Do not worry: your Lord has provided a stream at your feet, and if you shake the palm tree toward you, it will deliver ripe dates for your, so eat, drink, and rejoice.' (Q 19:22–6)*

Besides vividly indicating just how painful giving birth can be (apparently an experience that can make one wish to be dead and long forgotten), the Qur'an's description here is a fascinating example of what we might call intertextuality, the way in which texts from various traditions sort

---

[604] Ibn 'Arabi, *Fut*.III.36. As quoted in Chodkiewicz, *Seal of the Saints*, p.76.

[605] For more of St. John of Damascus's writings on icons, see: 'Apologia Against Those Who Decry Holy Images, *Fordham University Internet History Sourcebook*, https://sourcebooks.fordham.edu/basis/johndamascus-images.asp (accessed May 10, 2023).

of dialogue with (or echo) one another. Mostafa Akyol notes how the Qur'an's account, though deviating from Gospel versions, intriguingly resonates with other early Christian texts. The Protoevangelium of James, for example, a second-century text popular among Christians in the East, describes Jesus born not in Bethlehem, but in a desert cave outside of the town, alone – as in the Qur'an's account.[606] We also find the second-century Infancy Gospel of Matthew describing Mary eating from a palm tree and drinking from a miraculous spring, though not during Jesus' birth.

Of further interest here is the connection between the Qur'an, these earlier Christian narratives of the birth of Jesus, and a much older Greek myth: Callimachus's (d.*c*.240 BCE) *Hymn to Delos*, an account of the goddess Leto giving birth to the god Apollo. In the hymn, which was widely disseminated in Greek, Hellenistic and Roman contexts, a distressed Leto flees to the island of Delos in hopes of hiding away from Hera's anger. With notable parallels to later Christian and Qur'anic narratives, Leto sits by a palm tree along the Inopos River, expresses the pain of childbirth and delivers a holy child (Apollo).[607]

Although these connections could lead to the conclusion that the Qur'an is simply, as suggested by its critics, a pastiche of Christian and other Near Eastern sources,[608] Akyol highlights a recent archeological discovery that interestingly corresponds with the Qur'anic and Christian accounts. In 1997 Israeli archeologists uncovered a famous lost church, the Kathisma of the Theotokos, in the desert outside Bethlehem, said to mark the place where Mary gave birth to Jesus.[609]

---

606 Mustafa Akyol, 'Jesus' Birth between Islam and Christianity', *New Lines Magazine*, December 23, 2022, https://newlinesmag.com/essays/the-palm-and-the-spring/ (accessed January 8, 2023).

607 Suleiman A. Mourad, 'Mary in the Qur'an: A Reexamination of her Presentation', in *The Qur'an in its Historical Context*, edited by Gabriel Said Reynolds (New York, 2008), p.168.

608 The Qur'an further includes miracle stories not found in the Bible, such as Jesus speaking as an infant (Q 19:29–31), stories found in various Christian traditions, though not in the canonical Gospels.

609 The third Church Council in Ephesus (431 CE) affirmed that the Virgin Mary is *Theotokos*, the 'Godbearer' or 'Mother of God'. Kallistos Ware notes that this title of Mary's affirms Christ's divinity, namely that in giving birth to Jesus, '*God was born*. The Virgin is Mother ... of a single, undivided person who is God and man at once.' Ware, *The Orthodox Way*, p.71.

A sixth-century Christian pilgrimage guide detailed a spring at the site where pilgrims took water, said to have first flowed when Mary stopped there.[610]

Regardless of precisely where it took place, for Ibn 'Arabi, Jesus's virgin birth in a sense closes the circle of human creation. Paraphrasing Ibn 'Arabi's perspective on this, scholar of Islam and feminist theory Sa'diyya Shaikh explains that 'the creation of Jesus from a female (Mary) without a male proposes a gendered counterpoint to the creation of Eve from a male (Adam) without a female'.[611] This also makes Jesus a totally unique kind of human being, none other having this status in the Islamic tradition, as one born of a woman but without a human father. In his *The Meccan Revelations* Ibn 'Arabi situates Jesus, Mary, Adam and Eve together as follows:

> So he created Jesus from Mary and, thus, Mary was in the rank of Adam and Jesus in the rank of Eve. Therefore, just as there was a female created from male, there was also a male created from female. Thus, he sealed [the matter] in a similar manner to the way he began it: he [ended] by creating a son without a father, just as Eve was without a mother. So, Jesus and Eve were siblings and Adam and Mary were parents for them.[612]

We may also point out a notable gender parity here, in Ibn 'Arabi's situating Jesus and Eve as siblings and Adam and Mary as parents, all sharing a 'rank' or 'station' as a result of their special roles and natures. We further see in this passage that Ibn 'Arabi understands Jesus to be a uniquely *spiritualized* human, due to his spirit-based paternity.[613] As we saw at the beginning of this chapter, *lahut* is the principle of

---

610 Mustafa Akyol, 'Jesus' Birth between Islam and Christianity'.
611 Shaikh, *Sufi Narratives of Intimacy,* p.196.
612 Ibn 'Arabi, *Fut.*I.209. As quoted in Ali Hussain, 'Sainthood between the Ineffable and Social Practice', 77.
613 It is interesting to note that Jesus is not the only historical figure and spiritual founder to be associated with a miraculous birth. Padmasambhava's – the yogi-founder of the Nyingma school of Tibetan Buddhism – very name indicates this, meaning the 'Lotus-Born' – with some accounts of his life suggesting that he was miraculously born out of a lotus with neither human mother nor father. See Ngaqayng Zangpo, *Guru Rinpoche: His Life and Times* (Ithaca, NY, 2002), pp.22–3.

life – for Ibn 'Arabi life and spirit are one and the same. Jesus then is not only uniquely spiritualized but uniquely *alive* and *enlivening*: hence his raising of Lazarus, as recounted in both the Gospels and the Qur'an, in addition to a further Qur'anic narrative of Jesus breathing life into a bird he had formed of clay. In all cases, we see Jesus in these stories bringing the presence of life to where it is absent.[614] Ibn 'Arabi writes in his chapter on Jesus in the *Gemstones*, 'God purified his body and spirit and made him like Himself in creative power.' We should emphasize the 'like Himself' here, for Ibn 'Arabi also notes that 'the Real alone' holds the secret of life's arising and reviving.[615]

Perhaps in relation to Jesus' status as a special being who is profoundly alive, the Qur'an asserts in its fourth chapter that, regarding Jesus, *they did not slay him; nor did they crucify him, it only appeared so to them, and God raised him up unto Himself, and God is the Powerful, the Wise* (Q 4:157–8). Scholar of Islamic thought Todd Lawson notes that the Arabic phrase for 'it appeared so to them' or *shubbiha lahum*, is vague enough to have inspired various interpretations among early Muslim commentators. Some suggested that perhaps a disciple of Jesus like Judas was crucified in his place, or that God made Jesus only appear to be killed, when in actuality he was raised up to God, as a spiritual form, a form he will exist as until he returns at the end of time, in the Islamic tradition's own version of the Second Coming.[616]

It is worth noting here that the Qur'an's account can be read as at least somewhat corresponding with an early Christian belief known as Docetism from the Greek verb *dokeo*, meaning 'to seem' or 'to appear', a belief found in the apocryphal *Acts of John*, wherein Christ describes his crucifixion as merely an appearance rather than a reality.[617] However, in another verse, the Qur'an appears to reflect the more conventional Gospel narratives of Jesus' death and resurrection, when it quotes Jesus as saying, *Peace be upon me, the day I was born,*

---

614 Stephen Hirtenstein, 'Reviving the Dead: Ibn 'Arabi as Heir of Jesus', *Journal of the Muhyiddin Ibn 'Arabi Society*, 57 (2015), 43.

615 Ibid., 44.

616 Todd Lawson, *The Crucifixion and the Qur'an: A Study in the History of Muslim Thought* (Oxford, 2009), p.3.

617 Ibid., pp.3–4.

the day I die, and the day I am raised up alive (Q 19:33). Some Muslim commentators have read this as describing Jesus's actual death, which will follow his Second Coming before the end of the world, and his raising up will be on Judgment Day following the world's conclusion.[618]

Between Spirit and Law: Jesus, Sufism and Shari'a

Jesus is something of a quintessential Sufi, with his intensive spirituality, gentleness and love, his passionate refusal to compromise the truth and his consequent conflict with the legalistic clerical class. Not surprisingly, the 'amount of Jesus-related material in Sufism is overwhelming'.[619] Early Sufis like Harith al-Muhasibi (d.857) show a familiarity with Gospel teachings, such as the Sermon on the Mount, and several Sufis shared various sayings on asceticism and the spiritual life unique to the Islamic tradition that are attributed to Jesus. For example, we find Sufis relating the following saying of Jesus, on the futile and ultimately destructive nature of seeking happiness in external things: 'The seeker after the world is like one who would drink from the sea; the more he drinks the more thirsty he becomes – until it kills him in the end.'[620] Illustrating a more general Islamic understanding of Christ's nature, Sunni Islam's most famous theologian, Abu Hamid al-Ghazali, described Jesus as the 'prophet of the heart'.[621]

Recall that, as we discussed in the third chapter on Shu'ayb, the Qur'an articulates humanity's religious history in terms of prophets, 124,000 of which were sent to the world's various peoples between Adam and Muhammad. A key notion of Ibn 'Arabi's understanding of this is that God's friends (saints) all inherit their knowledge, power and spiritual orientation from a particular prophet – each prophet having their own unique kind of spirituality. It follows that, in each age, the earth is populated by 124,000 saints, each inheriting a particular style

---

618 Parinder, *Jesus in the Qur'an*, p.105.
619 Leirvik, *Images of Jesus Christ in Islam*, p.84.
620 Ibid., p.87.
621 Tarif Khalidi, *The Muslim Jesus* (Cambridge, MA, 2003), p.164.

of enlightenment or mode of wisdom from one of these prophets.⁶²² Ibn 'Arabi refers to some saints as *Musawi*, meaning 'Moses-like', 'related to Moses' or 'of Moses', and others as *'Isawi* – in the mode of Jesus. He even describes some as inheriting from several different prophets.⁶²³ This diversity of prophetic personality means that saints inherit wisdom in a wide range of styles, and hence embody wisdom according to a range of archetypes or modes. *'Isawi* spiritual types are, like Christ, also given a powerful spiritual energy that allows them to perform miraculous actions of healing and life-restoration. Ibn 'Arabi characterizes Jesus' spirituality as: 'renunciation of worldly affairs (*zuhd*), spiritual divesting and freedom (*tajrid*), itinerant wandering (*siyaha*), the preference for poverty over wealth (*faqr*), purity and purification (*tahara, takhlis*)'.⁶²⁴ He further describes the *'Isawis* as having a universal compassion for all regardless of religion or culture:

> One of the signs of the [*'Isawis*] is: if you want to recognize them, then observe every person who has kind compassion toward the world and affectionate concern for the people, whoever it may be, and whatever religion one may have, and whatever culture one shows – and an unreserved approval of them for God's sake.⁶²⁵

It is interesting to note here that Ibn 'Arabi himself entered the Sufi way through Jesus, whom he describes as 'my first teacher, the master through whom I returned to God'.⁶²⁶ He further relates encountering Jesus 'many times in ecstasies, and through him I have turned [from sin]'.⁶²⁷ As a result, for the first 18 years on the path Ibn 'Arabi was basically *'Isawi* in orientation, which included a somewhat ascetic abandonment of worldly pursuits, and even the avoidance of any sort of romantic relationship. He notably describes lacking all interest in

---

622 Chittick, *Ibn 'Arabi: Heir to the Prophets*, p.14.
623 Addas, *Quest for the Red Sulphur*, p.277.
624 Hirtenstein, 'Reviving the Dead', 43.
625 Ibn 'Arabi, *Fut*.III.36, as translated by Winkel, *The Openings Revealed in Mecca, Books 3 & 4*, p.293.
626 Ibn 'Arabi, *Fut*.II.49. As quoted in Zachary Markwith, 'Jesus and Christic Sanctity in Ibn 'Arabi and Early Islamic Spirituality', *Journal of the Muyhiddin Ibn 'Arabi Society*, 57 (2015), 92.
627 Ibn 'Arabi, *Fut*.II.49. As quoted in Elmore, *Islamic Sainthood in the Fullness of Time*, p.35.

romance and sexuality during the initial stages of the spiritual path, focused almost exclusively on reality's deeper dimensions.[628] However, he would eventually come to inherit his sagacity and sanctity from Muhammad, after which he was drawn to love, marriage and sexuality, extolling their profound spiritual value (something we will discuss at greater length in the following chapter). Regardless, he maintained that he had a close, special relationship with Christ throughout his entire life, sharing that Jesus 'is immensely kind towards me and does not neglect me for an instant'.[629]

As Jesus was crucified (or at least appeared to be) for his uncompromising truth and fealty to spirit over clerical convention, he became, for Sufis, an icon for those Sufi martyrs who themselves were executed for statements deemed to be in contravention of conventional orthodoxies – they were often understood to be *'Isawi* in orientation. Most famously, the 'Abbasid authorities executed Mansur al-Hallaj on March 26, 922, after a lengthy series of heresy trials. Hailing from Fars, Iran, Hallaj traveled widely, and for a time was a disciple of al-Junayd, perhaps the most renowned of early (orthodox) Sufis. Unlike his famously circumspect teacher, however, al-Hallaj spoke Sufi secrets publicly, and the resulting controversies not only cost him his life, but brought home to later Sufis the importance of keeping deeper teachings from those who may misunderstand them:

> Al-Hallaj called openly upon the people of Baghdad to seek God within their own hearts, realize the inner meanings of external rites, and challenge injustices which many religious and political elites were all too willing to tolerate. Abandoning caution, al Hallaj took to preaching spontaneously, jubilantly in the markets and mosque entrances of Baghdad.[630]

Although it is often suggested that his execution was for identifying himself with one of God's Names, in saying *'ana al-Haqq'* or 'I am the Truth' (something that Jesus also said), scholar of Sufism Carl

---

628 See, for example, Ibn 'Arabi, *Fut*.IV.84. As quoted in *The Tao of Islam*, p.186.
629 Addas, *Quest for the Red Sulpher*, p.39.
630 Dickson and Sharify-Funk, *Unveiling Sufism*, p.188.

W. Ernst notes that Hallaj was actually condemned to death on a technicality: 'the last straw was his opinion that those lacking the means to undertake the hajj, the pilgrimage to Mecca, could create a symbolic Kaʿaba in their homes, which would fulfill this religious duty'.[631] Al-Hallaj would go on to become Sufism's most celebrated martyr, even among the more law-oriented Sufis.[632] Scholar of Islam Zachary Markwith describes al-Hallaj as 'arguably the most striking example of Christic sanctity in Islamic history'.[633] This is not hard to appreciate, as very much like the Gospel portrayals of Christ, he spoke truth to power, revealed his hidden unity with God and was tortured, crucified and ultimately killed as a result. Interestingly, during his execution, he is said to have uttered the Qur'anic verse we mentioned above regarding Jesus, that, *'they did not slay him, nor did they crucify him, it only appeared so to them'*.[634]

The case of al-Hallaj raises an important – and too often misconstrued – issue, on Sufism's relationship to Islamic law or shariʿa. Although we have mentioned shariʿa before in this book and even went over some of its basic principles in the fourth chapter on Jonah, it is worth discussing the term a bit further here before considering Sufi approaches to it. The term shariʿa basically means a path to a source of water, such as a well, watering hole or river. Linguistically this actually tells us quite a bit about how Muslims have traditionally conceived of the law, as a path to life in this world and the next. In its most essential meaning, the shariʿa is the sacred balance inherent in life, and God's guidance on how humans can live in alignment with it. As scholar of Sufism Samer Dajani notes, the Qur'an itself makes this connection between guidance and life explicit in several places, such as

---

631 The notion that Hallaj was executed for saying, 'I am the Truth,' is traced back to the most complete classical biography of him, by Farid al-Din ʿAttar (d.1220), at the conclusion of his *Memoir of the Saints*. Carl W. Ernst translator and author of 'Introduction', in *Hallaj: Poems of a Sufi Martyr* (Evanston, IL, 2018), pp.4–5.

632 Ernst notes that stalwart early representatives of 'orthodox' Sufism, such as Abu al-Qasim al-Qushayri and ʿAli al-Hujwiri, valued Hallaj's writings, and regarded him as a master of the way, even if (as with al-Qushayri) this admiration was somewhat surreptitious in nature. Ibid., p.3.

633 Markwith, 'Jesus and Christic Sanctity in Ibn ʿArabi and Early Islamic Spirituality', 105.

634 Lawson, *The Crucifixion and the Qurʾan*, p.5.

8:24: *Believers, respond to God and His Messenger when he calls you to that which gives you life.*

Shari'a, in its meanings of 'path' or 'road', is used in the Qur'an to refer to religions, suggesting that God has given the world's peoples different shari'as to follow. In verse 5:48, for example, the Qur'an says, *For all [peoples] we have made a law (shir'atan) and a method/ way (minhajan)*, and notes that God could have made humanity one community but has instead made cultures and religions diverse throughout the world. For Muslims, the particular shari'a revealed to Muhammad is singular in essence, though from very early on, its human interpretations were acknowledged to be, inevitably, many. Hence, we see the discipline of Islamic jurisprudence or *fiqh* (literally 'understanding') develop in Islam's early centuries, embodied in several schools of legal methodology, each known as a *madhhab*, agreeing on most major issues but with notable differences between them. Although in common parlance the terms shari'a and *fiqh* are used interchangeably, for legal specialists the distinction between the two is critical, as it allows for an acknowledgment of the inevitably approximate nature of human interpretations of God's law – *fiqh* is always a human *attempt* to understand and apply God's guidance, the shari'a. A Muslim legal specialist gives an opinion (*fatwa*) on what they believe to be the best understanding of God's guidance in relation to a particular human action (whether it is encouraged, allowed or prohibited, for example), and yet they acknowledge that another opinion may in fact be more correct.

For their part, Sufis have historically fallen along a spectrum of approaches to shari'a, ranging from a) an understanding of Sufism that assumes a commitment to living according to the classical articulations of Islamic law (*fiqh*) – usually via adherence to one of the established schools of law, to b) an approach that decenters the law as a set of guidelines that are ultimately transcended when spiritual realization occurs, to c) outright and even ostentatious rejection of Islamic legal norms in the name of breaking through convention and hypocrisy.⁶³⁵ In an article I wrote on the subject, I called these juristic, supersessionist and formless tendencies within Sufism.⁶³⁶

Perhaps the majority of Sufis historically would have understood the deeper reality (*haqiqa*) of Islamic teachings as realized *through* a close adherence to Islamic law (juristic Sufism). And yet, as Shahab Ahmed's (d.2015) now classic work *What is Islam?* (2015), illustrates, for many Sufis in the classical period, Sufism was understood rather to be distinctly *above* the shari'a: Sufism was thought to be the deeper understanding of Islam that rendered the laws secondary or even redundant (supersessionist Sufism). Ahmad calls this 'Sufi-philosophical amalgam', a sort of 'religion above religion', and highlights its dominant cultural influence in the 'Balkan-to-Bengal' region in the medieval and early modern periods. An excellent example of this understanding of Sufism and shari'a is found in Rumi's *Masnavi*, where he writes on this as follows:

> The Law [*sharī'at*] is like a candle that shows the way: Without the candle in hand, there is no setting forth on the road. And when you are on the road: that journey is the Way [*tarīqat*]; and when you have reached the destination, that is the Real-Truth [*ḥaqīqat*]. It is in this regard that they say 'If the Real-Truths are manifest, the laws are nullified [*law ẓaharat al-ḥaqā'iq baṭalat al-sharā'i'*]', as when copper becomes gold, or was gold originally, it does not need the

---

635 From the ninth to the thirteenth centuries, various networks of Muslim mystics in the Mediterranean and Central Asian regions emerged that almost totally rejected shari'a norms, practicing an essentially formless spirituality that often self-consciously rejected Islamic rituals and rules. Ahmet T. Karamustafa labels these Sufis 'antinomian', for their, in some cases, total rejection of the law. This basically antinomian Sufism was discussed by Muslim observers relatively early in Islamic history, with Abu 'Asim al-Nasa'i (d.867) labeling them *fikriyya* – 'meditationists' or 'contemplatives' – those who believed they could reach God directly through meditation, and others for whom the love of God has consumed them entirely such that they held the law no longer applies to them. Such Sufis basically prioritized the inward experience of God far above outward acts of religious obedience. Later, the terms *darvish* (beggar) and *qalandar* (uncultured or wild) would be applied to these non-conformist Sufis, who would flourish as a larger movement in the medieval period. Ahmet T. Karamustafa, 'Antinomian Sufis', in *The Cambridge Companion to Sufism*, edited by Lloyd Ridgeon (New York, 2015), p.102.

636 William Rory Dickson, 'Sufism and *Sharia*: Contextualizing Contemporary Sufi Expressions', *Religions*, 13:5 (2022), https://www.mdpi.com/2077-1444/13/5/449 (accessed February 17, 2023).

alchemy that is the Law ...[637]

Here we find Rumi articulating the shariʿa as necessary at the beginning of the path, an irreplaceable light that sets one off in the right direction, and even alchemically facilitates the transformation of the lower self (copper) into a spiritualized one (gold). However, once it has done its work, and the self has become realized, the law is ultimately transcended/superseded. We can see here that it is not so much that Rumi rejects the law, but rather he decenters it such that it becomes a preliminary stage and a means to an end, rather than an end in and of itself.

This is illustrated clearly in biographies of Rumi, which record a fascinating response of his to some local clerics who accosted him about his master Shams Tabrizi's (d.c.1248) wine-drinking, and hence breaking the (almost universally agreed upon) shariʿa prohibition on consuming alcohol.[638] It is said that, when these jurists approached Rumi about Shams's violation of the law, Rumi used an Islamic legal argument to counter them. He pointed out to the jurists that, according to the Islamic laws regulating the purity of water, a drop of wine renders a basin of water impure and hence not something that can be used for drinking or washing oneself with in preparation for prayer. However, an entire 'wine-skin' can be poured into a river, not affecting its purity – you can dump gallons of wine into a river and, according to Islamic legal norms, that river water is still permissible to use for drinking and washing, as the wine is so diluted by the volume of water that it cannot possibly compromise its purity. Rumi suggested to the questioning jurists that even barley bread is forbidden for them, as their selves are as small as a basin, and hence easily polluted with even the smallest trace of alcohol, whereas the 'rule of the river' applies to Shams, in his spiritual vastness, and hence 'everything is permitted' for him: like the river Shams can drink as much as he wants

---

637 Rumi, *Masnavi* V.1–3. As quoted in Shahab Ahmed, *What is Islam?*, p.21.

638 For a good overview of early Islamic legal debates over alcohol consumption, see Najam Haider, 'Contesting Intoxication: Early Juristic Debates over the Lawfulness of Alcoholic Beverages', *Islamic Law and Society*, 20 (2013), 48–89.

and cannot pollute himself.⁶³⁹ As Ahmed points out, this argument of Rumi's is also 'Islamic', as it takes its ultimate reference point to be Islamic law, though understood in a manner that differs from that of his more legalistic challengers.

Even when Sufis were those that understood the authentic Muhammadan way as one grounded in a close adherence to the outward dictates of Islamic law, they tended to emphasize mercy, flexibility and the avoidance of 'overburdening believers with obligations and prohibitions that God did not intend for people'.⁶⁴⁰ We might call this a quintessentially Christic (or *'Isawi*) approach to the law, as Jesus himself says in the Gospels that he has not come to abolish the law but to fulfill it (Matthew 5:17), and consistently resisted legalistic interpretations that inhibited the free flowing of life. For most Sufis, the true scholar of the law, the true *faqih*, 'was not he who memorised rote knowledge of a list of rulings, but he whose illumined heart gave him deep understanding of what was right and wrong'.⁶⁴¹

Ibn 'Arabi actually had his own approach to the law that does not quite fit with any of the prominent Sunni schools, such as the Hanafi, Maliki, Shafi'i and Hanbali. In one sense he was exceptional in this respect, as probably most Sufis historically followed one of the schools of law, which tended to become established in particular regions of the Islamic world. Sufis in the Islamic West (today countries like Morocco, Mauritania, Tunisia and Algeria), for instance, tended to be adherents of the Maliki school of law, as this was the school that came to predominate in that region, whereas Sufis in Turkey and India would have largely been Hanafis, the school that was most established in those countries. In another sense, Ibn 'Arabi's trans-school approach to the law reflects a long Sufi tradition of not identifying with any particular school, seeing the Sufi method as one that takes the practitioner beyond the understandings found in the legal schools. Early Sufi master and author Abu al-Qasim al-Qushayri, for example, suggested that it did not befit the Sufi to adhere to one of the schools,

---

639 Ahmed, *What is Islam?*, p.100.
640 Dajani, *Sufis and Shari'a*, p.5.
641 Ibid., p.43.

when the realized one could spiritually see the deeper truth about the Qur'an and Sunnah, a sight that jurists lacked access to, as they were not those who had fully opened the eye of the heart, as we spoke of in chapter five: 'The Sufis had spiritual insight and certainty; therefore, they could plainly see what was hidden from the jurists who had to search for it by way of either traditions (*naql* and *athar*) or rational thought (*'aql* and *fikr*).'[642]

Although Ibn 'Arabi's approach to the law certainly emphasized mercy, flexibility and openness, it was also methodologically in line with some of the more conservative and even literalist approaches, such as those of the *ahl al-hadith* or Traditionalists, like Ahmad Ibn Hanbal (d.855) and Muhammad al-Bukhari (d.870). For Ibn 'Arabi, the best way to access the true shari'a was a methodology that closely adhered to the *letter* of the sacred texts, as the Traditionalists advocated.[643] However, he also believed that adherence to the letter should coincide with adherence to the *inward spirit and meaning* of revelation: hence his preference for rulings that facilitated ease, alongside his understanding of human life as characterized by a general permissibility (that is, all things are assumed permissible unless explicit textual evidence clearly suggests the contrary), and his emphasis on God's forgiveness and hence the need for humans to similarly foreground mercy and pardon in the law.[644]

The Difference between God and Lord

See how subtle and precise is this spiritual, divine message! [Jesus said,] 'Worship Allah,' using the Name Allah, because of the diversity of worshippers in their religious practices and the differences in their religions. He did not specify one name [of God's] to the exclusion of others. Rather, he used the Name that gathers

---

642 Ibid., p.54.

643 Ibn 'Arabi has further been associated with the somewhat literalist or Zahiri *madhhab* of the Andalusian jurist Abu Muhammad Ibn Hazm (d.1064), though to what degree exactly has long been debated. For more on this subject, see Elmore, *Islamic Sainthood in the Fullness of Time*, pp.41–5.

644 Ibid., pp.136–66.

them all together. Then he said, 'My Lord and your Lord.' It is known that His relationship to a given existent through His being Lord is not identical with the relationship He has with another.[645]

In this passage from the *Gemstones*, Ibn 'Arabi homes in on a dialog in the Qur'an between God and Jesus, in the scripture's fifth chapter (*Surah al-Ma'idah*). Following an account of various miracles performed by Jesus, including speaking as an infant, healing blindness and leprosy, breathing life into a bird he had made of clay and spontaneously providing a feast for his disciples, God questions Jesus as to whether he called upon people to worship himself and his mother *as gods besides God* (Q 5:116). Jesus emphatically responds, *Glory be to You! I would never utter that which I have no right to ... I said only what you commanded me to: 'worship Allah: my Lord and your Lord'* (Q 5:117).

Izutsu characterizes the distinction between God as God, and God as Lord, as 'one of the cardinal elements of Ibn 'Arabi's thought'.[646] Ibn 'Arabi, ever one to read the Qur'an as closely as possible, in his belief that every word choice, every letter, is purposeful, reads in this short phrase of Jesus a metaphysical description of the unity of Reality and diversity of religions, or the singularity of Allah and diversity of lords.

As we discussed in this book's first chapter on Adam, Ibn 'Arabi holds that the name Allah includes all of the Names of God within Itself. Hence when Jesus refers to 'Allah' he means the all-comprehensive Name, indicating the Real as such, beyond any *particular* name, form, quality, theology, doctrine, law, religion, practice etc. This singular, universal Essence is what ultimately is, and hence any who have genuine realization, enlightenment or insight are knowing this transcendent One. At this level there is one truth, one religion, what Rumi calls the Religion of Love, which is simply the reality of God.[647] However, this transcendent Real is Being undefined, totally variable, manifesting as every form, and only ever known *through* a particular

---

645 Ibn 'Arabi, *Fusus*, p.135.
646 Izutsu, *Sufism and Taoism*, p.110.
647 Rumi writes, 'The religion of love is separate from all religions, for lovers the only religion is God.' *Masnavi* II.1770.

form, as it presents Itself to an individual, and hence that individual (i.e. *every* individual) experiences Allah in relation to themselves, and that relational form of God is what Ibn 'Arabi calls a *particular Lord* (in Arabic *rabb*). We might also say here that Jesus' concise statement in the Qur'an acknowledges the simultaneous unity of the Real, and diversity of its expressions in various religions, beliefs and paths. As the ancient Hindu scripture, the *Rig Veda*, concisely states (1.164.46), 'To the One, the wise give many names.'

Unlike Allah, who is always revealing Himself in new ways, someone's Lord has a certain static quality to it, as defined by the particular Name of God that an individual relates to Allah through, and this Name is bound by the quality that particularizes it, that makes it a unique Name distinct from the others. Each person then has a different Lord, that is totally unique to them, and hence each has a different window onto the Real, or we might say the Real reveals itself to each in a unique form, based upon the individual's own essential nature and receptivity. Correspondingly, no one knows Allah as such in totality or as pure unity. Although in one sense we may think of each person as having their own Lord, in another sense their Lord changes based upon the way in which they relate to Allah throughout their lives: hence someone suffering illness and seeking relief is seeking the Real as *al-Shafi'*, the Healer, while one engaged in working for their livelihood is relating to the Real as *al-Razzaq*, the Provider. Whichever way we choose to engage our life situation, whatever we pursue and seek, is the Name and Lord of the Real we relate to in that moment, though our self is also a general 'shape' that has its own more 'static' Lord. In his chapter in the *Gemstones* on Ishmael, Ibn 'Arabi states simply that it is impossible for an existent being to know God beyond their particular Lord, or to know all the lords. He further notes:

> Happy is the one whose Lord is pleased with them, and indeed every being is approved by their Lord. ... However, it does not necessarily follow that every being will be pleasing to the Lord of another, for they only relate to one Lord, not all.[648]

---

648 Ibn 'Arabi, *Fusus*, p.74.

This passage indicates why we might say that, from one perspective, every creature is pleasing to God, or that God's love encompasses all without any exception whatsoever. One's own Lord is God's unique face toward one's soul, and hence the Lord knows it, and its tendencies, history and qualities more intimately than the soul knows itself. A Lord is thus always pleased with the soul it connects with, knowing and loving the soul with all of its idiosyncratic beauties and foibles.

In the 1985 film *Ladyhawk*, for example, there is a scene that nicely illustrates this. The movie's protagonist is a pickpocket named Phillipe Gaston, deftly played by Matthew Broderick. At one point he swears off practicing his professional thieving. However, despite his vow he just can't seem to help himself and ends up picking another pocket. He then declares to God, 'I know I promised, Lord, *never again*. But I also know that *You* know what a weak-willed person I am.'[649] Although we can certainly appreciate Phillipe's attempt to secure a kind of moral insurance, and even go along with him in assuming that, as his Lord indeed knows of his weak will, that He also remains pleased with him, this does not mean that Phillipe is totally 'off the hook'. According to Ibn 'Arabi, if one soul violates the rights of another, harms them and hence engages in actions that we may call evil, they will not be pleasing to *that other soul's* Lord, as they have harmed this other soul, whose Lord will call them to account. Perhaps it is only those rare, perfected individuals, like Jesus, who have become a lens through which the light of the Real can shine unencumbered, who are pleasing not only to their own Lord, but the *Lord of Lords*, the One, in totality, *Allah*.[650] As we will see in the next, and final chapter, although Jesus is for Muslims a totally unique being and profound manifestation of God's Word and Spirit, it is to Muhammad that Muslims look for the most *comprehensive* or complete paradigm of this sort of human perfection.

---

649 I have to thank Naniece Ibrahim for sharing with me this illustrative anecdote from the film *Ladyhawk* during our discussion of this part of the chapter.

650 Dagli, *The Ringstones of Wisdom*, p.81.

8

Muhammad and the Wisdom of Singularity: Marrying Sense and Spirit

I am dust on the path of Muhammad, the Chosen One.[651]

Who is Muhammad?

For his followers, the Prophet Muhammad is not just a person who lived in Arabia between the late sixth century and early seventh, tasked by God with delivering His final revelation to humanity. His remarkable role in history is of course deeply significant for them, and yet Muhammad is something much more. He is a beloved model of compassion, nobility and humility, one that Muslims strive to embody in their everyday lives. Muhammad echoes within them when they leave things better than they found them, when they reach out to comfort the sick and ease the worries of the troubled, when they protect those in harm's way or when they pray at night and fast during the day and are charitable as often as they can be. Muhammad is still more, however. He is a living presence of love, a subtle spiritual reality that can be encountered here and now. This deeper reality of Muhammad is acknowledged in each of the five daily prayers of Islam, when Muslims send a greeting of peace *directly* to the Prophet, saying, 'al-salamu 'alayka ayyuha'n nabi', or 'Peace be unto you O Prophet', connecting with his spiritual presence in an immediate way. We can also recall here that Ibn 'Arabi received *The Gemstones of Wisdom* from

---

651 Jalal al-Din Rumi, Quatrain No. 1173, translated by Ibrahim Gamard and Ravan Farhadi in *The Quatrains of Rumi: Ruba'iyat-e Jalaluddin Muhammad Balkhi-Rumi* (San Rafael, CA, 2008), p.2.

the hand of Muhammad himself, the Prophet perpetually accessible to the purified and devout, in dream and vision.[652] Nur al-Jerrahi explains the intimate, living reality of Muhammad for believers:

> We place our hand upon our heart when we speak his most beautiful name, Muhammad, because he is the true human heart – the essence of our own mystical heart, hidden far behind the heart of life throbbing within the human breast. He is not in the desert of Arabia, but in the heart. Love him, and you will love all persons abundantly.[653]

As the loving essence of the heart, Muslims experience a profound sense of intimacy with the Prophet, akin to the closeness of family, or even more so. His model of humanity and spiritual reality are celebrated in every Muslim culture, through song, art and story. For a variety of theological and historical reasons, however, Muhammad has not always been appreciated in the historically Christian societies that we call the West, nor has his role in Muslim spirituality been well understood.[654] The centuries of geopolitical rivalry between Muslim and Christian dynasties in the greater Mediterranean region have created a kind of historical baggage when it comes to all things Islamic, and especially so in regard to the Prophet. There is a widespread lack of understanding not only who Muhammad *was* but also who he *is* for Muslims – his deep meaning for them and their profound love for him.

Kecia Ali, scholar of Islamic history and law, observes that, in the early stages of the European Enlightenment, it wasn't uncommon to find Moses, Jesus and Muhammad considered together. Some

---

652 In a well-established hadith with several chains of transmission, the Prophet Muhammad said, 'Whoever sees me in a dream has truly seen me, for Satan cannot assume my form.' See Muhammad al-Tirmidhi, *Al-Shama'il al-Muhammadiyya: 415 Hadiths on the Beauty and Perfection of the Prophet Muhammad*, translated by Abdul Aziz Suraqah and Mohammed Aslam (New York, 2019), pp.268–9.

653 Hixon, *Atom from the Sun of Knowledge*, p.108.

654 Kecia Ali notes that, although Muslims and non-Muslims have had various understandings of Muhammad that have changed over time, the divide between how Muslims and non-Muslims understand Muhammad has actually grown since the 19th century, a division that has arisen from both polemical narratives of Muhammad during the colonial period, and Muslim responses to these narratives, which have, in effect, reconstituted how Muslims themselves understand him. Kecia Ali, *The Lives of Muhammad* (Cambridge, MA, 2014), p.2.

Enlightenment authors who were critical of religion disparaged them as collective emblems of a superstitious time past. However, in the late 19th century, after Buddhism 'made its debut on the stage of world religions', European commentators on religion replaced Moses with the Buddha, placing him next to Jesus and Muhammad to create a sort of archetypal trifecta.[655] As Buddhism, Christianity and Islam are the three most successful missionary faiths in history (those that have actively sought converts and expanded into lands far outside of their origin) and together they can count about 60 percent of humanity as their members, it isn't all that surprising that still today, Jesus, Buddha and Muhammad remain probably the world's three most recognizable religious archetypes.

For many contemporary people in the West, the Buddha tends to be more immediately intelligible as a spiritual icon than the Prophet Muhammad. One reason for this is simply that the Buddha more closely resembles Christ, or the Christic paradigm: both Jesus and the Buddha were somewhat *other-worldly* in nature, either never marrying, as in the case of Jesus, or leaving family to pursue enlightenment, as the Buddha did, and neither taking on roles of political or military leadership. In contrast to their monastic mode, Muhammad was *fully involved* with every conceivable aspect of life in the world, as a shepherd and trader, a husband, father and friend, a political leader and a warrior, and a legislator and counselor. In these respects, Muhammad more closely resembles Moses, though, as Ali notes, in the modern era Moses does not have the prominence he once did in Western public consciousness.

Moses and Muhammad's total involvement in what might be seen as secular affairs can conflict with certain notions of what a spiritual person should be like – perhaps ideally meditating alone in a mountain cave or desert, with romance and politics the furthest thing from their minds. And indeed, as scholar of Islam Carl W. Ernst notes, in the medieval period, 'the two biggest Christian criticisms of the Prophet Muhammad were undoubtedly in relation to his military activities

---

655 Ali, *The Lives of Muhammad*, pp.203–5.

and his marriages'.[656] For Muslims, however, this is precisely why the Prophet Muhammad offers such a uniquely powerful spiritual paradigm: in his own person he connects the highest spirituality to every aspect of human life, including some of its most challenging and earthly elements. This is also why he is beloved by Muslims both as a) a very human, historical person, one who struggled and loved and led a community, and shared his life with his friends and family, as well as b) an enlightened spiritual presence and principle going totally beyond his earthly existence.

Ibn 'Arabi begins this chapter of the *Gemstones* by explaining why Muhammad is associated with the Wisdom of Singularity or Uniqueness (*Fardiyya*), with his dual role as human prophet and metaphysical reality:

> His wisdom is singular because he is the most perfect existent among the human species. This is why he begins the affair and seals it. He was a prophet 'while Adam was still in-between water and clay.' Then he was the Seal of the Prophets in his elemental constitution ... [Muhammad], peace be upon him, is the most visible proof of his lord. He was further given comprehensive words, which are the realities of the names which Adam was taught.[657]

Ibn 'Arabi points to both aspects of Muhammad in this passage. First, he references a hadith found in several collections, where Muhammad states that he was a prophet while Adam was 'between water and clay', or in other versions 'between soul and body'.[658] Regardless of the exact wording, such sayings clearly point to Muhammad's existence as a prophetic reality existing before, not just his own earthly manifestation, but even prior to the appearance of

---

656 Carl W. Ernst, *Following Muhammad: Rethinking Islam in the Contemporary World* (Chapel Hill, 2003), p.14.

657 Ibn 'Arabi, *Fusus*, p.202.

658 Although there are several examples, some of the more oft-referenced are found in the *Musnad al-Shamiyyin* and the *Jami' al-Tirmidhi* (3609). This particular hadith, perhaps because of its metaphysical implications, drew concerted debate, with Ibn Taymiyya attacking it as a forgery, though he made an exception for the versions shared by Ibn Hanbal and al-Tirmidhi, which use the language of Adam 'between soul and body' as opposed to 'water and clay'. Chodkiewicz, *Seal of the Saints*, pp.60–1.

humanity itself. This situates him somewhat along the lines of the *logos* in the Western tradition, or the *Hiranyagarbha* in the Hindu tradition, concepts that we will consider a bit later on in this chapter. Muslims would later refer to this deeper dimension of Muhammad using a variety of terms, though the most popular among Sufis have been the Muhammadan Light (*Nur Muhammadi*) as well as the Muhammadan Reality (*al-Haqiqa al-Muhammadiyya*). Second, we see in the passage above that Ibn 'Arabi refers to Muhammad as the historical person who seals prophecy in this terrestrial term – the last of the great prophets sent to humanity before the conclusion of our cosmic cycle. Third, he says that Muhammad is a visible proof of God and a bearer of comprehensive words – both of which relate to Ibn 'Arabi's key notion of the Perfect or Universal Human (*al-insan al-kamil*). In what follows we will first consider who Muhammad was as a historical individual and human prophet, before exploring his deeper significance within Sufi philosophy, as the Muhammadan Light and Perfect Human.

Prophet and Paradigm: Muhammad Ibn 'Abd Allah

The Qur'an describes Muhammad in several ways: as a Messenger of God (Q 69:40), a spiritual and moral guide (Q 62:2) and a judge among the believers (Q 4:65).[659] It also calls upon Muslims to emulate the Prophet Muhammad as a spiritually efficacious model, stating: *Truly, in the Messenger of God you have a beautiful example for those who hope for God and the Last Day, and remember God frequently* (Q 33:21). For those who long for the Real and orient themselves beyond the ephemeral toward the Eternal, whose hearts frequently recall our transcendent Origin, Muhammad offers them a paradigm for a life lived accordingly. The Qur'an then calls upon those who of us who wish to not only live, but to live beautifully, to look to Muhammad as an example.

---

659 Khalil Andani helpfully breaks down the Qur'an's various descriptions of Muhammad thematically – see 'Metaphysics of Muhammad: The Nur Muhammad from Imam Ja'far al-Sadiq (d. 148/765) to Nasir al-Din al-Tusi (d. 672/1274)', *Journal of Sufi Studies*, 8 (2019), 101–2.

The Qur'an further says that Muhammad is a person of rare, elevated character: *And truly you are of a sublime character* (Q 68:4), referring to him here using the powerful Arabic word *'azim*, which I've translated as 'sublime' but whose Arabic root includes meanings of magnitude, elevation and beauty, perhaps something like a mountain peak in its magnificence and splendor. *'Azim* awakens and uplifts. It is by nature significant and impactful. Ibn 'Arabi further defines the Prophet's character simply as 'the Qur'an', and says that he assumed 'the divine names as his own traits'.[660] The historical Prophet Muhammad was something like a walking scripture, the embodiment of truth and a human vessel for God's own beautiful qualities. It follows that the Prophet's companions and the early generations that followed them were keen to know *everything* they could about who he was, what he said, or did and, in general, how he lived. This overall body of information about Muhammad is generally summed up using the term *Sunnah*: meaning his Way, his habit, custom and approach.

The widespread Muslim focus on Muhammad's Way further led, in Islam's first centuries, to a collective effort of remembrance, recording and transmitting his life in various reports (hadith), with Muslims paying particularly close attention to reports that shed light on his character. This led to a genre of hadith literature describing his qualities, both physical and spiritual.[661] A great example of this sort of hadith comes to us from a Bedouin woman named 'Atika bint Khalid al-Khuza'iyya, who used to give food and drink to travelers going between Mecca and Medina, around the half-way point, where she encountered the Prophet. She said he was dignified when silent and overcome with glory when speaking; he was beautiful and powerful

---

660 Ibn 'Arabi, *Fut*.III.61. As quoted in Chittick, *Sufi Path of Knowledge*, p.241.

661 One of the most celebrated of these collected by Muhammad al-Tirmidhi (d.892), with his *al-Shama'il al-Muhammadiyya*, a collection of 415 hadith that offer a series of windows onto the physical characteristics and personal qualities of the Prophet Muhammad. Michael Muhammad Knight observes that physical descriptions of Muhammad (such as those found in the *Shama'il*) share some interesting similarities and differences. Reports of him being of medium height are consistent across the board, as are reports of his hair somewhat between straightness and curls, with dark-colored eyes and prominent eye lashes. He is similarly universally described as having a somewhat unique gait, walking as though descending from a height. Accounts of his skin color differ, however, ranging from white to light or medium brown. *Muhammad: Forty Introductions* (New York, 2019), p.67.

from afar and yet sweet and kind up close, with measured, careful words, always surrounded by friends.[662]

As we go through the various reports that make up the early Muslim community's collective remembrance of Muhammad, we encounter, again and again, a mild, gentle and even shy person, one who lived simply, owning barely anything,[663] praying and fasting almost constantly, who was ever generous, and, perhaps above all, possessed a remarkable warmth and compassion. The numerous accounts of his familial relationships agree that the Prophet Muhammad cared profoundly for his wives and children, and was affectionate and often playful with them. The Prophet was reportedly asked by some male visitors if he kissed his children, and when he affirmed that he indeed did, they said, 'But we, by God, never kiss them.' He responded, 'What can I do if God has removed mercy from you?'[664]

His patience, kindness and forbearance with people were legendary, with one of his most oft-repeated admonitions being, simply, 'Do not get angry.'[665] There is a wonderful report about a sort of 'country bumpkin' coming in from the desert who strolls into the Prophet Muhammad's Mosque and proceeds to urinate in the corner. Muhammad's companions are understandably upset and move to stop this man from completing his, at the very least, inconsiderate act, but the Prophet calls them to not disturb him and let him finish relieving himself, and then goes and personally washes the area after the man moves on.[666] The hadith literature suggests that Muhammad's tenderness extended to animals as well. In one report the Prophet came across a camel being put to work in a garden, dragging itself, with tears of exhaustion in its eyes. Moved by the animal's plight, Muhammad gently wiped the camel's tears and held its head until it had calmed down. He then called to find out whose animal it was, and when the owner showed up, the Prophet reprimanded him, asking, 'Do you not

---

662 Ernst, *Following Muhammad*, p.78.
663 He is reputed to have said, '*faqri fakhri*', which literally translates as, 'My poverty is my pride.'
664 *Sunan Ibn Majah*, 3665.
665 Knight, *Muhammad: Forty Introductions*, p.96.
666 This hadith is found in Ahmad ibn Hanbal's *Musnad*, 13117.

fear God with this animal, that God has given you? It complains to me that you starve and exhaust it.'[667]

Alongside collections devoted to the Prophet's elevated character, in Islam's first centuries efforts to remember Muhammad crystalized into another genre of devotional literature known as the *sira*, or biography.[668] Although stories of Muhammad's life were told and retold among his followers and their successors, it was only a century after his death that the first proper biography of the Prophet was composed. We no longer have this original biography by Ibn Ishaq (d.767) and yet we do have Ibn Hisham's (d.833) later recension, a text that would prove paradigmatic for all later prophetic biographies. Ibn Hisham's work, alongside the various hadith that include biographical anecdotes, together offer a rich, detailed account of Muhammad's life, and here I will simply outline some of the narrative's contours in broad strokes, for those who may not be familiar with it.

Muhammad[669] was born in the year 570 in a remote trading outpost in Arabia called Mecca.[670] As the ancient home of the Ka'aba – the black square shrine said to have been built by Abraham and his son Ishmael – Mecca hosted an annual pilgrimage that brought trade and festivity

---

667 Knight, *Muhammad: Forty Introductions*, pp.207–8.

668 The genre of prophetic biography evolved from an earlier genre known as *maghazi* literature, which celebrated Muhammad's heroism in battle and as the brave leader of his people in Medina. Walid A. Saleh, 'The Arabian Context of Muhammad's Life', in *The Cambridge Companion to Muhammad*, edited by Jonathan E. Brockopp (New York, 2010), p.27. Sira literature would further draw upon the poems of Hassan ibn Thabit (d.674), one of the Prophet's companions, who would eulogize Muhammad and important events in the life of the Muslim community. Annemarie Schimmel, *And Muhammad is His Messenger* (Charlotte, 1985), p.9.

669 We should note here that Muhammad is also known by several other epithets in the Islamic tradition. He is also called *Ahmad* (the Praised or Praising one), *al-Mustafa* (the Chosen one), *Habib Allah* (the Beloved of God) and *'Abd Allah* (the Servant of God).

670 The Qur'an calls Mecca '*a valley without cultivation*' (14:37). In the 19th century, Spanish soldier and spy Domingo Badia, also known as Ali Bey (d.1818), described it as 'a sandy valley, surrounded on all sides by naked mountains, without brook, river or any running water; without trees, plants or any species of vegetation.' As quoted in Francis E. Peters, *Muhammad and the Origins of Islam* (Albany, NY, 1994), p.1.

to the otherwise quiet settlement.⁶⁷¹ Although Arabia is actually a *huge* landmass (larger than either India or Europe), it is almost entirely desert, making it largely uninhabited. The lack of rivers or other sources of water further made the peninsula pretty much inaccessible to outside armies, and hence, despite being surrounded by ancient civilizations and empires like the Romans and Persians, Arabia was almost completely isolated, at least compared to adjacent regions.⁶⁷²

Muhammad was born to Amina (d.577) and 'Abd Allah (d.570), and consequently his full Arabic name is Muhammad ibn 'Abd Allah, *ibn* here meaning 'son of'. His parents were of the Banu Hashim clan of the Quraysh tribe, a noble clan that traced its descent to Abraham through Ishmael. Early Muslim sources suggest that Muhammad was orphaned quite young, with his father dying months prior to his birth and his mother dying when he was only six. He first fell under the protection of his grandfather, 'Abd al-Muttalib (d.578), and after his grandfather died, was cared for by his uncle, Abu Talib (d.619). As a young man Muhammad reportedly worked as a shepherd and found employment taking camel caravans north from Mecca to Syria for trade. One caravan owner was an older widow named Khadija (d.619), who was struck by Muhammad's gentle, sincere character and had a friend of hers basically let him know that if he proposed marriage she would not decline.⁶⁷³ He received the message and they married (when

---

671 Peters notes that, although Mecca is often portrayed as laying at an intersection of natural trade routes, 'it in fact does not', with the natural trade route intersection well east of the settlement. This fact, combined with the barrenness of the area, lends weight to the argument that Mecca's significance as a settlement is rooted in the holiness of the Ka'aba. Ibid., p.24.

672 There were of course connections between Arabia and the broader Near East, through trade and missionaries and such, but overall Arabia existed largely outside of the cultural spheres of surrounding civilizations. Saleh, 'The Arabian Context of Muhammad's Life', p.21.

673 Khadija apparently consulted her friend Nufaysa, who approached Muhammad and asked why he was not yet married. He replied that he did not have the means, and Nufaysa asked him if that were not an issue, would he be interested? He asked who she had in mind, and when she said Khadija, Muhammad expressed a keen interest, and Nufaysa returned to Khadija with the good news. Khadija then arranged a meeting with Muhammad, where she declared her love for him, for his moderation, never taking sides in conflicts, for his trustworthiness and beauty of character, and offered herself to him in marriage. He accepted and they agreed to speak to their respective uncles to make wedding arrangements. Martin Lings, *Muhammad: His Life Based on the Earliest Sources* (Rochester, VT, 2006 [1983]), pp.35–6.

he was 25 and she 40), and by all accounts shared a profound, beautiful companionship. Notably, Khadija gave birth to Fatima (d.632), who would later marry 'Ali, giving Muhammad his only grandsons, Hasan (d.670) and Husayn (d.680), figures venerated by all Muslims, but especially by Shi'i communities, as the line of guidance embodied in the Imams – spiritual, ethical and political – goes through them. Muhammad would not marry again until after Khadija's death.[674]

One of the interesting facts about Muhammad's life (especially for Sufis) is that, as a young man, he was a committed spiritual seeker. During his marriage to Khadija, Muhammad was repeatedly drawn to spiritual retreat (*khalwa*), spending time meditating and praying in caves outside of Mecca. Later Muslims considered him to be one of the *hanifiyya*, those among the Arabs who, like Abraham, were lovers of God but subscribed to no particular religion or sectarian community (recall our discussion of the Qur'an's description of Abraham as a *hanif* in the second chapter).[675] The majority of Arabs had their own tribal gods, and there were some longstanding Jewish tribes in Arabia, as well as some scattered Christian communities, though Muhammad did not identify with any of them, and was instead, as a *hanif,* an unaffiliated monotheist and seeker. As he pursued spiritual retreat over the years, he began having clear, vivid, veridical dreams,[676] and eventually, in the year 610, at the poignant age of 40, Muhammad had a terrifying encounter with Gabriel, the Archangel of Revelation, in a cave outside of Mecca called Hira, on what would later be known as the *Jabal al-Nur*, or 'Mountain of Light'. According to the most widely accepted report passed down to us from Muhammad's later wife A'isha, the Angel commanded Muhammad to recite, and when he pleaded that

---

[674] Muslim biographical sources suggest that Muhammad and Khadija had four daughters – Ruqayya, Zaynab, Umm Kulthum and Fatima – as well as one son, al-Qasim, who died in infancy.

[675] Saleh, 'The Arabian Context', p.31. Ibn Ishaq records several individuals who identified as *hanif* in Mecca and its surrounding environs, whom he describes as unaffiliated monotheists seeking the original way of Abraham. Ibn Ishaq, *The Life of Muhammad: A Translation of Ibn Ishaq's 'Sirat Rasul Allah'*, Introduction and Commentary by Alfred Guillaume (Oxford, 1955), pp.98–9.

[676] A'isha related that Muhammad's experience of prophecy commenced with several *al-ru'ya al-sadiqa* or 'true dreams', such that whatever he dreamed would 'come true like the bright light of dawn'. *Sahih al-Bukhari* 6982.

he did not know how or what to recite, the Angel gripped him and told him: *Recite, in the Name of your Lord who creates. Creates man from a clot. Recite; and your Lord is most Bountiful. Who teaches by the pen. Teaches man what he knew not* (Q 96:1–5). Though at first he was unsure of what to make of the encounter, with the steadfast support of Khadija, he accepted the weighty call to prophecy, and began sharing the revelations he received from God via Gabriel with his family.

After some years privately sharing the verses of the Qur'an with his family and close friends, Muhammad received a call from God to *Arise and warn* (Q 74:2). He began publicly calling Meccans to worship God, and warning them of the coming Day of Judgment when their actions will be carefully weighed and requited. His rejection of the tribal gods of the Arabs, his critique of their blood feuds and his condemnation of their contempt for the weak and boasting of feats and wealth, did not go over well. The elites of the Quraysh attempted to ridicule him, boycott him and his followers, and even have him assassinated. But the power of the Qur'an and the sincerity of his character won over more and more to the fold of Islam, starting with the weak and marginalized, but eventually including the powerful and wealthy. The burgeoning community remained untenable in Mecca, however, with concerted and often violent opposition from Meccan elites, so Muhammad and his followers sought refuge elsewhere, and eventually found it in Yathrib, a city of date-palm groves north of Mecca, where various pagan Arab and Jewish tribes lived, farmed and frequently feuded. They hoped that Muhammad could bring some peace to the town, and in the year 622 his followers and eventually the Prophet himself made what was called a *hijra* or migration there, which marks the beginning of the Islamic or *hijri* calendar. The city of Yathrib would come to be known by Muslims simply as 'the City', or *al-Madina*, and sometimes the *Madinat al-Nabi* (the City of the Prophet), *Madinat al-Sharif* (the Noble City) or *Madinat al-Munawwara* (the Illuminated City). Going forward I will simply refer to it as Medina.

In Medina the Prophet Muhammad took on the role not only of divine messenger and spiritual guide, but also community leader,[677] and eventually, when warfare broke out between the Muslims and Meccans, a leader in battle. Three major battles were fought between Muslims and their pagan Meccan opponents,[678] and eventually the Meccans realized that Muhammad's growing body of believers and secure tribal alliances made their position untenable, and they surrendered in 630, with Muhammad triumphantly returning to Mecca and, in a notable departure from tribal custom, declaring a general amnesty for his opponents. He entered the Ka'aba, the holy shrine of Mecca, reciting a verse of the Qur'an (Q 17:81), *The Truth has come and falsehood has vanished. Truly the false is ever vanishing,* and, using his staff, he destroyed the idols therein, reconsecrating the House to the worship of God, as it was intended by its original builders, Abraham and Ishmael. Some reports suggest that there were icons of Jesus and Mary, as well as Abraham in the Ka'aba, which he preserved.[679]

His prophetic mission was now complete, and Muhammad returned to Medina. Two years later, however, he would make what was known as his Farewell Pilgrimage to Mecca, during which he received the final revelation of the Qur'an (Q 5:3): *Today I have perfected for you your religion and completed My blessing upon you, and have chosen for you Islam as religion.* Having fulfilled his arduous role as Messenger, Muhammad would then go back to his home in Medina where he would die a few weeks later, in the arms of his beloved wife A'isha. Upon his death, the verses of the Qur'an that had been written and memorized among thousands of his followers (with many having memorized the entire Qur'an), were soon collected into a standard

---

677 After the death of his beloved Khadija, the Prophet Muhammad married several times, often to secure tribal alliances, or to care for widows of fallen soldiers. Later in life he married A'isha, the daughter of his closest companion Abu Bakr, and she would go on after the Prophet's death to function as an important community leader and transmitter of knowledge about Muhammad's Way. The Qur'an refers to the Prophet's wives as the *Mothers of the Believers* (Q 33:6).

678 For the best accounts of these battles found in English, see Lings's *Muhammad: His Life Based on the Earliest Sources*, chapters 41-5, and 49-60.

679 Lings, *Muhammad*, pp.313-14.

version, which would some years later be promulgated among the whole community.[680]

The Prophet Muhammad's Three Beloveds

Ibn 'Arabi builds much of his chapter on the Prophet Muhammad in the *Gemstones* around a saying of Muhammad's, found in one of the canonical hadith collections, known as the *Sunan* of Ahmad al-Nasa'i (d.915). At first glance it may seem, perhaps, a strange choice among the thousands of the Prophet's recorded sayings. However, as one delves into the final chapter of Ibn 'Arabi's most important work, the metaphysical depths of this short hadith become apparent. In his collection, al-Nasa'i records a report traced back to Anas ibn Malik (d.709), that the Prophet said: 'Three things from your world were made beloved to me: women and perfume, and the coolness of my eye is found in prayer.'[681]

The first thing we can note here is that Muhammad refers not to 'my world' or 'our world', but rather to '*your world*', as though he is not *from it*, or *of it*, like a stranger who has appeared in a realm that he is not native to, speaking to its inhabitants as a foreigner. We might suggest here that Muhammad is speaking in this hadith from the perspective of the Muhammadan Reality. Along these same lines, he does not refer simply to three loves, but rather to three that 'were made beloved' to him, again indicating a sort of spiritual detachment from our world, as a foreign place that he is not by nature inclined to,

---

680 The particulars of this general narrative that I've just provided are all found in the earliest sources we have on the Prophet Muhammad's life. However, as Kecia Ali highlights, their *particular ordering* and *emphases*, found not only in my own rendering here, but in 'most biographies – whether in Arabic or English, whether by Muslims or non-Muslims', in text books, news articles and documentaries, are actually *only a few centuries old*. Before that, non-Muslims, particularly pre-modern Christian opponents of Islam, wrote polemical accounts of Muhammad that liberally mixed fact and fiction, while Muslims themselves wrote very different accounts reflecting their own sectarian interests, in many cases emphasizing miraculous events, or choosing particular themes of his life to focus on for various devotional reasons. Ali, *The Lives of Muhammad*, pp.8–9.

681 *Sunan al-Nasa'i* 3939. The version here better translates as: 'Made beloved to me from the world are women and perfume, and the coolness of my eye is in prayer.' https://sunnah.com/nasai:3939 (accessed February 21, 2023).

though three things of it were made beloved to him during his time here, for the profound wisdom they hold. The second thing to note is something that Ibn 'Arabi discusses in his chapter on Muhammad in the *Gemstones* but is not apparent from the English translation of the hadith:

> Truly [the Prophet], upon him peace, gives precedence in this report to the feminine over the masculine as he intended to highlight its importance. Thus, he said 'three' (*thalath*) in the feminine plural form and not 'three' (*thalatha*) in the masculine form, even though he mentions 'perfume', which is a masculine noun. The Arabs usually make the masculine prevail over the feminine and thus one would say 'the Faṭimas and Zayd went out' using a masculine plural verb, not the feminine plural. So, the Arabs make the masculine prevail grammatically over the feminine even though there is only one masculine noun among several feminine nouns. [Muhammad] was an Arab, and so he, peace be upon him, deliberately observed the specific meaning that he wanted to convey, taking into consideration God's intention to make women beloved to him, though he did not choose this love. God taught him what he did not know and bestowed upon him a sublime grace, and hence the Prophet made the feminine gender prevail over the masculine gender by saying 'three' in the feminine form.[682]

As Ibn 'Arabi describes here, according to the rules of grammar of the Arabic language the Prophet Muhammad should have used the masculine form of 'three' in this saying. However, he *chose* to use the feminine form, with great purpose, as the Prophet wanted to highlight the dignity, power and elevation of femininity, and to honor the fact that God made women beloved to him, and that this love was itself a sublime (*'azim*) grace, an overflowing gift full of wisdom.

As discussed in the chapter on Adam, although Ibn 'Arabi understands woman as metaphysically derived *from* man, he understands her to be the choicest or best part (*naqawa*), and hence having a degree of elevation *above* man, just as he understands man

---
682 Ibn 'Arabi, *Fusus*, pp.209-10.

to have a degree of elevation above woman, as her root and origin.[683] Despite these relative hierarchies, Ibn 'Arabi, in stark contrast to his contemporaries, relentlessly affirms the *utter and total equality* of men and women in terms of their basic essence and spiritual potential, stating clearly that 'everything that a man can attain – spiritual stations, levels, or qualities – can be attained by women', including the highest manifestations of sainthood, spiritual power and enlightenment.[684] For Ibn 'Arabi, our differences and hierarchies are incidental, not essential, with our deepest reality a shared elevation beyond the secondary causes of material existence. It was also for this reason that Ibn 'Arabi notably differed from the vast majority of Islamic jurists in affirming women's unrestricted right to lead both men and women in *salat*, something that remains controversial to this day for many Muslims.[685]

Ibn 'Arabi interprets the Prophet's love of women as encompassing the entire spectrum of relationship, from the sensual to the spiritual, noting the ways in which these are interwoven in our lives. We can begin here with what is most immediately available to us as beings, with the physical or sensual. In particular Ibn 'Arabi points to the uniquely encompassing passion we encounter in sexual union:

> There is no union, in the elemental structure [of the human being], greater than sexual union. For this reason, passion permeates every part of a person. This total permeation explains why one must perform the major ablution, which encompasses all human parts, just as one perishes in desire for the other when this desire is fulfilled.[686]

Ibn 'Arabi describes sexual union as involving a totalizing desire that encompasses one's entire being, with all of one's parts alive to its vibrancy. He interestingly uses the term *fana'* – which literally means

---

683 Shaikh, *Sufi Narratives of Intimacy*, p.175.

684 Ibn 'Arabi, *Fut*.III.89. As quoted in Shaikh, *Sufi Narratives of Intimacy*, p.84.

685 For more on Ibn 'Arabi's fascinating arguments on this subject, and for a general overview of the question of women leading *salat*, see Ahmed Elewa and Laury Silvers, '"I Am One of the People": A Survey and Analysis of Legal Arguments on Women-Led Prayer in Islam', *Journal of Law and Religion*, 26 (2010), 141–71.

686 Ibn 'Arabi, *Fusus*, p.207.

'annihilation'. When united with the beloved, one is *annihilated* in desire, totally absorbed such that one basically disappears in passion, perishing in it.[687] He continues to note that, as a result of this total involvement of the person in passion, according to the Islamic legal tradition one cannot return to a state of ritual purity for prayer after sexual union until they engage in *ghusl* – a complete ablution or washing of the body – to purify the totality of oneself for prayer, just as the totality of oneself was absorbed in passion.[688]

Women were beloved to the Prophet Muhammad in a way that included this sensual aspect of relationship, and yet the reason for his love went far beyond it, being a love that is ultimately metaphysical in its significance. Ibn 'Arabi says that God showed the Prophet Muhammad that the highest peak of spirituality is found in the contemplation of the feminine, as women harmoniously represent both active and receptive polarities in existence, and hence offer the best possible form or expression of the Real:

> This is why he, the peace and blessings of God be upon him, loved women: for the perfect vision of the Real within them. For the Real can never be witnessed disengaged from some matter, as God in Essence is independent of the worlds. Since the situation is impossible in this respect and witnessing takes place only in some matter, then the witnessing of the Real in women is the most sublime and perfect witnessing.[689]

Although God transcends all image and form, God cannot be known in this transcendent aspect, but rather only encountered when He reveals Himself to us through one or another of the manifest realities we encounter in life. Ibn 'Arabi suggests here that Muhammad loved women, not only in terms of the annihilating passion of sexual union, or for the joy of their companionship, but ultimately because,

---

[687] There is, interestingly, some correspondence here with the French term *la petite mort*, or 'little death', which initially referred to a momentary loss of consciousness, but in the 19th century came to be used in reference to sexual orgasm.

[688] This contrasts with the lesser requirement of ablution or *wudu'* – a washing of the hands, mouth and nose, face, forearms and feet, something undertaken if one has slept or gone to the bathroom.

[689] Ibn 'Arabi, *Fusus*, p.207.

out of all realities in our world, the feminine offers the most perfect vision of the Real.

One of the more beautiful aspects of the Muhammadan paradigm is this multidimensional marriage of sense and soul, an interweaving of life's physical and metaphysical aspects in a holistically human way. For Muslims, the Prophet Muhammad embodies a total integration of the highest spiritual realization with all facets of our world and human existence. Hence, his example shows us that romance, love and passion can offer an unparalleled means of understanding the Real, provided we engage with them in a way attuned to their deeper significance. For men who love women, the beauty and profundity of God's image can best be best witnessed in them, and hence, 'he who loves women as the Prophet loved them has loved God'.[690] Ibn 'Arabi explains this a bit further:

> He loved them for their degree and for their being a locus of receptivity ... Whoever loves women in accordance with this definition possesses divine love. He who loves them only because of natural desires is deprived of knowledge of these desires. They are then like a form possessing no spirit.[691]

Sa'diyya Shaikh argues that Ibn 'Arabi – with his interpretation of the Prophet Muhammad's love for women as rooted in the idea that God is best witnessed in the 'embodied reality of women' – offers us a 'clear inversion', a total over-turning of the all too common 'devaluations of women and their bodies' that we encounter not only in some expressions of Islamic culture, but really in almost every cultural history we can think of.[692] Ibn'Arabi is also careful to note here that a sort of basic love of women resulting from mere natural desire misses the point entirely and even misses the beauty of desire itself, experiencing only the dead form of desire as opposed to its living

---

690 Ibn 'Arabi, *Fut*.IV.84. As quoted in Murata, *The Tao of Islam*, p.185. Although it is not clear to me how far Ibn 'Arabi would expand this notion beyond his account of men's contemplation of God in women, we could certainly consider a shared contemplative principle here among all lovers of any gender or sexuality.
691 Ibn 'Arabi, *Fusus*, pp.208–9.
692 Shaikh, *Sufi Narratives of Intimacy*, p.179.

spirit. What happens in romantic love, if understood in its deepest meaning, goes way beyond physical instinct, and is rather something connected with the very meaning and essence of the universe, as it is in fact a symbol of the whole divine order. Rumi expresses the profundity of the feminine poetically, even radically, in his celebratory praise of woman: 'She is the radiance of God, she is not your beloved. She is the Creator – you could say that she is not created.'[693]

The hadith regarding Muhammad's three beloveds more generally points to the possibility of finding the most profound spirituality in all aspects of life, particularly *through* our embodied existence, perhaps best illustrated by the Prophet Muhammad's love of beautiful scent, to which we now turn. Ibn 'Arabi interestingly connects the Prophet's love of women to his love of scent, by noting, 'As for the wisdom of perfume and its placement after women, it is that the scents of creation come from women, and the sweetest scent is the embrace of the beloved, as the proverb states.'[694] For Ibn 'Arabi, the Prophet's love of scent naturally follows his love for women, for women's manifestation of cosmic generativity, the metaphorical 'scents of creation', as well as the sensual beauty of intimacy, which includes the intoxication of the scent of the beloved's embrace.[695] We will also see, however, that scent, among all of the senses, offers us the most direct means of accessing the deeper dimensions of our own selves: it is the sense that most immediately connects to spirituality.

Although at times overshadowed by other, more extroverted senses, like sight and sound, smell is one of the more mysterious, if not the most mysterious of our bodily senses. Smell is an intimate companion of memory and emotion. American author and disability activist Hellen Keller (d.1968) elegantly accounts for this mysterious power of smell to foster a sort of interdimensional travel:

---

693 Rumi, *Masnavi* I.2437. As quoted in Murata, *The Tao of Islam*, p.185.
694 Ibn 'Arabi, *Fusus*, p.210.
695 Nettler quite nicely sums up the interrelationship of the sensual and spiritual here: 'Women, perfume, women's perfume, the divine breaths of the Merciful God (*al-Rahman*) ... all of these, intertwined with, reflecting, and indeed identified with one another, create a story of profane and sacred love of physical and metaphysical import.' Nettler, *Sufi Metaphysics and Qur'anic Prophets*, p.194.

> Smell is a potent wizard that transports us across thousands of miles and all the years we have lived. The odors of fruits waft me to my southern home, to my childhood frolics in the peach orchard. Other odors, instantaneous and fleeting, cause my heart to dilate joyously or contract with remembered grief. Even as I think of smells, my nose is full of scents that start awake sweet memories of summers gone and ripening fields far away.[696]

This inrush of memory that smell provokes, as Keller describes, is the literary 'Proustian moment'. French novelist Marcel Proust (d.1922) recounts in his 1913 tome *In Search of Lost Time* a sensory moment that 'triggers a rush of memories often long past, or even seemingly forgotten'.[697] For Proust, this moment happens when he lifts a spoonful of tea to his mouth, with some madeleine crumbs dissolving in it. Neuroscience suggests that it was most likely not the taste of the spoonful but its *scent* that set off the flood of memory he then experienced (and in fact a great deal of taste is actually itself scent, which is why we can't taste much when we have a cold). Our brain anatomy shows us that, of all our senses, the sense of smell most *directly* connects to our limbic system, and, in particular, to the amygdala and hippocampus, the parts most closely associated with memory and emotion. Hence, as poet and author Diane Ackerman observes, we 'hit a tripwire of smell, and memories explode all at once'.[698]

Probably most of us have had our own Kellerian or Proustian moment, where we come across the scent of a long-lost lover's fragrance, or our nose fills with the fresh smell of a spring day just after the rain, and we are immediately transported back in time to a world of memory, feeling and experience we may not have realized remains within us still. Interestingly, smell is the first sense to fully develop in

---

696 Hellen Keller, as quoted by Diane Ackerman, *A Natural History of the Senses* (New York, 1995), p.3.

697 For a solid, brief overview of the science of scent, see Colleen Walsh, 'What the Nose Knows', *The Harvard Gazette*, February 27, 2020, https://news.harvard.edu/gazette/story/2020/02/how-scent-emotion-and-memory-are-intertwined-and-exploited/ (accessed March 15, 2023).

698 Ackerman, *A Natural History of the Senses*, p.5.

the womb and it remains the strongest until sight takes over at about the age of ten. Scent, it turns out, is the sense of origin. Ackerman further observes that scent is, like the sacred, totally beyond our ability to describe. Although we live in a world of scents – 'smells coat us, swirl around us, enter our bodies, emanate from us'[699] – we struggle to even remotely describe them: 'smells are our dearest kin, but we cannot remember their names'.[700]

Considering the power of scent to orient us toward the deepest parts of our own being, and even to the sacred itself, it is not surprising that the Prophet Muhammad's various companions all confirm that beautiful fragrances, whether perfume or incense, were beloved to him. He frequently wore beautiful scents and encouraged his followers to do so as well. To this day, it is common in mosques and Sufi centers for attendees to pass around perfumed oils to share, or rose water, and even the Ka'aba itself in Mecca is washed with rose water. It is also worth noting here that wearing a pleasant fragrance is first and foremost something that benefits others – it is a kind of consideration, beautifying the sensory experience of those around you, even more so than yourself.

The Prophet further recommended that his followers burn incense and pointed to Indian incense (*al-'ud al-Hind*) specifically, for healing. He frequently burned *bukhoor*,[701] fragrant wood chips or tree sap soaked in scented oils that produce a deep fragrance when lit, providing a rich sensory setting for prayer and meditation.[702] Incense of some form or another is generally used the world over, in various sacred contexts and ceremonies, as scent's ability to connect with emotion and memory means that it can function as a doorway to deeper dimensions of our own consciousness: *sense and spirt are synthesized in scent*. It follows that to love scent is to love the spiritual through the

---

699 Ibid., p.7.
700 Ibid.
701 See *Sahih al-Bukhari* 5692, 5693. Omid Safi, 'Come to Your Senses! On Perfume, Incense, and Spirituality in Islam,' *Bayt al-Fann*, https://www.baytalfann.com/post/come-to-your-senses-on-perfume-incense-and-spirituality-in-islam-omid-safi (accessed March 15, 2023).
702 Meena Sharify-Funk shared with me that Abdul Aziz Said was particularly fond of *bukhoor*, and especially loved and shared that which came from Oman.

sensual. Hence, we see that both women and scent are made beloved to the Prophet for the wisdom in them; the way in which they exist as beautiful doorways onto the deeper dimensions of the Real. Ibn 'Arabi is careful to point out this distinction between the Prophet loving and having something made beloved to him, with the connection to God foremost here: 'This is why he said "made beloved to me" and did not say "I love," from himself, for his love was attached to his Lord, whose image he is.'[703]

Ibn 'Arabi draws our attention to the larger principle found at the heart of the Muhammadan paradigm, in both his love of women and beautiful fragrances, in observing, 'Only the good in everything was made beloved to the Messenger of God, may God give him peace and blessings, and everything is just that.'[704] Simply put, the Prophet Muhammad always saw the good in everything. This is because everything is, in essence, good, and the more enlightened you are, the more this becomes apparent. Although he was, in a way, not of our world, the Prophet loved this world for the goodness found in every one of its aspects, whether this goodness is readily apparent, or more subtle, implicit and even hidden in nature.

A wonderful hadith that illustrates seeing the good even when it can be hard to find, describes the Prophet and his companions coming across the rotting carcass of a dog. The companions each in their own way express how awful the sight is, and how terrible the smell. This is totally understandable and our own reactions to it would very likely align with theirs. In contrast, however, the Prophet observes, 'but look at how beautifully white its teeth are!' – seeing the good in *everything*, including what most would deem to be something horrible.[705] This is not to say that the Prophet Muhammad ignored the bad, and Ibn 'Arabi clarifies this point explicitly:

---

703 Ibn 'Arabi, *Fusus*, p.207.
704 Ibid., p.212.
705 I could not find the original source for this hadith, but it is described in Chodkiewicz, *Seal of the Saints*, p.80. This narrative has also been attributed to Jesus. Al-Ghazali mentions this story but with Jesus in his *Ihya 'Ulum al-Din* 3.140. Apparently, Ignaz Goldziher (d.1921) believed that this story had a Buddhist origin. See Khalidi, *The Muslim Jesus*, p.122.

There is no temperament that only perceives a single reality in everything. Every human temperament perceives both good and bad … [but] his occupation with perceiving the good in a thing diverted him from sensing what is bad in it.[706]

We see here that it is not as though the Prophet was somehow unaware of the bad in things, or that he did not have his own dislikes. All human temperaments, as Ibn 'Arabi observes, have their share of preferences and dislikes, attractions and repulsions. As a human being the Prophet Muhammad was, of course, no exception to this general rule. Ibn 'Arabi makes mention of a hadith that indicates that the Prophet did not like the smell of garlic. However, he notes that Muhammad did not say 'I dislike garlic' in and of itself, but rather he said it was only its raw smell, an element manifested from it, that he disliked.[707] We can recall here that this resonates with Ibn 'Arabi's discussion of blameworthiness and praiseworthiness in Chapter Two, on Abraham, where he notes that these qualities only arise due to particular conditions and expressions. So, he concludes, despite having his own dislikes, as any other person does, the Prophet Muhammad occupied himself with *loving the good in things* such that he was *diverted from noticing the bad*.

Undoubtedly, living a life of constant prayer played an important role in this orientation. Ever-remembering the Source of all good no doubt fosters an appreciation of its manifestation in existence, and hence in the hadith of his three beloveds, the Prophet Muhammad says that the third thing made beloved to him, or the 'coolness' of his eye (*qurrat 'ayni*) – an Arabic expression that means tranquility, peace or serenity – is *salat,* or prayer. The first thing we may note here is that he considers prayer something of this world. It is something we as creatures of this world do, though it acts as a bridge to and dialog with the beyond. So, what is it exactly and how does it bring us peace? Ibn 'Arabi defines prayer as a reciprocity between the human and God, a sort of conversation (*munajat*) that is both intimate and cosmic in

---

706 Ibn 'Arabi, *Fusus,* p.212.
707 Ibid., pp.444–5.

nature. The dialogical nature of prayer is keenly represented by the very heart of the Islamic *salat,* its core component: the recitation of the first chapter of the Qur'an, called *al-Fatiha,* which literally means 'the Opening'.

Al-Fatiha opens in at least two senses. As the Qur'an's first *surah* or chapter, the Fatiha opens the sacred text itself. And, as the foundational component of the *salat,* it opens the human soul to God. It is probably safe to say that the Fatiha is to Islam what the Lord's Prayer is to Christianity: a short prayer encompassing the entire relationship between God and humanity. Muslims hold it to be an especially powerful chapter of the Qur'an, and the Qur'an itself calls the Fatiha the *Seven Oft-Repeated* (Q 15:87), referring to its seven constituent verses. It is a prayer recited throughout a Muslim's life, for protection, healing and to mark special occasions.[708] The Fatiha is also called the *Surah al-Salah,* as it is recited during each *rak'a,* each cycle of standing, bowing and prostrating during the performance of Islam's ritual prayer. As the dawn prayer consists of two *raka'at,* the noon, afternoon and evening four each, while the sunset prayer consists of three, a practicing Muslim will, at the very least, recite the Fatiha *seventeen* times a day (and hence its 'oft-repeated' nature). The Fatiha can be translated as follows (Q 1:1–7):

> *In the Name of God, the Compassionate, the Merciful.*
> *Praise be to God, Lord of the worlds,*
> *The Compassionate, the Merciful.*
> *Owner of the Day of Judgment.*
> *It is You we worship and from You we seek help.*
> *Guide us on the straight path,*
> *The path of those You have blessed,*
> *Not those who draw wrath or wander astray.*

In commenting on the Fatiha, Ibn 'Arabi begins with a well-known *hadith qudsi,* wherein God told the Prophet that the prayer is divided

---

708 In his *Ruh al-Qudus,* Ibn 'Arabi shares, in his account of Sufi masters he met in Andalusia, that his elderly teacher Fatima bint ibn al-Muthanna had a special relationship with the Fatiha – God in a sense gave it her such that she could 'wield its power' whenever she wanted. Austin, *Sufis of Andalusia,* p.143.

into two parts, one for God, and one for His servant.[709] In the prayer's first half, the worshipper praises, glorifies and submits to God. In the second, the servant beseeches God for aid, guidance and blessing. God says, in this hadith, that the servant will have what they request. Ibn 'Arabi points out the mutuality here between God and the human being, and then shifts to highlight this intimate mutuality by drawing upon another *hadith qudsi*, where God says, 'I am with the one who remembers Me.'[710] Ibn 'Arabi interprets this quite literally, and says that if one *truly* remembers God with the entirety of oneself, when prayer is performed at its highest state, that one will not only communicate with God, but become a person who will actually have a sublime vision (*ru'ya*) of God, spiritually witnessing (*mushahada*) Him.[711] As we will see in the last section of this chapter, Ibn 'Arabi simultaneously lauds these visions as the very perfection of prayer, while also situating them as, ultimately, our own projection and creation.

Ibn 'Arabi also observes that the bodily positions comprising *salat* correspond with larger cosmic processes, performing the human being's role as a microcosmic synthesis of all life in an embodied way. In terms of the cosmic process, this is, most fundamentally, the transformation of the unmanifest into the manifest, which Ibn 'Arabi says occurs through the three kinds of movement in the cosmos: ascending, static (or horizontal) and descending, and that the standing, bowing and prostrating during *salat* embody these three movements. His mention here of these three interestingly corresponds quite closely to the Samkhya system of Hindu philosophy, which names the three primordial *gunas* or cosmic tendencies as: *sattva*, representing an ascending, elevated movement; *rajas*, which is static or balanced; and *tamas*, which has a downward trajectory.[712] Hence when the human being performs the ritual prayer, they are in a sense performing the

---

709 Found in the *Muwatta* (3.41) of Imam Malik ibn Anas (d.795), one of the earliest hadith collections, this particular section of the hadith that Ibn 'Arabi refers to, is as follows: 'I have divided the prayer into two halves between Me and my servant. One half of it is for Me and one half of it is for my servant, and My servant has what he asks.'

710 *Sahih al-Bukhari* 7405.

711 Ibn 'Arabi, *Fusus*, p.214.

712 For a more detailed overview of the *gunas*, see K. B. Ramakrishna Rao, 'The Gunas of Prakrti According to the Samkhya Philosophy', *Philosophy East and West*, 13:1 (1963), 61–71.

Adamic function, integrating the entire creative process, as well as creation itself: while standing at the beginning of a *rak'a* one represents the human, while bowing, animals, and in prostration, plants and inanimate objects. Ibn 'Arabi suggests that the source for the Prophet's love of prayer, is both a) that it, involving body, mind, speech and spirit, expresses the essential human role in the cosmos (prayer brings peace as it is a ritual embodiment of what we really are), and b) if done with our whole being, allows for 'witnessing the Beloved, which causes comfort for the lover's eyes'.[713]

He then concludes his discussion by again emphasizing prayer's dialogical aspect, this time suggesting that it is not only we who pray to God, but that God also prays upon us, stating concisely that 'the prayer is from us and from Him'.[714] Although in English it might sound a bit strange to suggest that prayer is not only something that we do, but that God does as well, it's important to keep in mind here that in Arabic the word *salat* has a broader meaning, including not only prayer but also, perhaps more importantly, blessing. Hence the Qur'an says that God, the angels and even all animals perform *salat*, though the precise meaning of the term shifts according to the nature of the one performing it. In some cases, *salat* means something closer to blessing while in others it is more explicitly referencing prayer, and particularly the formal daily worship that the Prophet taught his followers. The Qur'an (Q 33:43) maintains that God is the One who '*yussali 'alaykum*', who '*prays over/blesses you all*', and adds that the angels do as well. And in verse 24:41, it says that all beings in the heavens and the earth, including all the animals, glorify God, specifying that '*each knows its [form of] salat*', that each type of being has its own form of blessing/prayer. Perhaps the most oft-repeated imperative in the Qur'an is to 'establish' the *salat*, or maintain the practice of regular prayer, to punctuate life with devotion and blessing.

---

713 Ibn 'Arabi, *Fusus*, p.217.
714 Ibid.

The Reality of Muhammad and the Nature of the Cosmos

Ibn 'Arabi connects the triplicity in the hadith discussed above – with the Prophet's three beloveds – to Muhammad's uniqueness: 'The first odd prime number is three, and the prime numbers that follow it are derived from it.'[715] Hence Muhammad is, like the number three itself, unique – an entity from which similarly unique phenomena derive. We can see this here as a symbol of his status as a prophetic reality that is unique in its comprehensiveness, a reality that other similar prophetic phenomena derive from.[716] He is pointing here to Muhammad as the original 'light' or 'reality' through which the cosmos and humanity emerge, and more particularly the niche of prophecy, from which all other prophets derive. To understand this notion, we will first look to the Greek conception of *logos*, which shares several important characteristics with later Islamic ideas about Muhammad.

The Greek work *logos* is derived from *lego*, which means 'I say', and hence the cognate *logos* means most simply 'word', 'speech' or 'discourse'. Over time it became associated with a larger family of meanings that include logic, principle, reasoning and proportion. In surveying the historical permutations of *logos*, philosopher and physician Raymond Tallis observes that it is not so much a word as it is 'a semantic field of nodes here and there specified in particular translations'.[717]

Within Western thought, we can trace *logos* as a philosophical concept all the way back to early Greek philosopher Heraclitus (fifth

---

715 Ibid., p.202.

716 Muslims have understood the Prophet Muhammad's comprehensive nature as a kind of synthesis of the various prophetic models. A tradition related by Abu Sa'd al-Kargushi (d.1016), for example, suggests that at his birth, the Prophet's mother, Amina, heard a heavenly voice saying: 'Bestow upon him the purity of Adam, the sweetness of Noah, the intimate friendship of Abraham, the word of Solomon, the beauty of Joseph, the good news given to Jacob, the voice of David, the patience of Job, the abnegation of John the Baptist, the generosity of Jesus. Immerse him in each prophetic virtue (*akhlaq al-nabiyyin*).' Al-Kargushi, *Sharaf al-Mustafa*, ed. Abu Asim Nabil al-Ghamri (Mecca, 2003), Volume 1, 359. As quoted in Chiabotti, 'The Abrahamic heritage in medieval Sufism, Part 1', pp.83–4.

717 Raymond Tallis, *Logos: The Mystery of How We Make Sense of the World* (Newcastle, 2018), pp.32–3.

century BCE), who lived half a millennium before Christ. Based in Ephesus (in modern-day Turkey), Heraclitus was known as the 'philosopher of flux', emphasizing the way that all things change, apparently the originator of the famous saying that we can 'never step in the same river twice'.[718] He also had quite a bit to say about the *logos*, and saw it as the reason, intelligence and order that we find in the cosmos and within ourselves: it is the singular timeless truth underlying everything, and hence anyone who knows truth, encounters this singular *logos*, and yet, he says, we tend to think of it as our own private insight.[719] In later Platonic thought we similarly find the *logos* coming to mean something like intellect, and then, for the Stoics, the *logos* 'was the source of all the activity and rationality of an ordered world that was both intelligible and intelligent'.[720] We may even say then that the *logos* is the very principle of intelligibility.

Logos takes a particularly pregnant turn with the Jewish thinker Philo Alexandrinus (d.*c*.45–50), or Philo of Alexandria as he is known in English. He was a mystic, scholar and rabbi in Roman Egypt. Philo brilliantly integrated this Greek philosophical notion of *logos* into an Abrahamic revelatory framework, an integration that would prove totally decisive for Christianity. Philo understood the *logos* to be, in a sense, God's own intelligence, pattern and method, and even metaphorically describes the *logos* as the 'First-Born Son of the Uncreated Father'.[721] This 'First-Born' *logos* is the template for all that comes after, the entire cosmos being its derivative. With the rise of Christianity in the Near East, we see Philo's metaphor of God and *logos,* as Father and Son, solidify into Trinitarian doctrine, with God the Father and Christ the Son. Recall that the Gospel of John (1:1) opens with the line, 'In the beginning was the *logos*, and the *logos* was with God and the *logos* was God.' The *logos* here is usually translated

---

718 This saying is actually attributed to Heraclitus by Plato, though his works suggest something along these lines. For more on this see Daniel W. Graham, 'Heraclitus', *The Stanford Encyclopedia of Philosophy* (Summer 2021 Edition), https://plato.stanford.edu/cgi-bin/encyclopedia/archinfo.cgi?entry=heraclitus (accessed April 25, 2023).

719 Ibid.

720 Tallis, *Logos*, p.36.

721 Ibid., p.37.

as the Word, in English, signifying Christ. We also see here how the *logos,* paradoxically, both is and is not God.

Moving east, there is an intriguingly similar notion with the ancient Indian *Hiranyagarbha,* or 'Golden Embryo'. The Vedas suggest that the *Hiranyagarbha* is the first to emerge from the unqualified Absolute, the 'first born', the World Soul or universal consciousness, the first cosmic light through which the world itself is created. According to Vedanta philosophy, 'Hiranyagarbha's subtle body is the universal mind or cosmic intelligence', and all beings emerge from its reality.[722] It would later be described as the first incarnation or manifestation of God, the primordial *avatara.* The science of yoga is ultimately traced back to *Hiranyagarbha* as an entity that can also function as a kind of prophetic teacher, and like the *logos,* is hence a source of knowledge, science and understanding.[723]

The idea of the Muhammadan Light, or *al-Nur al-Muhammadi*, shares several pointed parallels with both Philo's *logos* and the Vedic *Hiranyagarbha.* Before considering this concept, however, it's worth tracing its genealogy in early Islamic history. The notion of the Muhammadan Light was first written about by Sahl al-Tustari (d.896), a seminal early Sufi who came from Tustar, a Western Persian province near present-day Iraq. He was apparently something of a precocious philosopher, nagging the local scholars about questions existential, to no avail. His family then sent him to Basra, where they hoped the more renowned scholars there could satisfy the young Tustari. However, he found the Basran learned fell short as well: their intellectual acumen, though perhaps a step up, simply could not calm the fiery dragon of inquiry that drove him. He was soon directed to the storied island of 'Abbadan, just south of Basra, with its many Sufis who lived there in retreat.[724] It was finally here, on 'Abbadan, that Tustari encountered those who knew not only the books and doctrines and the outward

---

722 Kali, *Svetasvataropanisad: The Knowledge That Liberates,* p.191.

723 Pir Zia Inayat Khan, *Mingled Waters: Sufism and the Mystical Unity of Religions* (New Lebanon, NY, 2017), p.19.

724 The first center of spiritual retreat on the island had actually been established more than a century earlier by none other than Hasan al-Basri (whom we briefly discussed in the second chapter on Abraham). Bowering, *The Mystical Vision of Existence in Classical Islam,* p.48.

appearances of things, but their *inner meaning* and *existential reality*, as well. He found the deeper answers he was looking for and stayed on with the Sufis there for some time.⁷²⁵

Tustari later went on a pilgrimage to Mecca, where he fortuitously met the mysterious African sage known as Dhu'l-Nun al-Misri (d.859).⁷²⁶ A Nubian from the South of Egypt, Dhu'l-Nun is basically the fountainhead of later Sufism, with Sufis of the generations that followed citing him as their spiritual ancestor.⁷²⁷ Although it is not always easy to figure out who exactly he was based on the available sources, several works of 'alchemy, magic, and medicine' are attributed to Dhu'l-Nun, and he is probably the key link connecting the Hermeticism and alchemical traditions of ancient Egypt with Islam.⁷²⁸ The sources we do have on him suggest that he was born and raised in Akhmim (or Panopolis in Graeco-Roman times), an ancient temple city and center of alchemy, where he reportedly gained the ability to read the hieroglyphs found on the walls of Akhmim's temples. He traveled widely, encountering many Sufi masters, and himself becoming one of the most renowned masters of his time, despite facing opposition from some of the establishment jurists and theologians. Dhu'l-Nun was a matrix of multiple systems of knowledge, esoteric and exoteric, so I suppose it's not all that surprising that he would draw the ire of those

---

725 Ibn 'Arabi has his own interesting account of Tustari's journey. He appears to be the first to suggest that the question to which Tustari sought the answer was 'the heart's prostration'. Apparently, as a young man Tustari had a profound spiritual experience of his heart totally bowing, in a mode of prostration (*sujud*), and, mystified by this, had asked Sufis in Basra if they could explain what this prostration of the heart was, or if the heart ever rises from it, and could get no answer, as none had experienced that particular state. In 'Abbadan, however, he encountered a master, who, when Tustari asked him if the heart prostrates, simply said: 'forever'. Tustari ended up studying with him for some time. Ibid.

726 Dhu'l-Nun is a nickname, with his actual name being Abu al-Fayd Thawban ibn Ibrahim. Ibn 'Arabi actually wrote an entire book on Dhu'l-Nun, *Al-Kawkab al-durri fi manaqib Dhi al-Nun al-Misri*, or *The Illuminated Star Regarding the Virtues of Dhu'l-Nun al-Misri*. Binyamin Abrahamov, *Ibn al-'Arabi and the Sufis* (Oxford, 2014), p.19.

727 In his *The Meccan Revelations*, Ibn 'Arabi describes the 'knowledgeable ones of this community' who 'guard the spiritual states (*ahwal*)' of Muhammad 'and the mysteries (*asrar*) of his knowledge (*'ulum*)', as including 'Ali, Ibn Abbas, Salman al-Farsi, Abu Hurayra and Hudhayfa, among Muhammad's companions, Hasan al-Basri and Malik ibn Dinar among their successors, and Shayban al-Ra'i, and Dhu'l-Nun among those who succeed them. Translated by Winkel, *The Openings Revealed in Mecca, Books 1 and 2*, p.581.

728 Julian Baldick, *Mystical Islam: An Introduction to Sufism* (New York, 1989), p.35.

whose understanding remained trapped in dogmas and externalities.

Dhu'l-Nun is further said to be one of the first Sufis to define the particular mode of Sufi knowledge as *ma'rifa*, and to discuss the spiritual states (*ahwal*) and stations (*maqamat*) that one encounters along the spiritual path – something we will get into further in the next section of this chapter. Ibn 'Arabi notably only wrote two books focused in their entirety on a particular Sufi, and one of those is Dhu'l-Nun.[729] Ibn 'Arabi describes the Egyptian sage as someone very well-traveled, who learned from all, was gentle, careful and totally and completely devoted to God.[730] Tustari apparently did not speak publicly about mystical matters until after Dhu'l-Nun's death, as his respect for his master was such that he did not feel comfortable teaching Sufism as long as Dhu'l-Nun was alive.

Recall from Chapter Five that Suhrawardi understood Islamic Sufism to be a confluence of two ancient lines of wisdom, one Egyptian-Greek and the other Persian. He traces the Egyptian-Greek line of wisdom through Dhu'l-Nun and then to Tustari.[731] Suhrawardi's claim that his own light-based or *Ishraqi* philosophy can be traced all the way back to the ancients interestingly finds some support here, with Tustari's light-based philosophy ostensibly being inherited from Dhu'l-Nun, who provides the link back to ancient Egypt. We can also point out that Tustari's notion of the Nur Muhammad notably resembles earlier Greek mystical-philosophical notions of the *logos*. Although we could then see this as an outside transmission of ancient Egyptian and Greek wisdom *into* Islam, both Suhrawardi's and Tustari's philosophies of light can also be connected back to one of the most important verses in the Qur'an, known as the Verse of Light (Q 24:35):

> *God is the Light of the heavens and the earth. The likeness of His Light is a niche, within it a lamp. The lamp is in a glass, the glass like*

---

729 The other was on Abu Yazid al-Bistami, but it is nonextant.

730 He relates that Dhu'l-Nun described the sign of one brought near to God is that they are patient (*sabr*) in tribulation, grateful (*shukr*) when blessed and always in a state of *dhikr*, of recalling their origin, oriented to what has always been. Abrahamov, *Ibn al-'Arabi and the Sufis*, pp.20–1.

731 A secret, gnostic line of wisdom from al-Misri and Tustari is said to continue in the lineage of Ahmad al-Rifa'i (d.1182). Ibid., pp.52–4.

a glittering star kindled from a blessed olive tree, neither of the East nor of the West. Its oil almost shining, though no fire has touched it. Light upon light. God guides to His Light whomever He will.

Tustari connects Muhammad to *'the likeness of his Light'*, a connection that actually goes all the way back to one of the first commentators on the Qur'an, Muqatil bin Sulayman, who says that Muhammad is the lamp described in the verse above, evidently drawing upon another Qur'anic verse (Q 33:46) that describes Muhammad as a *shining lamp* or an *illuminating torch*.[732] In verse 5:15, the Qur'an says that *a light has come to you from God*, and another early commentator, Muhammad al-Tabari (d.923), says this is also a reference to the Prophet.[733] We further have a whole host of hadith reports that associate Muhammad with light in various forms, so thinking of Muhammad in terms of metaphysical light is not something that can simply be traced to earlier traditions, but also has roots in a variety of Islamic sources.

Tustari explicates the metaphysical origin of this light, and says that Muhammad existed as God's first creation, the primordial light, for 'a thousand thousand years before the beginning of creation'.[734] God's Essence – the first transcendent, unknowable Luminosity, expresses itself, prior to the creation of the cosmos, as a 'likeness', a light drawn from its own, one that exists in a state of adoration of and prostration toward the Essence from which it emerges.[735] This primordial light, an expression of the essential mystery at the heart of existence, is a kind of prime matter from which all other existents descend, in a hierarchy beginning with the other prophets, then the saints, then the rest of humanity, then the cosmos, all created from this light, and hence Ibn

---

732 Carl W. Ernst, 'Muhammad as the Pole of Existence', in *The Cambridge Companion to Muhammad*, edited by Jonathan E. Brockopp (New York, 2010), p.127.

733 Chodkiewicz, *Seal of the Saints*, p.61.

734 Ernst, *Cambridge Companion to Muhammad.*, p.128.

735 Annemarie Schimmel connects this theology of Muhammad's luminous nature to a famous prayer of his, beloved by Muslims: 'O God, place light in my heart, and light in my soul, light upon my tongue, light in my eyes and light in my ears, place light at my right, light at my left, light behind me and light before me, light above me and light beneath me. Place light in my nerves, and light in my flesh, light in my blood, light in my hair and light in my skin! Give me light, increase my light, make me light!' *And Muhammad is His Messenger*, p.125.

'Arabi describes the Prophetic Light as 'the Sun of Existence'.[736] It is the first creation, and has long been identified in various ancient systems with the Intellect, or pure intelligence. The Prophet Muhammad is reported to have said that the Intellect was the first thing created by God.[737] In both Neoplatonic and Sufi philosophical terms this is the First Intellect or *al-'aql al-awwal*. Ibn 'Arabi tends to refer to this as the Muhammadan Reality, or *al-haqiqa al-Muhammadiyya*.[738] He describes its *logos*-like nature as a 'copy'[739] of the Real, with humanity and the universe descending copies of this first copy:

> For [the Reality of] Muhammad (May God bless and keep him!) is a copy of the Real with marks of distinction, and Adam, in turn, is a copy from him entirely; while we, we are a copy of them both (Peace be upon them!), and the world, both earthly and heavenly, is a copy of us – and there the pens run dry.[740]

Just as the Neoplatonic First Intellect or Vedic Hiranyagarbha is *passive* in relation to the One from which it emanates, and yet *active* in relation to everything else that emanates from itself, so, for Ibn 'Arabi, the Muhammadan Reality is a pure servant in relationship to Allah, but lordly in relation to all else that derives from it, including every human and cosmic reality, without restriction.[741] Hence, Izutsu points out that this Reality of Muhammad is not so much an archetype, but the 'unifying principle of all archetypes', and 'universal Consciousness' itself.[742] We can see here that, for Sufi philosophers, Muhammad, as a metaphysical principle, goes light years beyond his physical, human manifestation, and exists rather as the *logos*, the primordial light of

---

736 Ibid., p.127.
737 Ali, *Philosophical Sufism*, p.90.
738 The connecting bridge between Tustari's notion of the Muhammadan Light, and Ibn 'Arabi's own understanding of the Muhammadan Reality, may be an earlier Andalusian Sufi, Ibn Barrajan (d.1141). For more on Ibn Barrajan, see Yousef Casewit, *The Mystics of al-Andalus: Ibn Barrajan and Islamic Thought in the Twelfth Century* (Cambridge, 2017).
739 Ibn 'Arabi, *Fut*.II.390. The Arabic word he uses here is *nuskhah*, which means a copy, replica, transcription or inscription. Elmore, *Islamic Sainthood in the Fullness of Time*, p.620.
740 Ibn 'Arabi, '*Anqa' Mughrib*, p.377. As quoted in Elmore, *Islamic Sainthood in the Fullness of Time*, p.80.
741 Izutsu, *Sufism and Taoism*, p.238.
742 Ibid., p.236.

awareness, the fundamental principle of intellect, *nous*, the foundation of every intelligible and sensible reality.

The Path and its Culmination: States and Stations

Earlier in the chapter we saw that Ibn 'Arabi understands Muhammad not only as a historical prophet and metaphysical reality, but also as a fully realized or completed human being, one given 'comprehensive words' and taught the actualities of the names God taught Adam. These names have been interpreted by Sufis as signaling the human being's potential for enlightenment, for comprehensive knowledge or full realization. Ibn 'Arabi says that Muhammad is the peak of this Adamic potential, fully realized and completed. It follows that he names this state of full enlightenment the *Muhammadan Station*.

Before looking at what this station is all about, we should consider first what exactly a station (or in Arabic, *maqam*) is, and how it differs from a temporary state or *hal*. As just mentioned, Dhu'l-Nun was probably the first Sufi to discuss this question of states and stations, though he wasn't the only one.[743] Mapping out precisely what these states and stations are, and which are encountered as the aspirant progresses through the spiritual path, was one of the first things that the formulators of Sufism engaged in, more generally.[744] Dhu'l-Nun is reported to have said that the true knower or gnostic, the true *'arif*, 'never stays constantly in the same state, but stays constantly with his Lord in all states',[745] indicating that states are the ever-fluctuating tones of experience we go through, which can, in a sense, become amplified as one engages in intensive spiritual practice. Dhu'l-Nun

---

743 Abu 'Abd al-Rahman al-Sulami says that Dhu'l-Nun was the first to classify the states and stations of the *ahl al-wilaya*, or people of sanctity, though others like Abu Sulayman al-Darani (d.830) and al-Muhasibi (d.857) have been associated with the early development of these classifications. Atif Khalil, *Repentance and the Return to God: Tawba in Early Sufism* (Albany, NY, 2018), p.80.

744 Scholar of Islamic thought and Sufism, Atif Khalil, notes that, besides *maqam*, early Sufis also used the term *manzil* (plural *manazil*), which means a 'place of dwelling'. However, *maqam* came to predominate, likely as it more clearly affirms the permanency of a genuine realization, whereas *manzil* can have more temporary connotations. Ibid., 78.

745 Shah-Kazemi, 'The Notion and Significance of *Ma'rifa* in Sufism', p.170.

also describes, rather poetically, how the aspirant progresses through discrete stations along the path, each of which, unlike a state, is a more permanent mode of being. He says that the Sufi begins first by 'planting the trees of their sins where they can see them', and then showering them 'with the water of their repentance (*tawba*)', so that the trees 'bear the fruit of regret (*nadam*)', after which they develop patience (*sabr*), then through scrupulous carefulness of action and awareness of self (*wara'*), they develop genuine renunciation (*zuhd*), or nonattachment to external objects and desires. He outlines a sort of spiritual ladder whereby one squarely faces one's own negativity and limitations, bringing them to light, before developing a genuine and committed intention to transcend them, and then crafting a way of life that effectively counteracts these negative tendencies of the lower self, which draws the heart away from its own spiritual Essence.[746]

Building on Dhu'l-Nun's early articulations of the path, later Sufis would elaborate in detail on what these rest-stops along the way consist of. We see Abu Nasr al-Sarraj (d.988), for example, in his early Sufi manual, *Kitab al-Luma'*, elaborate on Dhu'l-Nun's stations, describing a seven-station progression for the Sufi, beginning with repentance (*tawba*), or turning toward God and away from distraction, moving then to a carefulness in living, and a keen self-awareness, known as scrupulousness (*wara'*), which then leads to detachment from worldly pursuits or renunciation (*zuhd*), an embrace of material simplicity or poverty (*faqr*), the development of patience (*sabr*), trust in God (*tawakkul*) and finally contentment (*rida'*), a deep peace with whatever life brings.[747]

In his foundational Sufi manual, the *Risala*, al-Qushayri provides what would become the sort of 'textbook' definition of state and station for Sufis. Here he defines the state as 'a mode of consciousness that comes upon the heart' – it is a passing experience or level of awareness, notably one that *happens to you*, not something you make happen yourself – a *hal* or state occurs 'without a person's intending

---

746 Khalil, *Repentance and the Return to God*, p.81.
747 Ibid.

it, attracting it, or trying to gain it'.[748] We might think of these as a kind of spontaneous insight: an experience of peace or joy, a kind of spiritual 'aha' moment, one that anyone, anywhere, at any time can have, without requisite qualification or preceding labor. Whereas a *hal* is bestowed upon one, a *maqam*, in contrast, is something that one has to *work for*, that one attains. As al-Qushayri says, 'states are freely given while stations are gained with *majhud* (the expending of effort)',[749] here using a derivative of jihad, which, as we discussed in Chapter Four, means at root to strive or struggle.

Now, as states are given, they can also be taken away. By definition they are transient and hence not reliable gauges of spiritual progress. We make a real mistake when we assume that the spontaneous insights and creativity and joy that randomly shower upon us are somehow our own. A station, on the other hand, is basically secure, and is, at least in one sense, genuinely *ours*; although achieving a station, a higher level of awareness, peace and insight usually takes consistent work. Once it is achieved it is not something that can be taken away, as it is essentially what one has become, what one now *is*. Al-Qushayri continues to explain that the successful practitioner of spirituality will encounter stations as a sort of developmental staircase: a particular station can only be attained after the one prior to it has been securely realized – the path builds upon the foundations of what one has integrated prior. For example, he notes that the state of *tawakkul*, total trust in God as one's life unfolds, can only be attained after one has become contented (*rida'*) with whatever life brings.[750]

A Psychedelic Interlude: States without Stations?

Although the at times intricate Sufi discussions of states and stations may seem a bit arcane to some, or at least of concern only to those committed practitioners of the Sufi path, their analysis of spiritual progress may have some real applicability to a significant debate that has emerged globally in recent decades, namely the

---

748 Michael Sells, *Early Islamic Mysticism*, p.103.
749 Ibid.
750 Ibid., p.102.

debate over the potential psychological-spiritual benefits (and dangers) of psychedelics.[751] Although for centuries several Indigenous communities in North America have utilized psychoactive cacti and fungi for spiritual insight and healing,[752] these substances, more generally referred to as psychedelics, really only hit the mainstream in North America and Europe in the 1960s. British philosopher Aldous Huxley was a forerunner in this respect, writing one of the first accounts of a psychedelic experience, in his now classic work on the subject, *The Doors of Perception* (1955), titled after a quote of William Blake's: 'If the doors of perception were cleansed, everything would appear to man as it is, infinite.'[753]

An hour and a half after ingesting mescaline (the active agent in the peyote cactus), Huxley describes intently watching a vase of flowers, suddenly perceiving how each existent thing in our world intersects with the infinite. He relates that during this experience, he realized that the flowers were

> a transience that was yet eternal life, a perpetual perishing that was at the same time pure Being, a bundle of minute, unique particulars in which, by some unspeakable and yet self-evident paradox, was to be seen the divine source of all existence ... The Beatific Vision, *Sat Chit Ananda*, Being–Awareness–Bliss – for the first time I understood, not on a verbal level, not by inchoate hints or at a distance, but precisely and completely what those prodigious

---

751 Huston Smith points out that the term 'psychedelic' means 'mind-manifesting', a meaning that he thinks has value, though for him the term is too closely tied to the 1960s counterculture, and hence not appropriate for the reverential use of such substances. Instead, he proposes *entheogen*, which means something like 'God-containing' or 'God-enabling'. Huston Smith, *Cleansing the Doors of Perception: The Religious Significance of Entheogenic Plants and Chemicals* (New York, 2000), pp.xvi–xvii.

752 Michael Pollan observes that, for centuries, some Indigenous peoples of Mexico and Central America treated psilocybin-containing-mushrooms as a sacrament, with the Aztecs calling them *teonanacatl* or the 'flesh of the gods'. Their use, however, was 'brutally suppressed by the Roman Catholic Church after the Spanish conquest and driven underground'. Michael Pollan, *How to Change Your Mind: What The New Science of Psychedelics Teaches Us about Consciousness, Dying, Addiction, Depression, and Transcendence* (New York, 2018), p.3.

753 William Blake, *The Marriage of Heaven and Hell* (Boston, 1906), p.26.

syllables referred to.[754]

About a decade after Huxley's book was published, psychedelics would basically explode onto the Western cultural scene, especially with the popularization of lysergic acid (LSD).[755] The impacts of this psychedelic revolution still echo among us to this day. The history of alternative religions in the West, for instance, is closely tied to psychedelics, as many of the Boomer generation in particular developed an interest in things like meditation and mysticism, yoga, Sufism and Zen after having psychedelic experiences like Huxley's.[756] Perhaps most famously, The Beatles themselves exemplified this larger trend, with George Harrison (d.2001) pursuing a lifelong commitment to Hindu meditation and devotional practice following psychedelic experiences.

There remains a concerted debate among spiritual practitioners over the nature of psychedelic experiences, however, and their significance within the larger context of spiritual development. On the one hand, there seems to be a broad agreement among seekers who have encountered them that psychedelics can open the 'doors of perception', as Huxley wrote about so eloquently, leading to an awareness of deeper aspects of consciousness, not normally accessible. However, there is much less agreement over whether or not psychedelics offer *sustainable* spiritual benefit, whether or not they can, in and of themselves, constitute a spiritual path. In short, there appears to be significant evidence that psychedelics can help

---

754 Aldous Huxley, *The Doors of Perception* and *Heaven and Hell* (New York, 2004), pp.17–18. He draws upon the Vedantic characterization of the ultimate state as pure Being (*Sat*), Awareness (*Chit*) and Bliss (*Ananda*).

755 Albert Hofmann (d.2008) famously (and accidentally) discovered lysergic acid while working on a drug to stimulate circulation, employed by the Swiss pharmaceutical firm Sandoz. It was only after he accidentally ingested some that he found he had synthesized something *quite* different from what he had intended. Pollan, *How to Change Your Mind*, pp.1–2.

756 Scholars of Buddhism in North America note that, in some Buddhist groups in the 1990s, the majority of practitioners had come to Buddhism following psychedelic experiences. Charles T. Tart, for example, found that, in surveying almost 70 Buddhist practitioners of the Rigpa Fellowship in 1990, almost 80 percent reported having had prior experiences with psychedelics. Charles T. Tart, 'Psychedelics on the Path: Help or Hindrance?', in *Zig Zag Zen: Buddhism and Psychedelics*, edited by Allan Hunt Badiner and Alex Grey (San Francisco, 2002), pp.169–71.

foster spiritual *states*[757] but it is much less clear that they can offer more long-term transformation, or foster the attainment of sustained spiritual *stations*. The only exception here may be when they are taken within the context of a broader path, as one might find in the Native American Church, for instance, in which peyote is used sacramentally and communally, as part of a long-term commitment to healing and moral development.[758]

In the absence of such a path, those who have sought enlightenment from psychedelics have generally hit a wall. Before he was known as Ram Dass – the popular American spiritual teacher whom I've quoted in Chapter Four – he was Richard Alpert, a Harvard psychology professor. Along with his colleague Timothy Leary (d.1996), Alpert was a pioneer in psychedelic research. After Leary shared that he had learned more about the human mind in six hours on psilocybin-containing mushrooms than he had in all of his years of academic research, Alpert was understandably intrigued and, in 1961, first joined Leary on a psychedelic journey. Alpert shares that 'it changed my life in the sense that it undercut the models I had of who I thought I was', allowing him to experience a deep place in himself beyond all of his various social roles and identities. He says this place within, although at first terrifyingly absent of all the identities that he thought made him a unique person, was also a bare, unqualified *presence*:

---

[757] One of the first studies in this regard was the 'Good Friday Experiment', also known as the Marsh Chapel Experiment, conducted by a graduate student at Harvard Divinity School (and later minister and psychiatrist) Walter Pahnke (d.1971). His experiment took place on April 20, 1962, at Marsh Chapel at Boston University. It was double-blind, with one group receiving a placebo, and another psilocybin, all attending a Good Friday service at the chapel. Most of those who received psilocybin, including Huston Smith, reported profound religious experiences. For more on this experiment, see Walter N. Pahnke's PhD Thesis, 'Drugs and Mysticism: An Analysis of the Relationship between Psychedelic Drugs and the Mystical Consciousness', Harvard University, Cambridge, Massachusetts, June 1963, https://maps.org/images/pdf/books/pahnke/walter_pahnke_drugs_and_mysticism.pdf (accessed May 3, 2023). Later, in 2002, Roland R. Griffiths, a medical researcher at Johns Hopkins University, conducted an arguably more systematic experiment on psilocybin and spiritual experience, largely confirming Pahnke's findings. For an overview of Griffiths' results, as well as links to his article and scientific commentaries on it, see Eric Vohr, 'Hopkins Scientists Show Hallucinogen in Mushrooms Creates Universal "Mystical" Experience', Johns Hopkins Medicine, June 11, 2006, https://www.hopkinsmedicine.org/Press_releases/2006/07_11_06.html (accessed May 3, 2023).

[758] For a brief overview of the Church, see: https://pluralism.org/native-american-church (accessed April 17, 2023).

'Instead of being "good" or "this" or "that" or "achiever" or anything, I experienced a place in myself where I just say, "I am", not "I am this" or "that", just "I am".'[759] At first Leary and Alpert believed that psychedelics might offer permanent access to this state of pure consciousness, a kind of silver bullet for psychological transformation and liberation. However, Alpert describes that, after five years, he kept hitting this wall of limitations in his own (extensive) experimentation with psychedelics as, no matter how much he did and under which varying circumstances, he kept 'coming down'. Every time he knocked down his psychological walls they popped right back up again:

> In these few years we had gotten over the feeling that one experience was going to make you enlightened forever. We saw that it wasn't going to be that simple. And for five years I dealt with the matter of 'coming down'. ... And it was a terribly frustrating experience, as if you came into the kingdom of heaven and you saw how it all was and you felt these new states of awareness, and you were cast out again.[760]

Alpert's transcendent psychedelic experiences never quite translated into a sustainable way of being: these heightened states of awareness never became a permanent station, and he started looking for the possibility of going beyond what psychedelics offered. He eventually made his way to India, hoping to find someone who could take him beyond the wall he had been metaphorically banging his head against, and finally, he met who would become his guru, Neem Karoli Baba (d.1973). He shares that, with Karoli Baba, he had finally 'met a being who didn't come down'.[761] Alpert found someone who had stabilized higher spiritual states as his permanent station, his actual being. As Huston Smith put it, the purpose of religious practice is

---

759 Ram Dass, as quoted in the documentary film *Becoming Nobody*, directed by Jamie Catto (2019).
760 Ram Dass, *Be Here Now* (San Cristobal, NM, 1971).
761 As quoted in *Becoming Nobody*.

not 'altered states' but 'altered traits'[762] – it is this very stabilization of higher modes of awareness, consciousness and ethical refinement that is the goal, rather than encountering such modes in a more, perhaps, touristic way. In addition, once one has in fact stabilized a more aware, loving, sacred way of being, they are able to transmit this to others, as long as they are open to receiving and integrating this transmission.

Although a much longer, more laborious process than ingesting a psychedelic, a consistent path of spiritual practice brings, ultimately, permanent realization, and hence the Sufi emphasis on stations over states. We also find this emphasis within Buddhist teachings (among others), which suggest that the aspirant on the spiritual path is to avoid becoming attached to passing states and visions and experiences, however exalted and sublime, or terrifying and bizarre, and keep going until the placeless place is reached.[763] Until we get to where (or perhaps 'nowhere') we're going, it's best to avoid getting obsessed by what we see along the way. The spiritual traveler is a kind of nomad: we can set up our tent for a few nights, but must always keep going, keep moving on.

We should note here that this long process of spiritual traveling, of personal development fostered by practice and struggle, facing one's own limitations and setbacks, and continually trying again (and again), sort of *cooks* the personality into maturity, giving it a spaciousness, stability and dexterity. This maturity then serves as a container that allows intensive, potentially destabilizing experiences of alterity to be absorbed and integrated. Without this mature, personal stability, some of the intensive experiences that psychedelics foster can prove to be overwhelming, leading to short-term, and in some cases long-term psychological snags and issues. We now turn to consider

---

762 As quoted by Marilyn Berlin Snell, 'The World of Religion According to Huston Smith', Mother Jones, November/December 1997, https://www.motherjones.com/politics/1997/11/world-religion-according-huston-smith/ (accessed April 17, 2023).

763 Poet and Vajrayana practitioner Allen Ginsberg relates an encounter he had with Tibetan Lama Dudjom Rinpoche, sharing with him some of his psychedelic experiences. Rinpoche advised him: 'If you see something horrible, don't cling to it; if you see something beautiful, don't cling ot it.' 'The Lion For Real – Three Renditions'. *The Allen Ginsberg Project*, https://allenginsberg.org/2014/12/the-lion-for-real-three-renditions/ (accessed April 17, 2023).

how Ibn 'Arabi understands the *final* station on the path, the *maqam* of Muhammad, the placeless place.

The Path of Blame

For Ibn 'Arabi, Muhammad represents the pinnacle of human completion; a living integration of the entirety of Divine Names; a full realization of every enlightened quality, encompassing all of reality's dimensions, and yet mysteriously going beyond them. This comprehensive, encompassing nature is a kind of paradoxical emptiness that makes room for an abundant fullness, lived in a beautiful ordinariness and simplicity. The complete human, the *insan al-kamil*, has attained 'the Great Peace';[764] they have found the placeless-place, and totally dissolved into Being. They are profoundly fluid as a result, existing in a state of harmony with every possible situation, seamlessly blending into the larger context. The Muhammadan, Ibn 'Arabi tells us, 'does not become designated by a station which is attributed to him. On the contrary, in every breath, in every moment, and in every state, he takes the form which is required by that breath, moment, and state.'[765]

Perhaps some of the best illustrations of this fluid, dynamic and subtle Muhammadan station can be found in traditional Chinese landscape paintings. Informed by Daoist philosophy, such paintings often include, among the gently depicted rivers and mountains, a person who can almost be overlooked as they quite naturally and elegantly blend into the overall picture.[766] Daoist philosopher Zhuangzi (d. late fourth century BCE) describes the station of the perfected one as a complete naturalness:

> His mind is content with being in whatever situation it happens to be. His outward appearance is still and calm … Sometimes he is

---

[764] Shaykh Ahmad al-'Alawi is reported to have said, in response to a questioner: 'Some people are set at rest by very little; others find their satisfaction in religion; some require more; it is not only peace of mind that they must have, but the Great Peace, which brings with it the plenitude of the Spirit.' Lings, *A Sufi Saint of the Twentieth-Century*, p.26.

[765] Ibn 'Arabi, *Fut*.IV.76. As quoted in Chittick, *Sufi Path of Knowledge*, p.377.

[766] See Miranda Shaw, 'Buddhist and Taoist Influences on Chinese Landscape Painting', *Journal of the History of Ideas*, 49:2 (1988), 183–206.

coldly relentless like autumn; sometimes he is warmly amiable like spring. Joy and anger come and go as naturally as the four seasons do in Nature. Keeping perfect harmony with all things, he does not know any limit.[767]

Ibn 'Arabi associates the Muhammadan station, in particular, with the Malamatiyya or People of Blame (*ahl al-malama*). Although I briefly mentioned the Malamatiyya in the Introduction, it is worth discussing them further here, as they can help us get a richer sense of the Muhammadan spiritual paradigm.

To begin, if we think of those mystics and guides who exhibit a kind of spiritual fireworks – possessing a scintillating charisma, performing miracles or accomplishing great feats of fasting and prayer and meditation – the spiritual Olympians standing tall on the podiums of piety – the Malamatiyya are the very opposite of these folks, instead living a kind of inconspicuous sanctity. Ibn 'Arabi says the Malamatiyya are 'those who know and are not known', as 'their states conceal their stations' and hence they 'flow with the common people'.[768] They are something like clay statues hiding a solid gold core underneath, anonymous and easily overlooked, their value rarely appreciated. He also says that they are the sages who 'put things in their proper places'.[769] They give each thing its due, never exaggerating

---

767 Izutsu, *Sufism and Taoism*, p.454.
768 Ibn 'Arabi, *Fut*.II.16. As quoted in Chittick, *Sufi Path of Knowledge*, p.372.
769 Ibid., p.373.

or minimizing what is owed, and largely leave creation as it is.[770]

The term Malamatiyya itself comes from the Arabic root *lam-waw-mim*, from which we derive the word *malama,* meaning blame. The word is used in the Qur'an in some telling ways. First of all, we can recall from Chapter Three on Shu'ayb that the Qur'an names the second stage of the self the *nafs al-lawwama* (Q 5:59) or the *blaming self* – the self that has developed a critical sense of its own failings. This self's ability to face its own issues, limitations and destructive tendencies, if pursued, opens the doorway to discovering what lies beyond this mundane self, the discovery of its own deeper nature, which leads to the *nafs al-mulhama,* the inspired (and inspiring) self. In verse 5:54, the Qur'an describes those who strive in God's path as *fearing not the blame of any blamer.* For the Malamatiyya (and for Ibn 'Arabi), those who strive in God's way and fear not the blame of those who attack them, are first and foremost the Prophet Muhammad and his companions, and hence the Malamatiyya consider Muhammad to be the first of their way.[771]

Early Sufi works suggest that the distinguishing characteristic of

---

[770] The Malamatiyya emerged in Khorasan, a region of Central Asia found at the intersection of (today) Iran, Afghanistan, Uzbekistan and Tajikistan. Scholar of Sufism Annabel Keeler notes that, for Muslims, the region 'came to be known as the land whose product is saints' as some of the faiths greatest luminaries came from there, including early Sufis like Hakim al-Tirmidhi and Abu Yazid al-Bistami, and later ones like Abu'l-Hasan al-Kharaqani (d.1033) and Ahmad al-Ghazali (d.1126). Khorasan was also host to a variety of Islamic spiritual movements, including some that were ostentatiously pious and ascetical (like the Karramiyya), while others focused on inculcating a code of chivalry (*futuwwa*), possibly having some influence on later knightly orders in Europe. The term 'Sufism' took hold in Khorasan about a century or two after it did in Mesopotamia, and, to a large degree, the term's acceptance in the region can be traced to one of the key early formulators of Sufism, al-Sulami. Besides his outsized influence in shaping the early Sufi tradition, with works documenting its history, luminaries and techniques, Sulami also played an important role in sort of fusing Mesopotamian Sufism with the Malamati tradition of Khorasan, such that they eventually fell together under the term 'Sufi' in the centuries that followed. Sulami was born, lived and died in Nishapur, the cultural, political and economic capital of the Khorasan region, and the center of the Malamati movement. There he gained an expertise in the Shafi'i school of Islamic law as well as the study of hadith, hence having impeccable Sunni credentials. He was also a student of Nishapur's foremost Malamati, Abu Sahl al-Su'luki (d.977), and wrote the first work fully outlining their path, his *al-Risalat al-Malamatiyya,* from which we can gather much about the Malamati way. Annabel Keeler, *Sufi Hermeneutics: The Qur'an Commentary of Rashid al-Din Maybudi* (New York, 2006), pp.107–8. Also see Nicholas Heer and Kenneth L. Honerkamp, *Three Early Sufi Texts: A Treatise on the Heart, Stations of the Righteous, and The Stumblings of Those Aspiring* (Louisville, 2003), pp.87–91

[771] Heer and Honerkamp, *Three Early Sufi Texts,* p.92.

the way of the Malamatiyya is a concern to avoid pretentious religiosity and undercut any sort of spiritual materialism (or using spirituality for egotistical ends).[772] In other words, their main concern is total *sincerity*, to avoid all kinds of narcissism, hypocrisy, self-aggrandizement, self-consciousness and self-righteousness; any sense of, 'Ah yes, what a lovely spiritual practice I have going. I can't believe how refined and impressive and special I'm becoming. If I keep this up, I'll be a perfectly sculpted, spiritual genius in no time!' Their concern over this kind of spiritual egotism grew from a keen awareness that we all have 'clay feet' as the saying goes. As al-Sulami writes, 'the locus of created being will never be devoid of defects'.[773] Besides our own inevitable personal flaws as creatures, we also have a marked tendency to try and co-opt any kind of spirituality in the service of ego, and hence the People of Blame were keenly focused on *self-awareness*, casting the spotlight of attention within, vigilantly searching the self to weed out the roots of egotism and pretension, wherever they grow. They were also deeply wary of spiritual experiences and states. Much like their Buddhist counterparts we mentioned above, the Malamatiyya tended to disregard the significance of spiritual states entirely, seeing them as a kind of ostentation to be dismissed. The person of blame then is 'one who has no interior pretension nor exterior affectation. His inner secret, between him and God, is not apparent to his own heart, how then could it be to other creatures?'[774]

Al-Sulami shares that the Malamati path is thus built on five principles: 1) humble adherence to scriptural guidelines, 2) always behaving respectfully and kindly, 3) disdain for the ego, 4) discounting one's own piety or spiritual states, and 5) hiding one's state in God.[775] One of their methods utilized to achieve these ends was to behave in ways that, at times, made them appear irreligious, idiotic or even

---

772 This helpful term 'spiritual materialism' was coined by Chogyam Trunpga, to name the human tendency to use spirituality not to 'step out of the bureaucracy of ego', but rather to prop it up and strengthen it, with a growing collection of spiritual 'stuff'. Chogyam Trungpa, *Cutting through Spiritual Materialism* (Boston, 2002 [1973]), p.16.
773 Heer, Honerkamp, *Three Early Sufi Texts*, p.96.
774 Ibid., p.97.
775 Ibid., p.98.

just ordinary and boring. And yet this blameworthiness was carefully cultivated as a way of concealing their own exalted sanctity (even from themselves), such that neither their ego could parasitically feed off of a sense of celebrity and spiritual specialness, nor would they attract those who get starry-eyed over saintly sorts. This may also have been a kind of self-preservation, as historically we humans tend to crucify those we deify: flying below the radar is a great way to avoid getting shot down. And yet their approach cannot be reduced to this security found in anonymity, having a much deeper function of cutting out the roots of spiritual egotism before they can grow, curtailing the deadlier enemy within, rather than concern with any secondary enemy without.

In his book *The Knowing Heart* (1999) Kabir Helminski relates a wonderful story that a friend shared with him, about a deeply realized Turkish Sufi teacher. The friend's account of his time with this master brilliantly illustrates the entire Malamati dynamic. This particular teacher apparently lived in a rundown shack in a poor neighborhood, but possessed several relics from the great Sufi masters of the past, from various Sufi orders. Helminski's friend was one of a small circle of students who wanted to spend all of their time with this relatively hidden teacher. They had found no one more profound in all of their seeking, and wanted others to benefit from his rare wisdom and hence pleaded that he sort of 'go public' and increase his following. One day they were with him attending prayers in the city's great mosque, and as they left a pigeon just dropped dead from the sky on the mosque's steps in front of them. The master gently picked up the little bird, and lovingly breathed out a long '*Huuuuuuuu…*' and the bird came back to life and flew back into the sky.

This understandably attracted a lot of talk and attention, and quite rapidly the master's circle grew large, as word got out about his miracle. The students found themselves regretful though, as they no longer had much time with their teacher, as he was now surrounded by throngs of seekers and admirers. Then, weeks later, while they and the other new followers were all performing the night prayer with the master, he loudly farted. Disrupting prayer this way would have been embarrassing for a regular believer, but for the many new followers this was simply intolerable coming from a purported holy man, and in a short time most had left. The small circle of original followers now had their master back, and one night while they were conversing alone together, he said, 'You see, my sons, those who come because of a pigeon, leave because of a fart!'[776] We can see here quite clearly the counter-intuitive wisdom in incurring blame: the master's real followers stay regardless of miracle or faux pas, whereas a great many others come and go because of them.

The Level of Muhammad: The Station of No Station

According to Ibn 'Arabi, in the final analysis, the Station of Muhammad, the pinnacle of spiritual realization, is actually the 'station of no station', or *maqam la maqam* – a placeless place, or perspective-less perspective, that itself integrates and honors all possible perspectives and places within it, while going totally beyond them all. It is a kind of pure universality that both transcends and yet includes every possible particularity. He describes those perfected ones of this station as follows: 'The people of perfection have realized all stations and states and passed beyond these of the station above both majesty and beauty, so they have no attribute and no description.'[777] Just as the Essence of the Real is beyond all attribute and description, so the fully realized human, the Muhammadan, is a kind of 'copy' of the Real, and hence is also without attribute, and cannot be described at all.

Ibn 'Arabi points out that all of us are ever pursuing goals (and we can think here of our various pursuits of career, relationship, education, entertainment, experience, spirituality, etc.). As such, we are always reaching some station, a place of landing, after which we find soon find ourselves looking for a new place to arrive at, and 'hence', Ibn 'Arabi writes, 'the possessors of stations are those whose aspirations have become limited to certain goals and ends', that, after they are reached, new ones are sought, endlessly. In contrast, 'the Muhammadan has no such property and witnesses no such goal.

---

776 Helminski, *The Knowing Heart*, pp.240-1.
777 Ibn 'Arabi, *Fut*.II.133. As quoted in Chittick, *Sufi Path of Knowledge*, p.376.

His vastness is the vastness of the Real, and the Real has no goal in Himself which His Being might ultimately reach.'[778] Unlike the rest of us, those living the Station of Muhammad are without goal, direction or attribute. This is precisely why Muhammad most comprehensively embodies human perfection and the completion of wisdom: it is not so much that Muhammad has a *superior* perspective or higher station, but rather that his *absence* of a static perspective, his having gone totally beyond any permanent station, allows him to integrate all perspectives and stations, giving each their due – knowing the way in which they reflect and obscure God's reality. The celebrated Mahayana scripture known as the *Heart Sutra* ends with a mantra that quite beautifully illustrates this station: '*Gate, gate, paragate, parasamgate, bodhi svaha!*' This can be translated as, 'Gone, gone, gone beyond, totally gone beyond, enlightenment, hail!'[779]

For Ibn 'Arabi, the Muhammadan Station of complete realization (*tahqiq*) is also defined as 'giving things their *haqq*'.[780] Each existent entity, each person, animal and object has a *haqq*, a reality, that demands its right or its due, which must be given for us to live correctly, and to honor what should be honored. This, interestingly, also includes people's beliefs.

> We say, regarding beliefs: one praises none other than the god of their own belief, attaching oneself to it. ... This god of belief is the product of one's thought; it is one's own creation. One's praise of what they believe in is just praise of one's self. This is why people disparage the beliefs of others; if they were just, they would not do so. The one who worships the god of his own making is clearly ignorant of this, opposing the beliefs of others, in their own gods. Had this one known al-Junayd's saying, 'the water's color is that of its vessel', he would have approved everyone's belief and known God

---

778 Ibid.
779 For an overview of the *Heart Sutra* and this mantra, see Donald S. Lopez, Jr. 'What's in a Mantra? A Close Look at the *Heart Sutra*', *Tricycle: The Buddhist Review*, Summer 2008, https://tricycle.org/magazine/whats-mantra/, (accessed May 12, 2023).
780 Chittick, 'The Central Point', p.34.

in every belief and form.[781]

In this fascinating passage in the *Gemstones*, Ibn 'Arabi shares an understanding of belief in God that may be a bit unsettling for some believers. In his *Futuhat* he elaborates on this point, stating that creatures simply cannot worship the Real, but rather can only worship their own concept of the Real, which is 'nothing but a created thing'.[782] Ibn 'Arabi's analysis corresponds quite closely with one of the more compelling articulations of atheism in the Western philosophical tradition, that of German philosopher Ludwig Feuerbach (d.1872). In his best-known work, *The Essence of Christianity* (1841), Feuerbach argues that theology is basically just anthropology, in that everything we say about God is really just a projection of our own human nature onto an imaginary, external entity: we create God in our own image, he would suggest, rather than the other way around.[783] Here we find Ibn 'Arabi saying very much the same thing. Every person on earth who believes in God creates a version of God – a god – that they have somehow conceived and imagined, drawing from the contents of their own self, its concepts and qualities, and hence what they worship is actually a product of themselves, or we may even say (and Ibn 'Arabi says this) that they *worship their own self*. We can also extend this to include everyone who has any sort of belief whatsoever about reality: all are, in fact, projecting their own qualities onto reality; everyone, in one sense, is a worshipper of their own self.

If Ibn 'Arabi would have simply stopped there, it appears that he would be very much on the same page with Feuerbach. However, despite everyone only ever worshipping a projection of their own qualities, Ibn 'Arabi adds that, that which they worship actually becomes a receptacle for the Real: as Junayd says in the passage above, water takes on the color of whatever vessel it is poured into. Each person delimits the Real according to their own belief, philosophy, dogma or ideology.

---

781 Ibn 'Arabi, *Fusus*, p.218.

782 Ibn 'Arabi, *Fut*.IV.386. As quoted in Chittick, *Sufi Path of Knowledge*, p.341.

783 Feuerbach writes that 'in religion man contemplates his own latent nature. Hence it must be shown that this antithesis, this differencing of God and man, with which religion begins, is a differencing of man with his own nature.' Ludwig Feuerbach, *The Essence of Christianity*, translated by George Eliot (Walnut, CA, 2008), p.1.

And although the Real transcends each delimitation completely, it yet manifests through them all, taking on the color of every belief. Out of benevolence (*rahma*) God conforms to each one's belief – each knot tied in reality – and hence God 'ties Himself in a knot' to accommodate each creature's belief.[784]

Ibn ʿArabi then counsels an embrace of every belief as loci for witnessing the Real in all of its infinite manifestations: 'He who is more perfect than the perfect is he who believes every belief concerning Him.' The Muhammadan 'recognizes Him in faith, in proofs, and in heresy ... So if you want your eye to hit the mark, witness Him with every eye, for He pervades all things through self-disclosure. In every form He has a face and in every knower a state.'[785]

The Sufi who has realized this Muhammadan Station honors every manifestation of the sacred, and (metaphorically) bows to all of its forms, whether Vishnu, Christ or Buddha, seeing the singular sacred reality they represent, each showing a different face of the Absolute, but none with a monopoly of representation. Each orthodoxy is, from another perspective, a heresy, and vice versa. Regardless, all reveal the One in different ways. As I have pointed to in a few places in this book, there is a great synchronicity between Ibn ʿArabi and Rumi. Though their respective writing styles diverge, their message is a shared one. Rumi writes, echoing Ibn ʿArabi on this subject:

> *Beyond Islam and infidelity, there is a field.*
> *In the midst of that expanse, we have found a love.*
> *The knower of God who reaches there will bow completely.*
> *For there is no Islam, no infidelity, nor any 'where' in that place.*[786]

---

784 Chittick, *Sufi Path of Knowledge*, p.340.
785 Ibn ʿArabi, *Fut*.II.211. As quoted in Chittick, *Sufi Path of Knowledge*, p.349.
786 I have somewhat combined the translation of quatrain 395 in Rumi's *Divan-i Shams-i Tabrizi*, offered in Asghar Seyed-Gohrab, 'Rumi's Antinomian Poetic Philosophy', *Mawlana Rumi Review* (January 2020), https://brill.com/view/journals/mrr/9/1-2/article-p159_9.xml?language=en#FN000085, with the translation by Ibrahim Gamard, found in 'Apparently Irreligious Verses in the Works of Mawlana Rumi', published on his Dar al-Masnavi website, https://aalequtub.files.wordpress.com/2018/04/apparently-irreligious-verses.pdf (both accessed April 23, 2023).

The Muhammadan then, having arrived at the place without 'where', the destination without end or limit or sign, the field beyond all belief and non-belief, witnesses every conceivable belief, across time and culture, and recognizes that, underlying them all, is the singular truth that God has inscribed on his Throne, that His mercy prevails over all beings that have existed, exist now or will ever exist. The universe, as God manifest, is a reflection of mercy; it is inherently good, and none within it fall outside of God's compassion, and all in their individual uniqueness are honored for that very individuality:

> Since God is the root of the diversity of beliefs within the cosmos, and since He has also brought about the existence of everything in the cosmos in a constitution not possessed by anything else, everyone's final place of return is to mercy. For it is He who created them and brought them into existence, within the Breath of the Merciful.[787]

This Breath of the Merciful is a kind of existential exhalation of God's mercy, a benevolent breathing out, with each existent, every being, a unique letter formed upon this breath; the Merciful giving being to all in their irreducible idiosyncrasy. We are all individual letters, our families are words, and our communities, sentences; our collective histories and movements, chapters.[788] The Sublime Eternity exhales this grand saga, letters and words and sentences without end, and then inhales, and draws us back, sending prophets and friends to call us – in all of our infinite, beautiful diversity – back to the loving Oneness that we truly are. It remains up to us, however, to respond to their call.

---

787 Ibn 'Arabi, *Fut*.III.465. As quoted in Chittick, *Sufi Path of Knowledge*, p.338. Stephen Hirtenstein notes that the passage here is more literally translated as 'final place of return' rather than 'will end up with'.

788 In commenting on Ibn 'Arabi's articulation of the Breath of the Merciful, or *Nafas al-Rahman*, Chittick describes the metaphor of letters, words and sentences a bit differently than I have done, suggesting that 'every part of every existent thing is a letter', while the creature as a whole is a word, their entire life trajectory is a sentence and the world that they are a part of is a book. Regardless of how we employ these analogies, for Ibn 'Arabi, all existent things are God's words, and though the words themselves only appear for an instant before disappearing forever, God's speech itself is eternal. Chittick, *Sufi Path of Knowledge*, p.19.

Index

A

Aaron (Harun, prophet), 124, 126, 235
'abd Allah (servant of God), 46, 302
Abraham (Ibrahim, prophet), 28, 44, 49, 54, 93–100, 105, 111, 113, 119, 120, 124, 126, 128–129, 190, 252, 256, 302–304, 306, 316, 320, 322
Abu Bakr, 28, 306
Abu Hurayra, 44, 238, 323,
Abu Madyan, 139, 161
adab, 45, 250
Adam (prophet), 53–54, 58–63, 74–76, 87–91, 101, 115, 124, 126, 128, 148, 189, 190, 195, 199, 212, 222–223, 280, 282, 291, 298, 308, 319–320, 326–327
al-'Adawiyya, Rabi'a, 29–30
Advaita Vedanta, 66–67, 71, 322
Ahmed, Shahab, 46, 287–288
A'isha (wife of Prophet Muhammad), 304, 306
Akbarian, 52, 156
akhira / afterlife, 24, 31–32, 161, 181, 184–186, 210–211
al-'Alawi, Ahmad, 100, 335
'alam al-mithal (World of Images / Likenesses), 73, 223
alchemy, 47, 61, 126–127, 204, 226, 288, 323
Alexander the Great, 202, 235–237
Alexandria, 202, 208–209, 321
Ali, Asad, 11, 42–43, 257
'Ali ibn Abi Talib, 27–28, 101, 304, 323
al-'Alim (the Knower), 44, 217
Allah, 23, 44–46, 70, 72, 76, 87–88, 91, 97, 99, 130, 136, 156–157, 166, 175–176, 179, 241, 246, 258, 275, 290–293, 302, 326

Allegory of the Cave, 218–219
Amina (mother of Prophet Muhammad), 303, 320
al-Andalus (Andalusia), 1, 46–48, 187, 326
angels, 32, 59, 87–91, 156, 193, 197–200, 220, 226, 228, 246, 319
animals, 60, 81–82, 97, 116, 134, 162, 166, 219–222, 301–302, 319, 341
'Anqa' Mughrib 34, 77, 326
'aql (intellect), 134, 157, 223, 290, 326
Arabia (Arabian Peninsula), 2, 26, 49, 95, 170, 295–296, 302–304
'arif / 'arifun (knower / knowers), 91, 218, 327
Aristotle, 48, 115, 210, 219, 222
'arsh (throne), 138, 187
astrology (*'ilm al-nujum*), 197, 204
atheism, 13, 117, 130, 224–225, 342
Attar, Farid al-Din, 258, 285
'ayn (a'yan) thabita (fixed entity), 73, 112, 223
'azim (sublime, magnificent), 300, 308

B

Baba, Neem Karoli, 100, 333
Badiou, Alain, 219
Badr al-Din of Simawna, 185
Baghdad, 30, 140, 242, 284
Bahalil, 241
Baha al-Din (father of Rumi), 176–177
baraka (blessing energy), 26–27, 36–37, 245
barzakh (in-between, limit), 150, 195, 222, 277
Basra, 29, 322–323
al-Basri, Hasan, 109–110, 322–323
al-Batin (the Invisible / Hidden), 102, 149

Bawa Muhaiyaddeen, 35, 129, 142, 178–179
Being, 5–8, 13, 32, 34–36, 48, 62–66, 68–72, 74–84, 86–87, 90–91, 95, 99, 100–101, 103–105, 108, 111–113, 118–120, 137, 149–150, 153, 178–179, 189, 199, 207–208, 212, 223, 225–228, 254, 269, 291–292, 314, 322, 328, 330–331, 335, 338, 341, 344
Berger, Peter, 115–116
Bible, 14, 23, 41, 120, 124, 134, 161, 163, 194, 196–197, 199, 206, 208, 227, 234–235, 252, 279
al-Bistami, Abu Yazid, 46, 87, 138, 324, 337
Bonaventure, 214–215
Brahman (Absolute), 67, 72, 77
Buddha, 77–78, 107, 125, 129, 140, 297, 343
Buddhism, 14, 16, 66, 77, 84, 106–107, 110, 140, 151, 261, 280, 297, 331

C

category error, 215–216
Catholic Church, 48, 93, 115, 171, 214, 244, 330
Chalmers, David J., 267–268
Christ (see Jesus)
Christianity, 25, 39, 67, 93–94, 106, 167, 170, 200, 209–210, 214, 240, 244, 261, 271–272, 278, 297, 317, 321, 342
Church, 11, 13, 167, 171, 176, 196, 200, 240, 273, 279, 332
Corbin, Henry, 26, 202, 206, 222–223
Crucifixion, 281

D

Damascus, 2, 11, 20, 42, 49, 183, 278
Daoism, 14, 65–66, 138, 335
dar al-harb (Abode of War), 169, 171
dar al-islam (Abode of Islam), 169, 171

David (Dawud, prophet), 54, 123–124, 163–164, 320
Day of Judgment, 305, 317
Dee, John, 200–201
dervish (*darvish*), 32, 45, 145, 204, 287
Descartes, René, 36, 265–266
destiny, 17, 32, 55, 105–109, 111, 114, 116–117
dhat (essence), 20, 71, 153
dhawq (taste), 1, 20, 33, 108, 261
dreams, 224, 226, 229, 245, 304
Dudjom Rinpoche, 66, 334

E

Eckhart, Meister, 67, 71,
ego, 46, 103, 132, 135, 145–147, 240, 338–339
Einstein, Albert, 223–224, 231–232, 271–272
Elijah (Ilyas, prophet), 54, 73, 124, 193–195, 219, 221, 228, 236, 270
enlightenment, 9, 15, 17, 26, 40, 59–60, 66, 146, 198, 244, 282, 297, 309, 327, 332, 341
Enlightenment, the, 125, 255, 296–297
Enmeduranki, 199–200
Enneads, 67, 210, 267
Enoch (Idris, prophet), 54, 78–79, 124, 126, 193–201, 206, 208, 212, 216, 219–221, 228, 236
Enoch, Book of, 196–198, 200
Eve (*Hawwa'*), 59–60, 280
Ezra ('Uzayr, prophet), 33, 124

F

fana' (annihilation), 41, 147, 309
faqr (poverty), 283, 301, 328
al-Farsi, Salman, 28, 323
fass (bezel / gemstone), 53–54
Fatima (daughter of Prophet Muhammad), 28, 304
fatwa, pl. *fatawa* (Islamic legal ruling(s)), 19, 51, 173, 286

Ficino, Marsilio, 78, 206–207
fiqh (jurisprudence), 32, 168, 286
fitra (original human nature), 35, 95, 130, 189
Five Pillars of Islam, 32, 178
free will, 105, 109–111, 114
Fusus al-hikam (The Gemstones of Wisdom), 6, 10, 18–20, 49, 51–55, 58, 63, 269, 295–296
Futuhat al-Makkiyya (The Meccan Revelations), 19, 33, 61, 179, 212, 229, 241, 245, 342

G

Gabriel (angel), 31, 114, 198, 276–278, 304–305
Genesis, Book of, 58, 94, 195, 197
al-Ghani (the Rich Beyond Need), 86, 148
ghayb (unseen, hidden), 65, 153
al-Ghazali, Abu Hamid, 4, 31–32, 126, 165, 218, 282, 315
Gospels, 40, 44, 130, 270, 272–273, 278–279, 281, 289
Great Chain of Being, 70, 208

H

hadarat (presences / planes), 71–73
hadith, 27, 31–32, 35, 44, 60, 128, 137, 166, 174–176, 186–188, 195, 241–242, 244, 277, 290, 296, 298, 300–302, 307–308, 312, 315–318, 325, 337
hadith qudsi (divine tradition), 137, 317–318
hal (spiritual state), 327–329
al-Halim (the Lovingly Gentle / Kind), 85, 96
hanif (pure monotheist), 95, 304
haqiqa (reality), 146, 287
al-Haqiqa al-Muhammadiyya (The Muhammadan Reality), 54, 299, 326
haqq (truth, right), 63, 65, 150, 341
al-Haqq (the Real), 11, 23, 63–65, 130, 139, 153, 284

Hasan (grandson of Prophet Muhammad), 28, 304
al-Hayy (the Living), 44, 249
Heaven (*jannah*), 42, 44, 59, 66, 89, 126, 134, 140, 185–186, 188, 190, 198–199, 201, 216, 272, 319, 324, 326, 333
Hebrew(s), 58, 95, 158, 161, 194–197, 202, 234–235, 237, 250, 252, 270
Hell (*jahanam*), 30, 47, 142, 185–187, 189–190
Helminski, Kabir, 46, 132, 144–145, 339
Hermes Trismegistus, 193, 212, 201–204, 206–208, 212
Hermetica, 203–204, 206–207
Hermeticism, 47, 115, 213, 323
hieroglyphs, 73, 200–202, 323
Hijri calendar, 20, 305
hikma (wisdom), 27, 36–37, 54
Hinduism, 16, 84, 106, 261
Hiranyagarbha (Golden Embryo), 299, 322, 326
Hixon, Lex (Nur al-Jerrahi), 129, 186, 296
Hu (He / divine essence), 71–72, 153
al-Hujwiri, 'Ali, 16, 285
humanism, 19, 114, 117
Husayn (grandson of Prophet Muhammad), 28, 304
Huxley, Aldous, 78, 330–331

I

Iblis (Satan), 59, 276, 296
Ibn Hanbal, Ahmad, 290, 298, 301
Ibn Hisham, 195, 302
Ibn Ishaq, 302, 304
Ibn Muthanna, Fatima bint, 47, 180, 317
Ibn Taymiyya, Taqi al-Din Ahmad, 4, 19, 208, 298
ihsan (spiritual excellence), 31–32
'ilm (knowledge, science), 29, 31, 197, 217

Imaginal Realm (imaginatrix), 222–229
Imagination, 66, 82, 175, 185, 188, 219–229
Imam, 64, 237, 299, 318
Inayat Khan, Hazrat, 33, 60, 167, 182, 185–186
Inayat Khan, Noor, 167–168
Inayat Khan, Zia, 129, 206
al-insan al-kamil (perfect, universal human), 79, 81, 99, 208, 299, 335
Iran, 46, 204, 244, 284, 337
Iraq, 23, 29, 46, 206, 322
'Iraqi, Fakhr al-Din, 100–101, 105, 231
Isaac (Ishaq), 28, 94–95, 124, 222
'Isawi (mode of Jesus / Christic), 283–284, 289
ishara (allusion), 33
Ishmael (Isma'il), 28, 94–97, 124, 292, 302–303, 306
'ishq (passionate love / desire), 22, 29, 105, 258
Ishraqi philosophy (Illuminationism), 205, 324
Islam, 30–37
i'tiqad (belief), 153–154

J

Jacob (Ya'qub, prophet), 124, 227, 320
al-Jaza'iri, 'Abd al-Qadir, 156, 173
Jesus (Yeshua / 'Isa), 10, 14, 20, 24, 36, 40, 47, 54, 60, 65, 72, 123–124, 126, 128–130, 148, 206, 247, 262, 265, 269–285, 289–293, 296–297, 306, 315, 320
jihad (struggle), 164–168, 170, 172–176, 329
al-Jilani, 'Abd al-Qadir, 107, 140, 241–243, 248–249
jinn, 59, 114, 226, 246, 256
Job (Ayyub, prophet), 123, 320
John the Baptist (Yahya, prophet), 54, 124, 126, 271, 320

Jonah (Yunus, prophet), 23, 45, 54, 120, 124, 161–163, 181, 187, 285
Joseph (Yusuf, prophet), 124, 229, 320
Junayd al-Baghdadi, 138, 284, 342
Jung, Carl, 240–241

K

Ka'aba, 96–97, 256–257, 285, 302–303, 314,
Kabbalah, 115, 200
kamal (perfection), 79, 182
karma, 84, 106–107, 110
kashf (unveiling), 33, 145, 221
Keller, Hellen, 312–313
Khadija (wife of Prophet Muhammad), 303–306
khalifa (successor, representative), 27, 59,
khalil (friend), 97–98
khalwa (retreat), 47, 261, 304
Khidr, 49, 235–241, 243–245, 249–250, 270
Khorasan, 244, 337

L

lahut (godliness / divinity), 269–270, 275, 280
Lal, Radha Mohan, 64, 100
Laozi, 65–66
Leary, Timothy, 332–333
logos (word, speech), 54, 134, 275, 299, 320–322, 324, 326–327
love, 7, 14, 17, 19, 21–22, 24, 29–30, 35–36, 38, 41, 46–47, 50, 55, 74, 84–85, 93, 97–98, 100, 105, 120, 127, 130, 133–134, 136, 177, 186–189, 191, 209, 216, 243, 247, 254–256, 258–262, 272–273, 282, 284, 287, 291, 293, 295–296, 303, 308–312, 314–315, 319, 343
Luqman (prophet), 85–86, 124

M

madhhab (Islamic legal school), 286, 290
madhhab-i 'ishq (Way of Love), 22, 105, 258
magic, 47, 196–197, 199–205, 208, 323
majnun, 139, 241, 256
Majnun (Qays ibn al-Mulawwah), 256–257
Malamatiyya, 37, 41–41, 336–339
maqam (station), 97, 114, 139, 147, 324, 327, 329, 335, 340,
maqam la maqam (Station of No-Station), 147, 340
maqasid (goals or ends of the law), 164–165
ma'rifa (gnosis), 34, 145, 217–218, 324,
Maryam (Mary), 60, 124, 269, 274–280, 306
Maslow, Abraham, 144, 179
Masnavi, 24, 34, 44, 159, 177, 287–288, 291, 312
Massignon, Louis, 64, 93
Mecca, 32, 96–97, 170, 177, 245, 256, 285, 300, 302–306, 314, 323
de' Medici, Cosimo, 78, 206
Medina (*Madina*), 28, 300, 302, 305–306
meditation, 14, 18, 21, 24, 28, 38, 65–66, 135, 143–144, 181, 286, 314, 330–331, 336
Mesopotamia (*Balad bayn al-nahrayn*), 35, 127, 194, 199, 201, 337
metaphysics, 63, 211, 219
Metatron (*Mitatrush*), 197, 199, 220
microcosm, 76, 207–208
mind–body problem, 265–269
Mirandola, Pico della, 114–115, 117–118
al-Misri, Dhu'l Nun, 10, 64, 206, 217, 323–324, 327–328
monotheism, 93–94, 110, 112, 207,
Moses (Musa), 20–21, 36, 47, 49, 54, 74, 95, 105, 123–124, 126, 128–129, 142, 191, 197, 202, 206–207, 231, 234–241, 243, 249–255, 283, 296–297
mosque, 15, 28, 49, 179, 284, 301, 339
Muhammad ibn 'Abdullah (prophet), 18, 20–21, 24–28, 31–32, 35–36, 40, 44–47, 54, 59–60, 64, 88, 94, 96, 124, 128–129, 134, 136–137, 140, 147, 165–166, 169–170, 172, 174, 177–178, 183, 187, 195, 198, 206, 212, 228–229, 234–236, 238, 242, 245, 246–248, 253, 256–259, 261–262, 277, 282, 284, 286, 289, 293, 295–312, 314–316, 320, 322–327, 335–337, 340–344
Muhammadan Station, 327, 335–336, 340–344
al-Muhasibi, Harith, 282, 327
mushahada (witnessing), 34, 73, 318
mysticism, 4, 17, 47, 64, 67, 200, 202, 208, 225, 331

N

nafs (self), 35, 131, 135, 141–148, 172, 185, 312, 337
nasut (humanity / human nature), 269–270
Neoplatonism, 67, 208–210, 213
nirguna (beyond attribute), 67, 72
Noah (Nuh, prophet), 123–124, 128–129, 193, 197, 207, 220, 320
nubuwwa (prophethood), 247–248, 275
al-Nur (the Light), 44, 178
Nur Muhammadi (Muhammadan Light), 299, 322, 324
Nyingma, 66, 107, 280

O

Ottomans, 2, 19, 50–51, 171–172, 185, 232
Ozak, Muzaffer, 22, 36–37, 130

P

perennial philosophy, 78–79, 129, 195, 206
Persia, 29, 201, 205–206, 209, 237
Pharoah, 142, 234–235, 250
philosophy, 2–8, 10, 14–19, 21–22, 32, 47–48, 52, 54–55, 62–63, 65–67, 69, 71, 78–80, 84, 115, 117, 129, 154, 195, 202, 205–206, 208–210, 212, 219, 223, 225, 232, 267, 277, 299, 318, 322, 324, 335, 342
philosophical Sufism, 19, 52, 70
Plato, 69, 78, 80, 115, 202, 204, 206, 209–213, 218–220, 321
Platonic Academy, 78, 210
Plotinus, 67, 80, 208–210, 267
prayer, 11, 24–26, 28, 31–32, 40, 48, 81, 96–97, 130, 135, 143–144, 158, 175–179, 242, 288, 307, 309–310, 314, 316–319, 336, 339
predestination, 110–111, 113
Prisca Theologica, 78, 195, 207
psychedelics, 329–334
psychology, 63, 78, 86, 130–148, 162, 167, 332
Pythagoras, 204, 206

Q

qadar (destiny), 107–109, 113
qalb (heart), 131–133, 140, 158
al-Qarani, Uways, 245–246
al-Qashani, 'Abd al-Razzaq, 52, 65, 132, 188, 220
al-Qaysari, Dawud, 38, 50, 52, 54, 69, 71, 80
al-Qunawi, Sadr al-Din, 20, 51–52, 63, 65, 100, 105, 107, 275
Qur'an, 18, 20–23, 27–30, 37–38, 40–44, 46, 52–53, 59–60, 72, 79, 81, 84–91, 94–97, 102, 114, 120, 123–124, 128–135, 137–138, 140–141, 146–149, 154, 157, 161, 163, 166, 168–169, 173, 175–176, 182, 184, 186–187, 189–190, 194–195, 197, 208–212, 217, 227–229, 234–236, 238, 241, 243–245, 249–250, 252–254, 257, 261, 271, 274–279, 281–282, 286, 290–292, 299–300, 302, 304–306, 312, 317, 319, 324–325, 337
Quraysh, 303, 305
al-Qushayri, 'Abd al-Karim / Abu al-Qasim, 141, 285, 289, 328–329

R

rabb (Lord), 35, 72, 292
rahma (mercy), 98, 165, 187, 343
al-Rahman (the Merciful), 44, 312, 344
Ramadan, 26, 31, 46
Ram Dass (Richard Alpert), 100, 183–184, 332–333
rasul (messenger), 128, 247, 274
rationalism, 219, 255
rationality, 241, 321
religion, 3–4, 6–8, 13–16, 19, 22, 26, 29–30, 33, 37, 39–40, 44, 47, 58, 65, 77–79, 88, 90–91, 93–95, 105–106, 115, 118, 125, 129, 142–144, 148, 151, 154, 156, 159, 167, 170–171, 181–182, 195, 202–204, 207, 213, 218, 225–227, 234, 244, 254, 272, 283, 286–287, 290–292, 297, 304, 306, 331, 335, 342
Renaissance, 3, 78, 114–115, 194–195, 200, 206–207
al-Rifa'i, Ahmad, 206, 324
Romanticism, 254–256, 258
ruh (spirit), 131–132, 275
Ruh al-Qudus, 46, 141, 244, 246, 317,
Rumi, Jalal al-Din, 3, 16, 23–24, 34, 38, 43–45, 123, 142, 152, 158–159, 176–177, 180, 236, 287–289, 291, 295, 312, 343
ru'ya (vision), 304, 318

S

sabr (patience), 87, 324, 328
al-Sadiq, Ja'far, 28, 41, 64
Said, Abdul Aziz, 9, 35, 127, 175, 191, 314
salat (ritual prayer / blessing), 96, 135, 175–176, 178–180, 309, 316–319
Sartre, Jean-Paul, 117–118
scripture, 32, 36, 40, 43–44, 67, 124, 128, 152, 228, 234, 247–248, 257, 292, 300, 341
shahada (visible world, witness), 153, 167
Shankara, Adi, 66–67, 72
shari'a (divine law), 17, 26, 103–104, 142, 144, 147, 165, 173–174, 282, 285–288
Sharify-Funk, Meena, 9, 16, 35, 42, 183, 191, 314
Shi'ism, 27–28, 64, 205, 304
Shu'ayb, 54, 79, 124, 137, 139, 157–158, 186, 234, 253, 282, 337
shukr (gratitude), 85–87, 324
Smith, Huston, 14, 271, 330, 332–334
Solomon (Sulayman, prophet), 123–124, 163, 272, 320
spiritual experience, 13, 20, 24, 35, 47–48, 52, 221, 228, 323, 332, 338
spiritual materialism, 338
Suhrawardi, Shihab al-Din, 204–206, 223, 324
al-Sulami, 'Abd al-Rahman, 29, 141, 327, 337–338
Sulayman, Muqatil bin, 195, 325
Sunnah, 21, 177, 290, 300,
synagogue, 167, 176

T

Tabrizi, Shams, 236, 288, 343
tahqiq (realization), 34, 52, 65, 341
tajalli (self-manifestation), 71, 136, 153
tamam (completion), 79, 182
taqyid (binding), 91, 153
tariqa (spiritual path), 143–144
tasawwuf (Sufism), 17, 29, 45
tawba (repentance), 135, 327–328
tawhid (unity / oneness), 175, 275–276
theology, 11, 13, 17, 32, 48, 63, 67, 110, 210, 265, 274, 291, 325, 342
Thoth, 203–204, 206
Tibetan Buddhism (Vajrayana), 14, 66, 77, 100, 107, 240, 280, 334,
al-Tirmidhi, al-Hakim, 133, 244–248, 337
Torah, 44, 58–60, 94, 195, 199, 235, 271–272
Trinity, 274–275
Trungpa, Chogyam, 240, 338
al-Tustari, Sahl, 94, 206, 332
Tweedie, Irina, 64, 100

U

Upanishads, 67, 69, 71, 77, 84, 107

V

Vedas, 67, 292, 322
Victor, Hugh of, 214

W

walaya (friendship / sainthood), 38, 243–244, 247–249
wali (friend / saint), 38, 243, 247–249
Wilber, Ken, 215, 225
wine, 24, 88, 152, 186, 256, 288
wujud (being), 62, 70, 105, 111, 119, 149, 189, 191, 208

Y

yeshe cholwa ('crazy wisdom'), 240
yoga, 143, 322, 331

Z

al-Zahir (the Outwardly Manifest), 102, 149
Zen, 126, 151, 181, 331
Zhuangzi, 138, 335
zuhd (renunciation), 283, 328

www.ingramcontent.com/pod-product-compliance
Lightning Source LLC
Chambersburg PA
CBHW061424300426
44114CB00014B/1528